BRITISH RAILWAYS
Locomotives 1948

A 'West Country' on exchange duty. No. 34006 *Bude* arrives at Marylebone on Tuesday 1st June 1948 on an express from Manchester. This locomotive entered traffic in July 1945 at Exmouth Junction, but was not rebuilt, the streamlined casing remaining throughout its life. Withdrawal came in March 1967 from Salisbury depot.

Photomatic

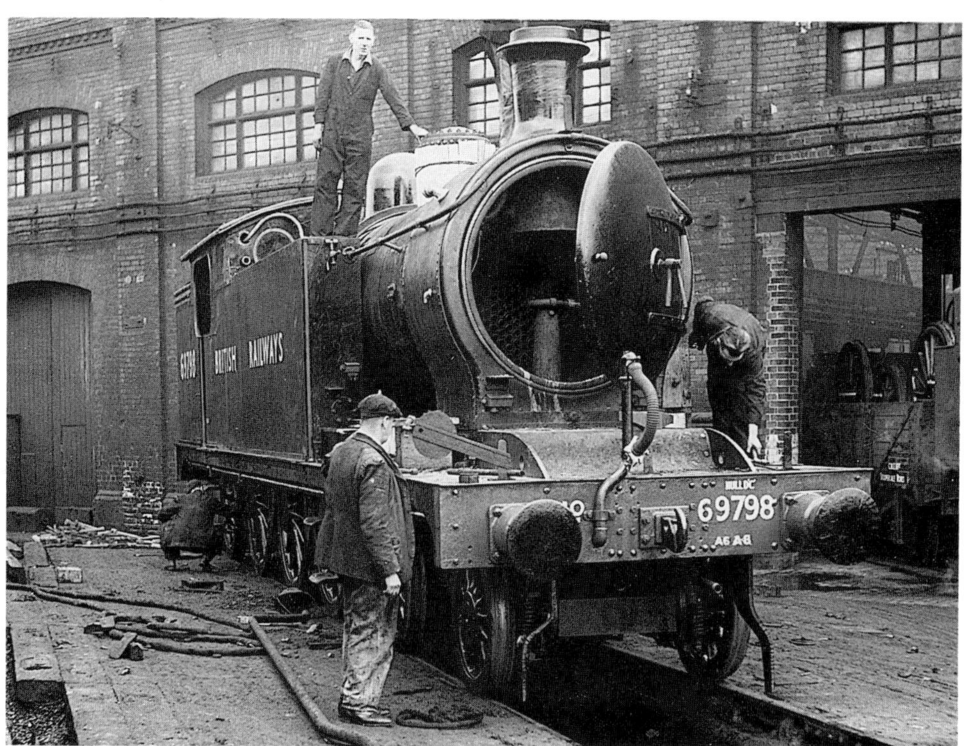

Darlington Works in June 1948. Work progressing on A6 class 4-6-2T No. 6979 Whoever painted the buffer beam made tw mistakes, for the engine is shown as class A8 whic had been crossed out. Also, the allocation is quote as Hull Dairycoates, but this was a Botan Gardens locomotive! This was the final allocatic when withdrawn on 6th February 1951. The la active member of the class, No. 69796, also retire at Botanic Gardens on 30th March 1953. The cla dated back to 1907 and were known as th "Whitby Tanks" as they were built for use on th hilly Whitby to Scarborough line. They wer originally built as 2-cylinder 4-6-0Ts, but wer rebuilt to 4-6-2Ts in 1915. This was to provide extr coal and water capacity for the hard work the were called on to perform. They virtuall monopolised the line for which they were built fc nearly 25 years, as it was not until 1934 that th Class A8 engines began to take over. The A6s wer known around the Whitby/Scarborough area a "Willies"!

G. W. Sharp

'Claughton' class 4-6-0 No. 6004 at Liverpool Edge Hill shed on Sunday 4th April 1948. This was the sole survivor of a class originally totalling 130 engines built between 1913 and 1922. Withdrawal came during the week ended 23rd April 1949 from Edge Hill, and the engine was cut up at Crewe Works on 10th August. It never carried its BR number 46004.

H.A. Gamble

BRITISH RAILWAYS
Locomotives 1948

Chris Banks

Oxford Publishing Co.

A FOULIS-OPC Railway Book

British Library Cataloguing in Publication Data
Banks, Chris
British Railways Locomotives – 1948.
1. Great Britain. Railway services: British Rail.
Locomotives, history
I. Title
625.260941

ISBN 0 86093 466 7

Library of Congress catalog card number
90-81742

Published by:
Haynes Publishing Group
Sparkford, Near Yeovil, Somerset. BA22 7JJ

Haynes Publications Inc.
861 Lawrence Drive, Newbury Park, California 91320, USA.

Printed by J.H. Haynes & Co. Ltd.

Above: 2884 class 2-8-0 No. 3803 arriving at Hornsey yard on a freight from Peterborough on Wednesday 25th August 1948. This was one of the interchange workings and the LMS dynamometer recording coach is behind the engine. No. 3803 was put into traffic in January 1939 and first allocated to Tyseley. The final allocation was Severn Tunnel Junction and was withdrawn in July 1963. This was one of the second batch of these Swindon built engines provided with a more enclosed cab with side windows. No. 3803 survives today, undergoing restoration at Tyseley for use on the Dart Valley Railway.

Photomatic

Title page: Paddington is the unlikely setting for A4 class No. 60033 *Seagull* leaving on a 'down' express. It is April 1948 and the Pacific is about to depart on a Plymouth working during the exchange trials. It was standing in for *Mallard* which had developed a mechanical fault. Built at Doncaster in June 1938 as No. 4902 it went new to King's Cross shed. It was also based at King's Cross when withdrawal came on 31st December 1962.

Photomatic

Opposite: Manchester Trafford Park shed in March 1948. At home is N5 class 0-6-2T No. E9343. This was a design for the Manchester, Sheffield & Lincolnshire Railway by T. Parker and first introduced in 1891, this example being built in 1900. Renumbered 69343 during the week ended 5th February 1949, withdrawal took place on 11th January 1960 from Mexborough shed.

Photomatic

Contents

Exmouth Junction shed on Sunday 29th August 1948. 0415 class 4-4-2T No. 30584 enjoys a rest from weekday work. This locomotive survived until 1961 being withdrawn in February and later cut up at Eastleigh Works.

G. W. Sharpe

Sheffield Millhouses shed proudly displays 'Jubilee' No. 45561 *Saskatchewan* in June 1948 in lined black livery. Hiding her face from the camera is 2P class 4-4-0 No. 423. Both engines were based at Bristol Barrow Road shed, and perhaps they had worked in together. The Stanier 'Jubilee' was built by the North British Locomotive Co. (builder's No. 24119) and entered traffic in July 1934 at Crewe North, and received its name in 1936. Withdrawal took effect during the week ended 19th September 1964 from Derby shed. The 2P was renumbered 40423 during the week ended 25th June 1949 and was withdrawn during the first week of September 1952 from Gloucester Barnwood.

G.W. Sharpe

Introduction

ON THURSDAY, 1st January 1948 British Railways was born. The four main constituent railway companies comprised: the Great Western, the London, Midland & Scottish, the Southern, and the London & North Eastern. All were merged into a new body officially known as "The Railway Executive"

Little ceremony took place at midnight on 31st December 1947, other than the sounding of engine whistles by drivers on duty on night trains. The last LMS train to arrive at Euston on 31st December 1947 was from Blackpool, hauled by 'Jubilee' No. 5574 *India* which arrived at 11.55pm. 'Patriot' No. 5508 had the honour of heading the first BR departure just after midnight, at 12.02am to Crewe. Over at Paddington the GWR passed into history with the departure of the 11.50pm to Penzance, headed by 'Castle' No. 5037 *Monmouth Castle*. Then at 12.05am No. 5032 *Usk Castle* ventured out with the first BR train to Birkenhead and exploded numerous detonators as it left Platform 3. What happened at the other termini is not recorded. Financially, winding up the companies did not take place until 10th June 1949 for the Southern, and 23rd December 1949 for the other three.

Nationalisation

Nationalisation of the railways had really commenced after the July 1945 general election, when the Labour Government, under Clement Attlee, had a large enough majority to push the bill through. The Transport Bill, as it was known, received Royal assent on 6th August 1947 after its second reading took place in the House of Commons in December 1946. The respective railway company boards made their opposition to the bill known in no uncertain terms, as did the Conservative Party - but all to no avail.

The Britain of 1948, into which the new nationalised railway was launched, was still recovering from the effects of the war. Rationing was still in force; indeed, on 27th March the Government announced a cut in the cheese ration from two to one and a half ounces per week! On 8th April Hugh Gaitskell, the fuel minister, announced that motorists would be rationed to 90 miles per month from 1st June. On 25th April the weekly milk ration went up a pint to three and a half; further good news was that jam rationing would cease from 5th December! It was the year for nationalisation of the electricity industry and the creation of the National Health Service.

The Locomotives

British Railways inherited 20,023 steam locomotives of 448 different designs. Many were in a run down state and of pre-Grouping design. Diesel and electric locomotives totalled only 70 engines, with 40 diesel railcars and 2,006 electric motor units. One of the first tasks of the Railway Executive was to plan and design replacement locomotives for the large number of elderly machines that were overdue for withdrawal. As is well known, this resulted in the Standard classes of locomotives being built, with the first, *Britannia* 4-6-2 No. 70000 appearing in 1951. Until then, new locomotives added to stock, perpetuated the designs of the "Big Four" pre-nationalisation companies, while ex-LMS locomotive types had a direct influence on the coming Standard engines. A type already in existence, which was to form the largest Standard class, was the "Austerity" 2-8-0. This design was as a direct result of the war. The order to designer R. A. Riddles was to produce a tough freight locomotive with no frills to fill a serious gap in available motive power during the war. At the point of nationalisation, the LNER already owned 200 of these engines, but the large majority were still under the control of the War Department. Some were still overseas, but were gradually shipped in and placed in store until workshops could cope with their repair. They were eventually taken into stock and renumbered. A second "Austerity" class was the 2-10-0s from the same design office. During the war these remained in this country and in August 1945 Nos 73774 to 73791 were recorded working from March depot in East Anglia. In 1948 only two were allocated to Carlisle Kingmoor, the remaining 23 being in store in the south of England. They were put through Brighton and Eastleigh works, renumbered, and allocated to Scotland.

The LMS Stanier 2-8-0 was also used abroad during the war, many never to return. In April 1948 39 did return from the Middle East, all carrying their War Department numbers. They were all placed in store in the old carriage sheds at Crewe, and after repair entered traffic during 1949. (For completeness these locomotives are listed with their allotted BR numbers and shown as "in store".) Another batch of engines that arrived back in 1948 after war service in France were five LMS 3F "Jinty" 0-6-0Ts. Two arrived by train ferry on Sunday 15th August and the remaining three on 5th September. All were despatched to Derby Works and were reported to be in a very bad state of repair – and full of bullet-holes!

The 1948 Inter-Change Trials

The locomotive exchange trials that took place during 1948 will always be a subject for debate. The real object of the exercise was to gather information that could be used to help towards producing the proposed Standard locomotives. It was also a public relations exercise that announced the "go ahead" approach of the new railway management. In actual fact, very little seems to have been gained from the exercise other than the confirmation that a modern design of steam locomotive, irrespective of its parent company, would perform well anywhere in the hands of a skilled and competent crew. It did succeed in creating a great deal of interest in the railway industry and injected some colour into a rather sombre scene.

Inter-Regional Transfers

During 1948, inter-regional transfers began to take place. These were not connected with the exchange trials. However, before we look at this interesting subject, one particularly unusual set of allocations must be mentioned. Bradford Manningham shed was not a location normally associated with Caledonian 0-4-4T engines, yet on 1st January four of this type were on allocation: Nos 15130, 15169, 15192 and 15227. During the week ended 22nd March 1947 15169 and 15227 had arrived on loan, and became officially transferred by 26th April. They joined

15130 and 15192 which had been sent on loan on 14th December 1946 and permanently allocated during January 1947. They had come as replacements for the Stanier 2P class 0-4-4Ts shedded at Manningham and sub-shed Ilkley. All returned to more usual haunts during the week ended 7th August 1948 when they were transferred to Dundee West.

The first unusual transfer under BR also featured Dundee West. The engines involved were "Tilbury" tank engines Nos 2153 (41971) and 2156 (41974) which moved from Shoeburyness and Plaistow respectively to Dundee during January 1948. They joined sister engines 2154 (41972) and 2155 (41973) that had arrived on the very eve of Nationalisation. They were greatly disliked by the Scottish crews, and Dundee rid itself of one, No. 2153, to Stirling during the week ended 20th March. After being renumbered, all four moved south during June, officially to Skipton. They got no further than Carlisle Durran Hill shed where they languished in store until withdrawal in February 1955. Why they remained all this time without turning a wheel in traffic is a mystery. Perhaps the authorities forgot they were there!

During the week of 17th April two almost new Fairburn 2-6-4Ts, Nos 42198 and 42199, went from Stirling to the Southern Region. They operated from various sheds as a prelude to this type being allocated to the Southern. They had returned to Stirling by 3rd July. Cricklewood received J50 class 0-6-0T No. E8950 from Stratford at the end of May and it was tried out on yard shunting. It returned to Stratford during the week ended 24th July. Stratford itself had a try out with Class 4F 2-6-0 No. 43011 which had arrived by 19th June from Derby. It returned home during the week ended 24th July. Sister engine, No. 43018 had a short stay at Colwick and Ardsley during the year, before returning to Nottingham. Class 2F 2-6-0s also moved to new depots on trial: No. 46416 going to Colwick from Bank Hall and on to New England; No. 46417 to Stratford; Nos 46418 and 46419 to Darlington. All had returned to their LMR sheds by August.

Liveries

Locomotive liveries were announced early in 1948. The Railway Executive declared that, subject to final decision, they proposed to paint the most important main-line passenger engines blue, ordinary passenger engines green, and other engines black. On Friday 30th January, Kensington Addison Road station was the venue for inspection by officials of locomotives and stock painted in experimental livery. The locomotives were: ex-LMS Class 5 4-6-0s Nos 4762 (Southern Railway malachite green, unlined shaded lettering), 4763 (LNER green, lined black and white), 4764 (GWR green, lined gold and black, white lettering), 5292 (black, lined red, white lettering) and Southern electric locomotive CC2 (pale blue, lined silver and black, silver lettering). All were lettered with the inscription "British Railways" in full. A further display occurred on Tuesday 6th April at Marylebone station. The locomotives were: ex-LNER A3 class No. 60091 *Captain Cuttle* (painted Royal blue, lined yellow), ex-LNER B17 class No. 61661 *Sheffield Wednesday* (very light green with yellow lining), and ex-LMS Class 5 No. 45292, now renumbered (black with full LNWR lining-out). All had smokebox number plates and red buffer beams. In true LNWR style No. 45292 had a black line painted around the buffer beam. Thought was then given to the emblem to be used, and B1s Nos 61001 *Eland* and 61009 *Hartebeeste* were placed on view at Liverpool Street station on Monday 19th April with different versions of the "Lion and Wheel" emblem on their tenders. Until a final decision was made, "British Railways" in full was added to repainted locomotives throughout 1948.

Repainting was carried out at main works and different varieties of lettering were used, depending on which works undertook the job. For instance, the first to be lettered "British Railways" from Wolverhampton Works was GWR 2-6-2T No. 6126 which emerged in February, the lettering being hand-painted in yellow edged with red. Derby Works turned out new 2-6-4T No. M2191 on 20th January with "British Railways" in straw coloured lettering. St Rollox were turning out engines with the lettering in plain white; Inverurie continued to letter engines "LNER" until 19th March when J35 No. 64485 left correctly lettered with its new ownership. Cowlairs continued until mid-March with LNER lettering, N15 class 0-6-2T No. 69187 being the first to emerge with "British Railways" in yellow on the tank sides. Gorton Works also continued with LNER lettering until mid-February when the new name was used for the first time on N5 class 0-6-2Ts E9300, E9310, E9322 and E9349. Doncaster turned out new A2 class Pacific No. E527 in January correctly lettered, the first to bear "British Railways" from this works, and Eastleigh's first departure in the new name was Bulleid Pacific No. S21C158. The honour at Swindon fell to 'Hall' class 4-6-0 No. 4946 *Moseley Hall* and at Crewe Class 5 No. M4820. After a year or so the "Lion and Wheel" totem was adopted and dark, Great Western green for top-link express engines and LNWR black for the remainder became standard.

Re-numbering

A consistent locomotive numbering scheme was an early priority to bring all the stock into a unified system. For the first three months of the year "W" was added to ex-GWR locomotive numbers, "S" to ex-Southern, "M" to ex-LMS and "E" to ex-LNER. This was short lived and only lasted until April when the finalised system was adopted. It was agreed that the ex-GWR engines would remain unaltered, the ex-Southern would have their numbers increased by 30000, LMS engines by 40000 and LNER by 60000. Renumbering was at first carried out at the main works as locomotives passed through for repair. Several locomotives turned out from Brighton after the announcement of the new numbering scheme were numbered with the five figure numbers, but having a comma between the second and third figures. In most cases this was soon painted out, but 'Schools' class 4-4-0 No. 30,903 *Charterhouse* ran so numbered for some months.

The numbers carried on 1st January 1948 were, of course, the ones allotted by the former companies. For clarity, all the numbers shown in this volume are the ones allocated under British Railways. A word of explanation is therefore needed to show how the numbers that did not fit into the general scheme were catered for. All these numbers are shown, where this applied, in the second column of figures. If we look at some examples, company by company, this will hopefully be easy to follow.

The GWR was in the process of renumbering certain locomotives from the Cardiff Valleys' division when Nationalisation came along. The renumbering was carried out under BR, an example being GWR No. 792 which became BR No. 193. Other locomotives carried temporary numbers to show that they had been converted to oil burners. 'Hall' class No. 5955 *Garth Hall* is an example and carried the number 3950. The Southern also had some anomalies – No. 3029 becoming 30564 for example.

Bulleid's unique scheme for his Q1 class and Pacifics was also abandoned, No. C1 becoming 33001 and 21C101 to 34001. The LMS had the biggest collection of locomotives that did not fit the system. Indeed, 31 locomotives were not allocated BR numbers at all but were on the stock books on 1st January. All were down for imminent withdrawal, an example being Johnson 0-4-4T No. 1307. In contrast, the LNER had few engines that did not readily fit into the new system, due to the complete renumbering of the fleet carried out under Thompson in 1946. One exception was the unique W1 class 4-6-4 No. 10000 which became 60700. (Had 60000 been added to this number it would have clashed with the first Standard locomotive.) The "Austerity" 2-8-0s owned by the LNER were also renumbered with the addition of 60000. However, not all were dealt with in this way, only 133 being so numbered during 1948 and 1949, the remaining 67 going straight into the later 90000 series, along with those acquired by BR from the War Department. Details of all locomotive renumberings during 1948 are included in this volume. Renumbering also included the provision of smokebox door number plates for all locomotives. For a time, however, the number was painted on the buffer beams on locomotives that were not of LMS origin. One odd exception was the ex-LNWR 0-8-0s which never carried front number plates, along with the other locomotives from this source. Perhaps this was Crewe Works showing its independence when all around were showing conformity! Renumbering took many years to complete. The last LMS engine to be dealt with was No. 51537 and this was not until 4th September 1954.

Power Classification

Locomotive power classifications were an area where the LMS influence ruled. Their system was adopted for all locomotives from 1949. This was a system of showing whether a locomotive was for freight traffic or passenger and the higher the number, the more powerful the engine was in relation to its tractive effort. "2P" meant class 2 passenger, "5P5F" was class 5 passenger and freight and "8F" class 8 freight locomotive. The classification "MT" was brought into use, meaning "mixed traffic" engine and replaced the use of "P" and "F" in the same code.

Depot Allocations

The locomotive allocations in this book are as at 1st January 1948. The only locomotives not included are service stock numbered outside the main series.

On 1st January the ex-LMS depots used a system of coding divided into districts with a number and letter, the parent depot for the district carrying the letter "A". Engines carried their home code on a plate at the base of the smokebox door. It was the practice at some Scottish sheds to place the shedplate at the top. The Southern GWR and LNER had no "number and letter" system, their depots being given alphabetical codes. These were not always carried on locomotives, but when it was it was painted on the buffer beam, main frames, or inside the cab. Once again the LMS influence showed through and the shedplate system was extended to the whole of British Railways. The first to be dealt with was the Scottish Region. From 1st January 1949 all the ex-LMS and ex-LNER depots were brought together and well known codes such as 64A, St Margaret's, or 66A Glasgow Polmadie were formed. The other regions were dealt with in 1950.

As well as the main depots, there were a number of sub-sheds that carried no code of their own – engines being supplied from the parent main shed. The definition of a sub-shed as laid down by British Railways was "a place where men may sign on and off only, with no need of a shed or engines, but there must be a register". Consequently, although shown as official sub-sheds, at some locations no actual shed buildings existed. An example was Hardengreen which was a sub to Edinburgh St Margaret's. Most did have some form of building with engines stabled overnight and at weekends. Sub-sheds are shown under their main parent depots in the shed list details.

Locomotive Names

Named locomotives are denoted by a * after the number and a complete list of names carried is included. In a few instances the names were not actually carried on 1st January, but their eventual naming is included for completeness.

Finally, a word about the photographs chosen. All have been taken during the first four years of British Railways, many during the first two. It would be difficult to show an example of every class of locomotive in a book this size, but as wide a selection as possible has been included.

The aim has been to include as much information as possible in one volume. For the first time the locomotive allocations, withdrawals, additions and renumberings during the first year of British Railways are all included together. It has been a mammoth task, all done without the aid of a computer! My special thanks must go to my wife Jean for putting up with the innumerable hours that I have spent sifting through countless documents to find the information needed, and scattering of books and papers all over the house. At last, all is complete and family life can return to normal. That is until I start on the next project! . . .

Chris Banks
Hinckley, Leics

Ex-GWR Engine Depots and Codes
as at 1st January 1948

Code	Depot
ABDR	ABERDARE
ABEEG	ABERBEEG
ABH	ABERYSTWYTH
AYN	ABERCYNON
BAN	BANBURY
BCN	BRECON
	Builth Wells
BHD	BIRKENHEAD
	(Shared with LMS Depot)
BRD	BRISTOL BATH ROAD
	Bath
	Wells
	Weston-Super-Mare
	Yatton
BRY	BARRY
CARM	CARMARTHEN
	Newcastle Emlyn
CDF	CARDIFF CANTON
CED	CARDIFF EAST DOCK
CH	CAEHARRIS
CHEL	CHELTENHAM (MALVERN ROAD)
	Brimscombe
	Chalford
	Cirencester
CHR	CHESTER
CHYS	CARDIFF CATHAYS
CNYD	CROES NEWYDD (WREXHAM)
	Bala
	Trawsfyndd
	Penmaenpool
DG	DANYGRAIG, SWANSEA
DID	DIDCOT
	Newbury
	Wallingford
	Winchester
DYD	DUFFRYN YARD, PORT TALBOT
EXE	EXETER
	Tiverton Junction
FDL	FERNDALE (CARDIFF VALLEYS)
FGD	FISHGUARD (GOODWICK)
GLO	GLOUCESTER HORTON ROAD
HFD	HEREFORD
	Kington
	Ledbury
	Leominster
	Ross-on-Wye
KDR	KIDDERMINSTER
LA	PLYMOUTH LAIRA
	Princetown
	Launceston
LDR	SWANSEA LANDORE
LLY	LLANELLY
	Burry Port
	Pantyffynnon
LMTN	LEAMINGTON SPA
LTS	LLANTRISANT
LYD	LYDNEY
	Tetbury
MCH	MACHYNLLETH
	Aberayron
	Portmadoc
	Pwllheli
MTHR	MERTHYR
NA	NEWTON ABBOT
	Ashburton
	Kingsbridge
NEA	NEATH
	Glyn Neath
	Neath N & B
NEY	NEYLAND
	Milford Haven
NPT	NEWPORT EBBW JUNCTION
OSW	OSWESTRY
	Llanfyllin
	Llanidloes
	Moat Lane
	Welshpool
OXF	OXFORD
	Abingdon
	Fairford
OXY	WOLVERHAMPTON OXLEY
PDN	OLD OAK COMMON, LONDON
PILL	NEWPORT PILL
PPRD	PONTYPOOL ROAD
	Branches Fork
	Pontrilas
PZ	PENZANCE
	Helston
	St Ives
RDG	READING
	Basingstoke
	Henley
RHY	RHYMNEY
	Dowlais Central
RYR	RADYR JUNCTION, CARDIFF
SALOP	SHREWSBURY
	(Shared with LMS Depot)
	Ludlow
SBZ	ST BLAZEY
	Bodmin
	Moorswater
SDN	SWINDON
	Andover Junction
	Chippenham
	Malmesbury
SED	SWANSEA EAST DOCK
SHL	SOUTHALL
	Staines
SLO	SLOUGH
	Aylesbury
	Marlow
	Watlington
SPM	BRISTOL ST PHILIP'S MARSH
SRD	WOLVERHAMPTON STAFFORD ROAD
STB	STOURBRIDGE
STJ	SEVERN TUNNEL JUNCTION
TDU	TONDU
	Bridgend
THT	TREHERBERT
	Pwllyrhebog
TN	TAUNTON
	Barnstaple
	Bridgwater
	Minehead
TR	TRURO
TYS	BIRMINGHAM TYSELEY
	Stratford-on-Avon
WES	WESTBURY
	Frome
	Salisbury
WEY	WEYMOUTH
	Bridport

WLN	WELLINGTON
	Crewe Gresty Lane
	Much Wenlock
WOS	WORCESTER
	Evesham
	Kingham
WTD	WHITLAND
	Cardigan
	Pembroke Dock
YEO	YEOVIL PEN MILL

Ex-Southern Railway Engine Depots and Codes
as at 1st January 1948

AFD	ASHFORD
	Canterbury West (CAN)
BA	BRICKLAYERS ARMS, LONDON
BAS	BASINGSTOKE
BAT	STEWARTS LANE, LONDON
BM	BOURNEMOUTH CENTRAL
	Hamworthy Junction (HAM)
	Swanage (SWE)
BPL	BARNSTAPLE
	Ilfracombe (ILF)
	Torrington (TOR)
BTN	BRIGHTON
	Newhaven (NHN)
DOR	DORCHESTER
	Weymouth (WEY)
DOV	DOVER MARINE
	Folkestone Junction (FOL)
EBN	EASTBOURNE
ELH	EASTLEIGH
	Andover Junction (AND)
	Lymington (LYM)
	Winchester (WIN)
EXJ	EXMOUTH JUNCTION
	Bude (BUD)
	Exmouth (EXM)
	Launceston (LCN)
	Lyme Regis (LR)
	Okehampton (OKE)
	Seaton (SEA)
FAV	FAVERSHAM
FEL	FELTHAM
FRA	FRATTON
	Gosport (GOS)
	Midhurst (MID)
GFD	GUILDFORD
	Ash (ASH)
	Bordon (BOR)
GIL	GILLINGHAM
HIT	HITHER GREEN
HOR	HORSHAM
	Bognor Regis (BOG)
9E	NINE ELMS, LONDON
NOR	NORWOOD JUNCTION
PLY	PLYMOUTH FRIARY
	Callington (CAL)
RAM	RAMSGATE
RED	REDHILL
RDG	READING
SAL	SALISBURY
SOT	SOUTHAMPTON DOCKS
STL	ST LEONARDS
3B	THREE BRIDGES
TON	TONBRIDGE
TWW	TUNBRIDGE WELLS WEST
WAD	WADEBRIDGE
YEO	YEOVIL TOWN
	Templecombe Upper (TEM)

Isle of Wight:

NPT	NEWPORT
RYD	RYDE

Ex-LMS Engine Depots and Codes
as at 1st January 1948

1A	WILLESDEN
1B	CAMDEN
1C	WATFORD
2A	RUGBY
	Market Harborough
	Seaton
2B	BLETCHLEY
	Cambridge
	Leighton Buzzard
	Oxford
	Newport Pagnell
	Aylesbury
2C	NORTHAMPTON
2D	NUNEATON
2E	WARWICK
2F	COVENTRY
3A	BESCOT
3B	BUSHBURY, WOLVERHAMPTON
3C	WALSALL
3D	ASTON, BIRMINGHAM
3E	MONUMENT LANE, BIRMINGHAM
4A	SHREWSBURY
	Coalport
	Ludlow
	Clee Hill
	Craven Arms
	Knighton
	Builth Road
4B	SWANSEA VICTORIA
	Llandovery
4C	UPPER BANK
	Brecon
	Gurnos
4D	ABERGAVENNY
4E	TREDEGAR
5A	CREWE NORTH
	Whitchurch
5B	CREWE SOUTH
5C	STAFFORD
5D	STOKE
5E	ALSAGER
5F	UTTOXETER

6A CHESTER
6B MOLD JUNCTION
6C BIRKENHEAD

7A LLANDUDNO JUNCTION
7B BANGOR
7C HOLYHEAD
7D RHYL
Denbigh

8A LIVERPOOL EDGE HILL
8B WARRINGTON DALLAM
Arpley
Over and Wharton
8C SPEKE JUNCTION
8D WIDNES

9A MANCHESTER LONGSIGHT
9B STOCKPORT EDGELEY
9C MACCLESFIELD
9D BUXTON
Cromford
Middleton
Sheep Pasture

10A WIGAN SPRINGS BRANCH
10B PRESTON
10C MANCHESTER PATRICROFT
10D PLODDER LANE
10E SUTTON OAK

11A CARNFORTH
11B BARROW
Lakeside
Coniston
11D OXENHOLME
11E TEBAY

12A CARLISLE KINGMOOR
12B CARLISLE UPPERBY
12C PENRITH
12D WORKINGTON
12E MOOR ROW
12F BEATTOCK
12G DUMFRIES
Kirkcudbright
12H STRANRAER
Newton Stewart

13A PLAISTOW
13B DEVONS ROAD
13C TILBURY
13D SHOEBURYNESS
13E UPMINSTER

14A CRICKLEWOOD
14B KENTISH TOWN
14C ST ALBANS

15A WELLINGBOROUGH
15B KETTERING
15C LEICESTER MIDLAND
15D BEDFORD

16A NOTTINGHAM
Southwell
Lincoln
16B PETERBOROUGH SPITAL
16C KIRKBY-IN-ASHFIELD
16D MANSFIELD

17A DERBY
17B BURTON-ON-TRENT
Overseal-
17C COALVILLE
17D ROWSLEY

18A TOTON
18B WESTHOUSES
18C HASLAND
18D STAVELEY BARROW HILL
Sheepbridge

19A SHEFFIELD GRIMESTHORPE
19B SHEFFIELD MILLHOUSES
19C CANKLOW
19D HEATON MERSEY
19E MANCHESTER BELLE VUE
19G MANCHESTER TRAFFORD PARK

20A LEEDS HOLBECK
20B STOURTON
20C ROYSTON
20D NORMANTON
20E BRADFORD MANNINGHAM
Ilkley
20F SKIPTON
Ingleton
Keighley
20G HELLIFIELD
20H LANCASTER

21A SALTLEY, BIRMINGHAM
21B BOURNVILLE, BIRMINGHAM
Redditch
21C BROMSGROVE
21D STRATFORD-ON-AVON

22A BRISTOL BARROW ROAD
22B GLOUCESTER BARNWOOD
Dursley
Tewkesbury
22C BATH GREEN PARK
Branksome
Radstock
22D TEMPLECOMBE
22E HIGHBRIDGE
Wells

23A LIVERPOOL BANK HALL
23B AINTREE
23C SOUTHPORT
23D WIGAN L&Y

24A ACCRINGTON
24B ROSE GROVE
24C LOSTOCK HALL
24D LOWER DARWEN
24E BLACKPOOL
24F FLEETWOOD

25A WAKEFIELD
25B HUDDERSFIELD
25C GOOLE
25D MIRFIELD
25E SOWERBY BRIDGE
25F LOW MOOR
25G FARNLEY JUNCTION

26A MANCHESTER NEWTON HEATH
26B MANCHESTER AGECROFT
26C BOLTON
26D BURY
26E BACUP
26F LEES, OLDHAM

27A GLASGOW POLMADIE
27B GREENOCK LADYBURN
Greenock Princes Pier
27C HAMILTON

28A MOTHERWELL
28B EDINBURGH DALRY ROAD
28C CARSTAIRS

29A PERTH
Aberfeldy
Blair Atholl
Crieff
29B ABERDEEN FERRYHILL
29C DUNDEE WEST
29D FORFAR
Arbroath

Brechin
Killin

30A GLASGOW CORKERHILL
30B HURLFORD
Muirkirk
Beith
30C ARDROSSAN
30D AYR

31A GLASGOW ST ROLLOX
31B STIRLING
31C OBAN
Ballachulish
31D GRANGEMOUTH
31E GLASGOW DAWSHOLM

Dumbarton
Yoker

32A INVERNESS
Dingwall
Fortrose
Kyle of Lochalsh
Tain
Dornoch
Helmsdale
Wick
Thurso
32B AVIEMORE
32C FORRES

CW CREWE WORKS
HW HORWICH WORKS

Ex-LNER Engine Depots and Codes
as at 1st January 1948

Southern Area

ANN ANNESLEY
ARD ARDSLEY

BFD BRADFORD (BOWLING JUNCTION)
BID BIDSTON
BOS BOSTON
BRN BARNSLEY
BSE BURY ST EDMUNDS
Sudbury

CAM CAMBRIDGE
Ely
Huntingdon East
Saffron Walden
Thaxted
CHR CHESTER (NORTHGATE)
CLK COLWICK
Derby (Friargate)
COL COLCHESTER
Braintree
Clacton
Kelverdon
Maldon
Walton-on-Naze
COP LEEDS COPLEY HILL

DON DONCASTER

FRO FRODINGHAM

GOR GORTON, MANCHESTER
Dinting
Hayfield
Macclesfield
GRA GRANTHAM
Newark

HAT HATFIELD
HIT HITCHIN
HSY HORNSEY

IMM IMMINGHAM
IPS IPSWICH
Aldeburgh
Felixstowe Beach
Framlingham
Laxfield
Stowmarket

KL KING'S LYNN
Hunstanton
Wisbech
KX KING'S CROSS

LEI LEICESTER CENTRAL
Leicester Belgrave Rd
LIN LINCOLN
LIV LIVERPOOL BRUNSWICK
Southport
Warrington
Widnes
LNG LANGWITH JUNCTION
LOW LOWESTOFT
LTH LOUTH

MAR MARCH
MC MELTON CONSTABLE
Cromer Beach
Norwich City
MEX MEXBOROUGH

NEA NEASDEN
Aylesbury
Chesham
NOR NORWICH
Cromer
Dereham
Swaffham
Wells
Wymondham
NTH NORTHWICH
NWE PETERBOROUGH NEW ENGLAND
Bourne
Spalding
Stamford

PKS PARKESTON

RET RETFORD (GREAT CENTRAL & GREAT NORTHERN)

SHF SHEFFIELD DARNALL
SL SOUTH LYNN
STP STOCKPORT, HEATON MERSEY (Shared with LMS Depot)
STR STRATFORD, LONDON
Bishop's Stortford
Brentwood
Buntingford
Chelmsford
Enfield Town
Epping
Hertford East
Palace Gates
Southend Victoria
Southminster
Spitalfields
Ware
Wickford
Wood Street, Walthamstow

STV STAVELEY (GREAT CENTRAL)

TFD MANCHESTER TRAFFORD PARK
(Shared with LMS Depot)
TUX TUXFORD

WAL WALTON-ON-THE-HILL, LIVERPOOL
WFD WOODFORD HALSE
WIG WIGAN, LOWER INCE
WRX WREXHAM, RHOSDDU

YAR YARMOUTH SOUTH TOWN
Yarmouth Vauxhall
YB YARMOUTH BEACH

Departmental Stock:
BOSE BOSTON ENGINEERING WORKS
DONW DONCASTER WORKS
LOWS LOWESTOFT SLEEPER WORKS
STRW STRATFORD WORKS

North East Area
AUK WEST AUCKLAND
Wearhead (WHD)

BLA BLAYDON
Alston (ALS)
Hexham (HEX)
Reedsmouth (RMH)
BOR BOROUGH GARDENS
BRI BRIDLINGTON

CON CONSETT
CUD CUDWORTH

DAR DARLINGTON
Middleton-in-Teesdale (MIT)

GHD GATESHEAD
Bowes Bridge (BOW)

HAV HAVERTON HILL
HLB HULL BOTANIC GARDENS
HLD HULL DAIRYCOATES
HLS HULL SPRINGHEAD
Hull Alexandra Dock (HLA)
HTN HEATON

KBY KIRKBY STEPHEN

MAL MALTON
Pickering (PKG)
MID MIDDLESBROUGH
Guisborough (GUI)

NBH NORTH BLYTH
South Blyth (SBH)
Rothbury (RBY)
NEV LEEDS NEVILLE HILL
Ilkley (ILK)
NLN NORTHALLERTON
Leyburn (LEY)
NPT NEWPORT

PMN PERCY MAIN

SAL SALTBURN
SBK STARBECK
Pateley Bridge (PAT)
SCA SCARBOROUGH
SEL SELBY
SKN STOCKTON-ON-TEES
SUN SUNDERLAND
Durham (DUR)

TDK TYNE DOCK
Pelton Level (PEL)
TWD TWEEDMOUTH
Alnmouth (ALN)

WBY WHITBY
WHL WEST HARTLEPOOL

YK YORK
Normanton (NMN)
(Shared with LMS Depot)

Departmental Stock:
DARF DARLINGTON FAVERDALE WORKS
DARG DARLINGTON GENEVA P.W. DEPOT
YKE YORK ENGINEERING YARD

Scottish Area
ABD ABERDEEN FERRYHILL
(Shared with LMS Depot)

BGT BATHGATE
Morningside

CAR CARLISLE CANAL

DEE DUNDEE (TAY BRIDGE)
Arbroath
Montrose
St Andrews
Tayport
DFU DUNFERMLINE UPPER
Loch Leven
Kelty

EFD GLASGOW EASTFIELD
Aberfoyle
Arrochar
Balloch
Kilsyth
Lennoxtown
Stobcross

FW FORT WILLIAM
Mallaig

HAY EDINBURGH HAYMARKET
HAW HAWICK
Jedburgh
Kelso
Riccarton Junction
St Boswells

KEI KEITH
Banff
Elgin Boat of Garten
KIT ABERDEEN KITTYBREWSTER
Ballater
Fraserburgh
Macduff
Peterhead

KPS GLASGOW KIPPS (COATBRIDGE)

PKD GLASGOW PARKHEAD
Helensburgh
POL POLMONT
Kinneil
PTH PERTH
STG STIRLING (SHORE ROAD)
Alloa
STM EDINBURGH ST MARGARET'S
Dunbar
Galashiels
Hardengreen
Longniddry
North Berwick
Peebles
Penicuik
Polton
Seafield

THJ THORNTON JUNCTION
Anstruther
Burntisland
Ladybank
Methil

Ex-GWR **Treherbert** shed on Sunday 3rd July 1949 with the usual selection of 0-6-2Ts shyly looking away from the camera. The allocation on 1st January 1948 was 29 locomotives, which was later boosted to around 40 with the addition of the Ferndale allocation when this became a sub-shed in 1950. The shed opened in 1931 and closed on 1st March 1965.

N. E. Preedy

Bournemouth shed in 1950 with Nos 34074 *46 Squadron* and 30740 *Merlin* nearest the camera. The buildings dated back to the mid-1930s and had replaced an earlier depot. Situated alongside the Central Station, it occupied a rather cramped site. A sign asking for "Quiet Please" was attached to the boundary wall for many years, reminding enginemen of the proximity of the nearby houses. On 1st January 1948 the allocation was 58 locomotives and steam remained active at the shed until the end of this form of traction on the Southern Region. Closure came on 9th July 1967.

Author's collection

Bath Green Park shed on Saturday 20th May 1950. Locomotives visible are: Nos 53802, 44096, 53807, 53808 and 53809. This ex-Somerset & Dorset shed was constructed mainly of wood and could accommodate up to 18 locomotives under cover on four roads. Next to it was the ex-Midland shed, a two road structure built of stone. The allocation on 1st January 1948 was 50 locomotives. A visit to the shed on Saturday 11th November 1950 at 2.15pm found the following present: Nos 40509, 40563, 40564, 40569, 40601, 40696, 40697, 40698, 41240, 41242, 43013, 43853, 44557, 44558, 44559, 44560, 44945, 45440, 45639, 47275, 47316, 53802, 53805, 53807 and 53809. Out at Radstock sub-shed on this date, visited at 3.35pm, were: Nos 47191, 47465, 47496, 47542, 47557 and 51202. Bath Green Park closed on 7th March 1966.

N. E. Preedy

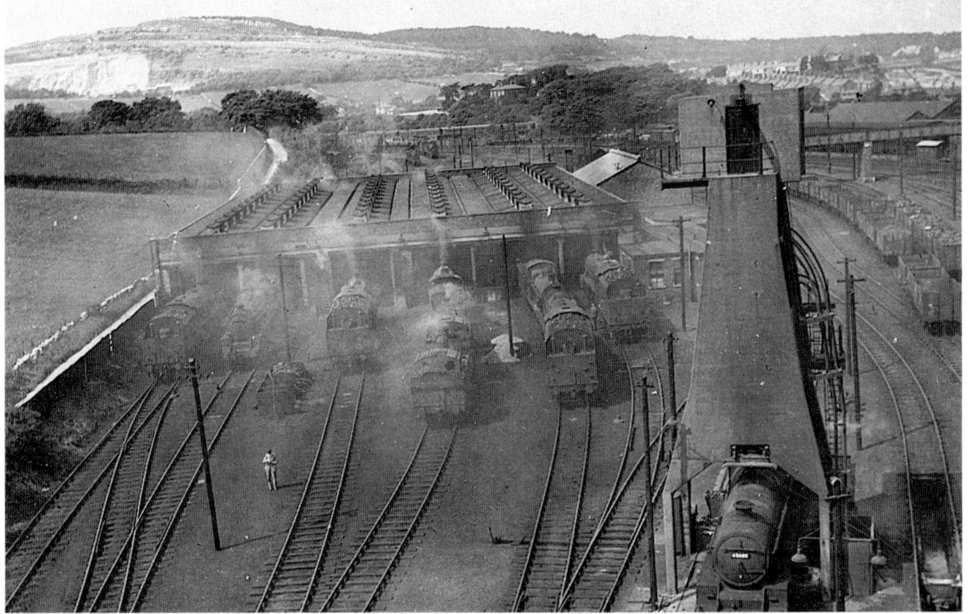

Carnforth shed on Sunday 24th June 1951 viewed from the top of the coaler. Opened on 18th December 1944 by the LMS it replaced the older, ex-Midland and LNWR buildings. On 1st January 1948 the allocation consisted of 48 locomotives. A visit to the shed on Sunday 13th November 1949 at 4.45pm found the following engines present: Nos 40001, 40041, 40068, 42393, 42428, 42573, 42601, 42711, 42983, 43009, 43851, 44060, 44075, 44083, 44374, 44385, 44399, 44510, 44709, 45050, 45129, 45193, 45306, 45343, 45388, 45392, 45426, 45427, 45550, 47317, 47339, 47406, 47407, 47409, 47410, 47605, 48555, 48708, 49075, 49109, 49112, 49130, 49151, 49241, 49252 and 49314. The shed closed on 5th August 1968 and is now part of the Steamtown Carnforth preservation complex.

K. C. H. Fairey

Spalding sub-shed in May 1948 with J6 class 0-6-0 No. 4217 outside. Of M&GN origin, in BR days locomotives were supplied from Peterborough New England. As the Ivatt 4MT 2-6-0s became widespread, a number were allocated to duties at Spalding. A visit to the shed on Sunday 8th April 1951 found the following present: Nos 43060, 43066, 43067, 43081, 43085, 43086, 43088, 64171, 64275 and 64278. It is interesting to compare this with a visit on Sunday 31st May 1953 when at the shed were: Nos 43062, 43081, 43086, 43087, 64171, 64172, 64207, 64210, 64216, 64219, 64275, 64279, 64359, 68786 and 68876. Spalding closed on 7th March 1960.

Photomatic

British Railways Locomotive Numbers and Allocations 1st January 1948

Ex-Great Western Railway Locomotives

STROUDLEY "TERRIER"
0-6-0T EX-WESTON CLEVEDON AND PORTISHEAD RAILWAY

5* SPM
6 SPM

0-6-0PT EX-CLEOBURY MORTIMER AND DITTON PRIORS LIGHT RAILWAY

28 KDR
29 KDR

0-6-2T EX-RHYMNEY RAILWAY

30 RYR
31 CED
32 RYR
33 CED
34 RYR
35 RYR
36 CED
37 CED
38 RYR
39 RHY
40 RYR
41 RYR
42 RYR
43 RYR
44 RYR
46 RYR
47 CED
51 CED

0-6-2T EX-RHYMNEY RAILWAY CLASS "A"

52 CED
53 CED
54 CED
55 CED
56 RYR
57 BRY
58 BRY
59 BRY
60 DG
61 CED
62 PILL
63 RYR
64 RYR
65 ABDR
66 CED
67 RHY
68 CED
69 DYD
70 DYD
71 DG
72 CED
73 CED
74 CED
75 NEA

0-6-2T EX-RHYMNEY RAILWAY CLASSES "P" AND "P1"

76 RHY
77 RHY
78 RHY
79 RHY
80 RHY
81 RHY
82 RHY
83 CH

0-6-0T EX-RHYMNEY RAILWAY CLASSES "S" AND "S1"

90 CED
91 605 CED
92 CED
93 CED
94 CED
95 610 CED
96 611 CED

0-6-2T EX-CARDIFF RAILWAY

155 CED

0-6-2T EX-PORT TALBOT RAILWAY

184 DYD

0-6-2ST EX-ALEXANDRA DOCKS RAILWAY

190 PILL

0-6-0T EX-TAFF VALE RAILWAY "H" CLASS

193 792 THT
194 793 THT
195 794 THT

0-6-2T EX-BARRY RAILWAY "B" CLASS

198 RYR

0-6-2T EX-TAFF VALE RAILWAY "04" CLASS

200 CDF
201 301 CHYS
202 302 THT
203 310 CDF
204 ABDR
205 CDF
206 314 ABDR
207 FDL
208 317 CDF
209 CDF
210 CED
211 320 CH

0-6-2T EX-BARRY RAILWAY "B" CLASS

212 CED
213 BRY

0-6-2T EX-TAFF VALE RAILWAY "04" CLASS

215 321 FDL
216 324 FDL
217 333 MTHR
218 409 FDL
219 414 AYN
220 420 CDF

0-6-2T EX-BARRY RAILWAY "B" CLASS

231 BRY

0-6-2T EX-TAFF VALE RAILWAY "04" CLASS

236 AYN

0-6-2T EX-BARRY RAILWAY "B" CLASS

238 CDF
240 RYR
246 RYR
248 BRY
258 RYR
259 CED
261 BRY
262 BRY
263 BRY
265 BRY
267 BRY
268 BRY
269 CED
270 BRY
271 BRY
272 BRY
274 BRY
275 BRY
276 BRY
277 BRY

0-6-2T EX-TAFF VALE RAILWAY "04" CLASS

278 FDL
279 FDL
280 CDF
281 AYN
282 ABDR
283 FDL
284 ABDR
285 CED
286 BRY
287 AYN
288 AYN
289 SED
290 THT
291 DYD
292 RHY
293 RYR
294 DYD
295 AYN
296 DYD
297 CED
298 FDL
299 FDL

0-6-2T EX-TAFF VALE RAILWAY "A" CLASS

303 THT
304 402 AYN
305 CHYS
306 404 BRY
307 406 CHYS
308 408 SED
309 438 SED
312 439 BRY
316 440 BRY
322 BRY
335 CDF
337 AYN
343 CHYS
344 CHYS
345 BRY
346 CHYS
347 CHYS
348 CHYS
349 PPRD
351 AYN
352 THT
356 AYN
357 CDF

0-6-0T EX-LLANELLY AND MYNYDD MAWR RAILWAY

359* DG

0-6-2T EX-TAFF VALE RAILWAY "A" CLASS

360 CHYS
361 BRY
362 ABDR
364 CHYS
365 THT
366 THT
367 CHYS
368 THT
370 RHY
371 CHYS
372 BRY
373 THT
374 ABDR
375 RHY
376 CHYS
377 BRY
378 THT
379 BRY
380 AYN
381 CDF
382 BRY
383 CHYS
384 CHYS
385 PPRD
386 BRY
387 BRY
388 BRY
389 BRY
390 CHYS
391 CHYS
393 CHYS
394 BRY
397 AYN
398 RHY
399 THT

0-6-2T EX-TAFF VALE RAILWAY "03" CLASS

410 CDF
411 CDF

0-6-2T EX-BRECON AND MERTHYR RAILWAY

421 11 PILL
422 STJ
423 332 STJ
424 504 PILL
425 PILL
426 PILL
428 DYD

0-6-2T EX-BRECON AND MERTHYR RAILWAY

431 1372 NPT
432 1373 NPT
433 RYR
434 1375 CHYS
435 1668 NPT
436 1670 NPT

0-6-0T EX-ALEXANDRA DOCKS RAILWAY

666 PILL
667 PILL

0-6-0ST EX-ALEXANDRA DOCKS RAILWAY

680 OSW

0-6-0PT EX-CARDIFF RAILWAY

681 CED
682 CED
683 CED
684 CED

0-6-0T EX-BARRY RAILWAY "D" CLASS

783 BRY
784 BRY

0-6-0T EX-LLANELLY AND MYNYDD MAWR RAILWAY

803 DG

0-6-0 EX-CAMBRIAN RAILWAY "15" CLASS

844 OSW
849 OSW
855 OSW
864 MCH
873 OSW
887 OSW
892 OSW
893 OSW
894 MCH
895 OSW
896 OSW

0-6-0PT "1854" CLASS

906 NEA
907 DID

0-6-0PT "1901" CLASS

992 SDN

4-6-0 "1000" COUNTY CLASS

1000* PDN
1001* NA
1002* BRD
1003* PDN
1004* LA
1005* BRD
1006* LA
1007* BRD
1008* PDN
1009* LA
1010* PDN
1011* BRD
1012* PDN
1013* BRD
1014* BRD
1015* PDN

1016* SRD
1017* SRD
1018* NA
1019* PZ
1020* EXE
1021* PDN
1022* PZ
1023* TR
1024* SRD
1025* SRD
1026* PDN
1027* WES
1028* BRD
1029* SRD

0-4-0T
"1101" CLASS

1101 DG
1102 DG
1103 DG
1104 DG
1105 DG
1106 DG

0-4-0ST
EX-SWANSEA HARBOUR TRUST

1140 701 SED
1141 929 DG
1142 943 DG
1143 968 DG
1144 974 SED
1145 1098 DG

0-6-0ST
EX-SWANSEA HARBOUR TRUST

1146 1085 DG
1147 1086 DG

0-4-0ST
EX-POWLESLAND AND MASON

1150 696 SED
1151 779 DG
1152 935 SED
1153 942 DG

2-4-0T
EX-CAMBRIAN RAILWAY

1196 OSW
1197 OSW

2-6-2T
EX-ALEXANDRA DOCKS RAILWAY

1205 LTS
1206 HFD

2-4-0T
EX-LISKEARD AND LOOE RAILWAY

1308* OSW

0-6-0ST
EX-WHITLAND AND CARDIGAN RAILWAY

1331 OSW

2-4-0
EX-MIDLAND AND SOUTH WESTERN JUNCTION RAILWAY

1334 DID
1335 RDG
1336 RDG

0-4-0ST
EX-CARDIFF RAILWAY

1338 TN

0-8-2T
EX-PORT TALBOT RAILWAY

1358 DG

0-6-0ST
"1361" CLASS

1361 LA
1362 NA
1363 LA
1364 LA
1365 LA

0-6-0PT
"1366" CLASS

1366 SDN
1367 WEY
1368 WEY
1369 SDN
1370 WEY
1371 SDN

0-4-2T
"1400" CLASS

1400 SDN
1401 CNYD
1402 CHEL
1403 WEY
1404 HFD
1405 EXE
1406 GLO
1407 RDG
1408 WOS
1409 LYD
1410 STB
1411 CNYD
1412 OSW
1413 GLO
1414 STB
1415 BRD
1416 CNYD
1417 OSW
1418 WOS
1419 FGD
1420 CHYS
1421 NPT
1422 PPRD
1423 FGD
1424 GLO
1425 CHYS
1426 SLO
1427 NA
1428 CNYD
1429 EXE
1430 BRD
1431 FGD
1432 OSW
1433 SDN
1434 CHR
1435 EXE
1436 SDN
1437 SLO
1438 STB
1439 NA
1440 EXE
1441 LYD
1442 SLO
1443 SHL
1444 RDG
1445 HFD
1446 SDN
1447 RDG
1448 OXF
1449 EXE
1450 OXF
1451 EXE
1452 FGD
1453 SDN
1454 WEY
1455 HFD
1456 LYD
1457 CNYD
1458 BAN
1459 OSW
1460 HFD
1461 AYN
1462 SHL
1463 BRD
1464 GLO
1465 MCH
1466 NA
1467 WEY
1468 EXE
1469 EXE
1470 NA
1471 LTS
1472 CARM
1473 BAN
1474 MCH

0-6-0PT
"1501" CLASS

1531 OXF
1532 CNYD
1538 SPM
1542 SDN

0-6-0PT
"1854" CLASS

1705 CED
1706 CNYD
1709 PILL
1713 NPT
1715 NEA
1720 NPT
1726 PILL
1730 TDU
1731 SDN

0-6-0PT
"655" CLASS

1742 OXF
1745 STB
1747 CNYD
1749 STB

0-6-0PT
"1854" CLASS

1752 STJ
1753 TR
1754 DYD
1758 SDN
1760 TN
1762 OXY
1764 PILL
1769 ABDR

0-6-0PT
"655" CLASS

1773 CNYD
1780 CNYD
1782 TR
1789 WEY

0-6-0PT
"1854" CLASS

1799 LA

0-6-0PT
"1813" CLASS

1835 STB

0-6-0PT
"1854" CLASS

1855 NEA
1858 NEA
1861 DID
1862 NPT
1863 SRD
1867 DYD
1870 STJ
1878 MTHR
1884 CED
1888 CED
1889 CDF
1891 CDF
1894 NPT
1896 PILL
1897 CED
1900 SBZ

0-6-0PT
"1901" CLASS

1903 CARM
1907 LLY
1909 TN
1912 PDN
1917 BHD
1919 WOS
1925 SHL
1930 SBZ
1935 OXF
1941 CARM
1943 GLO
1945 DG
1949 BHD
1957 LLY
1964 WTD
1965 MCH
1967 LLY
1968 BHD
1969 SHL
1973 LA
1979 WTD
1989 GLO
1990 LA
1991 LLY
1993 BRY
1996 WTD
2000 AYN
2001 WOS
2002 LLY
2004 BHD
2006 BHD
2007 WOS
2008 CED
2009 GLO
2010 WTD
2011 WTD
2012 LLY
2013 WTD
2014 SDN
2016 WOS
2017 SDN
2018 WTD
2019 LLY

0-6-0PT
"2021" CLASS

2021 PPRD
2022 CED
2023 WES
2025 LYD
2026 HFD
2027 LLY
2029 HFD
2030 WLN
2031 SPM
2032 OSW
2033 PILL
2034 LYD
2035 PPRD
2037 WOS
2038 TN
2039 LYD
2040 HFD
2042 LLY
2043 LYD
2044 LYD
2045 LYD
2047 CARM
2048 CED
2050 SBZ
2051 WOS
2052 BHD
2053 WES
2054 OSW
2055 SLO
2056 CARM
2059 LLY
2060 SDN
2061 SRD
2063 NPT
2064 SPM
2065 BAN
2066 CHYS
2067 SRD
2068 OSW
2069 CARM
2070 SPM
2071 TYS
2072 BRD
2073 NPT
2075 OSW
2076 RDG
2079 DYD
2080 LYD
2081 LLY
2082 DG
2083 LLY
2085 LLY
2086 CED
2088 EXE
2089 BHD
2090 STB
2091 LYD
2092 STB
2093 KDR
2094 PPRD
2095 SRD
2096 HFD
2097 NA
2098 LLY
2099 HFD
2100 WOS
2101 WOS
2102 LYD
2104 BHD
2106 BHD
2107 STB
2108 BHD
2109 SRD
2110 SRD
2111 CARM
2112 SLO
2113 PILL
2114 LYD
2115 WOS
2117 ABDR
2121 LYD
2122 NPT
2123 CED
2124 CED
2126 LLY
2127 TN
2129 BHD
2130 CED

2131	LYD
2132	LYD
2134	DG
2135	SPM
2136	PILL
2137	LLY
2138	HFD
2140	CED
2141	CED
2144	LYD
2146	GLO
2147	CED
2148	PZ
2150	LLY
2151	MCH
2152	TYS
2153	LYD
2154	PILL
2155	LYD
2156	SRD
2159	PPRD
2160	LYD

0-6-0T
EX- BURRY PORT
AND GWENDRAETH
VALLEY RAILWAY

2162	LLY
2165	LLY
2166	SED
2167	LLY
2168	LLY
2176	LLY

0-6-0PT
"2181" CLASS

2181	SBZ
2182	SBZ
2183	CNYD
2184	CNYD
2185	STB
2186	STB
2187	STB
2188	CNYD
2189	STB
2190	CNYD

0-6-0T
EX-BURRY PORT
AND GWENDRAETH
VALLEY RAILWAY

2192*	NEA
2193*	LLY
2194*	TN
2195	SDN
2196*	LLY
2197*	LLY
2198	LLY

0-6-0
"2251" CLASS

2200	ABH
2201	OSW
2202	DID
2203	TYS
2204	MCH
2205	WOS
2206	TYS
2207	WOS
2208	RDG
2209	TYS
2210	OSW
2211	TN
2212	TN
2213	TN
2214	TN
2215	TN
2216	CARM
2217	CARM
2218	NPT
2219	MCH
2220	SPM
2221	DID
2222	DID
2223	ABH
2224	SDN
2225	SPM
2226	DID
2227	CNYD
2228	SALOP
2229	SALOP
2230	EXE
2231	SALOP
2232	SRD
2233	SALOP
2234	SALOP
2235	SALOP
2236	CARM
2237	WOS
2238	TYS
2239	NPT
2240	DID
2241	WOS
2242	WOS
2243	HFD
2244	OSW
2245	RDG
2246	STB
2247	WOS
2248	GLO
2249	OXF
2250	SDN
2251	SPM
2252	DID
2253	SPM
2254	CARM
2255	OSW
2256	BAN
2257	TYS
2258	SPM
2259	CNYD
2260	ABH
2261	TN
2262	CHR
2263	WOS
2264	RDG
2265	SPM
2266	TN
2267	TN
2268	TN
2269	SPM
2270	STB
2271	CARM
2272	CARM
2273	LDR
2274	WOS
2275	TN
2276	PDN
2277	WOS
2278	WOS
2279	STB
2280	NPT
2281	STB
2282	PDN
2283	ABH
2284	CARM
2285	SHL
2286	HFD
2287	CNYD
2288	WTD
2289	DID
2290	WOS
2291	CARM
2292	TYS
2293	SPM
2294	WOS
2295	BAN
2296	TYS
2297	TYS
2298	ABH
2299	RDG

0-6-0
"2301" DEAN GOODS
CLASS

2322	SPM
2323	MCH
2327	OSW
2339	WOS
2340	SPM
2343	BCN
2349	HFD
2350	LYD
2351	BCN
2354	OSW
2356	MCH
2382	OSW
2385	PPRD
2386	OSW
2401	BCN
2407	NPT
2408	BAN
2409	CARM
2411	CARM
2414	STJ
2426	SPM
2431	CARM
2444	BRD
2445	WES
2449	OSW
2452	BCN
2458	WOS
2460	STJ
2462	BRD
2464	MCH
2468	BCN
2474	CARM
2482	OSW
2483	OSW
2484	CDF
2513	CHR
2515	LYD
2516	OSW
2523	BCN
2532	DID
2534	SPM
2537	CDF
2538	CDF
2541	HFD
2543	OSW
2551	WOS
2556	OSW
2568	SDN
2569	BCN
2570	CDF
2572	MCH
2573	RDG
2578	SPM
2579	OXF

2-6-0
"2600" ABERDARE
CLASS

2612	BAN
2620	STB
2623	OXY
2643	BAN
2651	WOS
2655	STB
2656	GLO
2662	CHR
2665	OXY
2667	CDF
2669	PPRD
2680	HFD

0-6-0PT
"655" CLASS

2702	SPM
2704	CNYD
2706	STB
2707	LLY
2708	TN
2709	SPM
2712	STB
2713	CNYD
2714	HFD
2715	DYD
2716	CNYD
2717	CNYD
2719	TYS

0-6-0PT
"2721" CLASS

2721	DYD
2722	NEA
2724	CED
2728	PPRD
2730	LLY
2734	PILL
2738	PILL
2739	PPRD
2743	WOS
2744	SALOP
2745	SALOP
2746	LLY
2748	TN
2749	PPRD
2751	LLY
2752	PZ
2754	CED
2755	TN
2756	GLO
2757	SLO
2760	MTHR
2761	TDU
2764	PILL
2767	PPRD
2769	TDU
2771	STB
2772	LMTN
2774	WOS
2776	LA
2780	SBZ
2781	CED
2785	NA
2786	SPM
2787	PANT
2789	SED
2790	SLO
2791	SRD
2792	DYD
2793	PILL
2794	NPT
2795	NPT
2797	NEA
2798	DG
2799	WOS

2-8-0
"2800/2884" CLASS

2800		PPRD
2801		ABDR
2802		PPRD
2803		WES
2804		STJ
2805		BAN
2806		ABDR
2807		HFD
2808		ABDR
2809		STJ
2810		ABDR
2811		ABDR
2812		CHR
2813		PPRD
2814		TN
2815		STJ
2816		BAN
2817		WEY
2818		WES
2819		STJ
2820		CDF
2821		CDF
2822		ABDR
2823		ABDR
2824		STJ
2825		OXY
2826		PDN
2827		OXF
2828		ABDR
2829		STJ
2830		OXY
2831		ABDR
2832	4806	LLY
2833		BHD
2834	4808	LA
2835		PDN
2836		ABDR
2837		CDF
2838		STJ
2839	4804	SPM
2840		PDN
2841		ABDR
2842		NPT
2843		SHL
2844		SPM
2845	4809	PDN
2846		SPM
2847	4811	LA
2848	4807	LA
2849	4803	STJ
2850		PDN
2851		NPT
2852		STB
2853	4810	SPM
2854	4801	STJ
2855		PDN
2856		PDN
2857		LA
2858		SHL
2859		SPM
2860		CDF
2861		OXF
2862	4802	LLY
2863	4805	LLY
2864		CDF
2865		NPT
2866		NPT
2867		LA
2868		PDN
2869		BAN
2870		ABDR
2871		BAN
2872	4800	LLY
2873		EXE
2874		BAN
2875		PDN
2876		NPT
2877		CDF
2878		BAN
2879		NPT
2880		ABDR
2881		OXF
2882		BAN
2883		CHR
2884		STJ
2885		BAN
2886		CHR
2887		STJ

2888	4850	LLY
2889		CDF
2890		CDF
2891		CDF
2892		STJ
2893		PPRD
2894		NPT
2895		BHD
2896		NPT
2897		SALOP
2898		BAN
2899		BAN

4-6-0
"2900" SAINT CLASS

2902*	LMTN
2903*	TYS
2905*	CDF
2906*	CDF
2908*	SDN
2912*	WEY
2913*	SDN
2915*	CHR
2916*	TYS
2920*	HFD
2924*	HFD
2926*	CHR
2927*	SDN
2928*	WES
2929*	BRD
2930*	CHR
2931*	BRD
2932*	HFD
2933*	LMTN
2934*	SDN
2935*	SDN
2936*	NPT
2937*	HFD
2938*	GLO
2939*	BRD
2940*	CDF
2941*	WES
2942*	BRD
2943*	CDF
2944*	HFD
2945*	SDN
2946*	WES
2947*	SDN
2948*	HFD
2949*	SDN
2950*	BRD
2951*	HFD
2952*	STJ
2953*	CHR
2954*	SDN
2955*	WEY
2979*	NPT
2980*	GLO
2981*	BAN
2987*	HFD
2988*	TYS
2989*	CHR

2-8-0
R.O.D. CLASS

3002	PPRD
3004	CARM
3005	TYS
3006	CARM
3008	SRD
3009	CARM
3010	CARM
3011	CARM
3012	PPRD
3013	SPM
3014	WES
3015	CARM
3016	OXY
3017	SPM
3018	PPRD
3019	WES
3020	SRD
3021	WOS
3022	SPM
3023	PPRD
3024	OXY
3025	RDG
3026	CNYD
3027	WOS
3028	CNYD
3029	WOS
3030	WOS
3031	OXY
3032	WES
3033	OXY
3034	SPM
3035	WES
3036	ABDR
3037	PPRD
3038	CDF
3039	OXY
3040	PPRD
3041	SPM
3042	CDF
3043	SRD
3044	CDF
3046	SPM
3047	RDG
3048	WOS
3049	TYS

2-6-2T
"3100" CLASS

3100	TDU
3101	TYS
3102	OXY
3103	NPT
3104	OXY

2-6-2T
"3150" CLASS

3150	STJ
3151	TYS
3153	GLO
3154	STJ
3157	STJ
3158	TYS
3159	STJ
3160	SRD
3161	STJ
3163	STJ
3164	GLO
3165	STJ
3167	STJ
3168	STJ
3169	BHD
3170	STJ
3171	GLO
3172	STJ
3174	STJ
3175	GLO
3176	STJ
3177	STJ
3178	STJ
3180	TYS
3182	STJ
3183	STJ
3184	STJ
3185	STJ
3186	LA
3187	LA
3188	STJ
3189	STJ
3190	STJ

0-6-0
"2251" CLASS

3200	MCH
3201	MCH
3202	OSW
3203	CNYD
3204	GLO
3205	GLO
3206	CNYD
3207	MCH
3208	OSW
3209	HFD
3210	DID
3211	DID
3212	DID
3213	GLO
3214	WOS
3215	SDN
3216	BAN
3217	SALOP

4-4-0
"3300" BULLDOG
CLASS

3335	EXE
3341*	NA
3363*	WES
3364*	WES
3366	CHR
3376*	DID
3377	SALOP
3379*	GLO
3382	WOS
3383	NA
3386	RDG
3391*	LA
3393*	WOS
3395*	EXE
3396*	DID
3400*	NA
3401*	LA
3406*	PPRD
3407*	NA
3408*	DID
3417*	WLN
3418*	RDG
3419	DID
3421	SDN
3426	RDG
3430*	NA
3431	LA
3432	HFD
3438	WES
3440	WOS
3441*	LA
3442*	SALOP
3443*	TN
3444*	TN
3445*	LA
3446*	LA
3447*	NEY
3448*	DID
3449*	CHEL
3450*	STB
3451*	EXE
3452*	SDN
3453*	PPRD
3454*	HFD
3455*	NEA

2-4-0T
"3500" CLASS

3561	SDN
3562	SHL

0-4-2T
"1159" CLASS

3574	WOS
3575	STJ
3577	SED

2-4-0T
"3500" CLASS

3582	TN
3585	OXF
3586	LTS
3588	OXF
3589	OXF
3592	CARM
3597	CHYS
3599	RYR

0-6-0PT
"5700" CLASS

3600	PDN
3601	HFD
3602	SALOP
3603	EXE
3604	SPM
3605	ABDR
3606	EXE
3607	WOS
3608	OXF
3609	GLO
3610	ABDR
3611	NEA
3612	ABEEG
3613	TYS
3614	SPM
3615	SRD
3616	ABEEG
3617	LTS
3618	PDN
3619	PDN
3620	SHL
3621	NEA
3622	DID
3623	SPM
3624	TYS
3625	TYS
3626	BHD
3627	TDU
3628	PPRD
3629	LA
3630	BAN
3631	LMTN
3632	SPM
3633	SED
3634	NPT
3635	PDN
3636	NPT
3637	FGD
3638	BCN
3639	LA
3640	ABEEG
3641	SED
3642	LLY
3643	SPM
3644	PDN
3645	SDN
3646	PDN
3647	NPT
3648	PDN
3649	STB
3650	TYS
3651	PPRD
3652	SLO
3653	TYS
3654	NEY
3655	ABDR
3656	LTS
3657	TYS
3658	PDN
3659	PDN
3660	TYS
3661	DG
3662	NPT
3663	RGD
3664	TYS
3665	CHR
3666	SDN
3667	STB
3668	TDU
3669	PDN
3670	ABEEG
3671	YEO
3672	PDN
3673	TYS
3674	TDU
3675	LA
3676	SPM
3677	SLO
3678	LDR
3679	SED
3680	ABEEG
3681	SLO
3682	SDN
3683	ABEEG
3684	SDN
3685	PDN
3686	LA
3687	OXF
3688	PDN
3689	TYS
3690	PPRD
3691	LTS
3692	PPRD
3693	TYS
3694	BAN
3695	TDU
3696	WES
3697	RDG
3698	LLY
3699	TDU
3700	NPT
3701	LDR
3702	SALOP
3703	LTS
3704	SHL
3705	LA
3706	BCN
3707	CED
3708	CDF
3709	DID
3710	PDN
3711	PPRD
3712	NPT
3713	LDR
3714	NPT
3715	RDG
3716	CDF
3717	PPRD
3718	DYD
3719	LLY
3720	SPM
3721	DID
3722	OXF
3723	PDN
3724	SDN
3725	HFD
3726	NPT
3727	SHL
3728	HFD
3729	ABEEG
3730	PPRD
3731	WES
3732	WLN
3733	YEO
3734	PDN
3735	WES
3736	RDG
3737	SDN
3738	PDN
3739	SDN

No.		Shed
3740		STB
3741		OXF
3742		BHD
3743		TYS
3744		OXY
3745		OXY
3746		SPM
3747		ABDR
3748		SDN
3749		WLN
3750		SHL
3751		BAN
3752		LLY
3753		ABDR
3754		PDN
3755		CDF
3756		SRD
3757		NEA
3758		WES
3759		SPM
3760		SRD
3761		LLY
3762		CHR
3763		SPM
3764		SPM
3765		SPM
3766		PDN
3767		BCN
3768		LDR
3769		SLO
3770		RDG
3771		LLY
3772		TDU
3773		SPM
3774		NEA
3775		WLN
3776		ABEEG
3777		LLY
3778		SRD
3779		PPRD
3780		SDN
3781		DG
3782		SALOP
3783		RDG
3784		SPM
3785		LDR
3786		CHR
3787		LA
3788		SALOP
3789		HFD
3790		LA
3791		DYD
3792		OXY
3793		OXY
3794		EXE
3795		SPM
3796		NPT
3797		LDR
3798		SLO
3799		SHL

2-8-0
"2884" CLASS

No.		Shed
3800		NPT
3801		NPT
3802		BAN
3803		BAN
3804		NPT
3805		NPT
3806		STJ
3807		NPT
3808		STJ
3809		CDF
3810		NPT
3811		LA
3812		CDF
3813	4855	LA
3814		CDF
3815		STJ
3816		NPT
3817		CDF
3818	4852	STJ
3819		BAN
3820	4856	PDN
3821		BAN
3822		PPRD
3823		CDF
3824		CDF
3825		BAN
3826		PPRD
3827		BAN
3828		PPRD
3829		BAN
3830		NPT
3831	4857	NPT
3832		PDN
3833		NPT
3834		EXE
3835		OXF
3836		OXF
3837	4854	PDN
3838		OXF
3839	4853	PDN
3840		RDG
3841		RDG
3842		WES
3843		RDG
3844		RDG
3845		RDG
3846		RDG
3847		OXF
3848		OXF
3849		WES
3850		WES
3851		PDN
3852		PDN
3853		PDN
3854		SHL
3855		SHL
3856		SHL
3857		SHL
3858		SHL
3859		SHL
3860		SHL
3861		BAN
3862		PPRD
3863		WES
3864		LA
3865	4851	STJ
3866		OXF

4-6-0
"4000" STAR CLASS

No.	Shed
4003*	LDR
4004*	OXF
4007*	WOS
4012*	NA
4013*	CHR
4015*	SDN
4017*	SDN
4018*	SRD
4019*	BRD
4020*	BRD
4021*	OXF
4022	SDN
4023	LDR
4025	SRD
4026	TN
4028	WES
4030	BRD
4031*	SRD
4033*	BRD
4034*	BRD
4035*	BRD
4036*	SDN
4038*	WES
4039*	LDR
4040*	SALOP
4041*	BRD
4042*	BRD
4043*	BRD
4044*	SALOP
4045*	WES
4046*	SALOP
4047*	BRD
4048*	LDR
4049*	OXF
4050*	LDR
4051*	WOS
4052*	OXF
4053*	SRD
4054*	EXE
4055*	SDN
4056*	TN
4057*	SDN
4058*	TYS
4059*	GLO
4060*	SRD
4061*	SALOP
4062*	SDN

4-6-0
"4073" CASTLE
CLASS

No.	Shed
100A1*	PDN
111*	PDN
4000*	SRD
4016*	NA
4032*	LA
4037*	PDN
4073*	PDN
4074*	LDR
4075*	PDN
4076*	PDN
4077*	NA
4078*	LDR
4079*	HFD
4080*	BRD
4081*	LDR
4082*	GLO
4083*	CDF
4084*	BRD
4085*	RDG
4086*	WOS
4087*	LA
4088*	LA
4089*	BRD
4090*	LA
4091*	PDN
4092*	WOS
4093*	BRD
4094*	CDF
4095*	LDR
4096*	BRD
4097*	PZ
4098*	NA
4099*	NA

2-6-2T
"5101" CLASS

No.	Shed
4100	WOS
4101	TYS
4102	LMTN
4103	SRD
4104	STB
4105	SRD
4106	TYS
4107	TYS
4108	SRD
4109	NA
4110	SRD
4111	TYS
4112	LMTN
4113	TN
4114	WOS
4115	SRD
4116	TYS
4117	TN
4118	SALOP
4119	STJ
4120	BHD
4121	BHD
4122	BHD
4123	BHD
4124	BHD
4125	BHD
4126	BHD
4127	BHD
4128	BHD
4129	BHD
4130	STJ
4131	PPRD
4132	NEA
4133	NA
4134	LDR
4135	PPRD
4136	TN
4137	STJ
4138	PPRD
4139	WOS
4140	GLO
4141	CHEL
4142	BRD
4143	BRD
4144	STJ
4145	TDU
4146	STB
4147	TYS
4148	STJ
4149	STB
4150	STB
4151	BRD
4152	BRD
4153	KDR
4154	WLN
4155	BRD
4156	STJ
4157	TYS
4158	STJ
4159	CHR

2-8-0T
"4200" CLASS

No.	Shed
4200	STJ
4201	PILL
4203	NPT
4206	NPT
4207	LDR
4208	LTS
4211	PILL
4212	LDR
4213	LLY
4214	TDU
4215	SBZ
4217	ABEEG
4218	TDU
4221	NEA
4222	ABEEG
4223	CARM
4224	NPT
4225	NPT
4226	PILL
4227	CDF
4228	ABDR
4229	PILL
4230	NPT
4231	ABEEG
4232	NEA
4233	PILL
4235	PILL
4236	CDF
4237	PILL
4238	PPRD
4241	TDU
4242	NPT
4243	ABEEG
4246	PILL
4247	NPT
4248	NPT
4250	LDR
4251	TDU
4252	NEA
4253	PILL
4254	LLY
4255	DYD
4256	LDR
4257	ABDR
4258	PILL
4259	NEA
4260	NPT
4261	LTS
4262	STJ
4263	NPT
4264	ABDR
4265	LDR
4266	CARM
4267	ABEEG
4268	NPT
4269	PILL
4270	NPT
4271	NPT
4272	NEA
4273	TDU
4274	NEA
4275	PPRD
4276	NPT
4277	DYD
4278	LLY
4279	NEA
4280	PILL
4281	LLY
4282	SED
4283	SED
4284	NEA
4285	ABDR
4286	DYD
4287	ABEEG
4288	NEA
4289	NPT
4290	CDF
4291	PILL
4292	DYD
4293	NEA
4294	NPT
4295	LDR
4296	SED
4297	ABDR
4298	SBZ
4299	DG

2-6-0
"4300" CLASS

No.	Shed
4303	PPRD
4318	DID
4320	CHEL
4326	DID
4337	BHD
4353	BHD
4358	NEY
4365	WES
4375	CNYD
4377	WES
4381	SDN
4386	BHD

2-6-2T
"4400" CLASS

No.	Shed
4400	WLN
4401	WLN
4402	LA

4403 WLN
4404 TDU
4405 NA
4406 WLN
4407 LA
4408 TDU
4409 WLN
4410 EXE

2-6-2T
"4500/4575" CLASS

4500 PZ
4501 MCH
4502 SDN
4503 SBZ
4504 WOS
4505 SBZ
4506 WTD
4507 SDN
4508 WES
4509 PZ
4510 SDN
4511 MCH
4512 MCH
4513 MCH
4514 ABEEG
4515 WTD
4516 SBZ
4517 LA
4518 NPT
4519 WTD
4520 WES
4521 SDN
4522 ABEEG
4523 TR
4524 LA
4525 PZ
4526 NA
4527 WEY
4528 LA
4529 SBZ
4530 EXE
4531 LA
4532 TR
4533 PPRD
4534 GLO
4535 BRD
4536 BRD
4537 PZ
4538 SDN
4539 BRD
4540 PZ
4541 PPRD
4542 LA
4543 SDN
4544 SDN
4545 PZ
4546 WOS
4547 NA
4548 PZ
4549 MCH
4550 SDN
4551 SDN
4552 SBZ
4553 WTD
4554 TR
4555 MCH
4556 WTD
4557 TDU
4558 WOS
4559 SBZ
4560 MCH
4561 TR
4562 WEY
4563 BRD
4564 CHEL
4565 SBZ
4566 PZ
4567 CHEL
4568 SBZ
4569 TR
4570 SBZ
4571 MCH
4572 WES
4573 WES
4574 PZ
4575 MCH
4576 WTD
4577 BRD
4578 CHEL
4579 WTD
4580 BRD
4581 TR
4582 NA
4583 LA
4584 KDR
4585 SDN
4586 KDR
4587 NA
4588 TR
4589 TR
4590 SDN
4591 LA
4592 SDN
4593 NPT
4594 KDR
4595 BRD
4596 WOS
4597 ABEEG
4598 SBZ
4599 NPT

0-6-0PT
"5700" CLASS

4600 HFD
4601 DID
4602 SALOP
4603 SPM
4604 SHL
4605 TYS
4606 PDN
4607 SPM
4608 SHL
4609 PDN
4610 SHL
4611 PPRD
4612 SPM
4613 WOS
4614 WOS
4615 PDN
4616 CHYS
4617 SLO
4618 CED
4619 SPM
4620 TYS
4621 NEA
4622 CDF
4623 SALOP
4624 SPM
4625 KDR
4626 SPM
4627 GLO
4628 GLO
4629 WOS
4630 CED
4631 BAN
4632 MTHR
4633 CDF
4634 TDU
4635 MTHR
4636 WES
4637 CDF
4638 STB
4639 PPRD
4640 DYD
4641 KDR
4642 PDN
4643 TDU
4644 PDN
4645 OXF
4646 BAN
4647 SPM
4648 TYS
4649 RDG
4650 SLO
4651 SDN
4652 CDF
4653 LA
4654 NEY
4655 WEY
4656 LA
4657 HFD
4658 LA
4659 GLO
4660 WEY
4661 RDG
4662 PILL
4663 SHL
4664 WOS
4665 PDN
4666 PDN
4667 PDN
4668 PPRD
4669 TDU
4670 RDG
4671 NPT
4672 SALOP
4673 SHL
4674 LTS
4675 TDU
4676 OXF
4677 CDF
4678 HFD
4679 LA
4680 PDN
4681 DYD
4682 ABEEG
4683 TYS
4684 DYD
4685 ABEEG
4686 ABEEG
4687 STB
4688 RDG
4689 YEO
4690 RDG
4691 PDN
4692 RDG
4693 LA
4694 DG
4695 SHL
4696 STB
4697 SDN
4698 PDN
4699 PDN

2-8-0
"4700" CLASS

4700 PDN
4701 PDN
4702 PDN
4703 LA
4704 BHD
4705 PDN
4706 EXE
4707 PDN
4708 OXY

4-6-0
"4900" HALL CLASS

4900* PDN
4901* CDF
4902* OXF
4903* OXF
4904* OXY
4905* SDN
4906* TR
4907* 3903 PDN
4908* LLY
4909* BAN
4910* CARM
4912* PPRD
4913* CDF
4914* RDG
4915* CARM
4916* OXY
4917* TYS
4918* CHR
4919* SALOP
4920* RDG
4921* OXF
4922* CARM
4923* OXY
4924* TYS
4925* SDN
4926* WES
4927* WES
4928* OXF
4929* TR
4930* TYS
4931* RDG
4932* PPRD
4933* PPRD
4934* TYS
4935* PDN
4936* TR
4937* NEY
4938* OXF
4939* TYS
4940* SBZ
4941* NPT
4942* BRD
4943* PDN
4944* OXY
4945* SDN
4946* PZ
4947* PZ
4948* 3902 LA
4949* PZ
4950* SRD
4951* PDN
4952* CDF
4953* CDF
4954* TN
4955* OXY
4956* SDN
4957* NEY
4958* PDN
4959* TYS
4960* SRD
4961* PDN
4962* PDN
4963* WES
4964* OXY
4965* SPM
4966* LA
4967* TYS
4968* 3900 SPM
4969* SPM
4970* PZ
4971* 3901 LA
4972* 3904 LA
4973* OXF
4974* CDF
4975* CDF
4976* CHR
4977* GLO
4978* PDN
4979* CDF
4980* WOS
4981* CARM
4982* FGD
4983* NA
4984* CARM
4985* PDN
4986* SPM
4987* OXY
4988* WEY
4989* RDG
4990* SPM
4991* OXY
4992* TYS
4993* TYS
4994* RDG
4995* RDG
4996* OXY
4997* NEY
4998* PDN
4999* TYS

4-6-0
"4073" CASTLE CLASS

5000* PDN
5001* CDF
5002* LDR
5003* TN
5004* PDN
5005* CDF
5006* LDR
5007* CDF
5008* PDN
5009* LA
5010* CDF
5011* NA
5012* EXE
5013* LDR
5014* PDN
5015* SRD
5016* LDR
5017* WOS
5018* SRD
5019* BRD
5020* CDF
5021* SALOP
5022* PDN
5023* PDN
5024* BRD
5025* BRD
5026* LA
5027* PDN
5028* NA
5029* PDN
5030* CDF
5031* SRD
5032* SALOP
5033* CHR
5034* NA
5035* PDN
5036* PDN
5037* PDN
5038* PDN
5039* PDN
5040* PDN
5041* LA
5042* GLO
5043* PDN
5044* PDN
5045* PDN
5046* CDF
5047* NA
5048* BRD
5049* CDF
5050* LA
5051* LDR
5052* CDF
5053* SRD
5054* CDF
5055* PDN
5056* PDN
5057* LA
5058* NA

5059* EXE
5060* LA
5061* SALOP
5062* NA
5063* WOS
5064* SALOP
5065* PDN
5066* PDN
5067* SDN
5068* SDN
5069* PDN
5070* SRD
5071* NA
5072* LDR
5073* SALOP
5074* BRD
5075* SRD
5076* BRD
5077* TN
5078* NA
5079* LA
5080* CDF
5081* PDN
5082* BRD
5083* BRD
5084* BRD
5085* PDN
5086* SALOP
5087* PDN
5088* SRD
5089* LDR
5090* LA
5091* BRD
5092* WOS
5093* LDR
5094* NA
5095* LA
5096* BRD
5097* SALOP
5098* EXE
5099* PDN

2-6-2T
"5101" CLASS

5101 STB
5102 TYS
5103 SRD
5104 LMTN
5105 STB
5106 TYS
5107 STB
5108 NA
5109 LMTN
5110 KDR
5111 SRD
5112 WOS
5113 NA
5114 WOS
5117 CHR
5119 SHL
5121 TYS
5122 STB
5125 TYS
5127 WLN
5128 RHY
5129 TYS
5130 LMTN
5131 STB
5132 NA
5134 STB
5135 WLN
5136 STB
5137 WLN
5138 STB
5139 WLN
5140 SBZ
5141 STB
5142 NA
5143 SRD
5144 LMTN
5146 STB
5147 STB
5148 LA
5150 NA
5151 SRD
5152 TYS
5153 NA
5154 SALOP
5155 STB
5156 TYS
5157 NA
5158 SBZ
5159 THT
5160 STB
5161 LMTN
5162 TYS
5163 LMTN
5164 TYS
5165 STB
5166 TYS
5167 STB
5168 SALOP
5169 BRD
5170 STB
5171 TYS
5172 TN
5173 WOS
5174 CHR
5175 TYS
5176 CHR
5177 TYS
5178 WLN
5179 CHR
5180 STB
5181 CHR
5182 TYS
5183 STJ
5184 CHR
5185 LMTN
5186 CHR
5187 LMTN
5188 TYS
5189 STB
5190 TYS
5191 STB
5192 LMTN
5193 STB
5194 LMTN
5195 BRY
5196 STB
5197 STB
5198 TYS
5199 TYS

2-8-0T
"4200" CLASS

5200 CDF
5201 NPT
5202 TDU
5203 LLY
5204 LLY

2-8-0T
"5205" CLASS

5205 STJ
5206 NPT
5207 CARM
5208 NPT
5209 LLY
5210 SED
5211 LDR
5212 LLY
5213 LLY
5214 SED
5215 LLY
5216 DYD
5217 NPT
5218 NPT
5219 LDR
5220 LLY
5221 SED
5222 NPT
5223 LLY
5224 NPT
5225 NEA
5226 LLY
5227 SED
5228 LLY
5229 NPT
5230 LLY
5231 CARM
5232 SED
5233 NPT
5234 NPT
5235 PILL
5236 CDF
5237 ABDR
5238 NPT
5239 NEA
5240 LLY
5241 SPM
5242 NEA
5243 NPT
5244 PILL
5245 ABDR
5246 SED
5247 LLY
5248 LLY
5249 CDF
5250 DYD
5251 NPT
5252 PILL
5253 SED
5254 NEA
5255 NPT
5256 NPT
5257 DYD
5258 ABDR
5259 ABEEG
5260 DYD
5261 LLY
5262 STJ
5263 ABDR
5264 NPT

2-6-0
"4300" CLASS

5300 OXY
5302 BAN
5303 KDR
5305 WEY
5306 WES
5307 CDF
5309 WLN
5310 NEY
5311 WES
5312 GLO
5313 OXY
5314 WEY
5315 CNYD
5316 BHD
5317 BAN
5318 LA
5319 CNYD
5320 RDG
5321 EXE
5322 SDN
5323 OXF
5324 BAN
5325 BRD
5326 WES
5327 BRD
5328 WEY
5330 DID
5331 OXY
5332 WLN
5333 OXY
5334 CNYD
5335 CDF
5336 GLO
5337 WEY
5338 WEY
5339 CARM
5340 WEY
5341 LDR
5343 BRD
5344 CHR
5345 CHEL
5346 TYS
5347 GLO
5348 HFD
5349 BAN
5350 NA
5351 SPM
5353 NEY
5355 PPRD
5356 RDG
5357 NEY
5358 SPM
5359 WEY
5360 SHL
5361 BAN
5362 STJ
5364 NPT
5365 CNYD
5367 SDN
5368 NEY
5369 TYS
5370 TYS
5371 SDN
5372 NEY
5373 BAN
5374 SPM
5375 RDG
5376 LA
5377 HFD
5378 CDF
5379 OXY
5380 DID
5381 DID
5382 CDF
5384 WEY
5385 RDG
5386 OXY
5388 CDF
5390 OXY
5391 NA
5392 NEY
5393 8393 BHD
5394 GLO
5395 FGD
5396 SDN
5397 DID
5398 GLO
5399 CHR

0-6-0PT
"5400" CLASS

5400 LDR
5401 SHL
5402 WES
5403 WES
5404 BAN
5405 SHL
5406 WES
5407 BAN
5408 LDR
5409 SHL
5410 SHL
5411 SHL
5412 LA
5413 SHL
5414 SHL
5415 SHL
5416 SHL
5417 SHL
5418 SHL
5419 WES
5420 SHL
5421 SHL
5422 WES
5423 WES
5424 BAN

2-6-2T
"4575" CLASS

5500 TR
5501 TN
5502 SBZ
5503 TN
5504 TN
5505 NA
5506 BRD
5507 MCH
5508 WES
5509 WEY
5510 SDN
5511 BRD
5512 BRD
5513 WTD
5514 BRD
5515 CHEL
5516 NPT
5517 MCH
5518 KDR
5519 SBZ
5520 ABDR
5521 TN
5522 TN
5523 BRD
5524 MCH
5525 EXE
5526 TR
5527 BRD
5528 BRD
5529 YEO
5530 NA
5531 SBZ
5532 PPRD
5533 TN
5534 SDN
5535 BRD
5536 BRD
5537 TR
5538 CHEL
5539 BRD
5540 LA
5541 MCH
5542 TN
5543 TN
5544 WOS
5545 NPT
5546 BRD
5547 BRD
5548 BRD
5549 WTD
5550 NPT
5551 NA
5552 NA
5553 BRD
5554 WES
5555 BRD
5556 TDU
5557 NA
5558 BRD
5559 BRD
5560 ABH

5561 BRD
5562 TR
5563 SDN
5564 BRD
5565 YEO
5566 SDN
5567 LA
5568 WTD
5569 LA
5570 ABH
5571 TN
5572 BRD
5573 KDR
5574 CHEL

0-6-2T
"5600" CLASS

5600 FDL
5601 THT
5602 NPT
5603 NPT
5604 LDR
5605 CHYS
5606 OXY
5607 THT
5608 THT
5609 BRY
5610 FDL
5611 THT
5612 DYD
5613 THT
5614 CHYS
5615 THT
5616 OXF
5617 CHYS
5618 AYN
5619 AYN
5620 STJ
5621 BRY
5622 BRY
5623 CHYS
5624 CHYS
5625 STJ
5626 STJ
5627 BRY
5628 CDF
5629 DYD
5630 AYN
5631 LDR
5632 BRY
5633 TDU
5634 TYS
5635 RHY
5636 THT
5637 AYN
5638 NPT
5639 DYD
5640 RYR
5641 AYN
5642 SALOP
5643 AYN
5644 AYN
5645 STJ
5646 CHYS
5647 CHR
5648 BRY
5649 PPRD
5650 THT
5651 CHYS
5652 CH
5653 CH
5654 MTHR
5655 RYR
5656 DYD
5657 OXY
5658 CHYS
5659 CHYS
5660 RHY
5661 CHYS
5662 BRY
5663 THT
5664 BRY
5665 BRY
5666 CH
5667 BRY
5668 FDL
5669 AYN
5670 OXY
5671 CH
5672 CHYS
5673 SALOP
5674 CH
5675 LLY
5676 THT
5677 MTHR
5678 MTHR
5679 CDF
5680 THT
5681 CHYS
5682 AYN
5683 RHY
5684 OXY
5685 CDF
5686 AYN
5687 CHYS
5688 THT
5689 WES
5690 CHR
5691 THT
5692 RHY
5693 BRY
5694 CH
5695 THT
5696 RHY
5697 GLO
5698 CH
5699 BRY

0-6-0PT
"5700" CLASS

5700 TYS
5701 TYS
5702 LLY
5703 NEA
5704 SED
5705 LLY
5706 STJ
5707 TDU
5708 LTS
5709 NPT
5710 DID
5711 MTHR
5712 TYS
5713 DYD
5714 STJ
5715 SLO
5716 FGD
5717 PDN
5718 WES
5719 STB
5720 NEA
5721 MTHR
5722 LLY
5723 CHR
5724 BAN
5725 CHR
5726 STB
5727 SHL
5728 PPRD
5729 STJ
5730 DG
5731 DYD
5732 NPT
5733 ABEEG
5734 DYD
5735 DID
5736 BAN
5737 SLO
5738 TYS
5739 SRD
5740 PILL
5741 NPT
5742 TYS
5743 SED
5744 DID
5745 TYS
5746 NEA
5747 PILL
5748 OXY
5749 CDF
5750 SHL
5751 RDG
5752 DID
5753 SHL
5754 STB
5755 SHL
5756 TDU
5757 WES
5758 WLN
5759 LDR
5760 EXE
5761 RDG
5762 RDG
5763 RDG
5764 PDN
5765 HFD
5766 RDG
5767 YEO
5768 PPRD
5769 MTHR
5770 ABDR
5771 WES
5772 RDG
5773 DYD
5774 SALOP
5775 DG
5776 PILL
5777 LTS
5778 NEA
5779 TR
5780 OXY
5781 WES
5782 LLY
5783 SLO
5784 SPM
5785 WES
5786 ABEEG
5787 ABDR
5788 ABEEG
5789 ABEEG
5790 TYS
5791 CHR
5792 PPRD
5793 GLO
5794 STB
5795 STB
5796 ABDR
5797 TDU
5798 NA
5799 SHL

0-4-2T
"5800" CLASS

5800 SDN
5801 BCN
5802 SDN
5803 BRD
5804 SDN
5805 SDN
5806 OSW
5807 HFD
5808 HFD
5809 BRD
5810 CNYD
5811 CNYD
5812 TN
5813 BRD
5814 HFD
5815 WOS
5816 WOS
5817 HFD
5818 PPRD
5819 CARM

4-6-0
"4900" HALL CLASS

5900* WES
5901* RDG
5902* EXE
5903* DID
5904* OXF
5905* FGD
5906* NPT
5907* TYS
5908* LLY
5909* SRD
5910* CDF
5911* NPT
5912* CHR
5913* LDR
5914* WOS
5915* PZ
5916* OXY
5917* WOS
5918* OXY
5919* SRD
5920* OXY
5921* OXY
5922* PDN
5923* CHR
5924* WES
5925* WES
5926* SBZ
5927* SRD
5928* FGD
5929* NEY
5930* BAN
5931* PDN
5932* PDN
5933* RDG
5934* SDN
5935* DID
5936* PDN
5937* PDN
5938* PDN
5939* PDN
5940* PDN
5941* PDN
5942* SRD
5943* SDN
5944* SRD
5945* OXY
5946* CDF
5947* OXY
5948* RDG
5949* BRD
5950* TYS
5951* GLO
5952* PDN
5953* CDF
5954* BAN
5955* 3950 BRD
5956* RDG
5957* OXY
5958* CDF
5959* RDG
5960* OXF
5961* WES
5962* PDN
5963* CARM
5964* SPM
5965* GLO
5966* CHR
5967* BAN
5968* WEY
5969* WEY
5970* CDF
5971* WES
5972* CARM
5973* RDG
5974* WES
5975* PPRD
5976* 3951 SPM
5977* CDF
5978* SDN
5979* OXY
5980* GLO
5981* SALOP
5982* TN
5983* WOS
5984* SPM
5985* WES
5986* 3954 PDN
5987* PDN
5988* GLO
5989* OXY
5990* GLO
5991* BAN
5992* BAN
5993* TYS
5994* SALOP
5995* SRD
5996* PDN
5997* TYS
5998* LA
5999* TN

4-6-0
"6000" KING CLASS

6000* LA
6001* PDN
6002* LA
6003* PDN
6004* LA
6005* SRD
6006* SRD
6007* PDN
6008* SRD
6009* PDN
6010* LA
6011* SRD
6012* LA
6013* PDN
6014* PDN
6015* PDN
6016* LA
6017* LA
6018* NA
6019* LA
6020* LA
6021* PDN
6022* LA
6023* NA
6024* NA
6025* PDN
6026* LA
6027* NA
6028* NA
6029* LA

2-6-2T
"6100" CLASS

6100 SLO
6101 SLO
6102 SHL
6103 OXF
6104 SLO
6105 SLO
6106 SLO

6107	SLO
6108	SLO
6109	RDG
6110	SHL
6111	SLO
6112	PDN
6113	SLO
6114	SLO
6115	RDG
6116	SLO
6117	RDG
6118	SHL
6119	SLO
6120	PDN
6121	RDG
6122	OXF
6123	SLO
6124	SLO
6125	SHL
6126	SLO
6127	SLO
6128	SHL
6129	PDN
6130	RDG
6131	RDG
6132	PDN
6133	SLO
6134	PDN
6135	PDN
6136	RDG
6137	PDN
6138	OXF
6139	SHL
6140	RDG
6141	PDN
6142	PDN
6143	SLO
6144	PDN
6145	SLO
6146	SLO
6147	SHL
6148	SHL
6149	PDN
6150	SLO
6151	SLO
6152	SLO
6153	SLO
6154	RDG
6155	PDN
6156	SHL
6157	SLO
6158	PDN
6159	PDN
6160	SLO
6161	SLO
6162	RDG
6163	RDG
6164	SLO
6165	SHL
6166	PDN
6167	SLO
6168	PDN
6169	SHL

2-6-0
"4300" CLASS

6300	OXF
6301	EXE
6302	RDG
6303	CNYD
6304	LDR
6305	TN
6306	WOS
6307	SALOP
6308	CHR
6309	GLO
6310	CARM
6311	CHR
6312	RDG
6313	RDG
6314	WES
6316	CNYD
6317	TN
6318	PZ
6319	LA
6320	SDN
6321	SRD
6322	SDN
6323	TN
6324	WOS
6325	SHL
6326	CHEL
6327	CNYD
6328	TN
6329	DID
6330	SBZ
6331	CARM
6332	OXY
6333	PPRD
6334	RDG
6335	OXY
6336	TYS
6337	CHR
6338	SALOP
6339	CHR
6340	SDN
6341	CHEL
6342	OXY
6343	TN
6344	CARM
6345	NA
6346	BHD
6347	NEY
6348	SALOP
6349	HFD
6350	BHD
6351	WES
6352	HFD
6353	CDF
6354	PZ
6355	NEY
6356	SBZ
6357	SDN
6358	SDN
6359	DID
6360	SDN
6361	OXY
6362	OXY
6363	RDG
6364	TN
6365	WES
6366	RDG
6367	CARM
6368	WES
6369	WES
6370	PPRD
6371	NEY
6372	TN
6373	TR
6374	SDN
6375	WES
6376	BHD
6377	TN
6378	WOS
6379	DID
6380	CHR
6381	GLO
6382	WOS
6383	RDG
6384	SDN
6385	WOS
6386	STJ
6387	SDN
6388	SHL
6389	NEY
6390	BAN
6391	SRD
6392	CHR
6393	RDG
6394	TN
6395	HFD
6396	WOS
6397	EXE
6398	TN
6399	WES

0-6-0PT
"6400" CLASS

6400	PPRD
6401	AYN
6402	CHYS
6403	PPRD
6404	BHD
6405	BHD
6406	LA
6407	SHL
6408	MTHR
6409	NPT
6410	ABDR
6411	AYN
6412	LDR
6413	ABDR
6414	LA
6415	NPT
6416	CHYS
6417	LA
6418	SRD
6419	LA
6420	SBZ
6421	LA
6422	SRD
6423	CHYS
6424	PPRD
6425	LDR
6426	NPT
6427	MTHR
6428	NPT
6429	PPRD
6430	PPRD
6431	LDR
6432	PPRD
6433	CHYS
6434	MTHR
6435	CHYS
6436	CHYS
6437	ABDR
6438	AYN
6439	NPT

0-6-2T
"5600" CLASS

6600	OXY
6601	SPM
6602	BRY
6603	RYR
6604	LDR
6605	ABDR
6606	SALOP
6607	RYR
6608	RYR
6609	OXY
6610	OXY
6611	TYS
6612	NPT
6613	NEA
6614	BRY
6615	CHYS
6616	DYD
6617	STB
6618	RYR
6619	BRY
6620	BRY
6621	ABEEG
6622	CDF
6623	GLO
6624	CHR
6625	LMTN
6626	CHYS
6627	CHYS
6628	ABDR
6629	DYD
6630	TYS
6631	HFD
6632	LMTN
6633	SALOP
6634	PPRD
6635	CHYS
6636	PPRD
6637	BRY
6638	OXY
6639	STJ
6640	OXY
6641	BRY
6642	TDU
6643	BRY
6644	LMTN
6645	OXY
6646	STB
6647	BRY
6648	CHYS
6649	NPT
6650	LMTN
6651	PPRD
6652	ABDR
6653	BRY
6654	NPT
6655	CHYS
6656	SPM
6657	LMTN
6658	BRY
6659	CHYS
6660	CHYS
6661	CHYS
6662	BRY
6663	NPT
6664	RYR
6665	STB
6666	STJ
6667	STB
6668	BRY
6669	BRY
6670	SPM
6671	SPM
6672	NPT
6673	STJ
6674	STB
6675	TDU
6676	STJ
6677	STB
6678	STB
6679	LDR
6680	LDR
6681	GLO
6682	OXF
6683	SALOP
6684	STB
6685	TDU
6686	DYD
6687	PPRD
6688	DYD
6689	STJ
6690	WES
6691	CDF
6692	ABDR
6693	ABDR
6694	CNYD
6695	LDR
6696	BAN
6697	LMTN
6698	CNYD
6699	WES

0-6-0PT
"6700" CLASS

6700	CED
6701	CED
6702	CED
6703	CED
6704	CED
6705	CED
6706	CED
6707	CED
6708	CED
6709	CED
6710	PILL
6711	PILL
6712	BRY
6713	DG
6714	SED
6715	DYD
6716	SDN
6717	DYD
6718	DYD
6719	DYD
6720	DYD
6721	CED
6722	BRY
6723	BRY
6724	BRY
6725	PILL
6726	PILL
6727	PILL
6728	PILL
6729	PILL
6730	PILL
6731	PILL
6732	PILL
6733	BRY
6734	DG
6735	PILL
6736	BRY
6737	SDN
6738	BRY
6739	SDN
6740	BRY
6741	SDN
6742	PPRD
6743	PILL
6744	CED
6745	BRY
6746	BRY
6747	BRY
6748	BRY
6749	DYD
6750	BRY
6751	CED
6752	BRY
6753	BRY
6754	BRY
6755	PILL
6756	PILL
6757	STJ
6758	BRY
6759	PILL

4-6-0
"6800" GRANGE
CLASS

6800*	LDR
6801*	PZ
6802*	RDG
6803*	BAN
6804*	WES
6805*	CDF
6806*	LDR
6807*	WOS
6808*	PZ
6809*	SHL
6810*	CDF

6811*	CDF
6812*	SRD
6813*	NA
6814*	NA
6815*	STJ
6816*	BAN
6817*	CDF
6818*	CARM
6819*	BHD
6820*	PPRD
6821*	NPT
6822*	NA
6823*	FGD
6824*	CARM
6825*	PZ
6826*	SHL
6827*	CDF
6828*	LDR
6829*	NA
6830*	SPM
6831*	TYS
6832*	BAN
6833*	TYS
6834*	STJ
6835*	BAN
6836*	SPM
6837*	NPT
6838*	PZ
6839*	BAN
6840*	PPRD
6841*	BAN
6842*	SPM
6843*	TYS
6844*	SRD
6845*	WES
6846*	SPM
6847*	TYS
6848*	SRD
6849*	BAN
6850*	SPM
6851*	WOS
6852*	SPM
6853*	TYS
6854*	BAN
6855*	TYS
6856*	OXY
6857*	LDR
6858*	TYS
6859*	CHR
6860*	TYS
6861*	SPM
6862*	OXY
6863*	SPM
6864*	RDG
6865*	PDN
6866*	TYS
6867*	SPM
6868*	NPT
6869*	PDN
6870*	NPT
6871*	STJ
6872*	LDR
6873*	STJ
6874*	NPT
6875*	PPRD
6876*	SPM
6877*	WOS
6878*	BHD
6879*	OXY

4-6-0
"4900" HALL CLASS

6900*		PDN
6901*		SRD
6902*		SDN
6903*		LDR
6904*		TYS
6905*		HFD
6906*		BAN
6907*		LA
6908*		SRD
6909*		SPM
6910*		PDN
6911*		PZ
6912*		SPM
6913*		LA
6914*		TYS
6915*		OXY
6916*		WOS
6917*		GLO
6918*		LDR
6919*		CARM
6920*		HFD
6921*		WOS
6922*		SPM
6923*		DID
6924*		SRD
6925*		OXF
6926*		NPT
6927*		NPT
6928*		CDF
6929*		BAN
6930*		WOS
6931*		TR
6932*		OXY
6933*		OXF
6934*		NA
6935*		SDN
6936*		WOS
6937*		OXF
6938*		WOS
6939*		OXY
6940*		GLO
6941*		CHR
6942*		OXY
6943*		HFD
6944*		SPM
6945*		WEY
6946*		CDF
6947*		WOS
6948*		CDF
6949*	3955	LA
6950*		WOS
6951*		WOS
6952*		DID
6953*	3953	PDN
6954*		SPM
6955*		WES
6956*		OXY
6957*	3952	PDN
6958*		BRD

4-6-0
"6959" MODIFIED
HALL CLASS

6959*	PDN
6960*	PDN
6961*	PDN
6962*	PDN
6963*	SALOP
6964*	SRD
6965*	SDN
6966*	WES
6967*	OXY
6968*	RDG
6969*	CDF
6970*	OXY
6971*	BRD
6972*	BRD
6973*	PDN
6974*	PDN
6975*	OXY
6976*	SALOP
6977*	PDN
6978*	WES
6979*	BAN
6980*	SALOP

4-6-0
"4073" CASTLE
CLASS

7000*	NA
7001*	CDF
7002*	LDR
7003*	LDR
7004*	GLO
7005*	WOS
7006*	SALOP
7007*	SRD

2-8-2T
"7200" CLASS

7200	NA
7201	CDF
7202	STJ
7203	NPT
7204	DID
7205	ABDR
7206	PPRD
7207	OXY
7208	SPM
7209	STJ
7210	STJ
7211	SED
7212	NPT
7213	ABDR
7214	DID
7215	SPM
7216	STJ
7217	NPT
7218	LMTN
7219	CDF
7220	NA
7221	ABDR
7222	OXY
7223	STJ
7224	STJ
7225	LDR
7226	OXY
7227	OXY
7228	DID
7229	STJ
7230	PPRD
7231	NPT
7232	PPRD
7233	PPRD
7234	SPM
7235	PPRD
7236	OXY
7237	SPM
7238	OXY
7239	STJ
7240	OXY
7241	NPT
7242	ABDR
7243	OXY
7244	LDR
7245	NPT
7246	STJ
7247	NPT
7248	OXY
7249	NPT
7250	NA
7251	STJ
7252	DID
7253	NPT

2-6-0
"4300" CLASS

7300	WES
7301	WOS
7302	WES
7303	CHEL
7304	TN
7305	CNYD
7306	NEY
7307	OXY
7308	WOS
7309	WES
7310	CNYD
7311	OXY
7312	CHEL
7313	CHR
7314	TN
7315	SRD
7316	EXE
7317	OXY
7318	RDG
7319	SALOP
7320	RDG
7321	SDN

0-6-0PT
"7400" CLASS

7400	CARM
7401	CARM
7402	STB
7403	CNYD
7404	OXF
7405	OSW
7406	ABH
7407	CARM
7408	WEY
7409	CNYD
7410	OSW
7411	OXF
7412	OXF
7413	FGD
7414	CNYD
7415	SDN
7416	WOS
7417	WTD
7418	SDN
7419	CARM
7420	HFD
7421	TN
7422	TR
7423	ABDR
7424	SDN
7425	CARM
7426	PPRD
7427	NA
7428	STB
7429	STJ

0-6-0PT
"5700" CLASS

7700	KDR
7701	NEA
7702	LMTN
7703	ABEEG
7704	SED
7705	STB
7706	DYD
7707	HFD
7708	RDG
7709	SBZ
7710	DID
7711	SPM
7712	NPT
7713	PDN
7714	BHD
7715	SBZ
7716	EXE
7717	MTHR
7718	SPM
7719	SPM
7720	ABEEG
7721	LTS
7722	THT
7723	GLO
7724	PPRD
7725	TDU
7726	SPM
7727	WES
7728	SPM
7729	SPM
7730	SHL
7731	SHL
7732	SHL
7733	DYD
7734	PDN
7735	TYS
7736	NPT
7737	NEA
7738	PDN
7739	NEA
7740	ABEEG
7741	GLO
7742	NEA
7743	NEA
7744	DYD
7745	LLY
7746	TDU
7747	FGD
7748	ABDR
7749	SPM
7750	WOS
7751	CED
7752	TDU
7753	NPT
7754	PDN
7755	LLY
7756	SED
7757	NEA
7758	TYS
7759	OXY
7760	PDN
7761	EXE
7762	LA
7763	BAN
7764	STJ
7765	LLY
7766	MTHR
7767	NEA
7768	NPT
7769	NEA
7770	TDU
7771	NPT
7772	MTHR
7773	ABDR
7774	PILL
7775	TDU
7776	LLY
7777	RDG
7778	ABEEG
7779	SPM
7780	SPM
7781	NPT
7782	SPM
7783	SPM
7784	WES
7785	LLY
7786	NEA
7787	LDR
7788	RDG
7789	ABEEG
7790	SPM
7791	PDN
7792	SDN
7793	SPM
7794	SDN
7795	SPM
7796	OXY
7797	OXY
7798	TDU
7799	NEA

4-6-0
"7800" MANOR
CLASS

7800*	BAN
7801*	SPM
7802*	ABH
7803*	ABH
7804*	SPM
7805*	BAN
7806*	BAN
7807*	OSW
7808*	OSW
7809*	BRD
7810*	LMTN
7811*	BAN
7812*	BRD
7813*	OXY
7814*	BRD
7815*	GLO
7816*	NEY
7817*	CNYD
7818*	CHEL
7819*	OSW

2-6-2T
"8100" CLASS

8100	LMTN
8101	KDR
8102	WTD
8103	OSW
8104	NEA
8105	SPM
8106	WOS
8107	WTD
8108	TYS
8109	LMTN

0-6-0PT
"5700" CLASS

8700	TYS
8701	GLO
8702	SPM
8703	SPM
8704	STB
8705	SRD
8706	LLY
8707	PDN
8708	LLY
8709	LA
8710	NPT
8711	NPT
8712	TDU
8713	SPM
8714	SPM
8715	NEA
8716	PPRD
8717	GLO
8718	KDR
8719	LA
8720	DG
8721	TDU
8722	SPM
8723	ABEEG
8724	ABEEG
8725	BHD
8726	SRD
8727	KDR
8728	CDF
8729	BAN
8730	SPM
8731	GLO
8732	LLY
8733	SDN
8734	SRD
8735	PDN
8736	MTHR
8737	SPM
8738	PDN
8739	ABEEG
8740	CDF
8741	SPM
8742	STB
8743	CED
8744	WES
8745	WES
8746	SPM
8747	SPM
8748	TDU
8749	LLY
8750	PDN
8751	PDN
8752	SHL
8753	SHL
8754	PDN
8755	PPRD
8756	PDN
8757	PDN
8758	SHL
8759	PDN
8760	PDN
8761	PDN
8762	PDN
8763	PDN
8764	SHL
8765	PDN
8766	SPM
8767	PDN
8768	PDN
8769	PDN
8770	PDN
8771	PDN
8772	PDN
8773	PDN
8774	SHL
8775	NEA
8776	ABEEG
8777	TDU
8778	NPT
8779	SDN
8780	PDN
8781	GLO
8782	NEA
8783	SBZ
8784	TYS
8785	LLY
8786	NPT
8787	BAN
8788	PPRD
8789	LDR
8790	SPM
8791	STB
8792	STB
8793	SPM
8794	ABEEG
8795	SPM
8796	NPT
8797	STB
8798	OXY
8799	STJ

4-4-0
"9000" DUKEDOG
CLASS

9000	MCH
9001	OSW
9002	ABH
9003	OSW
9004	MCH
9005	MCH
9006	DID
9007	TYS
9008	TYS
9009	MCH
9010	TYS
9011	SDN
9012	MCH
9013	ABH
9014	MCH
9015	DID
9016	OSW
9017	ABH
9018	SDN
9019	TYS
9020	OSW
9021	ABH
9022	OSW
9023	SDN
9024	SALOP
9025	ABH
9026	OSW
9027	MCH
9028	OSW

4-4-0
"DUKE" CLASS

9054*	MCH
9064*	GLO
9065*	OSW
9072	MCH
9073*	SALOP
9076	SALOP
9083*	DID
9084*	STB
9087*	ABH
9089	GLO
9091*	MCH

2-6-0
"4300" CLASS

9300	SHL
9301	SHL
9302	PDN
9303	RDG
9304	RDG
9305	RDG
9306	PDN
9307	RDG
9308	PDN
9309	RDG
9310	PDN
9311	SHL
9312	OXY
9313	RDG
9314	OXY
9315	RDG
9316	OXF
9317	OXF
9318	RDG
9319	RDG

0-6-0PT
"9400" CLASS

9400	SDN
9401	PDN
9402	PDN
9403	PDN
9404	PDN
9405	PDN
9406	PDN
9407	PDN
9408	OXY
9409	PDN

0-6-0PT
"5700" CLASS

9600	SDN
9601	YEO
9602	FGD
9603	FGD
9604	SPM
9605	SPM
9606	SPM
9607	ABDR
9608	TYS
9609	ABDR
9610	TYS
9611	OXF
9612	WES
9613	STB
9614	BCN
9615	WES
9616	LTS
9617	DYD
9618	MTHR
9619	HFD
9620	SPM
9621	SRD
9622	MTHR
9623	NA
9624	WLN
9625	SED
9626	SPM
9627	NEA
9628	WES
9629	CDF
9630	WLN
9631	BRY
9632	NPT
9633	NA
9634	DYD
9635	TYS
9636	STB
9637	NPT
9638	MTHR
9639	WLN
9640	SLO
9641	SHL
9642	WEY
9643	MTHR
9644	NPT
9645	SED
9646	EXE
9647	EXE
9648	CDF
9649	TDU
9650	PPRD
9651	BHD
9652	NEY
9653	SLO
9654	OXF
9655	SBZ
9656	CNYD
9657	SALOP
9658	PDN
9659	PDN
9660	TDU
9661	PDN
9700	PDN
9701	PDN
9702	PDN
9703	PDN
9704	PDN
9705	PDN
9706	PDN
9707	PDN
9708	PDN
9709	PDN
9710	PDN
9711	LA
9712	ABDR
9713	CDF
9714	OXY
9715	OXY
9716	LA
9717	NA
9718	TN
9719	SALOP
9720	SDN
9721	SDN
9722	RDG
9723	ABEEG
9724	TYS
9725	PDN
9726	PDN
9727	GLO
9728	CHR
9729	SPM
9730	OXY
9731	NPT
9732	SPM
9733	TYS
9734	NEA
9735	DYD
9736	DYD
9737	DYD
9738	LDR
9739	OXY
9740	LMTN
9741	STB
9742	OXY
9743	LLY
9744	SED
9745	STJ
9746	LTS
9747	OXY
9748	TYS
9749	RDG
9750	NEA
9751	PDN
9752	OXY
9753	TYS
9754	PDN
9755	SHL
9756	NEA
9757	TN
9758	PDN
9759	CDF
9760	FGD
9761	LDR
9762	WES
9763	RDG
9764	SPM
9765	LA
9766	DYD
9767	STB
9768	OXY
9769	OXY
9770	LA
9771	YEO
9772	SDN
9773	SDN
9774	CHR
9775	LDR
9776	GLO
9777	LDR
9778	CDF
9779	NEA
9780	LTS
9781	SLO
9782	BAN
9783	NEA
9784	PDN
9785	DYD
9786	NEA
9787	LLY
9788	LLY
9789	SLO
9790	SDN
9791	RDG
9792	NEA
9793	TYS
9794	CHR
9795	SDN
9796	CDF
9797	PPRD
9798	TYS
9799	DYD

Ex-Southern Railway Locomotives

0-4-4T
T1 CLASS

30001	ELH
30002	ELH
30003	PLY
30005	ELH
30007	PLY
30008	ELH
30009	FEL
30010	SAL
30013	SAL
30020	FRA

0-4-4T
M7 CLASS

30021	BM
30022	GFD
30023	BPL
30024	EXJ
30025	EXJ
30026	GFD
30027	FRA
30028	BM
30029	ELH
30030	EXJ
30031	FEL
30032	EXJ
30033	9E
30034	EXJ
30035	PLY
30036	BPL
30037	EXJ
30038	9E
30039	EXJ
30040	BM
30041	SAL
30042	BPL
30043	GFD
30044	BPL
30045	FRA
30046	EXJ
30047	BM
30048	ELH
30049	EXJ
30050	BM
30051	BM
30052	BM
30053	ELH
30054	FRA
30055	EXJ
30056	GFD
30057	BM
30058	YEO
30059	BM
30060	GFD

0-6-0T
"U.S.A." CLASS

30061	SOT
30062	SOT
30063	SOT
30064	SOT
30065	SOT
30066	SOT
30067	SOT
30068	SOT
30069	SOT
30070	SOT
30071	SOT
30072	SOT
30073	SOT
30074	SOT

0-4-0T
B4 CLASS

30081*	SOT
30082	ELH
30083	DOV
30084	PLY
30085*	SOT
30086*	BAT
30087	ELH
30088	ELH
30089*	SOT
30090*	BAT
30091	PLY
30092	BM
30093*	BM
30094	PLY
30095*	PLY
30096*	ELH
30097*	SOT
30098*	SOT
30099	BM
30100	BM
30101*	SOT
30102*	ELH
30103	PLY

0-4-4T
M7 CLASS

30104	BM
30105	EXJ
30106	BM
30107	BM
30108	GFD
30109	ELH
30110	GFD
30111	BM
30112	BM

4-4-0
T9 CLASS

30113	FRA
30114	FRA
30115	FRA
30116	PLY
30117	SAL
30118	FRA
30119	9E
30120	ELH
30121	ELH
30122	SAL

0-4-4T
M7 CLASS

30123	9E
30124	EXJ
30125	ELH
30127	SAL
30128	ELH
30129	YEO
30130	9E
30131	BM
30132	9E
30133	EXJ

4-4-0
L11 CLASS

30134	YEO

4-4-0
K10 CLASS

30135	EXJ
30137	EXJ
30139	FEL
30140	FEL
30141	GFD
30142	9E
30143	YEO
30144	FEL
30145	YEO
30146	DOR

0-4-0T
B4 CLASS

30147*	SOT

4-4-0
L11 CLASS

30148	ELH

4-4-0
K10 CLASS

30150	ELH
30151	ELH
30152	YEO
30153	FEL

4-4-0
L11 CLASS

30154	ELH
30155	ELH
30156	DOR
30157	ELH
30158	FEL
30159	ELH

0-6-0T
G6 CLASS

30160	9E

4-4-0
L11 CLASS

30161	BM

0-6-0T
G6 CLASS

30162	DOR

4-4-0
L11 CLASS

30163	YEO
30164	FRA
30165	ELH
30166	FRA
30167	FEL
30168	BM
30169	BM
30170	FRA
30171	ELH
30172	FRA
30173	BM
30174	FEL
30175	ELH

0-4-0T
B4 CLASS

30176*	SOT

0-4-4T
02 CLASS

30177	DOR
30179	9E
30181	WAD
30182	PLY
30183	PLY
30192	EXJ
30193	EXJ
30197	PLY
30198	ELH
30199	EXJ
30200	ELH
30203	WAD
30204	9E
30207	EXJ
30212	9E
30213	ELH
30216	PLY
30221	DOR
30223	DOR
30224	EXJ
30225	ELH
30229	DOR
30230	EXJ
30231	ELH
30232	EXJ
30233	DOR
30236	PLY

0-6-0T
G6 CLASS

30237	SAL
30238	YEO
30239	BM
30240	ELH

0-4-4T
M7 CLASS

30241	9E
30242	ELH
30243	SAL
30244	9E
30245	EXJ
30246	GFD
30247	BPL
30248	9E
30249	9E
30250	BPL
30251	BM
30252	EXJ
30253	EXJ
30254	FEL
30255	EXJ
30256	EXJ

0-6-0T
G6 CLASS

30257	9E
30258	RDG
30259	9E
30260	RDG
30261	ELH
30262	GFD
30263	9E
30264	ELH
30265	BAS
30266	9E
30267	ELH
30268	GFD
30269	GFD
30270	GFD
30271	9E
30273	9E
30274	ELH
30275	ELH
30276	YEO
30277	ELH
30278	BAS
30279	SAL

4-4-0
T9 CLASS

30280	FRA
30281	DOR
30282	EXJ
30283	EXJ
30284	DOR
30285	SAL
30286	ELH
30287	FRA
30288	SAL
30289	PLY
30300	DOR
30301	EXJ
30302	ELH
30303	FRA
30304	FRA
30305	FRA

0-6-0
700 CLASS

30306	ELH

4-4-0
T9 CLASS

30307	BAS

0-6-0
700 CLASS

30308	GFD
30309	GFD

4-4-0
T9 CLASS

30310	YEO
30311	GFD
30312	SAL
30313	ELH
30314	FRA

0-6-0
700 CLASS

30315	SAL
30316	ELH
30317	SAL

0-4-4T
M7 CLASS

30318	BM
30319	9E
30320	EXJ
30321	BPL
30322	9E
30323	EXJ
30324	GFD

0-6-0
700 CLASS

30325	GFD
30326	GFD
30327	GFD

0-4-4T
M7 CLASS

30328	GFD

4-4-0
K10 CLASS

30329	EXJ

4-6-0
H15 CLASS

30330	SAL
30331	SAL
30332	SAL
30333	SAL
30334	SAL
30335	SAL

4-4-0
T9 CLASS

30336 ELH
30337 BM
30338 FRA

0-6-0
700 CLASS

30339 9E

4-4-0
K10 CLASS

30340 YEO
30341 ELH
30343 GFD
30345 ELH

0-6-0
700 CLASS

30346 GFD

0-6-0T
G6 CLASS

30348 BAS
30349 GFD

0-6-0
700 CLASS

30350 ELH

0-6-0T
G6 CLASS

30351 ELH

0-6-0
700 CLASS

30352 GFD

0-6-0T
G6 CLASS

30353 9E
30354 9E

0-6-0
700 CLASS

30355 SAL

0-4-4T
M7 CLASS

30356 EXJ
30357 ELH

0-4-4T
T1 CLASS

30361 SAL
30363 BM
30366 ELH
30367 ELH

0-6-0
700 CLASS

30368 BAS

0-4-4T
M7 CLASS

30374 EXJ
30375 EXJ
30376 EXJ
30377 EXJ
30378 GFD
30379 BM

4-4-0
K10 CLASS

30380 9E
30382 SAL
30383 FEL
30384 FRA
30385 FEL
30386 9E
30389 SAL
30390 9E
30391 9E
30392 9E
30393 ELH
30394 ELH

4-4-0
S11 CLASS

30395 ELH
30396 FRA
30397 ELH
30398 BM
30399 BM
30400 FRA
30401 FRA
30402 FRA
30403 FRA
30404 FRA

4-4-0
L11 CLASS

30405 SAL
30406 9E
30407 BAS
30408 EXJ
30409 EXJ
30410 DOR
30411 ELH
30412 YEO
30413 FRA
30414 FRA

4-4-0
L12 CLASS

30415 BM
30416 GFD
30417 FRA
30418 BAS
30419 GFD
30420 ELH
30421 SAL
30422 ELH
30423 ELH
30424 FRA
30425 FRA
30426 BAS
30427 9E
30428 ELH
30429 BM
30430 ELH
30431 9E
30432 SAL
30433 GFD
30434 GFD

4-4-0
L11 CLASS

30435 9E
30436 EXJ
30437 ELH
30438 GFD
30439 EXJ
30440 9E
30441 FRA
30442 9E

4-6-0
T14 CLASS

30443 9E
30444 9E
30445 9E
30446 9E
30447 9E

4-6-0
N15 'KING ARTHUR' CLASS

30448* SAL
30449* SAL
30450* SAL
30451* SAL
30452* SAL
30453* SAL
30454* SAL
30455* SAL
30456* SAL
30457* SAL

0-4-0T
0458 CLASS

30458* 3458 GFD

4-6-0
T14 CLASS

30459 9E
30460 9E
30461 9E
30462 9E

4-4-0
D15 CLASS

30463 ELH
30464 ELH
30465 ELH
30466 ELH
30467 ELH
30468 ELH
30469 ELH
30470 ELH
30471 ELH
30472 ELH

4-6-0
H15 CLASS

30473 ELH
30474 ELH
30475 SAL
30476 SAL
30477 9E
30478 ELH

0-4-4T
M7 CLASS

30479 ELH
30480 FRA
30481 GFD

4-6-0
H15 CLASS

30482 9E
30483 9E
30484 9E
30485 9E
30486 9E
30487 9E
30488 9E
30489 9E
30490 9E
30491 9E

4-8-0T
G16 CLASS

30492 FEL
30493 FEL
30494 FEL
30495 FEL

4-6-0
S15 CLASS

30496 FEL
30497 FEL
30498 FEL
30499 FEL
30500 FEL
30501 FEL
30502 FEL
30503 FEL
30504 FEL
30505 FEL
30506 FEL
30507 FEL
30508 FEL
30509 FEL
30510 FEL
30511 FEL
30512 FEL
30513 FEL
30514 FEL
30515 FEL

4-6-2T
H16 CLASS

30516 FEL
30517 FEL
30518 FEL
30519 FEL
30520 FEL

4-6-0
H15 CLASS

30521 ELH
30522 ELH
30523 ELH
30524 ELH

0-6-0
Q CLASS

30530 ELH
30531 TWW
30532 ELH
30533 RED
30534 TWW
30535 ELH
30536 ELH
30537 RED
30538 RED
30539 RED
30540 HOR
30541 3B
30542 3B
30543 HOR
30544 HOR
30545 RED
30546 RED
30547 RED
30548 BM
30549 BM

0-6-0
0395 CLASS

30564 3029 EXJ
30565 3083 GFD
30566 3101 ELH
30567 3154 FEL
30568 3155 GFD
30569 3163 FEL
30570 3167 FEL
30571 3397 ELH
30572 3400 FEL
30573 3433 FEL
30574 3436 GFD
30575 3439 GFD
30576 3440 +
30577 3441 SAL
30578 3442 GFD

+ On Loan to Kent and East Sussex Railway.

30579 3496 FEL
30580 3506 GFD
30581 3509 ELH

4-4-2T
0415 CLASS

30582 3125 EXJ
30583 3488 EXJ
30584 3520 EXJ

2-4-0T
0298 CLASS

30585 3314 WAD
30586 3329 WAD
30587 3298 WAD

0-4-0T
C14 CLASS

30588 3741 ELH
30589 3744 ELH

0-4-2
A12 CLASS

30618 GFD
30627 ELH
30629 ELH
30636 ELH

0-4-4T
M7 CLASS

30667 9E
30668 EXJ
30669 EXJ
30670 BPL
30671 EXJ
30672 9E
30673 9E
30674 ELH
30675 SAL
30676 9E

0-6-0
700 CLASS

30687 FEL
30688 FEL
30689 FEL
30690 SAL
30691 SAL
30692 9E
30693 BAS
30694 9E
30695 DOR
30696 BM
30697 FEL
30698 FEL
30699 9E
30700 BM
30701 9E

4-4-0
T9 CLASS

30702 YEO
30703 WAD
30704 GFD
30705 ELH
30706 BAS
30707 ELH
30708 BAS
30709 SAL
30710 YEO
30711 PLY
30712 YEO
30713 ELH
30714 YEO
30715 SAL
30716 YEO
30717 WAD
30718 9E

30719 BM
30721 SAL
30722 ELH
30723 EXJ
30724 EXJ
30725 EXJ
30726 GFD
30727 SAL
30728 BM
30729 SAL
30730 EXJ
30731 FRA
30732 FRA
30733 FRA

4-6-0
N15 "KING ARTHUR" CLASS

30736* BM
30737* ELH
30738* 9E
30739* ELH
30740* ELH
30741* ELH
30742* 9E
30743* BM
30744* SAL
30745* ELH
30746* SAL
30747* EXJ
30748* ELH
30749* ELH
30750* ELH
30751* ELH
30752* ELH
30753* 9E
30754* ELH
30755* 9E

0-6-0T
756 CLASS

30756* ELH

0-6-2T
757 CLASS

30757* PLY
30758* PLY

4-6-0
N15 "KING ARTHUR" CLASS

30763* BAT
30764* BAT
30765* BAT
30766* 9E
30767* DOV
30768* DOV
30769* DOV
30770* DOV
30771* DOV
30772* BM
30773* 9E
30774* 9E
30775* BAT
30776* BAT
30777* ELH
30778* BAT
30779* 9E
30780* BAT
30781* BAT
30782* 9E
30783* 9E
30784* ELH
30785* ELH
30786* 9E
30787* BM
30788* 9E
30789* BM
30790* BM
30791* 9E
30792* 9E
30793* BAT
30794* BAT
30795* BAT
30796* BAT
30797* BAT
30798* BA
30799* BA
30800* HIT
30801* AFD
30802* AFD
30803* AFD
30804* AFD
30805* AFD
30806* AFD

4-6-0
S15 CLASS

30823 EXJ
30824 EXJ
30825 EXJ
30826 EXJ
30827 EXJ
30828 SAL
30829 SAL
30830 SAL
30831 SAL
30832 SAL
30833 FEL
30834 FEL
30835 FEL
30836 FEL
30837 FEL
30838 FEL
30839 FEL
30840 FEL
30841 FEL
30842 FEL
30843 EXJ
30844 EXJ
30845 EXJ
30846 EXJ
30847 EXJ

4-6-0
"LORD NELSON" CLASS

30850* BM
30851* BM
30852* BM
30853* BM
30854* BM
30855* BM
30856* 9E
30857* 9E
30858* 9E
30859* 9E
30860* 9E
30861* 9E
30862* BM
30863* BM
30864* BM
30865* BM

4-4-0
V "SCHOOLS" CLASS

30900* STL
30901* STL
30902* STL
30903* STL
30904* STL
30905* STL
30906* STL
30907* STL
30908* STL
30909* STL
30910* STL
30911* RAM
30912* RAM
30913* RAM
30914* RAM
30915* RAM
30916* RAM
30917* RAM
30918* RAM
30919* RAM
30920* RAM
30921* BA
30922* BA
30923* BA
30924* DOV
30925* DOV
30926* DOV
30927* DOV
30928* BA
30929* BA
30930* BA
30931* BA
30932* BA
30933* BA
30934* BA
30935* BA
30936* BA
30937* BA
30938* BA
30939* BA

0-6-0T
EAST KENT RAILWAY

30948 4 +

0-8-0T
KENT & EAST SUSSEX RAILWAY

30949* 9E

0-8-0T
Z CLASS

30950 HIT
30951 HIT
30952 ELH
30953 HIT
30954 EXJ
30955 HIT
30956 HIT
30957 SAL

4-4-0
F1 CLASS

31002 GIL

0-6-0
01 CLASS

31003 GIL

0-6-0
C CLASS

31004 RAM

0-4-4T
H CLASS

31005 BAT

0-6-0
01 CLASS

31007 GIL

0-6-0T
R1 CLASS

31010 AFD

+On Loan to East Kent Railway.

4-4-0
B1 CLASS

31013 GIL

0-6-0
01 CLASS

31014 GIL

0-4-4T
H CLASS

31016 RAM

0-6-0
C CLASS

31018 HIT

4-4-0
E1 CLASS

31019 BAT

0-6-0T
P CLASS

31027 DOV

4-4-0
F1 CLASS

31028 HIT
31031 HIT

0-6-0
C CLASS

31033 BA

4-4-0
E CLASS

31036 BA

0-6-0
C CLASS

31037 STL
31038 STL

0-6-0
01 CLASS

31039 GIL
31041 STL

4-4-0
F1 CLASS
31042 RDG

0-6-0
01 CLASS

31044 HIT
31046 FAV

0-6-0T
R1 CLASS

31047 FOL

0-6-0
01 CLASS

31048 TON
31051 GIL

0-6-0
C CLASS

31054 HIT

4-4-0
D CLASS

31057 TON

0-6-0
C CLASS

31059 HIT
31061 HIT
31063 TON

0-6-0
01 CLASS

31064 GIL
31065 DOV
31066 GIL

4-4-0
E1 CLASS

31067 BAT

0-6-0
C CLASS

31068 HIT

0-6-0T
R1 CLASS

31069 AFD

0-6-0
C CLASS

31071 HIT

4-4-0
D CLASS

31075 STL

4-4-0
F1 CLASS

31078 RDG

0-6-0
01 CLASS

31080 RAM

0-6-0
C CLASS

31086 TON
31090 BA

4-4-0
D CLASS

31092 GIL

0-6-0
01 CLASS

31093 BA

0-6-0
C CLASS

31102 BA

4-4-0
F1 CLASS

31105 GIL

0-6-0
01 CLASS

31106 FAV

0-6-0T
R1 CLASS

31107 FOL

0-6-0
01 CLASS

31108 DOV
31109 HIT

0-6-0
C CLASS

31112 GIL
31113 HIT

0-6-0
01 CLASS

31123 AFD

0-6-0T
R1 CLASS

31127 FOL
31128 FOL

4-4-0
D1 CLASS

31145 BAT

0-6-0T
R1 CLASS

31147 AFD

0-6-0
C CLASS

31150 TON

4-4-0
F1 CLASS

31151 RAM

0-6-0T
R1 CLASS

31154 FOL

4-4-0
E CLASS

31157 HOR

0-4-4T
H CLASS

31158 AFD

4-4-0
E CLASS

31159 BA

4-4-0
E1 CLASS

31160 BAT

0-4-4T
H CLASS

31161 DOV
31162 BA

4-4-0
E1 CLASS

31163 BAT

0-4-4T
H CLASS

31164 RAM

4-4-0
E1 CLASS

31165 BAT

4-4-0
E CLASS

31166 BA

0-6-0T
R1 CLASS

31174 STL

4-4-0
E CLASS

31175 BA
31176 BA

0-4-4T
H CLASS

31177 BAT

0-6-0T
P CLASS

31178 BTN

4-4-0
E1 CLASS

31179 BAT

0-4-4T
H CLASS

31182 RAM
31184 BAT

0-6-0
C CLASS

31191 HIT

0-4-4T
H CLASS

31193 TON

4-4-0
F1 CLASS

31215 GIL

4-4-0
B1 CLASS

31217 RDG

0-6-0
C CLASS

31218 AFD
31219 TON
31221 TON
31223 BA
31225 TON
31227 TON
31229 FAV

4-4-0
F1 CLASS

31231 FAV

0-6-0
C CLASS

31234 GIL

0-6-0
01 CLASS

31238 GIL

0-4-4T
H CLASS

31239 AFD

0-6-0
C CLASS

31242 FAV
31243 HIT
31244 HIT
31245 HIT

4-4-0
D1 CLASS

31246 DOV
31247 BAT

0-6-0
01 CLASS

31248 HIT

0-6-0
C CLASS

31252 DOV
31253 HIT
31255 DOV
31256 GIL

31257 HIT

0-6-0
01 CLASS

31258 HIT

0-4-4T
H CLASS

31259 BAT

0-6-0
C CLASS

31260 FAV

0-4-4T
H CLASS

31261 AFD
31263 BAT
31265 RAM
31266 BAT

0-6-0
C CLASS

31267 GIL
31268 AFD

0-4-4T
H CLASS

31269 AFD

0-6-0
C CLASS

31270 HIT
31271 AFD
31272 TON

4-4-0
E CLASS

31273 HOR

0-4-4T
H CLASS

31274 AFD

4-4-0
E CLASS

31275 BA

0-4-4T
H CLASS
31276 DOV

0-6-0
C CLASS

31277 BA

0-4-4T
H CLASS

31278 GIL
31279 FAV

0-6-0
C CLASS

31280 BA
31287 BA
31291 DOV
31293 BAT
31294 BA

0-4-4T
H CLASS

31295 BAT

0-6-0
C CLASS

31297 BA
31298 HIT

0-4-0T
CRANE TANK

31302 BAT

0-4-4T
H CLASS

31305 AFD
31306 AFD
31307 BAT
31308 GIL
31309 FAV
31310 FAV
31311 BAT

4-4-0
E CLASS

31315 BA

0-6-0
01 CLASS

31316 RAM

0-6-0
C CLASS

31317 GIL

0-4-4T
H CLASS

31319 BAT
31320 TON
31321 BAT
31322 AFD

0-6-0T
P CLASS

31323 FOL

0-4-4T
H CLASS

31324 BA

0-6-0T
P CLASS

31325 DOV

0-4-4T
H CLASS

31326 BA
31327 TON
31328 BA
31329 BAT

0-6-0T
R1 CLASS

31335 STL
31337 FOL
31339 AFD
31340 FOL

0-6-0
01 CLASS

31369 FAV
31370 TON
31371 +
31372 +
31373 DOV
31374 HIT
31377 HIT
31378 GIL
31379 FAV
31380 TON
31381 DOV
31383 +
31384 GIL

+ On Loan to East Kent Railway.

31385 HIT
31386 HIT
31388 BA
31389 BA
31390 AFD
31391 GIL
31395 BA
31396 TON
31397 BA
31398 BA

2-6-0
N CLASS

31400 AFD
31401 AFD
31402 AFD
31403 AFD
31404 AFD
31405 BAT
31406 RED
31407 EXJ
31408 EXJ
31409 EXJ
31410 BAT
31411 BAT
31412 BAT
31413 BAT
31414 BAT

0-6-0
01 CLASS

31425 BA
31426 AFD
31428 BA
31429 BA
31430 GIL
31432 STL
31434 AFD
31437 TON
31438 FAV
31439 GIL

4-4-0
B1 CLASS

31440 FAV
31443 DOV
31445 BAT
31446 RDG
31448 FAV
31449 GIL
31450 DOV
31451 RAM
31452 RAM
31453 RAM
31454 BAT
31455 HIT
31457 HIT
31459 RDG

0-6-0
C CLASS

31460 BA
31461 TON

4-4-0
D1 CLASS

31470 DOV

4-4-0
D CLASS

31477 AFD

0-6-0
C CLASS

31480 HIT
31481 FAV
31486 HIT

4-4-0
D1 CLASS

31487 FAV

4-4-0
D CLASS

31488 TON

4-4-0
D1 CLASS

31489 FAV

4-4-0
D CLASS

31490 TON

4-4-0
E CLASS

31491 BA

4-4-0
D1 CLASS

31492 BAT

4-4-0
D CLASS

31493 FAV

4-4-0
D1 CLASS

31494 BAT

0-6-0
C CLASS

31495 FAV

4-4-0
D CLASS

31496 FAV

4-4-0
E1 CLASS

31497 BAT

0-6-0
C CLASS

31498 BAT

0-4-4T
H CLASS

31500 BA

4-4-0
D CLASS

31501 FAV

4-4-0
D1 CLASS

31502 FAV

0-4-4T
H CLASS

31503 TON

4-4-0
E1 CLASS

31504 BAT

4-4-0
D1 CLASS

31505 FAV

4-4-0
E1 CLASS

31506 BAT
31507 BAT

0-6-0
C CLASS

31508 BAT

4-4-0
D1 CLASS

31509 FAV

0-6-0
C CLASS

31510 GIL

4-4-0
E1 CLASS

31511 BAT

0-4-4T
H CLASS

31512 DOV

0-6-0
C CLASS

31513 TON

4-4-0
E CLASS

31514 BAT
31515 BAT
31516 BAT

0-4-4T
H CLASS

31517 DOV
31518 TON
31519 TON
31520 DOV
31521 RAM
31522 RAM
31523 RAM
31530 DOV
31531 DOV
31532 DOV
31533 BA
31540 TON
31541 BA
31542 BA
31543 TON
31544 9E

4-4-0
D1 CLASS

31545 DOV

0-4-4T
H CLASS

31546 BA

4-4-0
E CLASS

31547 BA

0-4-4T
H CLASS

31548 DOV

4-4-0
D CLASS

31549 AFD

0-4-4T
H CLASS

31550 BA
31551 9E
31552 9E
31553 9E
31554 BAT

0-6-0T
P CLASS

31555 DOV
31556 DOV
31557 BTN
31558 FOL

0-6-0
C CLASS

31572 HIT
31573 GIL

4-4-0
D CLASS

31574 AFD

0-6-0
C CLASS

31575 BAT
31576 BAT

4-4-0
D CLASS

31577 AFD

0-6-0
C CLASS

31578 BAT
31579 GIL
31580 TON
31581 HIT
31582 BAT
31583 GIL
31584 BA
31585 GIL

4-4-0
D CLASS

31586 TON

4-4-0
E CLASS

31587 RED

0-6-0
C CLASS

31588 GIL
31589 AFD
31590 TON

4-4-0
D CLASS

31591 TON

0-6-0
C CLASS

31592 RAM
31593 TON

0-6-4T
J CLASS

31595 AFD
31596 AFD
31597 AFD
31598 AFD
31599 AFD

0-6-0T
T CLASS

31602 BAT
31604 BAT

2-6-0
U CLASS

31610 RDG
31611 RDG
31612 SAL
31613 9E
31614 GFD
31615 RDG
31616 9E
31617 9E
31618 SAL
31619 9E
31620 RDG
31621 GFD
31622 BM
31623 GFD
31624 BM
31625 EXJ
31626 SAL
31627 BAS
31628 RDG
31629 BAS
31630 SAL
31631 FAV
31632 BAS
31633 BAS
31634 BAS
31635 EXJ
31636 SAL
31637 9E
31638 EXJ
31639 FAV

0-4-4T
R CLASS

31658 GIL
31659 GIL
31660 GIL
31661 BAT
31662 GIL
31663 GIL
31665 GIL
31666 GIL
31667 FAV
31670 TON
31671 TON
31672 TON
31673 DOV
31674 FAV
31675 TON

0-6-0
C CLASS

31681 BAT
31682 GIL
31683 BAT
31684 GIL

0-6-0T
S CLASS

31685 BA

0-6-0
C CLASS

31686 TON
31687 BA
31688 GIL
31689 HIT
31690 BAT
31691 FAV
31692 FAV
31693 BA
31694 BAT
31695 HIT

0-4-4T
R1 CLASS

31696 FEL
31697 GIL
31698 FEL
31699 FAV
31700 TON
31703 TON
31704 TON
31705 DOV
31706 BAT
31707 TON
31708 DOV
31709 FAV
31710 BAT

0-6-0
C CLASS

31711 AFD
31712 BAT
31713 GIL
31714 BAT
31715 FAV
31716 BAT
31717 BAT
31718 BAT
31719 BAT
31720 HIT
31721 AFD
31722 BAT
31723 BA
31724 BA
31725 BA

4-4-0
D1 CLASS

31727 DOV

4-4-0
D CLASS

31728 RED
31729 RED
31730 HOR
31731 TON
31732 TON
31733 TON
31734 TON

4-4-0
D1 CLASS

31735 DOV
31736 BAT

4-4-0
D CLASS

31737 STL
31738 STL

4-4-0
D1 CLASS

31739 FAV

4-4-0
D CLASS

31740 STL

4-4-0
D1 CLASS

31741 FAV
31743 BAT

4-4-0
D CLASS

31744 STL

4-4-0
D1 CLASS

31745 BAT

4-4-0
D CLASS

31746 GIL
31748 AFD

4-4-0
D1 CLASS

31749	BAT

4-4-0
D CLASS

31750	GIL

4-4-0
L1 CLASS

31753	DOV
31754	DOV
31755	DOV
31756	DOV
31757	DOV
31758	BA
31759	BA

4-4-0
L CLASS

31760	BAT
31761	TON
31762	TON
31763	TON
31764	BAT
31765	BAT
31766	STL
31767	STL
31768	STL
31769	BAT
31770	AFD
31771	AFD
31772	AFD
31773	AFD
31774	AFD
31775	AFD
31776	AFD
31777	RAM
31778	RAM
31779	RAM
31780	RAM
31781	RAM

4-4-0
L1 CLASS

31782	BA
31783	BA
31784	BA
31785	BA
31786	BA
31787	BA
31788	BA
31789	BA

2-6-0
U CLASS

31790	YEO
31791	YEO
31792	YEO
31793	YEO
31794	YEO
31795	YEO
31796	BM
31797	FRA
31798	GFD
31799	GFD
31800	GFD
31801	GFD
31802	GFD
31803	GFD
31804	GFD
31805	GFD
31806	GFD
31807	RDG
31808	FAV
31809	GFD

2-6-0
N CLASS

31810	BAT
31811	BAT
31812	BAT
31813	BAT
31814	NOR
31815	RED
31816	RED
31817	RED
31818	RED
31819	DOV
31820	DOV
31821	DOV

2-6-0
N1 CLASS

31822	STL

2-6-0
N CLASS

31823	DOV
31824	BA
31825	BA
31826	BA
31827	ELH
31828	EXJ
31829	ELH
31830	TON
31831	FRA
31832	EXJ
31833	EXJ
31834	EXJ
31835	EXJ
31836	EXJ
31837	EXJ
31838	EXJ
31839	EXJ
31840	EXJ
31841	EXJ
31842	EXJ
31843	RED
31844	NOR
31845	EXJ
31846	SAL
31847	EXJ
31848	SAL
31849	RED
31850	RDG
31851	RED
31852	RED
31853	EXJ
31854	RDG
31855	EXJ
31856	EXJ
31857	RDG
31858	RED
31859	TON
31860	RDG
31861	RDG
31862	TON
31863	RED
31864	RED
31865	BA
31866	ELH
31867	ELH
31868	RDG
31869	EXJ
31870	ELH
31871	EXJ
31872	SAL
31873	SAL
31874	EXJ
31875	EXJ

2-6-0
N1 CLASS

31876	STL
31877	STL
31878	HIT
31879	HIT
31880	HIT

2-6-0
U1 CLASS

31890	BTN
31891	BTN
31892	BTN
31893	BTN
31894	BTN
31895	RED
31896	RED
31897	RED
31898	RED
31899	RED
31900	BTN
31901	BA
31902	BA
31903	BAT
31904	BAT
31905	BAT
31906	BAT
31907	BAT
31908	BAT
31909	BAT
31910	BAT

2-6-4T
W CLASS

31911	HIT
31912	BAT
31913	HIT
31914	BAT
31915	BAT
31916	NOR
31917	NOR
31918	NOR
31919	NOR
31920	NOR
31921	HIT
31922	HIT
31923	HIT
31924	HIT
31925	HIT

4-4-2T
I1X CLASS

32001	TWW
32002	3B
32003	TWW
32004	TWW
32005	EBN
32006	TWW
32007	3B
32008	EBN
32009	EBN
32010	EBN

4-4-2T
I3 CLASS

32021	TWW
32022	TWW
32023	TWW
32025	TWW
32026	TWW
32027	TWW
32028	TWW
32029	TWW
32030	TWW

4-4-2
H1 CLASS

32037*	BTN
32038*	BTN
32039*	BTN

4-4-0
B4X CLASS

32043	BTN

4-4-0
B4 CLASS

32044	EBN

4-4-0
B4X CLASS

32045	HOR
32050	EBN

4-4-0
B4 CLASS

32051	HOR

4-4-0
B4X CLASS

32052	EBN

4-4-0
B4 CLASS

32054	EBN

4-4-0
B4X CLASS

32055	HOR
32056	BTN
32060	BTN

4-4-0
B4 CLASS

32062	EBN
32063	EBN

4-4-0
B4X CLASS

32067	HOR

4-4-0
B4 CLASS

32068	EBN

4-4-0
B4X CLASS

32070	EBN
32071	BTN
32072	BTN
32073	EBN

4-4-0
B4 CLASS

32074	HOR

4-4-2T
I3 CLASS

32075	BA
32076	BA
32077	BA
32078	3B
32079	3B
32080	3B
32081	3B
32082	3B
32083	EBN
32084	BTN
32085	BA
32086	BTN
32087	BA
32088	BTN
32089	BA
32090	EBN
32091	EBN

0-6-2T
E1R CLASS

32094	BPL
32095	BPL
32096	BPL

0-6-0T
E1 CLASS

32097	BA

0-6-0T
E2 CLASS

32100	BAT
32101	BAT
32102	BAT
32103	BAT
32104	BAT
32105	BAT
32106	BAT
32107	BAT
32108	DOV
32109	DOV

0-6-0T
E1 CLASS

32112	SOT
32113	TON
32122	BTN

0-6-2T
E1R CLASS

32124	EXJ

0-6-0T
E1 CLASS

32127	BTN
32128	BA
32129	TON
32133	ELH

0-6-2T
E1R CLASS

32135	EXJ

0-6-0T
E1 CLASS

32138	TON
32139	BTN
32141	BA
32142	BA
32145	TON
32147	ELH
32151	BA
32153	FRA
32156	SOT
32160	ELH
32162	SOT
32164	TON

0-6-2T
E3 CLASS

32165	BA
32166	BA
32167	NOR
32168	BA
32169	NOR
32170	BA

0-4-2T
D1 CLASS

32215	TWW
32234	EBN
32235	BTN
32239	ELH

32252 HOR
32253 TWW
32259 ELH
32269 FRA
32274 EBN
32283 HOR
32286 HOR
32289 HOR
32299 AFD

0-6-0
C3 CLASS

32300 HOR
32301 HOR
32302 NOR
32303 3B
32306 HOR
32307 HOR
32308 HOR
32309 NOR

4-6-2T
J1 CLASS

32325 TWW

4-6-2T
J2 CLASS

32326 TWW

4-6-0
N15X "REMEMBRANCE"
CLASS

32327* BAS
32328* BAS
32329* BAS
32330* BAS
32331* BAS
32332* BAS
32333* BAS

2-6-0
K CLASS

32337 FRA
32338 FRA
32339 BTN
32340 BTN
32341 BTN
32342 BTN
32343 BTN
32344 BTN
32345 BTN
32346 BTN
32347 BTN
32348 EBN
32349 EBN
32350 NOR
32351 NOR
32352 3B
32353 3B

0-4-2T
D1 CLASS

32358 EBN
32359 DOV
32361 ELH

0-4-4T
D3 CLASS

32364 AFD
32365 AFD
32366 HOR
32367 TON
32368 BTN
32370 TON
32371 STL
32372 BTN
32373 HOR
32374 TON
32376 BTN
32377 EBN
32378 TON
32379 STL
32380 AFD
32383 STL
32384 HOR
32385 BTN
32386 BTN
32387 HOR
32388 AFD
32389 HOR
32390 TWW
32391 EBN
32393 TWW
32394 STL
32395 EBN
32397 BTN
32398 TWW

0-6-2T
E5 CLASS

32399 HOR
32400 3B

0-6-2T
E5X CLASS

32401 HOR

0-6-2T
E5 CLASS

32402 EBN
32404 NOR
32405 3B
32406 EBN

0-6-2T
E6X CLASS

32407 NOR

0-6-2T
E6 CLASS

32408 BA
32409 ELH
32410 BA

0-6-2T
E6X CLASS

32411 NOR

0-6-2T
E6 CLASS

32412 BA
32413 BA
32414 NOR
32415 BA
32416 NOR
32417 NOR
32418 NOR

4-4-2
H2 CLASS

32421* NHN
32422* NHN
32423* NHN
32424* NHN
32425* NHN
32426* NHN

0-6-0
C2X CLASS

32434 NHN

0-6-0
C2 CLASS

32435 RED
32436 3B

0-6-0
C2X CLASS

32437 BTN
32438 BTN
32440 NOR
32441 3B
32442 BA
32443 BTN
32444 NOR
32445 3B
32446 BA
32447 NOR
32448 BA
32449 HOR
32450 RED
32451 3B

0-6-2T
E3 CLASS

32453 BA
32454 BA
32455 NOR
32456 NOR
32457 NOR
32458 BA
32459 BA
32460 BA
32461 BA
32462 BA

0-6-2T
E4 CLASS

32463 BA
32464 HOR
32465 3B

0-6-2T
E4X CLASS

32466 NOR

0-6-2T
E4 CLASS

32467 BA
32468 BA
32469 BA
32470 BTN
32471 BTN
32472 BA
32473 NOR
32474 BA
32475 NHN
32476 NOR

0-6-2T
E4X CLASS

32477 NOR
32478 NOR

0-6-2T
E4 CLASS

32479 NOR
32480 3B
32481 NOR
32482 NHN
32484 3B
32485 EBN
32486 BTN
32487 GFD
32488 TON

0-6-2T
E4X CLASS

32489 NOR

0-6-2T
E4 CLASS

32490 FRA
32491 BTN
32492 NHN
32493 NOR
32494 NHN
32495 NOR
32496 HOR
32497 3B
32498 NOR
32499 NHN
32500 GFD
32501 HOR
32502 NOR
32503 TON
32504 GFD
32505 BTN
32506 NOR
32507 RED
32508 NHN
32509 FRA
32510 ELH
32511 HOR
32512 TWW
32513 BTN
32514 BTN
32515 HOR
32516 3B
32517 RED
32518 EBN
32519 3B
32520 3B

0-6-0
C2X CLASS

32521 HOR
32522 3B
32523 BTN
32524 BA
32525 BA
32526 NOR
32527 3B
32528 BTN
32529 3B
32532 3B

0-6-0
C2 CLASS

32533 NHN

0-6-0
C2X CLASS

32534 NHN
32535 NOR
32536 NOR
32537 FRA
32538 EBN
32539 BTN
32540 NOR
32541 RED
32543 BTN
32544 NOR
32545 3B
32546 BTN
32547 NOR
32548 FRA
32549 BA
32550 HOR
32551 BA
32552 3B
32553 3B
32554 FRA

0-6-2T
E4 CLASS

32556 HOR
32557 HOR
32558 BTN
32559 FRA
32560 RED
32561 NOR
32562 FRA
32563 NOR
32564 BA
32565 BA
32566 BTN

0-6-2T
E5 CLASS

32567 BTN
32568 RED

0-6-2T
E5X CLASS

32570 HOR

0-6-2T
E5 CLASS

32571 HOR
32572 3B
32573 HOR
32574 EBN
32575 EBN

0-6-2T
E5X CLASS

32576 BTN

0-6-2T
E4 CLASS

32577 BTN
32578 BA
32579 NOR
32580 TON
32581 TWW
32582 TWW

0-6-2T
E5 CLASS

32583 BTN
32584 HOR
32585 3B

0-6-2T
E5X CLASS

32586 RED

0-6-2T
E5 CLASS

32587 BTN
32588 EBN
32589 TWW
32590 TWW
32591 TWW
32592 RED
32593 3B
32594 HOR

4-4-2T
I1X CLASS

32595 EBN
32596 EBN
32598 3B
32599 3B
32601 3B
32602 3B
32603 TWW
32604 3B

0-4-2T
D1 CLASS

32605 EBN

0-6-0T
E1 CLASS

32606 BTN

0-6-2T
E1R CLASS

32608 BPL

0-6-0T
E1 CLASS

32609 ELH

0-6-2T
E1R CLASS

32610 BPL

0-6-0T
A1X "TERRIER" CLASS

32636 NHN
32640 FRA
32644 FRA
32647 NHN
32655 FRA
32659 FRA
32661 FRA
32662 FRA
32678 +

0-6-0T
E1 CLASS

32689 SOT
32690 FRA
32691 FRA
32694 FRA

+ On Loan to Kent and East Sussex Railway.

0-6-2T
E1R CLASS

32695 EXJ
32696 BPL
32697 EXJ

0-4-2T
D1 CLASS

32699 ELH

0-6-0
Q1 CLASS

33001 C1 GFD
33002 C2 GFD
33003 C3 GFD
33004 C4 GFD
33005 C5 GFD
33006 C6 GFD
33007 C7 GFD
33008 C8 GFD
33009 C9 GFD
33010 C10 GFD
33011 C11 GFD
33012 C12 GFD
33013 C13 GFD
33014 C14 ELH
33015 C15 ELH
33016 C16 ELH
33017 C17 ELH
33018 C18 ELH
33019 C19 ELH
33020 C20 ELH
33021 C21 ELH
33022 C22 ELH
33023 C23 ELH
33024 C24 ELH
33025 C25 ELH
33026 C26 TON
33027 C27 TON
33028 C28 TON
33029 C29 TON
33030 C30 TON
33031 C31 FEL
33032 C32 FEL
33033 C33 FEL
33034 C34 FEL
33035 C35 FEL
33036 C36 FEL
33037 C37 FEL
33038 C38 FEL
33039 C39 FEL
33040 C40 FEL

4-6-2
"WEST COUNTRY" CLASS

34001*21C101 EXJ
34002*21C102 EXJ
34003*21C103 EXJ
34004*21C104 EXJ
34005*21C105 EXJ
34006*21C106 EXJ
34007*21C107 EXJ
34008*21C108 EXJ
34009*21C109 EXJ
34010*21C110 EXJ
34011*21C111 EXJ
34012*21C112 EXJ
34013*21C113 EXJ
34014*21C114 EXJ
34015*21C115 EXJ
34016*21C116 EXJ
34017*21C117 EXJ
34018*21C118 EXJ
34019*21C119 EXJ
34020*21C120 EXJ
34021*21C121 EXJ
34022*21C122 9E
34023*21C123 9E
34024*21C124 EXJ
34025*21C125 EXJ
34026*21C126 EXJ
34027*21C127 EXJ
34028*21C128 EXJ
34029*21C129 EXJ
34030*21C130 RAM
34031*21C131 RAM
34032*21C132 RAM
34033*21C133 BAT
34034*21C134 BAT
34035*21C135 BAT
34036*21C136 BAT
34037*21C137 BAT
34038*21C138 BAT
34039*21C139 BAT
34040*21C140 BAT
34041*21C141 EXJ
34042*21C142 EXJ
34043*21C143 EXJ
34044*21C144 EXJ
34045*21C145 EXJ
34046*21C146 EXJ
34047*21C147 EXJ
34048*21C148 SAL

4-6-2
"BATTLE OF BRITAIN" CLASS

34049*21C149 SAL
34050*21C150 SAL
34051*21C151 SAL
34052*21C152 SAL
34053*21C153 SAL
34054*21C154 BAT
34055*21C155 BAT
34056*21C156 DOV
34057*21C157 DOV
34058*21C158 9E
34059*21C159 9E
34060*21C160 9E
34061*21C161 9E
34062*21C162 RAM
34063*21C163 RAM
34064*21C164 9E
34065*21C165 RAM
34066*21C166 RAM
34067*21C167 RAM
34068*21C168 RAM
34069*21C169 RAM
34070*21C170 RAM

4-6-2
"MERCHANT NAVY" CLASS

35001* 21C1 EXJ
35002* 21C2 EXJ
35003* 21C3 EXJ
35004* 21C4 EXJ
35005* 21C5 EXJ
35006* 21C6 SAL
35007* 21C7 SAL
35008* 21C8 SAL
35009* 21C9 SAL
35010* 21C10 SAL
35011* 21C11 9E
35012* 21C12 9E
35013* 21C13 9E
35014* 21C14 9E
35015* 21C15 9E
35016* 21C16 9E
35017* 21C17 9E
35018* 21C18 9E
35019* 21C19 9E
35020* 21C20 9E

Ex-Southern Railway Locomotives Allocated to the Isle of Wight

0-6-0T
E1 CLASS

W1* NPT
W2* NPT
W3* NPT
W4* NPT

0-6-0T
A1X "TERRIER" CLASS

W8* NPT
W13* NPT

0-4-4T
02 CLASS

W14* RYD
W15* RYD
W16* RYD
W17* RYD
W18* RYD
W19* RYD
W20* RYD
W21* RYD
W22* RYD
W23* RYD
W24* RYD
W25* NPT
W26* NPT
W27* NPT
W28* NPT
W29* NPT
W30* NPT
W31* NPT
W32* NPT
W33* NPT
W34* NPT

Ex-London, Midland & Scottish Railway Locomotives

FOWLER 2-6-2T 3P

40001 11A
40002 7A
40003 2A
40004 1C
40005 4A
40006 8A
40007 8A
40008 4A
40009 2E
40010 1C
40011 3C
40012 26F
40013 26A
40014 26A
40015 26A
40016 11E
40017 3C
40018 2D
40019 3C
40020 1C
40021 20G
40022 14B
40023 14A
40024 14C
40025 14A
40026 14A
40027 14B
40028 14B
40029 14A
40030 14A
40031 14A
40032 14A
40033 14A
40034 14C
40035 14B
40036 14B
40037 14B
40038 14A
40039 14C
40040 14B
40041 11A
40042 3C
40043 1C
40044 2E
40045 3C
40046 1C
40047 3B
40048 4A
40049 3B
40050 8A
40051 9A
40052 2A
40053 3B
40054 3B
40055 9B
40056 26F
40057 26F
40058 4A
40059 26F
40060 26F
40061 26F
40062 26F
40063 26A
40064 20G
40065 26A
40066 3B
40067 11B
40068 11B
40069 3C
40070 11E

STANIER 2-6-2T 3P

40071 9A
40072 7B
40073 7B
40074 19G
40075 19B
40076 5D
40077 9B
40078 5D
40079 14B
40080 8B
40081 8B
40082 19B
40083 7B
40084 8B
40085 5F
40086 5F
40087 7A
40088 19G
40089 19G
40090 19D
40091 14C

40092	14B
40093	19D
40094	19D
40095	19D
40096	14B
40097	21A
40098	14B
40099	14B
40100	14B
40101	6C
40102	6C
40103	11A
40104	6C
40105	21B
40106	9A
40107	9A
40108	9A
40109	2E
40110	6C
40111	14B
40112	14B
40113	19D
40114	14B
40115	21A
40116	15C
40117	21A
40118	19G
40119	22A
40120	15C
40121	6C
40122	5D
40123	7A
40124	7B
40125	5D
40126	5D
40127	5D
40128	5D
40129	6C
40130	6A
40131	6C
40132	6C
40133	7B
40134	7A
40135	2E
40136	6C
40137	7A
40138	9A
40139	19B
40140	16A
40141	15C
40142	22C
40143	2D
40144	2A
40145	15C
40146	15C
40147	19G
40148	14B
40149	14B
40150	27C
40151	27C
40152	27C
40153	27C
40154	27C
40155	14B
40156	5F
40157	5D
40158	27C
40159	28A
40160	14B
40161	14B
40162	21B
40163	16A
40164	14B
40165	15C
40166	14B
40167	14B
40168	21B
40169	20C
40170	12G
40171	14B
40172	14B
40173	21B
40174	22A
40175	21A
40176	31E
40177	31E
40178	16A
40179	21B
40180	16B
40181	20C
40182	15C
40183	20G
40184	20G
40185	31E
40186	31E
40187	31E
40188	31E
40189	31E
40190	24C
40191	24C
40192	24C
40193	16A
40194	24C
40195	25G
40196	25G
40197	25G
40198	24C
40199	24C
40200	28A
40201	2D
40202	2D
40203	2E
40204	2D
40205	2D
40206	2D
40207	8B
40208	2D
40209	7A

FOWLER 4-4-0 2P

40322	5A
40323	20F
40324	19A
40325	17A
40326	22D

JOHNSON/FOWLER 4-4-0 2P

40332	10C
40337	18C
40351	20A
40353	15A
40356	10B
40359	20A
40362	20C
40364	17B
40370	18C
40377	5C
40383	17A
40385	21A
40391	20E
40394	16A
40395	17B
40396	7A
40397	10A
40400	15C
40401	19A
40402	5B
40403	12B
40404	17A
40405	5B
40406	20F
40407	17A
40408	16B
40409	20F
40410	16B
40411	17A
40412	2C
40413	3C
40414	20F
40415	16A
40416	17A
40417	16A
40418	17A
40419	16A
40420	2C
40421	2C
40422	20F
40423	22A
40424	16D
40425	2A
40426	17A
40427	16A
40430	2D
40432	17B
40433	2D
40434	10C
40436	17B
40437	22B
40438	9D
40439	21B
40443	5C
40444	20C
40446	12B
40447	2D
40448	5B
40450	2A
40452	20F
40453	15D
40454	15B
40455	20A
40456	17B
40458	16A
40459	20G
40461	5C
40462	3C
40463	21A
40464	2D
40466	18C
40468	15C
40470	20G
40471	5A
40472	18C
40477	14B
40478	16A
40479	9D
40480	20C
40482	17A
40483	9D
40484	20F
40485	15C
40486	21A
40487	19B
40488	20H
40489	20E
40490	18C
40491	18C
40492	5A
40493	21A
40494	7D
40495	8A
40496	16A
40497	16B
40498	16A
40499	17D
40500	17B
40501	3C
40502	16A
40503	16D
40504	16A
40505	22C
40506	18C
40507	10C
40508	2D
40509	22D
40510	15A
40511	21A
40512	21A
40513	17A
40514	20C
40515	2A
40516	17A
40517	21B
40518	19B
40519	20A
40520	17D
40521	20A
40522	2A
40523	22B
40524	7A
40525	17B
40526	17B
40527	8D
40528	5C
40529	5A
40530	22B
40531	9A
40532	16B
40533	16B
40534	2C
40535	16A
40536	15C
40537	15B
40538	15C
40539	9A
40540	16A
40541	15C
40542	15C
40543	15C
40544	19B
40545	19B
40546	16A
40547	14B
40548	15A
40549	15C
40550	15B
40551	15D
40552	16B
40553	16A
40554	10B
40555	18C
40556	18C
40557	18C
40558	16B
40559	16A
40560	16A
40561	10A
40562	20E

L.M.S. 4-4-0 2P

40563	22D
40564	22D
40565	20H
40566	28C
40567	20E
40568	22C
40569	22C
40570	30B
40571	30B
40572	30B
40573	30B
40574	30D
40575	30D
40576	12G
40577	12G
40578	30C
40579	30C
40580	26E
40581	23A
40582	26A
40583	23A
40584	26A
40585	25C
40586	25C
40587	26E
40588	26A
40589	25C
40590	30D
40592	28C
40593	30B
40594	30A
40595	30A
40596	30A
40597	30B
40598	30A
40599	30A
40600	12H
40601	22C
40602	12A
40603	30A
40604	30A
40605	28C
40606	30C
40607	30C
40608	30C
40609	30C
40610	30D
40611	12H
40612	30B
40613	12A
40614	12G
40615	12A
40616	12H
40617	30B
40618	30B
40619	28C
40620	30A
40621	30A
40622	30A
40623	12H
40624	30C
40625	30C
40626	30C
40627	30A
40628	8A
40629	7D
40630	16D
40631	17B
40632	17A
40633	17B
40634	22D
40635	10C
40636	30A
40637	30A
40638	30D
40640	30D
40641	30A
40642	30A
40643	30B
40644	30B
40645	30B
40646	7D
40647	30D
40648	30D
40649	30A
40650	30A
40651	30A
40652	12B
40653	2C
40654	12B
40655	2A
40656	12D
40657	2C
40658	7A
40659	5A
40660	5A
40661	30B

40662	30B
40663	30B
40664	30D
40665	30B
40666	28C
40667	30C
40668	30C
40669	30C
40670	30D
40671	7A
40672	1C
40673	12B
40674	9A
40675	7A
40676	24A
40677	24D
40678	23D
40679	23D
40680	23D
40681	26E
40682	24A
40683	24A
40684	24D
40685	25C
40686	30B
40687	30B
40688	30B
40689	30B
40690	24D
40691	26E
40692	2C
40693	9D
40694	12D
40695	12D
40696	22C
40697	22C
40698	22C
40699	12B
40700	22C

JOHNSON 4-4-0 3P

40711	17A
40715	21A
40720	20A
40726	19C
40727	19C
40728	19A
40729	19A
40731	19B
40734	17A
40735	17A
40736	20A
40739	16A
40740	15C
40741	22A
40743	17A
40745	21A
40747	16A
40748	20A
40756	17A
40757	16A
40758	20A
40762	15D

L.M.S. COMPOUND
4-4-0 4P

40900	6A
40901	28C
40902	12G
40903	28C
40904	12G
40905	30A
40906	30A
40907	28C
40908	30D
40909	30A
40910	20A
40911	28B
40912	12G
40913	30A
40914	30A
40915	28C
40916	27A
40917	21B
40918	31A
40919	30A
40920	30A
40921	29A
40922	29A
40923	29A
40924	29A
40925	7A
40926	6A
40927	20A
40928	21A
40929	16A
40930	17A
40931	20H
40932	20G
40933	6A
40934	21B
40935	22A
40936	7A
40937	23A
40938	29A
40939	29A

DEELEY COMPOUND
4-4-0 4P

41000	17A
41001	22B
41002	16A
41003	17A
41004	20E
41005	20H
41006	20G
41007	15D
41008	15C
41009	15D
41010	15B
41011	15C
41012	16A
41013	15D
41014	19B
41015	16A
41016	19B
41017	15D
41018	14B
41019	22B
41020	20A
41021	19B
41022	20H
41023	14B
41024	19B
41025	22B
41026	19B
41027	22B
41028	22A
41029	21A
41030	22A
41031	15C
41032	16A
41033	17A
41034	15D
41035	21A
41036	17A
41037	19B
41038	15D
41039	22B
41040	20A
41041	15C
41042	15D
41043	20E
41044	15D

L.M.S. COMPOUND
4-4-0 4P

41045	20H
41046	21A
41047	15B
41048	20A
41049	17D
41050	14B
41051	14B
41052	19G
41053	20H
41054	14B
41055	17A
41056	20G
41057	17A
41058	22B
41059	17A
41060	17A
41061	21B
41062	19B
41063	19B
41064	21B
41065	20H
41066	19G
41067	20E
41068	20A
41069	20A
41070	15D
41071	15B
41072	19B
41073	21B
41074	22B
41075	19B
41076	19G
41077	14B
41078	22C
41079	19B
41080	20G
41081	20H
41082	16A
41083	17A
41084	17A
41085	23C
41086	7A
41087	20A
41088	17A
41089	15C
41090	2A
41091	15D
41092	12H
41093	7A
41094	16A
41095	20H
41096	16A
41097	22B
41098	6A
41099	29A
41100	24A
41101	24A
41102	24A
41103	26C
41104	26C
41105	2A
41106	6A
41107	6A
41108	6A
41109	12G
41110	30A
41111	3E
41112	5A
41113	9A
41114	7C
41115	5A
41116	3E
41117	14B
41118	7A
41119	7A
41120	6A
41121	6A
41122	9A
41123	7C
41124	7C
41125	29A
41126	31A
41127	30A
41128	31A
41129	12A
41130	28C
41131	27A
41132	30D
41133	30D
41134	29B
41135	12G
41136	28C
41137	20A
41138	30D
41139	12A
41140	12A
41141	12A
41142	12A
41143	12A
41144	20A
41145	28C
41146	12A
41147	28C
41148	30A
41149	30A
41150	7A
41151	5C
41152	2A
41153	3E
41154	3E
41155	30D
41156	7A
41157	6A
41158	6A
41159	9A
41160	5A
41161	7A
41162	6A
41163	6A
41164	6A
41165	2A
41166	9A
41167	5A
41168	9A
41169	6A
41170	6A
41171	12G
41172	3E
41173	5A
41174	2A
41175	12G
41176	29B
41177	28B
41178	28B
41179	12G
41180	28C
41181	19G
41182	30A
41183	30D
41184	29B
41185	24A
41186	25F
41187	24A
41188	23A
41189	25F
41190	26C
41191	26C
41192	24E
41193	23C
41194	24A
41195	24E
41196	23C
41197	24E
41198	24A
41199	26C

IVATT 2-6-2T 2P

41200	7B
41201	7B
41202	4D
41203	4D
41204	4E
41205	20G
41206	20G
41207	14B
41208	14B
41209	15D

JOHNSON 0-4-0ST OF

41516	17B
41518	18C
41523	17B

DEELEY 0-4-0T OF

41528	18D
41529	18D
41530	22B
41531	18C
41532	18C
41533	17B
41534	18D
41535	17A
41536	17B
41537	22B

JOHNSON 0-6-0T 1F

41660	14B
41661	14B
41664	14B
41666	16A
41668	14B
41671	14B
41672	14B
41674	14B
41676	4B
41682	16A
41686	16A
41690	19E
41695	17A
41699	21A
41702	19E
41706	22A
41708	18D
41710	18D
41711	18D
41712	14A
41713	14B
41714	6C
41718	17B
41720	22B
41724	14A
41725	4A
41726	17A
41727	22B
41734	6C
41739	20B
41745	20A
41747	18D
41748	20F
41749	18D
41752	18D
41753	18D
41754	17A
41756	19E
41759	20B
41762	16A

41763 18D
41767 20F
41768 19A
41769 4C
41770 17B
41773 17A
41777 21A
41779 17A
41780 6C
41781 20F
41788 17A
41793 20D
41794 20B
41795 17A
41797 19C
41803 18D
41804 18D
41805 20F
41811 14A
41813 19C
41814 19E
41818 6C
41820 20F
41824 4C
41826 16A
41829 14A
41833 17A
41835 19C
41838 20B
41839 17B
41842 20B
41844 20D
41846 16B
41847 17A
41852 4C
41853 6C
41854 14C
41855 19A
41856 21A
41857 19A
41859 17B
41860 4C
41865 17B
41869 19C
41870 22B
41873 18C
41874 22A
41875 17D
41878 17B
41879 21A
41885 16D
41889 15B
41890 20B
41893 4C
41895 16A

STANIER 0-4-4T 2P

41900 22C
41901 20H
41902 22C
41903 22C
41904 22C
41905 9B
41906 9B
41907 9B
41908 1C
41909 1C

L.T.&S. 4-4-2T 2P

41910 2092 18C
41911 2093 16A
41912 2094 18C
41913 2095 18C
41914 2096 16A
41915 2097 13C
41916 2098 16A
41917 2099 19C
41918 2100 13C
41919 2101 16A
41920 2102 18C
41921 2103 16A
41922 2104 16A
41923 2106 13C
41924 2107 13C
41925 2108 18C
41926 2109 19C

L.T.&S. 4-4-2T 3P

41928 2110 13C
41929 2111 13C
41930 2112 13A
41931 2113 13A
41932 2114 13A
41933 2115 13C
41934 2116 13D
41935 2117 13A
41936 2118 13C
41937 2119 13D
41938 2120 15C
41939 2121 13C
41940 2122 16D
41941 2123 13D
41942 2124 13A
41943 2125 16D
41944 2126 13A
41945 2127 13A
41946 2128 13C
41947 2129 16D
41948 2130 13A
41949 2131 13A
41950 2132 13A
41951 2133 13A
41952 2134 13A
41953 2135 13C
41954 2136 13A
41955 2137 13C
41956 2138 13C
41957 2139 13A
41958 2140 19C
41959 2141 13A
41960 2142 13C
41961 2143 16D
41962 2144 19C
41963 2145 13A
41964 2146 13C
41965 2147 13C
41966 2148 13C
41967 2149 13A
41968 2150 13D
41969 2151 13A
41970 2152 13A
41971 2153 13D
41972 2154 29C
41973 2155 29C
41974 2156 13A
41975 2157 13A
41976 2158 13A
41977 2159 13C
41978 2160 13D

L.T. & S. 0-6-2T 3F

41980 13C
41981 13A
41982 13A
41983 13A
41984 13A
41985 13A
41986 13A
41987 13A
41988 13A
41989 13A
41990 13A
41991 13D
41992 13D
41993 13A

FAIRBURN 2-6-4T 4P

42187 25F
42188 25F
42189 25F
42200 27A
42201 27A
42202 27A
42203 27A
42204 27A
42205 27A
42206 27A
42207 27A
42208 27A
42209 30C
42210 30C
42211 30C
42212 30C
42213 27A
42214 27A
42215 27A
42216 27A
42217 27C
42218 13C
42219 13C
42220 13C
42221 13C
42222 13D
42223 13D
42224 13D
42225 13A
42226 13A
42227 13A
42228 16A
42229 16A
42230 14B
42231 5D
42232 5D
42233 5D
42234 5D
42235 5D
42236 5D
42237 5D
42238 27A
42239 27A
42240 27A
42241 27A
42242 27A
42243 27A
42244 27A
42245 27A
42246 27A
42247 27A
42248 13A
42249 13A
42250 13A
42251 13A
42252 13A
42253 13A
42254 13A
42255 13A
42256 13A
42257 13A
42258 7B
42259 7B
42260 7B
42261 7B
42262 3E
42263 3E
42264 3E
42265 3E
42266 5A
42267 11A
42268 28B
42269 28B
42270 28B
42271 28B
42272 28B
42273 28B
42274 27A
42275 30A
42276 30A
42277 30A
42278 26A
42279 26A
42280 26A
42281 26A
42282 26A
42283 26A
42284 26A
42285 26A
42286 26A
42287 26A
42288 26A
42289 26A
42290 26A
42291 23C
42292 23C
42293 23C
42294 23C
42295 24A
42296 25F
42297 25F
42298 25F
42299 25F

FOWLER 2-6-4T 4P

42300 14C
42301 11D
42302 14C
42303 10A
42304 1C
42305 9C
42306 9D
42307 4B
42308 11E
42309 5A
42310 25B
42311 25B
42312 25B
42313 11D
42314 11D
42315 9D
42316 1A
42317 11D
42318 9D
42319 9C
42320 5D
42321 11B
42322 9A
42323 9C
42324 25B
42325 14B
42326 21A
42327 21B
42328 16A
42329 14B
42330 15C
42331 14B
42332 9B
42333 16A
42334 15C
42335 14C
42336 17B
42337 21A
42338 21B
42339 21B
42340 17A
42341 17A
42342 21B
42343 5D
42344 5D
42345 5C
42346 5C
42347 5C
42348 5E
42349 9C
42350 9A
42351 9A
42352 9B
42353 9B
42354 9B
42355 9C
42356 9C
42357 9C
42358 5F
42359 11B
42360 5D
42361 16A
42362 23D
42363 5F
42364 5D
42365 9D
42366 9D
42367 9D
42368 9D
42369 9C
42370 9D
42371 9D
42372 1A
42373 21B
42374 14C
42375 5D
42376 5D
42377 20E
42378 5D
42379 10A
42380 20E
42381 23D
42382 9C
42383 14B
42384 25B
42385 4B
42386 11B
42387 4B
42388 4B
42389 1C
42390 4B
42391 5C
42392 11B
42393 11B
42394 4B
42395 9A
42396 9A
42397 9A
42398 9A
42399 9A
42400 27B
42401 9A
42402 9A
42403 11E
42404 11E
42405 25D
42406 25F
42407 25F
42408 25B
42409 25F
42410 25B
42411 25B
42412 25B
42413 25B
42414 25B
42415 27B
42416 27B
42417 27B
42418 27B
42419 27B
42420 27B
42421 27B
42422 27B
42423 27B
42424 11E

STANIER 2-6-4T 4P

42425 6A

42426 8A
42427 11B
42428 11A
42429 11A
42430 11B
42431 11A
42432 11A
42433 24A
42434 24C
42435 24C
42436 24C
42437 24C
42438 24B
42439 24B
42440 3D
42441 3D
42442 2B
42443 1A
42444 3C
42445 1C
42446 1C
42447 5E
42448 3C
42449 3D
42450 3E
42451 3E
42452 3C
42453 8A
42454 10C
42455 10A
42456 10A
42457 11D
42458 2B
42459 8A
42460 7B
42461 9A
42462 11B
42463 9B
42464 11D
42465 10A
42466 3C
42467 9A
42468 5F
42469 5D
42470 3D
42471 5E
42472 23D
42473 26D
42474 26D
42475 24B
42476 26D
42477 26A
42478 9A
42479 14C
42480 24C
42481 24C
42482 1C
42483 24D
42484 24D
42485 24D
42486 26A
42487 2A
42488 3E
42489 3E
42490 24A
42491 26A
42492 26A
42493 11B
42494 5D

STANIER 3 CYLINDER 2-6-4T 4P

42500 13D
42501 13D
42502 13D
42503 13D
42504 13D
42505 13D
42506 13D
42507 13D
42508 13D
42509 13D
42510 13D
42511 13D
42512 13D
42513 13D
42514 13D
42515 13D
42516 13D
42517 13D
42518 13D
42519 13D
42520 13D
42521 13D
42522 13A
42523 13A
42524 13A
42525 13A
42526 13A
42527 13A
42528 13A
42529 13A
42530 13A
42531 13A
42532 13A
42533 13A
42534 13A
42535 13A
42536 13A

STANIER 2-6-4T 4P

42537 23D
42538 3D
42539 10A
42540 6A
42541 1C
42542 10C
42543 5D
42544 11A
42545 26C
42546 24B
42547 24B
42548 24A
42549 26A
42550 26F
42551 26A
42552 3D
42553 25D
42554 23D
42555 24B
42556 24C
42557 23D
42558 24B
42559 24D
42560 10C
42561 10C
42562 3C
42563 10A
42564 8A
42565 26C
42566 2B
42567 3E
42568 6A
42569 23D
42570 11B
42571 11B
42572 10A
42573 11B
42574 10C
42575 9A
42576 2A
42577 2A
42578 3D
42579 3E
42580 9A
42581 11B
42582 1C
42583 8B
42584 5D
42585 5D
42586 3C
42587 6A
42588 10A
42589 1C
42590 1C
42591 2B
42592 23D
42593 1C
42594 11B
42595 11D
42596 10C
42597 8A
42598 1C
42599 9A
42600 2B
42601 11A
42602 11B
42603 5D
42604 3C
42605 5D
42606 8B
42607 5D
42608 9A
42609 5D
42610 1C
42611 5E
42612 8A
42613 11A
42614 23D
42615 11A
42616 3D
42617 6A
42618 26A
42619 26A
42620 26A
42621 26A
42622 26A
42623 26A
42624 26A
42625 26A
42626 26A
42627 3C
42628 7B
42629 26D
42630 26A
42631 23D
42632 23D
42633 26C
42634 24A
42635 24B
42636 24E
42637 24E
42638 24E
42639 23A
42640 23D
42641 23D
42642 23D
42643 23A
42644 25F
42645 26B
42646 26B
42647 26B
42648 26B
42649 26E
42650 26E
42651 26E
42652 26C
42653 26C
42654 26C
42655 26C
42656 26C
42657 26C
42658 8A
42659 3E
42660 3C
42661 24C
42662 10C
42663 5D
42664 5D
42665 5D
42666 5D
42667 5D
42668 5D
42669 5D
42670 5D
42671 5D
42672 5D

FAIRBURN 2-6-4T 4P

42673 5D
42674 5D
42675 5D
42676 5D
42677 6A
42678 16A
42679 16A
42680 16A
42681 14C
42682 20E
42683 14B
42684 14C
42685 21A
42686 16A
42687 14B
42688 27A
42689 27A
42690 27A
42691 27A
42692 27A
42693 27A
42694 27A
42695 27A
42696 27A
42697 27B
42698 27A
42699 27A

HUGHES/FOWLER 2-6-0 5F

42700 26A
42701 26A
42702 26A
42703 26A
42704 26A
42705 26A
42706 26A
42707 26A
42708 26A
42709 26A
42710 26A
42711 26A
42712 24F
42713 26A
42714 26A
42715 26B
42716 26B
42717 26B
42718 26B
42719 26B
42720 26B
42721 26B
42722 26B
42723 26B
42724 26B
42725 26B
42726 25F
42727 25F
42728 25F
42729 25G
42730 25G
42731 25G
42732 25F
42733 25B
42734 26B
42735 27C
42736 31D
42737 31D
42738 29D
42739 30D
42740 27C
42741 27C
42742 12A
42743 12A
42744 12A
42745 12A
42746 12A
42747 1A
42748 12A
42749 12A
42750 26A
42751 12A
42752 12A
42753 26B
42754 21A
42755 26B
42756 17D
42757 17B
42758 21A
42759 20B
42760 17D
42761 19A
42762 20E
42763 17B
42764 21A
42765 19E
42766 26A
42767 17B
42768 17B
42769 19A
42770 20G
42771 20B
42772 9B
42773 9B
42774 17D
42775 9A
42776 9A
42777 2D
42778 9A
42779 3A
42780 12A
42781 2D
42782 3D
42783 2D
42784 21A
42785 5B
42786 1A
42787 1A
42788 8C
42789 26A
42790 21A
42791 20E
42792 15C
42793 21A
42794 14A
42795 20B
42796 26B
42797 19A
42798 20B
42799 21A
42800 29D
42801 29D
42802 12A
42803 12A
42804 28B
42805 30D
42806 30D
42807 28B
42808 30D
42809 30D

42810	8C
42811	3D
42812	1A
42813	9A
42814	2D
42815	8C
42816	20B
42817	1A
42818	21A
42819	26B
42820	26A
42821	25G
42822	21A
42823	16A
42824	21A
42825	21A
42826	21A
42827	21A
42828	25F
42829	21A
42830	12A
42831	12A
42832	12A
42833	12A
42834	12A
42835	12A
42836	12A
42837	12A
42838	26B
42839	14B
42840	24F
42841	24F
42842	24F
42843	25F
42844	25G
42845	17D
42846	17B
42847	17A
42848	9A
42849	9A
42850	21A
42851	3A
42852	9A
42853	3A
42854	9A
42855	14A
42856	5B
42857	21A
42858	9A
42859	9B
42860	26B
42861	25B
42862	25B
42863	25B
42864	26B
42865	25F
42866	25B
42867	24F
42868	26B
42869	25B
42870	1A
42871	26A
42872	17A
42873	17D
42874	17D
42875	12A
42876	12A
42877	12A
42878	12A
42879	30D
42880	12A
42881	12A
42882	12A
42883	12A
42884	12A
42885	1A
42886	9A
42887	9A
42888	2D
42889	9A
42890	21A
42891	3D
42892	3D
42893	20G
42894	3D
42895	20H
42896	19E
42897	17A
42898	17B
42899	16A
42900	21A
42901	26A
42902	17D
42903	21A
42904	19A
42905	12A
42906	12A
42907	12A
42908	12G
42909	12G
42910	30A
42911	30A
42912	30A
42913	30A
42914	30A
42915	30A
42916	30A
42917	30A
42918	12G
42919	12G
42920	5B
42921	3D
42922	22B
42923	9A
42924	9A
42925	9A
42926	8C
42927	30D
42928	20H
42929	3D
42930	9A
42931	1A
42932	2D
42933	8C
42934	8C
42935	9A
42936	9A
42937	9A
42938	9B
42939	5B
42940	1A
42941	2D
42942	9D
42943	9D
42944	5B

STANIER 2-6-0 5F

42945	6B
42946	8C
42947	5B
42948	7B
42949	2B
42950	5B
42951	7B
42952	5B
42953	6C
42954	7A
42955	5B
42956	5B
42957	2B
42958	2D
42959	2D
42960	5B
42961	5B
42962	5B
42963	3D
42964	2D
42965	6B
42966	3D
42967	6C
42968	5B
42969	6C
42970	6C
42971	7A
42972	8C
42973	2D
42974	8C
42975	6B
42976	6B
42977	5B
42978	8C
42979	6B
42980	5B
42981	2D
42982	5B
42983	5B
42984	7B

IVATT 2-6-0 4F

43000	5B
43001	5B
43002	5B

JOHNSON 0-6-0 3F

43137	20G
43174	15D
43178	22A
43180	19C
43181	19C
43183	15C
43185	15D
43186	20G
43187	20H
43188	17B
43189	11A
43191	17A
43192	16A
43193	16D
43194	22E
43200	17A
43201	21A
43203	21A
43204	22A
43205	15C
43207	8B
43208	19C
43210	21A
43211	18C
43212	18C
43213	22B
43214	17B
43216	22E
43218	22E
43219	18C
43222	15D
43223	21A
43224	18D
43225	21A
43226	20G
43228	22A
43231	20G
43232	15C
43233	20C
43234	18D
43235	18B
43237	11A
43239	16D
43240	18D
43241	19A
43242	18D
43243	19C
43244	17B
43245	14C
43246	14A
43247	17B
43248	22D
43249	16A
43250	20C
43251	20F
43252	18D
43253	16B
43254	18B
43256	17B
43257	22B
43258	22B
43259	18A
43260	22D
43261	14A
43263	22B
43265	14A
43266	18B
43267	20B
43268	9D
43269	9D
43271	9D
43273	17A
43274	9D
43275	9A
43277	21D
43278	9D
43281	9B
43282	9D
43283	8B
43284	21A
43286	17B
43287	18A
43290	17D
43292	18D
43293	20H
43294	18D
43295	20F
43296	9D
43297	18D
43298	18D
43299	18D
43300	19C
43301	20D
43305	18A
43306	17B
43307	20H
43308	17A
43309	18D
43310	18D
43312	17A
43313	14A
43314	8B
43315	17A
43317	16B
43318	17A
43319	16B
43321	21A
43323	17A
43324	17A
43325	19C
43326	15C
43327	18A
43329	11A
43330	20H
43331	18B
43332	20C
43333	15C
43334	19A
43335	20G
43336	21A
43337	20F
43338	17D
43339	21A
43340	17B
43341	16D
43342	17D
43344	22B
43351	20E
43355	21B
43356	22D
43357	8B
43359	21B
43361	19E
43364	17A
43367	15A
43368	17A
43369	16A
43370	17A
43371	16B
43373	22B
43374	21A
43378	16A
43379	18B
43381	21D
43386	18D
43387	9D
43388	17B
43389	8B
43392	20B
43394	4A
43395	17B
43396	7D
43398	8B
43399	16A
43400	14A
43401	20A
43402	17A
43405	18A
43406	17A
43408	14A
43410	3C
43411	15C
43419	22A
43427	22B
43428	15D
43429	17C
43431	16D
43433	21A
43435	21A
43436	22A
43439	22A
43440	14A
43441	21A
43443	21A
43444	22A
43446	20C
43448	14A
43449	20B
43453	18A
43454	20A
43456	20B
43457	9A
43458	16A
43459	17A
43462	22D
43463	19B
43464	22A
43468	19A
43469	17A
43474	15D
43476	20B
43482	17A
43484	21A
43490	21A
43491	21A
43494	16C
43496	17A
43497	20D
43499	18A
43502	3C
43506	22B
43507	22B
43509	20C
43510	17A
43514	20D
43515	18D

43520 21D
43521 21D
43522 16D
43523 21D
43524 18D
43529 16D
43531 21A
43538 16A
43540 21A
43544 21A
43546 18D
43548 17A
43550 17A
43553 20C
43558 16D
43562 21B
43565 14A
43568 21D
43570 11A
43572 17A
43573 4A
43574 17A
43575 18D
43578 17A
43579 20B
43580 18B
43581 4A
43582 17B
43583 21B
43584 17A
43585 20G
43586 20G
43587 16D
43593 22A
43594 21A
43595 19A
43596 19A
43598 17A
43599 18A
43600 4A
43604 22B
43605 19A
43607 19A
43608 17B
43612 19E
43615 8B
43618 4A
43619 17B
43620 21A
43621 21A
43622 18C
43623 17B
43624 21A
43627 21A
43629 14A
43630 19E
43631 18A
43633 18A
43634 16D
43636 19A
43637 16A
43638 19E
43639 20D
43644 21A
43645 22B
43650 18A
43651 16B
43652 16B
43653 15C
43656 20D
43657 8B
43658 17A
43660 19C
43661 19A
43662 19A
43664 19C
43665 20A
43667 21A
43668 21B
43669 19C
43673 21A
43674 21A
43675 21B
43676 15C
43678 20B
43679 4A
43680 21A
43681 20B
43682 17C
43683 19A
43684 21A
43686 21A
43687 21B
43690 21A
43693 21D
43698 21A
43705 20B
43709 17B
43710 15C
43711 16A
43712 22A
43714 20D
43715 19A
43717 9A
43721 15D
43723 19E
43724 16A
43727 16D
43728 15C
43729 16A
43731 19A
43734 22A
43735 17A
43737 20B
43742 20D
43745 17A
43747 19C
43748 15C
43749 19A
43751 18D
43753 15C
43754 22B
43755 19A
43756 19E
43757 11A
43759 17A
43760 11A
43762 16D
43763 17A
43765 16D
43766 15D
43767 21D
43769 18C
43770 20B
43771 18C
43772 19A
43773 16C

DEELEY 0-6-0 3F

43775 19A
43776 17A
43777 15D
43778 18A
43779 17C
43781 20G
43782 14A
43783 20E
43784 20F
43785 15D
43786 3C
43787 18A
43789 20C
43790 15C
43791 22B
43792 22D
43793 18A
43795 18A
43796 15A
43797 15A
43798 18A
43799 18A
43800 14A
43801 14C
43802 16D
43803 18A
43804 18A
43805 18A
43806 14A
43807 15C
43808 15A
43809 18D
43810 18A
43811 19D
43812 21A
43813 19C
43814 19C
43815 17B
43817 18A
43818 18A
43819 18A
43820 18A
43821 18A
43822 21D
43823 18A
43824 18A
43825 18A
43826 18A
43827 18A
43828 18A
43829 15C
43830 15A
43831 18A
43832 18A
43833 18A

FOWLER 0-6-0 4F

43835 17C
43836 19E
43837 17B
43838 17A
43839 17A
43840 17A
43841 2B
43842 9D
43843 21A
43844 19A
43845 21A
43846 22B
43847 17B
43848 31A
43849 31A
43850 18B
43851 20B
43852 20B
43853 22A
43854 16B
43855 20B
43856 18C
43857 18D
43858 21A
43859 16B
43860 18B
43861 15A
43862 18D
43863 18D
43864 16B
43865 17C
43866 18B
43867 18B
43868 12A
43869 16A
43870 15A
43871 20B
43872 17C
43873 21D
43874 16D
43875 22C
43876 15A
43877 7A
43878 20A
43879 21A
43880 18B
43881 17A
43882 18B
43883 31D
43884 28A
43885 18A
43886 18D
43887 22B
43888 15D
43889 15B
43890 18C
43891 21A
43892 17B
43893 20F
43894 16C
43895 16C
43896 19G
43897 24D
43898 16B
43899 30B
43900 18A
43901 14A
43902 12A
43903 20D
43904 20F
43905 13A
43906 19C
43907 16C
43908 19D
43909 15A
43910 15D
43911 21A
43912 21A
43913 20D
43914 18A
43915 2B
43916 17B
43917 17B
43918 17D
43919 17B
43920 16B
43921 17C
43922 12A
43923 18A
43924 22B
43925 17D
43926 14A
43927 19E
43928 22A
43929 17D
43930 17B
43931 20B
43932 22B
43933 16A
43934 14A
43935 14B
43936 18C
43937 15C
43938 17B
43939 18A
43940 21A
43941 21A
43942 20C
43943 18A
43944 20F
43945 19D
43946 21A
43947 14A
43948 16A
43949 21A
43950 19C
43951 21A
43952 19E
43953 22A
43954 16A
43955 17A
43956 16A
43957 16B
43958 16A
43959 18C
43960 20F
43961 18A
43962 16A
43963 20B
43964 14B
43965 15C
43966 18B
43967 15D
43968 21B
43969 16A
43970 18A
43971 15D
43972 17B
43973 12A
43974 18A
43975 18A
43976 17B
43977 15C
43978 22B
43979 18A
43980 16B
43981 16B
43982 15A
43983 16D
43984 20F
43985 19E
43986 21A
43987 20B
43988 18A
43989 20B
43990 18A
43991 17B
43992 18B
43993 18D
43994 16A
43995 18A
43996 12A
43997 16D
43998 20B
43999 20F
44000 20F
44001 12A
44002 17B
44003 20C
44004 16D
44005 16C
44006 19A
44007 20F
44008 12A
44009 12A
44010 19D
44011 28A
44012 18A
44013 19C
44014 18B
44015 19C
44016 12A
44017 17D
44018 17D
44019 9D
44020 20B
44021 16C
44022 19E
44023 17A
44024 17D
44025 19E
44026 21A

L.M.S. 0-6-0 4F

44027 3B

44028 14A
44029 14A
44030 16A
44031 17A
44032 20H
44033 15A
44034 15C
44035 17B
44036 19C
44037 20B
44038 25E
44039 16A
44040 19E
44041 20F
44042 25E
44043 18A
44044 20A
44045 22B
44046 17B
44047 17B
44048 17B
44049 21A
44050 17D
44051 14A
44052 14B
44053 18C
44054 18C
44055 16A
44056 23C
44057 3E
44058 3D
44059 11B
44060 11A
44061 3A
44062 23C
44063 5E
44064 12D
44065 6B
44066 18D
44067 5D
44068 5D
44069 3C
44070 18D
44071 19C
44072 2B
44073 6B
44074 9B
44075 12D
44076 2C
44077 3D
44078 9A
44079 10D
44080 9D
44081 12B
44082 16C
44083 11E
44084 21A
44085 17C
44086 12B
44087 17B
44088 21A
44089 18A
44090 19D
44091 18A
44092 21A
44093 5D
44094 20B
44095 16A
44096 22C
44097 16B
44098 20D
44099 20D
44100 17B
44101 17A
44102 22D
44103 17C
44104 18D
44105 25C
44106 18A
44107 18C
44108 21A
44109 17C
44110 19D
44111 19D
44112 22A
44113 16C
44114 19E
44115 3C
44116 1A
44117 19D
44118 11A
44119 10D
44120 11B
44121 12B
44122 18D
44123 15C
44124 17B
44125 10E
44126 11A
44127 19C
44128 19C
44129 18D
44130 18B
44131 16A
44132 16A
44133 18A
44134 17D
44135 22A
44136 18A
44137 21A
44138 21B
44139 21A
44140 16C
44141 20C
44142 17A
44143 17B
44144 19D
44145 21A
44146 22D
44147 18D
44148 17C
44149 20G
44150 18A
44151 20A
44152 16B
44153 20D
44154 18D
44155 16B
44156 17B
44157 18A
44158 16A
44159 30B
44160 15A
44161 20C
44162 18C
44163 17D
44164 16A
44165 19A
44166 17B
44167 22B
44168 17D
44169 22A
44170 17B
44171 17B
44172 17D
44173 19C
44174 17D
44175 22B
44176 21A
44177 17A
44178 19D
44179 20D
44180 16A
44181 12A
44182 18D
44183 12A
44184 21A
44185 21A
44186 21A
44187 18A
44188 18B
44189 12A
44190 21A
44191 18B
44192 12D
44193 29A
44194 31A
44195 17A
44196 29A
44197 20F
44198 30B
44199 12A
44200 21A
44201 20H
44202 16C
44203 21A
44204 21D
44205 16C
44206 16C
44207 21A
44208 1A
44209 17D
44210 14A
44211 19A
44212 19A
44213 21A
44214 17A
44215 16A
44216 20D
44217 20D
44218 16B
44219 3D
44220 23B
44221 25C
44222 20F
44223 16A
44224 21A
44225 24D
44226 17B
44227 17C
44228 13A
44229 22B
44230 16A
44231 15C
44232 19C
44233 18A
44234 27A
44235 22B
44236 19G
44237 19D
44238 16B
44239 16B
44240 24D
44241 18A
44242 15A
44243 14A
44244 18C
44245 20B
44246 17D
44247 16A
44248 21A
44249 17D
44250 18A
44251 29A
44252 17C
44253 31A
44254 31A
44255 31A
44256 31A
44257 31A
44258 29A
44259 13C
44260 17C
44261 19E
44262 17D
44263 17A
44264 16A
44265 17B
44266 22A
44267 16A
44268 16C
44269 22B
44270 17B
44271 19D
44272 22B
44273 16B
44274 18C
44275 16A
44276 20F
44277 20F
44278 15B
44279 17C
44280 20H
44281 27A
44282 20G
44283 31B
44284 19A
44285 19A
44286 19D
44287 15A
44288 18C
44289 21B
44290 20D
44291 24D
44292 11E
44293 16B
44294 18C
44295 17B
44296 16B
44297 13A
44298 14A
44299 20F
44300 5B
44301 5E
44302 3D
44303 9A
44304 21A
44305 7B
44306 11B
44307 5F
44308 9A
44309 9D
44310 5D
44311 26A
44312 30B
44313 16A
44314 29A
44315 12A
44316 17B
44317 21A
44318 28B
44319 30B
44320 31D
44321 18B
44322 29A
44323 30B
44324 12A
44325 30B
44326 12A
44327 17D
44328 29A
44329 30B
44330 31B
44331 31B
44332 15A
44333 21B
44334 19A
44335 20D
44336 20D
44337 20D
44338 20D
44339 3C
44340 9B
44341 10D
44342 5B
44343 5D
44344 5B
44345 3C
44346 12B
44347 11B
44348 1A
44349 5D
44350 3D
44351 11B
44352 10D
44353 5D
44354 2A
44355 19A
44356 10D
44357 9A
44358 10E
44359 5B
44360 9D
44361 11B
44362 15D
44363 5D
44364 12D
44365 9D
44366 2C
44367 6B
44368 11B
44369 5D
44370 1A
44371 19E
44372 1A
44373 5D
44374 11A
44375 11A
44376 18A
44377 5D
44378 5D
44379 10D
44380 5D
44381 1A
44382 9D
44383 5D
44384 5E
44385 12D
44386 10D
44387 5B
44388 5D
44389 7A
44390 12B
44391 5D
44392 2A
44393 5D
44394 16D
44395 2A
44396 1C
44397 1A
44398 24D
44399 12D
44400 20E
44401 16A
44402 17A
44403 15C
44404 20A
44405 20H
44406 21A
44407 19D
44408 16A
44409 17A
44410 18C
44411 22A
44412 16A
44413 21A
44414 16A
44415 16C
44416 16A
44417 22D

44418	19A
44419	17A
44420	17A
44421	19D
44422	22C
44423	15C
44424	22A
44425	14A
44426	19A
44427	21A
44428	17B
44429	17B
44430	17A
44431	20A
44432	17A
44433	17B
44434	17B
44435	17B
44436	17B
44437	19A
44438	2B
44439	3B
44440	1A
44441	1A
44442	1A
44443	1C
44444	9B
44445	7B
44446	20C
44447	2B
44448	5D
44449	12D
44450	5E
44451	1A
44452	5E
44453	5B
44454	3C
44455	2A
44456	2A
44457	19C
44458	16B
44459	19E
44460	24A
44461	5B
44462	23B
44463	16C
44464	25E
44465	15B
44466	22A
44467	20B
44468	20H
44469	11E
44470	18A
44471	23C
44472	16C
44473	10E
44474	23C
44475	21A
44476	16B
44477	19C
44478	5D
44479	24A
44480	16A
44481	23B
44482	17B
44483	24D
44484	5D
44485	25C
44486	25C
44487	11B
44488	3C
44489	5D
44490	3D
44491	2C
44492	3B
44493	6B
44494	5E
44495	12D
44496	5D
44497	1A
44498	5D
44499	5D
44500	5D
44501	20A
44502	5D
44503	5D
44504	5F
44505	12D
44506	3C
44507	1A
44508	5D
44509	16B
44510	11A
44511	2A
44512	3C
44513	5D
44514	3E
44515	21A
44516	21A
44517	3D
44518	16B
44519	16B
44520	21A
44521	16B
44522	16B
44523	22C
44524	21A
44525	21A
44526	17B
44527	17B
44528	17B
44529	14B
44530	13A
44531	14B
44532	14B
44533	16A
44534	22A
44535	22C
44536	22A
44537	22A
44538	21A
44539	17C
44540	17D
44541	23B
44542	17A
44543	26A
44544	26A
44545	21A
44546	16A
44547	18A
44548	9D
44549	2B
44550	19A
44551	17B
44552	18A
44553	22B
44554	20H
44555	20G
44556	20H
44557	22C
44558	22C
44559	22C
44560	22C
44561	22C
44562	20D
44563	14B
44564	17D
44565	17A
44566	17A
44567	21A
44568	19A
44569	22A
44570	20D
44571	21A
44572	19A
44573	19A
44574	15A
44575	15A
44576	22B
44577	16A
44578	16A
44579	20G
44580	21A
44581	14A
44582	15D
44583	21A
44584	21A
44585	22C
44586	20D
44587	21D
44588	17D
44589	16C
44590	18D
44591	21A
44592	3E
44593	12D
44594	11B
44595	5E
44596	2C
44597	17B
44598	16A
44599	17B
44600	17B
44601	17A
44602	17A
44603	20D
44604	20D
44605	17A
44606	21D

STANIER 4-6-0 5P5F

44758	5A
44759	5A
44760	5A
44761	5A
44762	5A
44763	5A
44764	5A
44765	5A
44766	5A
44767	5A
44768	29A
44769	29A
44770	29A
44771	32A
44772	32A
44773	32A
44774	20A
44775	20A
44776	14B
44777	14B
44778	24E
44779	24E
44780	25A
44781	26A
44782	26A
44783	12B
44784	12B
44785	12B
44786	12B
44787	12B
44788	5A
44789	5A
44790	5A
44791	28A
44792	28A
44793	27A
44794	27A
44795	12A
44796	29A
44797	29A
44798	32A
44799	32A
44800	6B
44801	5A
44802	19E
44803	19E
44804	22A
44805	21A
44806	21A
44807	5A
44808	5A
44809	17A
44810	21A
44811	21A
44812	22A
44813	21A
44814	21A
44815	17A
44816	14B
44817	14A
44818	17A
44819	17A
44820	20A
44821	20A
44822	14B
44823	20A
44824	20A
44825	16A
44826	22C
44827	5B
44828	20A
44829	18A
44830	22C
44831	2A
44832	5A
44833	5A
44834	5A
44835	5A
44836	5A
44837	5A
44838	5A
44839	17A
44840	21A
44841	16A
44842	21A
44843	22A
44844	5B
44845	19E
44846	14B
44847	20A
44848	20A
44849	20A
44850	20A
44851	17A
44852	21A
44853	20A
44854	20A
44855	22A
44856	20A
44857	20A
44858	19A
44859	19B
44860	7A
44861	16A
44862	5A
44863	5A
44864	5A
44865	5A
44866	2A
44867	2A
44868	12B
44869	12B
44870	9A
44871	9A
44872	3D
44873	3C
44874	5A
44875	5A
44876	12B
44877	12A
44878	12A
44879	12A
44880	31A
44881	31A
44882	12A
44883	12A
44884	12A
44885	29A
44886	12A
44887	23C
44888	26A
44889	26A
44890	26A
44891	26A
44892	10A
44893	26A
44894	26A
44895	26A
44896	25G
44897	8B
44898	12A
44899	12A
44900	12A
44901	12A
44902	12A
44903	12A
44904	8A
44905	12B
44906	12B
44907	12B
44908	5A
44909	2A
44910	2A
44911	7A
44912	25F
44913	3A
44914	3A
44915	2C
44916	2B
44917	14B
44918	16A
44919	21A
44920	21A
44921	19A
44922	31A
44923	31A
44924	29A
44925	29A
44926	23C
44927	24E
44928	24E
44929	24E
44930	24E
44931	28B
44932	24E
44933	26A
44934	26A
44935	8A
44936	12B
44937	9A
44938	9A
44939	12B
44940	26A
44941	8A
44942	3A
44943	20A
44944	19G
44945	22C
44946	23A
44947	24E
44948	24F
44949	25A
44950	24E
44951	26A
44952	5A
44953	28C
44954	5A
44955	28C
44956	31A

44957	31A
44958	29A
44959	29A
44960	29A
44961	29A
44962	17A
44963	19B
44964	19B
44965	19B
44966	21A
44967	5A
44968	2B
44969	9A
44970	9A
44971	19B
44972	29A
44973	29A
44974	29A
44975	29A
44976	29A
44977	29A
44978	27A
44979	27A
44980	27A
44981	14A
44982	23A
44983	20A
44984	14B
44985	14B
44986	20A
44987	26A
44988	24E
44989	23C
44990	23A
44991	32A
44992	32A
44993	12A
44994	12A
44995	31A
44996	31A
44997	2A
44998	2A
44999	2A
45000	2A
45001	8B
45002	2A
45003	2A
45004	2A
45005	12A
45006	12A
45007	28A
45008	28A
45009	12A
45010	29A
45011	29A
45012	28A
45013	12A
45014	12A
45015	12A
45016	28A
45017	12A
45018	28A
45019	10A
45020	2A
45021	10B
45022	12A
45023	12A
45024	1A
45025	2B
45026	8B
45027	1A
45028	5B
45029	28B
45030	10A
45031	19E
45032	8B
45033	2A
45034	2A
45035	8B
45036	29A
45037	10C
45038	5B
45039	11A
45040	20A
45041	5B
45042	6A
45043	20A
45044	5B
45045	8A
45046	12B
45047	30A
45048	5B
45049	30A
45050	11A
45051	3D
45052	2A
45053	32A
45054	8A
45055	10C
45056	22C
45057	2A
45058	3D
45059	16A
45060	5B
45061	23C
45062	25F
45063	25G
45064	5B
45065	20A
45066	32A
45067	5B
45068	20A
45069	5B
45070	1A
45071	1A
45072	5B
45073	5B
45074	5B
45075	25G
45076	25G
45077	25G
45078	25G
45079	26A
45080	25G
45081	12A
45082	12A
45083	12A
45084	12A
45085	29A
45086	29A
45087	29A
45088	17A
45089	5B
45090	32A
45091	10B
45092	20A
45093	5B
45094	8A
45095	8B
45096	12A
45097	5B
45098	32A
45099	25B
45100	12A
45101	24A
45102	26A
45103	26A
45104	26B
45105	26A
45106	12B
45107	24F
45108	5B
45109	8B
45110	7C
45111	7C
45112	7A
45113	7C
45114	5D
45115	31A
45116	31A
45117	31A
45118	12A
45119	12A
45120	28A
45121	28A
45122	32A
45123	32A
45124	32A
45125	29A
45126	12A
45127	12A
45128	5B
45129	12B
45130	2B
45131	5B
45132	3D
45133	12B
45134	5B
45135	10C
45136	32A
45137	10C
45138	32A
45139	12B
45140	1A
45141	10A
45142	10B
45143	5B
45144	3A
45145	5B
45146	5B
45147	10C
45148	5B
45149	8B
45150	2C
45151	12A
45152	12A
45153	31A
45154*	31A
45155	31A
45156*	31A
45157*	31A
45158*	31A
45159	31A
45160	32A
45161	29A
45162	29A
45163	29A
45164	29A
45165	29A
45166	29A
45167	29A
45168	30A
45169	12A
45170	29A
45171	29A
45172	29A
45173	29A
45174	29A
45175	29A
45176	31A
45177	31A
45178	31A
45179	31A
45180	4A
45181	5B
45182	10C
45183	5B
45184	12B
45185	10B
45186	21A
45187	20A
45188	10C
45189	5B
45190	4A
45191	2C
45192	32A
45193	12B
45194	30A
45195	5B
45196	8B
45197	5B
45198	5B
45199	10C
45200	23C
45201	25F
45202	26A
45203	26A
45204	25A
45205	25A
45206	25A
45207	25F
45208	25F
45209	25F
45210	25F
45211	25F
45212	24F
45213	29A
45214	24F
45215	25B
45216	23A
45217	23A
45218	25B
45219	26B
45220	26B
45221	25F
45222	26A
45223	26B
45224	26A
45225	23A
45226	23A
45227	23A
45228	23A
45229	23A
45230	12B
45231	10C
45232	26A
45233	26A
45234	26A
45235	5B
45236	5B
45237	25B
45238	25B
45239	5B
45240	5B
45241	12A
45242	5B
45243	12B
45244	12B
45245	4A
45246	12B
45247	6A
45248	5B
45249	7C
45250	2A
45251	30A
45252	8B
45253	7A
45254	5B
45255	5B
45256	8A
45257	5D
45258	12B
45259	10C
45260	20A
45261	17A
45262	19A
45263	19B
45264	14A
45265	21A
45266	12A
45267	14B
45268	21A
45269	21A
45270	5B
45271	5B
45272	22A
45273	21A
45274	21A
45275	6A
45276	20A
45277	14A
45278	5D
45279	14B
45280	20A
45281	4A
45282	2C
45283	4A
45284	19E
45285	17A
45286	6B
45287	3B
45288	6B
45289	20A
45290	10C
45291	11A
45292	4A
45293	12B
45294	9A
45295	12B
45296	12B
45297	6A
45298	8A
45299	12B
45300	5B
45301	7A
45302	10C
45303	7A
45304	10C
45305	5B
45306	11A
45307	12B
45308	3C
45309	27A
45310	1A
45311	12B
45312	10C
45313	7C
45314	2B
45315	10C
45316	2B
45317	5B
45318	4A
45319	32A
45320	32A
45321	8B
45322	3A
45323	12B
45324	5D
45325	5D
45326	5D
45327	12B
45328	6B
45329	10C
45330	4A
45331	2B
45332	8A
45333	11A
45334	23C
45335	23A
45336	23A
45337	26B
45338	26B
45339	25A
45340	25G
45341	25G
45342	14A
45343	11A
45344	8A
45345	10B
45346	7A

45347	8A
45348	12B
45349	3D
45350	8A
45351	8A
45352	5D
45353	1A
45354	12B
45355	31A
45356	31A
45357	29A
45358	31A
45359	31A
45360	32A
45361	32A
45362	31A
45363	12A
45364	12A
45365	29A
45366	29A
45367	24A
45368	12B
45369	5A
45370	7A
45371	12B
45372	2A
45373	10B
45374	5A
45375	2A
45376	8A
45377	10C
45378	12B
45379	2A
45380	8A
45381	5D
45382	6A
45383	6B
45384	4A
45385	6B
45386	10C
45387	8A
45388	12B
45389	29A
45390	3D
45391	2A
45392	11A
45393	12B
45394	2A
45395	3C
45396	24A
45397	3D
45398	8A
45399	8A
45400	8A
45401	10C
45402	10C
45403	6A
45404	2A
45405	3B
45406	4A
45407	19A
45408	10C
45409	12B
45410	8A
45411	10C
45412	5A
45413	10A
45414	12B
45415	23C
45416	12B
45417	3A
45418	3A
45419	2A
45420	10C
45421	10C
45422	5A
45423	31A
45424	10C

45425	10A
45426	10C
45427	11A
45428	12B
45429	12A
45430	2A
45431	1A
45432	12A
45433	3A
45434	3B
45435	23C
45436	5A
45437	3B
45438	10C
45439	12B
45440	22C
45441	2A
45442	10C
45443	12A
45444	10C
45445	4A
45446	3D
45447	21A
45448	2A
45449	10A
45450	12B
45451	12B
45452	29A
45453	28A
45454	12A
45455	12A
45456	29A
45457	29A
45458	29A
45459	29A
45460	29A
45461	28A
45462	28A
45463	29A
45464	29A
45465	29A
45466	29A
45467	29A
45468	31A
45469	29A
45470	29A
45471	31A
45472	29A
45473	29A
45474	29A
45475	29A
45476	32A
45477	32A
45478	32A
45479	32A
45480	31A
45481	31A
45482	12A
45483	28A
45484	27A
45485	27A
45486	27A
45487	27A
45488	28A
45489	30A
45490	30A
45491	30A
45492	4A
45493	5A
45494	12B
45495	3E
45496	28A
45497	28A
45498	28A
45499	28A

PATRIOT CLASS
4-6-0 5XP & 6P

45500*	8A
45501*	8A
45502*	10B
45503*	5A
45504*	5A
45505*	10B
45506	12B
45507*	5A
45508	5A
45509	1A
45510	1A
45511*	5A
45512*	5A
45513	10B
45514*	3B
45515*	10B
45516*	10B
45517	8A
45518*	12B
45519*	10B
45520*	8A
45521*	8A
45522*	5A
45523*	8A
45524*	10B
45525*	1A
45526*	8A
45527*	8A
45528	3B
45529	3B
45530*	9A
45531*	3B
45532*	5A
45533*	8A
45534*	20A
45535*	20A
45536*	10B
45537*	10B
45538*	20A
45539*	5A
45540*	3B
45541*	12B
45542	5A
45543*	8A
45544	10B
45545	8A
45546*	5A
45547	8A
45548*	5A
45549	5A
45550	12B
45551	5A

JUBILEE CLASS
4-6-0 5XP & 6P

45552*	9A
45553*	12B
45554*	16A
45555*	5A
45556*	9A
45557*	14B
45558*	5A
45559*	10C
45560*	30A
45561*	22A
45562*	20A
45563*	12B
45564*	12A
45565*	20A
45566*	20A
45567*	8A
45568*	20A
45569*	20A
45570*	22A
45571*	24E
45572*	22A
45573*	20A
45574*	24E
45575*	30A
45576*	30A
45577*	12A
45578*	5A
45579*	12A
45580*	12A
45581*	12A
45582*	12A
45583*	27A
45584*	27A
45585*	17A
45586*	8A
45587*	20A
45588*	24E
45589*	20A
45590*	19B
45591*	1A
45592*	8A
45593*	9A
45594*	19B
45595*	12B
45596*	5A
45597*	20A
45598*	14B
45599*	12B
45600*	5A
45601*	1B
45602*	17A
45603*	5A
45604*	20A
45605*	20A
45606*	1B
45607*	19B
45608*	20A
45609*	14B
45610*	17A
45611*	20A
45612*	14B
45613*	8A
45614*	14B
45615*	14B
45616*	14B
45617*	1B
45618*	19G
45619*	20A
45620*	20A
45621*	19B
45622*	19G
45623*	8A
45624*	12B
45625*	1A
45626*	19B
45627*	14B
45628*	19G
45629*	19G
45630*	5A
45631*	9A
45632*	5A
45633*	9A
45634*	8A
45635*	26A
45636*	16A
45637*	5A
45638*	9A
45639*	17A
45640*	16A
45641*	14B
45642*	26A
45643*	30A
45644*	30A
45645*	30A
45646*	30A
45647*	5A
45648*	14B
45649*	14B
45650*	14B
45651*	20A
45652*	19G
45653*	24E
45654*	14B
45655*	19G
45656*	17A
45657*	14B
45658*	20A
45659*	20A
45660*	20A
45661*	26A
45662*	22A
45663*	22A
45664*	19G
45665*	14B
45666*	8A
45667*	17A
45668*	10C
45669*	1B
45670*	10C
45671*	25G
45672*	8A
45673*	8A
45674*	5A
45675*	5A
45676*	5A
45677*	12B
45678*	12B
45679*	19B
45680*	9A
45681*	8A
45682*	22A
45683*	19B
45684*	5A
45685*	22A
45686*	5A
45687*	5A
45688*	5A
45689*	5A
45690*	22A
45691*	27A
45692*	27A
45693*	30A
45694*	22A
45695*	24E
45696*	19B
45697*	24E
45698*	23A
45699*	20A
45700*	26A
45701*	26A
45702*	25G
45703*	9A
45704*	25G
45705*	25G
45706*	26A
45707*	24E
45708*	25G
45709*	5A
45710*	26A
45711*	26A
45712*	26A
45713*	12A
45714*	12A
45715*	12A
45716*	12A
45717*	26A
45718*	12B
45719*	26A
45720*	10C
45721*	1A
45722*	5A
45723*	9A
45724*	8A
45725*	8A
45726*	10C
45727*	12A
45728*	12A
45729*	12A
45730*	12A
45731*	12A

45732*	12A
45733*	3B
45734*	3B
45735*	1B
45736*	1B
45737*	5A
45738*	3B
45739*	1A
45740*	9A
45741*	5A
45742*	3B

CLAUGHTON CLASS 4-6-0 5XP

46004	8A

ROYAL SCOT CLASS 4-6-0 6P

46100*	1B
46101*	1B
46102*	27A
46103*	20A
46104*	27A
46105*	27A
46106*	8A
46107*	27A
46108*	20A
46109*	20A
46110*	12B
46111*	8A
46112*	7C
46113*	5A
46114*	9A
46115*	5A
46116*	1B
46117*	20A
46118*	1B
46119*	1B
46120*	9A
46121*	9A
46122*	9A
46123*	1B
46124*	8A
46125*	5A
46126*	5A
46127*	7C
46128*	12B
46129*	9A
46130*	1B
46131*	9A
46132*	7C
46133*	20A
46134*	8A
46135*	8A
46136*	8A
46137*	12B
46138*	8A
46139*	1B
46140*	1B
46141*	1B
46142*	1B
46143*	27A
46144*	8A
46145*	9A
46146*	5A
46147*	5A
46148*	1B
46149*	9A
46150*	9A
46151*	1B
46152*	1B
46153*	1B
46154*	5A
46155*	5A
46156*	8A
46157*	7C
46158*	12B
46159*	1B
46160*	9A
46161*	5A
46162*	5A
46163*	5A
46164*	8A
46165*	5A
46166*	5A
46167*	5A
46168*	1B
46169*	9A
46170*	1B

PRINCESS ROYAL CLASS 4-6-2 7P

46200*	5A
46201*	5A
46202	1B
46203*	5A
46204*	5A
46205*	5A
46206*	5A
46207*	5A
46208*	5A
46209*	5A
46210*	5A
46211*	5A
46212*	5A

PRINCESS CORONATION CLASS 4-6-2 7P

46220*	27A
46221*	27A
46222*	27A
46223*	27A
46224*	27A
46225*	1B
46226*	12B
46227*	5A
46228*	12B
46229*	5A
46230*	27A
46231*	27A
46232*	27A
46233*	5A
46234*	5A
46235*	5A
46236*	5A
46237*	1B
46238*	12B
46239*	1B
46240*	1B
46241*	1B
46242*	27A
46243*	1B
46244*	1B
46245*	1B
46246*	1B
46247*	1B
46248*	1B
46249*	12B
46250*	12B
46251*	12B
46252*	5A
46253*	1B
46254*	1B
46255*	1B
46256*	5A

IVATT 2-6-0 2F

46400	15B
46401	15B
46402	15B
46403	15B
46404	15B
46405	25G
46406	25G
46407	25C
46408	25C
46409	25A
46410	24E
46411	24E
46412	24E
46413	24E
46414	4B
46415	4B
46416	23A
46417	23A
46418	26A
46419	26A

WEBB 2-4-2T 1P

46601	4A
46603	8B
46604	2B
46605	5A
46616 26616	2C
46620	4B
46628	10E
46632	7D
46635	12G
46637	10E
46639	12G
46643	7B
46654	3B
46656	27C
46658	7D
46661	3C
46663	8B
46666	2C
46669	2E
46673	2E
46676	10E
46679	3C
46680	5A
46681	7A
46682	10E
46683	2E
46686	1C
46687	7D
46688	8B
46691	7D
46692	10E
46701	7D
46710	8B
46711	5A
46712	7D
46718	8B
46727	7D
46738	9D
46740	4B
46742	2C
46747	7A
46749	2E
46757	3C

ASPINALL WIRRAL RLY. 2-4-2T 2P

46762	10B

WEBB 0-6-2T 2P

46876	5C
46878	3E
46881	3B
46883	12B
46899	7C
46900	8A
46906	8B
46909	2B
46912	2B
46917	8A
46920	8B
46922	3E
46924	8B
46926	7B
46931	3B

L.M.S. 0-4-0ST OF

47000	17B
47001	23A
47002	23A
47003	18C
47004	18C

FOWLER 0-6-0T 2F

47160	6C
47161	24F
47162	28B
47163	28B
47164	6C
47165	24F
47166	6C
47167	27B
47168	27B
47169	27B

SENTINEL 0-4-0T

47180	10E
47181	4A
47182	30D
47183	10E
47184	10E
47190	22A
47191	22C

JOHNSON 0-6-0T 3F

47200	14A
47201	14A
47202	16B
47203	14A
47204	14A
47205	14A
47206	14A
47207	14A
47208	14A
47209	14A
47210	14A
47211	14A
47212	14A
47213	14A
47214	14A
47215	14A
47216	14A
47217	14A
47218	14A
47219	14A
47220	14A
47221	14A
47222	14A
47223	14A
47224	14A
47225	14A
47226	14A
47227	14A
47228	14A
47229	14B
47230	4C
47231	17B
47232	4C
47233	17B
47234	21C
47235	19A
47236	19A
47237	22B
47238	15A
47239	20B
47240	14A
47241	14B
47242	14B
47243	14A
47244	14B
47245	14B
47246	14B
47247	18A
47248	14A
47249	18A
47250	14A
47251	14A
47252	15D
47253	17B
47254	20A
47255	20E
47256	4C
47257	17B
47258	4C
47259	4C

FOWLER L.M.S. 0-6-0T 3F

47260	14B
47261	14C
47262	14B
47263	14B
47264	15A
47265	15A
47266	5B
47267	9A
47268	8B
47269	16B
47270	16B
47271	20B
47272	18C
47273	21A
47274	15C
47275	22C
47276	21A
47277	16A
47278	18C
47279	15A
47280	5B
47281	1A
47282	14B
47283	14B
47284	8C
47285	2D
47286	2D
47287	11B
47288	2B
47289	9B
47290	12D
47291	10B
47292	12D
47293	10B
47294	5C
47295	12B
47296	10B
47297	6A
47298	2B
47299	2C
47300	13A
47301	21C
47302	13B
47303	21C
47304	13B
47305	21C
47306	13B
47307	13B
47308	21C
47309	8A
47310	13B
47311	13A
47312	13B
47313	21C
47314	13B
47315	13B
47316	22C
47317	11A
47318	2C
47319	10B
47320	5D
47321	7C
47322	11B

47323	11B
47324	6C
47325	8A
47326	12B
47327	1A
47328	13A
47329	30A
47330	5B
47331	27A
47332	27A
47333	15A
47334	20D
47335	20D
47336	19E
47337	12E
47338	5D
47339	11A
47340	12B
47341	9A
47342	1A
47343	9A
47344	5B
47345	9A
47346	9B
47347	9A
47348	13B
47349	13B
47350	13B
47351	13A
47352	8B
47353	6B
47354	1B
47355	1A
47356	1B
47357	1A
47358	1B
47359	1B
47360	2A
47361	1A
47362	1A
47363	3D
47364	3D
47365	3D
47366	3D
47367	2D
47368	7C
47369	9A
47370	5D
47371	6B
47372	6B
47373	6A
47374	6A
47375	6A
47376	8B
47377	12B
47378	2A
47379	2A
47380	1A
47381	20H
47382	3A
47383	6A
47384	5B
47385	8A
47386	24B
47387	8B
47388	8C
47389	6C
47390	12E
47391	12B
47392	5E
47393	10E
47394	9A
47395	1A
47396	3A
47397	3B
47398	3B
47399	3B
47400	9A

47401	10D
47402	8A
47403	12B
47404	8A
47405	20D
47406	11A
47407	11A
47408	12B
47409	11A
47410	11A
47411	13B
47412	1A
47413	3B
47414	5B
47415	12B
47416	5B
47417	17A
47418	20A
47419	20E
47420	20B
47421	20C
47422	16A
47423	18C
47424	18D
47425	21C
47426	18C
47427	14B
47428	14B
47429	14B
47430	1A
47431	5B
47432	14B
47433	14A
47434	14A
47435	14A
47436	18A
47437	15B
47438	16A
47439	8C
47440	19E
47441	15C
47442	15C
47443	20B
47444	5B
47445	5B
47446	15A
47447	14A
47448	20C
47449	17C
47450	6C
47451	5B
47452	2B
47453	10E
47454	18A
47455	18D
47457	17D
47458	13A
47459	17D
47460	17D
47461	17D
47462	20C
47463	20B
47464	17B
47465	22C
47466	18B
47467	1B
47468	20H
47469	20H
47470	20H
47471	20H
47472	6C
47473	3B
47474	1A
47475	1A
47476	7C
47477	4C
47478	4C
47479	4C

47480	4C
47481	4C
47482	13B
47483	13B
47484	13A
47485	16A
47486	13B
47487	13B
47488	13B
47489	13B
47490	13B
47491	13B
47492	13B
47493	13B
47494	13B
47495	13B
47496	22C
47497	13B
47498	13B
47499	13B
47500	13B
47501	13B
47502	13B
47503	11A
47504	6A
47505	13B
47506	13B
47507	6C
47508	25E
47509	25E
47510	25E
47511	13B
47512	13A
47513	19A
47514	13B
47515	13B
47516	13B
47517	13B
47518	13B
47519	3A
47520	1A
47521	2B
47522	1B
47523	5B
47524	5B
47525	12E
47526	5B
47527	1B
47528	9A
47529	1B
47530	6C
47531	1A
47532	20H
47533	15C
47534	15C
47535	18C
47536	27A
47537	27A
47538	20B
47539	16A
47540	27A
47541	32A
47542	22C
47543	15A
47544	22A
47545	19A
47546	19C
47547	19C
47548	14A
47549	15D
47550	22A
47551	18A
47552	16A
47554	15A
47555	18A
47556	12B
47557	22C
47558	13B

47559	13B
47560	13B
47561	13B
47562	13B
47563	13B
47564	13B
47565	21C
47566	16B
47567	25G
47568	25G
47569	25G
47570	25G
47571	25G
47572	26B
47573	26B
47574	26B
47575	24B
47576	24B
47577	26E
47578	26B
47579	26B
47580	26E
47581	20C
47582	26E
47583	26B
47584	26B
47585	26B
47586	26A
47587	5D
47588	5C
47589	+
47590	5B
47591	8B
47592	CW
47593	12D
47594	2D
47595	5E
47596	5D
47597	8A
47598	5C
47599	5D
47600	6A
47601	9B
47602	5B
47603	8A
47604	12D
47605	11A
47606	5C
47607	+
47608	5B
47609	5D
47610	5D
47611	+
47612	2C
47614	12B
47615	6B
47616	5B
47618	12B
47619	22B
47620	22B
47621	14A
47622	16B
47623	18A
47624	19A
47625	18D
47626	18D
47627	18D
47628	18D
47629	16A
47630	18A
47631	16A
47632	16A
47633	5B
47634	20C
47635	22B
47636	15A

NOTE: + In store.

47637	16A
47638	21A
47639	21A
47640	14B
47641	17B
47642	15A
47643	17B
47644	14B
47645	14B
47646	6B
47647	5D
47648	5D
47649	5C
47650	6B
47651	8A
47652	8B
47653	5C
47654	8B
47655	4C
47656	6B
47657	8B
47658	5D
47659	+
47660	+
47661	5E
47662	5E
47664	12B
47665	5B
47666	12B
47667	1B
47668	1B
47669	1B
47670	5C
47671	1B
47672	6C
47673	9A
47674	6C
47675	1A
47676	1A
47677	2A
47678	22A
47679	17D
47680	5B
47681	5B

WEBB 0-4-2ST 1F

47862	CW
47865	CW

BOWEN COOKE 0-8-2T 6F

47875	8C
47877	8C
47881	8C
47884	8C
47885	10A
47887	10C
47888	10A
47892	10C
47896	10A

BEAMES L.M.S. 0-8-4T 7F

47930	8A
47931	4B
47932	4B
47933	8A
47936	9D
47937	4B
47938	8A
47939	4E
47948	4B
47951	8A
47954	9D
47956	8A
47958	8A
47959	8A

BEYER-GARRATT 2-6-6-2T

No.		Shed
47967		18A
47968		18C
47969		18A
47970		18A
47971		18C
47972		18A
47973		18C
47974		18A
47975		18A
47976		18A
47977		18A
47978		18A
47979		18A
47980		18C
47981		18A
47982		18A
47983		18C
47984		18C
47985		18A
47986		18A
47987		18A
47988		18A
47989		18A
47990		18C
47991		18A
47992		18C
47993		18C
47994		18A
47995		18A
47996		18A
47997		18C
47998		18A
47999		18A

STANIER 2-8-0 8F

No.		Shed
48000		16C
48001		20A
48002		18A
48003		16A
48004		18A
48005		20G
48006		16C
48007		16C
48008		17C
48009		16C
48010		21A
48011		18B
48012	70577	+
48016	70591	+
48017		19A
48018	70582	+
48020	70579	+
48024		15A
48026		19C
48027		16C
48029		16C
48033		18A
48035		16D
48036		16C
48037		18A
48039	70588	+
48045	70573	+
48046	70599	+
48050		15A
48053		18D
48054		18D
48055		20H
48056		18B
48057		18B
48060		18B
48061	70614	+
48062		20C
48063		18B
48064		16A
48065		19C
48067		15B
48069		15B
48070		18A
48073		20A
48074		16C
48075		18A
48076		18B
48077	70611	+
48078		20C
48079		20C
48080		20C
48081		20F
48082		15A
48083		18B
48084		20D
48085		20C
48088		16D
48089		19D
48090		20A
48092		16C
48093		21A
48094	70606	+
48095		20C
48096		16C
48097		16C
48098		16C
48099		19D
48100		16C
48101		16C
48102		18B
48103		20C
48104		16C
48105		19A
48106		17C
48107		17C
48108		16C
48109		16C
48110		20A
48111		18D
48112		18A
48113		20C
48114		16C
48115		18B
48116		19A
48117		18A
48118		18B
48119		18A
48120		18D
48121		20A
48122		18D
48123		20D
48124		15B
48125		18B
48126		20A
48127		20A
48128		15A
48129		20A
48130		20D
48131		20D
48132		15C
48133		18A
48134		18D
48135		19D
48136		18B
48137		20A
48138		20A
48139		16C
48140		20B
48141		15B
48142		18A
48143		20A
48144		18A
48145		20G
48146		20D
48147		31D
48148		31D

NOTE: + In store.

No.		Shed
48149		31D
48150		31D
48151		31D
48152		31D
48153		31E
48154		19D
48155		31E
48156		28A
48157		17A
48158		16A
48159		20D
48160		20D
48161		20C
48162		20C
48163		28B
48164		20D
48165		4A
48166		16C
48167		15A
48168		18A
48169		20C
48170		16A
48171		1A
48172		1A
48173		1A
48174		1A
48175		4B
48176		20A
48177		15D
48178		18A
48179		19D
48180		15A
48181		15A
48182		18A
48183		28A
48184		28A
48185		28A
48186		28A
48187		28A
48188		28A
48189		20G
48190		19D
48191		5B
48192		15A
48193		16C
48194		18A
48195		18D
48196		18A
48197		18A
48198		15A
48199		18A
48200		18A
48201		18A
48202		18A
48203		18A
48204		18A
48205		18A
48206		16A
48207		16A
48208		19D
48209		19C
48210		18D
48211		15C
48212		18B
48213		18D
48214		16C
48215		16C
48216		19A
48217		16A
48218		16A
48219		19A
48220		19D
48221		18A
48222		15A
48223		16C
48224		16C
48225		16C
48246	70300	+
48247	70301	+
48248	70311	+
48249	70314	+
48250	70318	+
48251	70332	+
48252	70363	+
48253	70376	+
48254	70378	+
48255	70384	+
48256	70394	+
48257	70395	+
48258	70398	+
48259	70504	+
48260	70518	+
48261	70544	+
48262	70576	+
48263	70584	+
48264		15A
48265		17C
48266		20D
48267		16C
48268		16C
48269		15A
48270		16C
48271		20D
48272		16C
48273		5B
48274		20D
48275		19D
48276		20B
48277		20B
48278		1A
48279		16A
48280		18B
48281		15A
48282		16A
48283		16C
48284		19A
48285		15B
48286	70401	+
48287	70402	+
48288	70403	+
48289	70413	+
48290	70438	+
48291	70440	+
48292	70442	+
48293		16A
48294	70443	+
48295	70446	+
48296	70447	+
48297	70449	+
48301		28C
48302		28C
48303		28C
48304		18A
48305		15A
48306		20A
48307		4A
48308		4A
48309		2A
48310		5B
48311		18A
48312		24B
48313		18A
48314		19A
48315		19D
48316		19D
48317		20F
48318		5B
48319		24B
48320		5B
48321		28B
48322		17A
48323		18A
48324		18A
48325		4B
48326		9D
48327		4A
48328		4A
48329		19D
48330		19E
48331		28C
48332		18D
48333		18B
48334		15A
48335		4B
48336		21A
48337		21A
48338		15A
48339		24B
48340		5B
48341		18D
48342		18B
48343		4B
48344		4B
48345		5B
48346		18D
48347		4A
48348		19E
48349		19E
48350		18A
48351		21A
48352		20D
48353		18B
48354		20B
48355		15B
48356		15B
48357		20D
48358		18B
48359		15A
48360		15A
48361		18A
48362		18A
48363		15A
48364		15A
48365		15A
48366		4B
48367		18A
48368		1A
48369		4A
48370		18A
48371		15A
48372		1A
48373		4A
48374		15A
48375		4A
48376		20C
48377		20C
48378		16C
48379		16C
48380		16A
48381		16A
48382		16C
48383		16C
48384		18A
48385		23B
48386		25A
48387		18A
48388		18A
48389		21A
48390		17A
48391		18B
48392		16C
48393		16C
48394		20D
48395		20D
48396		20D
48397		15C
48398		15C
48399		15C
48400		21A
48401		21A
48402		21A
48403		21A
48404		17A
48405		21A

The GWR acquired two Stroudley "Terrier" 0-6-0Ts from the Weston, Clevedon & Portishead Railway in 1940. This is No. 5, dating from 1877 and seen here in store in Swindon stock shed with its *Portishead* nameplates removed in June 1951. It lasted until 1954, withdrawal taking place in March from Swindon shed.

G. W. Sharpe

Two 0-6-0PTs were acquired from the Cleobury Mortimer & Ditton Priors Railway by the GWR and numbered 28 and 29. Here No. 29 takes a rest at Kidderminster shed on Sunday 27th May 1951. Withdrawal took place in January 1954 from Kidderminster. Sister engine No. 28 went in November 1953 from Newport Ebbw Junction.

G. W. Sharpe

Ex-Rhymney Railway No. 3 R class 0-6-2T, GWR/BR No. 32, shunting at Cardiff Radyr yard on Monday 20th June 1949. It had not long to live for withdrawal came in February 1950 from Radyr shed.

G. W. Sharpe

Rhymney shed turntable is the setting for this photograph, taken on Tuesday 21st June 1949. Nearest the camera is ex-Rhymney Railway No. 43, an R1 class 0-6-2T. It had been rebuilt by the GWR with taper boiler and numbered 39. Behind is ex-Rhymney Railway No. 35 P class 0-6-2T, here with GWR/BR No. 78. Both were withdrawn in August 1955 from Cardiff East Dock. No. 78 was the last of its class and was cut up at Swindon in December.

G. W. Sharpe

Ex-works on Cardiff Cathays shed on 20th June 1949 is ex-Rhymney Railway No. 14 A class 0-6-2T. Rebuilt with GWR boiler and numbered 56, withdrawal came in September 1953 from Cardiff East Dock.

G. W. Sharpe

Another ex-Rhymney Railway A class 0-6-2T, here with earlier type boiler and numbered 61. Recorded at Cardiff East Dock shed on 20th June 1949, withdrawal came in February 1950 from the same depot.

G. W. Sharpe

Ex-Rhymney Railway No. 38 GWR/BR No. 81, P class 0-6-2T with GWR boiler at Cardiff East Dock shed on 20th June 1949, out of commission awaiting repair and return of the middle driving wheels. Withdrawal came in May 1954 from Merthyr shed.

G. W. Sharpe

Ex-Cardiff Railway No. 35 0-6-2T. This was the only one of its type to come into British Railways' stock and was the survivor of a class of three dating back to 1908. It was reboilered by the GWR and numbered 155. It is here seen at Cardiff East Dock shed on 20th June 1949 where it remained until withdrawal in September 1953.

G. W. Sharpe

The 1 in 13 Pwllyrhebog Incline on 21st June 1949. This was a colliery cable-worked line with the winding engine at the summit. The weight of the descending train counterbalanced that of the ascending, with the cable attached to the rear of the locomotive. A trio of 0-6-0Ts were built for the Taff Vale Railway by Kitsons in 1884 specially for working this line. Descending is BR No. 193, formerly GWR No. 792. It was withdrawn in February 1952 and sold to the National Coal Board.

G. W. Sharpe

A delightful study of another of the Taff Vale trio, No. 194, again in June 1949, at Tonypandy yard on shunting duties. Withdrawal came in November 1953 for scrap, and this was the last one to survive.
G. W. Sharpe

Ex-Taff Vale Railway No. 109 class 04 0-6-2T, recorded at Aberdare shed in 1949 with GWR boiler and numbered 204. Withdrawal came in July 1955 from Cardiff East Dock.
G. W. Sharpe

Another ex-Taff Vale Railway 04 class, this time with older type boiler. This scene was recorded at Duffryn Yard shed in June 1949 and shows No. 296. This was the engine's last home, being withdrawn in September the same year.
G. W. Sharpe

No. 270 on Barry shed on 20th June 1949. This was an ex-Barry Railway B class 0-6-2T, originally numbered 114 and was a design dating back to 1888. This one survived at Barry until April 1951.

G. W. Sharpe

Ex-Taff Vale Railway A class 0-6-2T, here with original round-topped side tanks at Barry shed in 1949. Numbered 361 with the GWR and British Railways, it was withdrawn from Cardiff Cathays in January 1957.

R. H. G. Simpson

Cardiff East Dock shed in June 1949 finds No. 611 taking a rest. Allocated BR number 96, renumbering did not take place until 16th December 1949. This was an ex-Rhymney Railway class S1 type, No. 114, and was withdrawn in April 1954 from East Dock.

G. W. Sharpe

No. 666 in 1950 at Newport Pill shed, from where withdrawal took place in April 1955. It was the last of its type to operate. With sister engine 667 (withdrawn in November 1954 from Pill) it came from the Alexandra Docks Railway. The original design however was one from The War Department and they were originally numbered ROD 604 and 602.

G. W. Sharpe

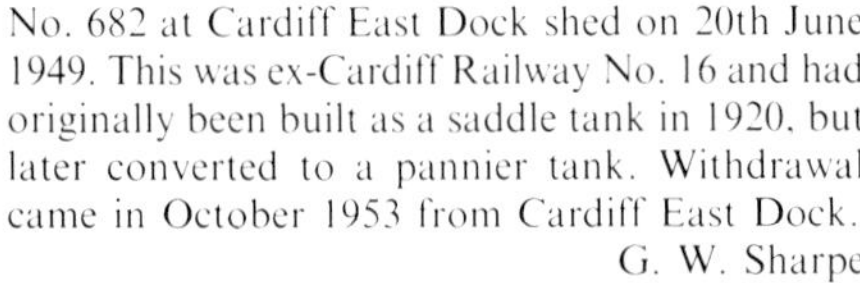

No. 682 at Cardiff East Dock shed on 20th June 1949. This was ex-Cardiff Railway No. 16 and had originally been built as a saddle tank in 1920, but later converted to a pannier tank. Withdrawal came in October 1953 from Cardiff East Dock.

G. W. Sharpe

Barry shed in 1948 finds 0-6-0T No. 783 enjoying the sunshine. This locomotive, and No. 784 illustrated next, were built in 1890 for the Barry Railway. They were originally numbered 50 and 51 respectively. No. 783 was withdrawn in August 1948 from Barry.

G. W. Sharpe

August 1949 and No. 784 has arrived at Swindon Works for scrapping from Barry. Note the detail differences compared with No. 783.
R. H. G. Simpson

Oswestry shed in 1951 finds ex-Cambrian Railways 0-6-0 No. 99 with British Railways on the tender and re-numbered 893. This example of the class was finally laid to rest in February 1953, Oswestry being its last allocation. The last survivor of this type, No. 855, was withdrawn in October 1954, also from Oswestry.
G. W. Sharpe

'County' class 4-6-0 No. 1027 *County of Stafford* at an unidentified location in 1949. New in March 1947 and first allocated to Westbury, withdrawal came in October 1963 from Swindon shed.
G. W. Sharpe

Didcot shed in 1948 finds No. 1334 in steam and awaiting work. This M&SWJR 2-4-0 dated back to 1894 and was withdrawn from Didcot in September 1952. The last survivor was No. 1336 which was taken out of service in March 1954 from Reading shed.

G. W. Sharpe

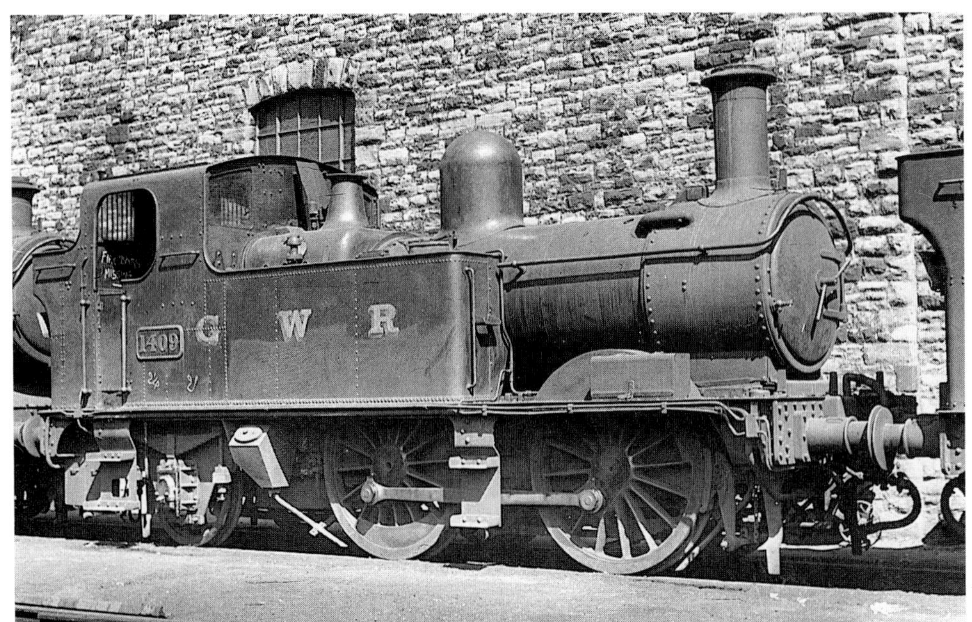

1400 class 0-4-2T No. 1409 at Hereford shed in May 1948. Built in October 1932 and originally numbered 4809, the engine's first home was Exeter. Withdrawal came in October 1963 from the LMS shed at Gloucester Barnwood.

Photomatic

Swindon Works scrap roads in March 1950 finds two elderly pannier tanks awaiting breaking up. On the left is 655 class No. 2712, last shed Stourbridge, and 2021 class No. 2113, last shed Newport Pill.

G. W. Sharpe

2600 class 2-6-0 No. 2620 at Stourbridge shed in 1948, paired with a ROD tender. Built in 1903, No. 2620 survived until August 1949, Stourbridge being its last home. Only one then remained, No. 2667 which went in October 1949 from Pontypool Road shed. The class had the unofficial name "Aberdare's" which stuck throughout their careers and came from their first duties on coal trains from Aberdare to Swindon.

R. H. G. Simpson

Swindon shed is the setting for this portrait of 2800 class 2-8-0 No. 2809 in 1948. Dating back to October 1905, withdrawal came in January 1960 from Plymouth Laira. This was one of the earlier type without a cab fitted with side windows, the later engines being classified as 2884.

R. H. G. Simpson

A sad sight on Swindon dump in December 1949 is 'Bulldog' 4-4-0 No. 3386 awaiting its turn for cutting up. It had been withdrawn the previous month from Reading shed. It had originally carried the name *Paddington*, but this had been removed in 1927.

G. W. Sharpe

Wolverhampton Stafford Road shed has 'Star' class 4-6-0 No. 4059 *Princess Patricia* in the yard in 1949. Built in 1914 she lasted until September 1952 when retired from Gloucester Horton Road. The last one to remain active, No. 4056 *Princess Margaret*, was not withdrawn until October 1957 from Swansea Landore.

G. W. Sharpe

'Castle' class 4-6-0 No. 111 *Viscount Churchill* at Old Oak Common shed in 1948. This locomotive had a fascinating history for it was a rebuild from the first British Pacific locomotive constructed at Swindon in 1908, numbered 111 and named *The Great Bear*. Withdrawal took place in September 1924. The locomotive was then rebuilt at Swindon into a standard 'Castle' class, retaining the same number but renamed. Final withdrawal took place in July 1953 from Plymouth Laira.

Photomatic

'Castle' class 4-6-0 No. 4091 *Dudley Castle* waits for the off at Leamington Spa on an 'up' express in July 1948, fresh from works. The livery is light green with red, cream and grey lining. A departure from former GWR practice is the lack of lining on the firebox and painting of the background of the nameplate and numberplate the same colour as the locomotive. No. 4091 was built in 1925 and withdrawn in January 1959 from Old Oak Common, and was one of the first of the class to go.

G. W. Sharpe

5101 class 2-6-2T No. 4165 on Hatton Bank in July 1950 with a local from Leamington Spa to Stratford-on-Avon. This was always a BR engine for it was built after Nationalisation. Withdrawal came during the week ended 9th October 1965 fom Oxley shed, then coded 2B and part of the London Midland Region.

R. H. G. Simpson

4400 class 2-6-2T No. 4404 at Kennington Junction, Oxford, on Wednesday 30th May 1951. The engine was returning to its home shed of Tondu after a visit to Wolverhampton Works, its birthplace in December 1905. It must have only been a light repair with no repaint, for withdrawal took place in March 1952 from Tondu.

R. H. G. Simpson

The standard GWR shunting machine, the 5700 class pannier tank. This example, No. 4620, is shown outside Llantrisant shed in June 1948 after being transferred from Tyseley in May. Tyseley was the engine's first allocation in June 1942 when new. Withdrawal took place in July 1965 from Newport Ebbw Junction.

R. H. G. Simpson

The approaches to Paddington in June 1948, with the washing from the nearby houses out drying and probably getting dirtier with all the passing traffic. 'Hall' class 4-6-0 No. 4995 *Easton Hall* runs past with an 'up' semi-fast from Reading. Built in 1931, this engine survived until June 1962, the last allocation being Southall.

Photomatic

Paddington after dark finds 'Castle' class 4-6-0 No. 5007 *Rougemont Castle* awaiting departure on a 'down' Cardiff in 1948. Dating back to 1927, this was another victim of the massive withdrawal of steam locomotives in 1962 when many old familiar friends disappeared for ever. A total of 2,929 locomotives were withdrawn that year and it was 5007's turn in September from Gloucester Horton Road shed.

G. W. Sharpe

Newport Pill shed, with the famous transporter bridge in the background, on 19th June 1949. 5205 class 2-8-0T No. 5252 takes a well earned Sunday rest. New in December 1925 it worked through until May 1965 when its fire was thrown out for the last time at Ebbw Junction shed.

G. W. Sharpe

Bristol Bath Road shed is the location on Sunday 29th May 1949 with 4575 class 2-6-2T No. 5523 alongside the coal stage ramp. These Prairie tanks were extremely useful engines and this type of wheel arrangement was extensively used on the GWR; indeed, more so than any other company. No. 5523 appeared in December 1927 and lasted until June 1960 finishing at St Blazey.

L. Hanson

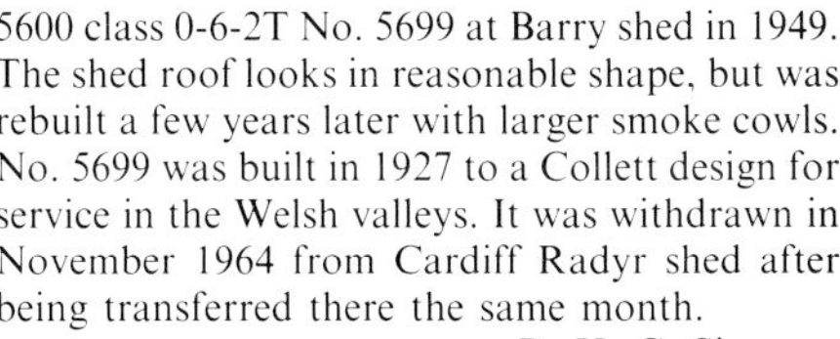
5600 class 0-6-2T No. 5699 at Barry shed in 1949. The shed roof looks in reasonable shape, but was rebuilt a few years later with larger smoke cowls. No. 5699 was built in 1927 to a Collett design for service in the Welsh valleys. It was withdrawn in November 1964 from Cardiff Radyr shed after being transferred there the same month.

R. H. G. Simpson

Collett 1927 design 'King' class 4-6-0 No. 6018 *King Henry VI* at Holloway on the 1.10pm King's Cross to Leeds express on Tuesday 18th May 1948 during the exchanges, with a dynamometer car recording the run. The 'King' was in its original condition with single chimney and low temperature superheater and was reported to have made the quickest time to this point compared with its rivals. Withdrawn along with the rest of the class in 1962, No. 6018 was scrapped in December from Old Oak Common, together with the other three last survivors.

Photomatic

A 'King' in more usual surroundings in 1948. No. 6021 *King Richard II* nears Paddington on an 'up' express. Old Oak Common was the engine's final home in September 1962.

Photomatic

6100 class 2-6-2T No. 6118 passing Kennington Junction signal box in 1948 on freight. Transfer had been effected in September 1948 from Southall to Didcot and so probably No. 6118 was not in the best condition and relegated to freight work instead of Paddington local passenger workings. Built in September 1931, withdrawal came in November 1963 from Reading.

R. H. G. Simpson

At home at Oxford shed in 1948 is 5600 class 0-6-2T No. 6682. Only two of this type were allocated to Oxford at this time, the other being No. 5616 of the earlier series. Built in 1928, No. 6682 was withdrawn in February 1964 from Cardiff East Dock.

R. H. G. Simpson

We revisit Newport Pill shed again on Sunday 19th June 1949 and find 0-6-0PT No. 6710 in extremely good condition, but bearing no ownership name on the side tanks. The allocation is shown on the footstep just below the frame. Dating from June 1930, No. 6710 spent its whole British Railways' working life at Newport Pill and was withdrawn in August 1957. These locomotives were known as the 6700 class, but were virtually identical to the 5700s. However, they were only fitted with a steam brake and no A.T.C. and so could only be used for shunting duties.

G. W. Sharpe

Collett 'Grange' class 4-6-0 No. 6802 *Bampton Grange* on its home shed, Reading, in September 1949. Built in October 1936 and delivered new to Old Oak Common, withdrawal came in August 1961 from Pontypool Road shed.

G. W. Sharpe

'Castle' class 4-6-0 No. 7014 *Caerhays Castle* on a 'down' express near Ealing when only a few weeks old in 1948. Run in from Swindon shed, No. 7014 moved to Bristol Bath Road shortly after being built in July and where the engine remained for many years. Withdrawn in February 1965 from Tyseley, which was then LMR property and coded 2A.

Photomatic

Newton Abbot shed in 1948 finds 7200 class 2-8-2T No. 7250 in steam and awaiting work over the South Devon banks. This locomotive had been rebuilt from 4200 class No. 4219 in March 1939 and then allocated to Swansea East Dock. Withdrawal came in September 1964 from Cardiff Radyr.

R. H. G. Simpson

4300 class 2-6-0 No. 7317 on Tyseley shed in September 1948. Reallocated from Oxley in August it remained at Tyseley until November 1960 and then moved to St Philip's Marsh, Bristol. Withdrawal came in December 1963 from Taunton.

R. H. G. Simpson

48406 19D
48407 19C
48408 24B
48409 16C
48410 14A
48411 19G
48412 20C
48413 16C
48414 14A
48415 14A
48416 24A
48417 21A
48418 18A
48419 20C
48420 21A
48421 16C
48422 2C
48423 2C
48424 21A
48425 26B
48426 2C
48427 4B
48428 5B
48429 25C
48430 19C
48431 20C
48432 17A
48433 1A
48434 19C
48435 24B
48436 24D
48437 26C
48438 1A
48439 20C
48440 19G
48441 25C
48442 16C
48443 20C
48444 26B
48445 2C
48446 26B
48447 25B
48448 24A
48449 25C
48450 19C
48451 9D
48452 25B
48453 26C
48454 4A
48455 25B
48456 24B
48457 5B
48458 24B
48459 24B
48460 26A
48461 23B
48462 26A
48463 24B
48464 9D
48465 5B
48466 5B
48467 5B
48468 26C
48469 23B
48470 24B
48471 24B
48472 24D
48473 4B
48474 4A
48475 24B
48476 1A
48477 5B
48478 5B
48479 24A
48490 18A
48491 15B
48492 15A
48493 18D
48494 18B
48495 18B
48500 25A
48501 25A
48502 25A
48503 25A
48504 25A
48505 25A
48506 25A
48507 25A
48508 25A
48509 25A
48510 25A
48511 25A
48512 25A
48513 25A
48514 25A
48515 25A
48516 25A
48517 25A
48518 25A
48519 25A
48520 25A
48521 25A
48522 25A
48523 24B
48524 24B
48525 24B
48526 24C
48527 24C
48528 24C
48529 24C
48530 16C
48531 15C
48532 20C
48533 14A
48534 18B
48535 18B
48536 18B
48537 18D
48538 18D
48539 18D
48540 20C
48541 14A
48542 20C
48543 17C
48544 18D
48545 20C
48546 20C
48547 20C
48548 19C
48549 18B
48550 2C
48551 4B
48552 16C
48553 5B
48554 1A
48555 5B
48556 4A
48557 2C
48558 9D
48559 5B
48600 1A
48601 1A
48602 1A
48603 1A
48604 18D
48605 1A
48606 18A
48607 18A
48608 16C
48609 18D
48610 1A
48611 18A
48612 1A
48613 4A
48614 16A
48615 18A
48616 16C
48617 15A
48618 18A
48619 15C
48620 18B
48621 16D
48622 16D
48623 18B
48624 1A
48625 15A
48626 1A
48627 15A
48628 1A
48629 1A
48630 1A
48631 4A
48632 1A
48633 1A
48634 1A
48635 16A
48636 18A
48637 18A
48638 18A
48639 16A
48640 17A
48641 16C
48642 19A
48643 16D
48644 15A
48645 15B
48646 15A
48647 17A
48648 1A
48649 2A
48650 18B
48651 15A
48652 18D
48653 16A
48654 17A
48655 18A
48656 1A
48657 1A
48658 1A
48659 2A
48660 1A
48661 18B
48662 18A
48663 18D
48664 4B
48665 4B
48666 16A
48667 19D
48668 15C
48669 21A
48670 20D
48671 15A
48672 18A
48673 4B
48674 4A
48675 16A
48676 19D
48677 17A
48678 15A
48679 1A
48680 19G
48681 18A
48682 19C
48683 19D
48684 1A
48685 18A
48686 18D
48687 21A
48688 4A
48689 4A
48690 18A
48691 4B
48692 15A
48693 2C
48694 15A
48695 15A
48696 16A
48697 19D
48698 19G
48699 15A
48700 20C
48701 16D
48702 20D
48703 18A
48704 15B
48705 24A
48706 23B
48707 23B
48708 5B
48709 15C
48710 24B
48711 24B
48712 9D
48713 24B
48714 24B
48715 24B
48716 5B
48717 4B
48718 24B
48719 24C
48720 24C
48721 24D
48722 25A
48723 5B
48724 25A
48725 25A
48726 25A
48727 25A
48728 15C
48729 5B
48730 25A
48731 5B
48732 25A
48733 25B
48734 5B
48735 25G
48736 4A
48737 25B
48738 25D
48739 25G
48740 5B
48741 5B
48742 5B
48743 4A
48744 5B
48745 5B
48746 5B
48747 5B
48748 5B
48749 5B
48750 5B
48751 25D
48752 25D
48753 5B
48754 25G
48755 25G
48756 26A
48757 5B
48758 5B
48759 26A
48760 26A
48761 26A
48762 26A
48763 26A
48764 5B
48765 26A
48766 26B
48767 26C
48768 26D
48769 26D
48770 5B
48771 5B
48772 5B

L.N.W.R. WHALE
4-6-0 4F

48801 10C
48824 10A
48834 10A

L.N.W.R. G1 AND
G2A 0-8-0 6F/7F

48892 2F
48893 4B
48894 2B
48895 4A
48896 2D
48897 2E
48898 8A
48899 4D
48901 2A
48902 2B
48903 10C
48904 8C
48905 3A
48906 5B
48907 8D
48908 8A
48909 3A
48910 2E
48911 2D
48912 10C
48913 2B
48914 2C
48915 1C
48917 3A
48918 10E
48920 10C
48921 4E
48922 2E
48924 2E
48925 2B
48926 2A
48927 8A
48929 2C
48930 10A
48931 2B
48932 4D
48933 8A
48934 11A
48935 2B
48936 2C
48939 8D
48940 5C
48941 10C
48942 8C
48943 1A
48944 8B
48945 4A
48948 4D
48950 6B
48951 2B
48952 2B
48953 1A
48954 10E
48962 5B
48964 1C
48966 8A
49002 9A
49003 3C
49004 2C
49005 2B
49006 4D
49007 2B
49008 8B
49009 9D
49010 9B
49011 3D
49012 1A
49013 2A

49014	10A
49015	3C
49016	8A
49017	3D
49018	20B
49019	4D
49020	8D
49021	1A
49022	3A
49023	10A
49024	10A
49025	3A
49026	10A
49027	8C
49028	4A
49029	10A
49030	10A
49031	3C
49032	8A
49033	4B
49034	3A
49035	4B
49036	3A
49037	2B
49038	8D
49039	3A
49040	3C
49041	1A
49042	2C
49043	10A
49044	3A
49045	3A
49046	4A
49047	6B
49048	3C
49049	2A
49050	3A
49051	4D
49052	6B
49053	10A
49054	9A
49055	19C
49056	3C
49057	8C
49058	8D
49059	9D
49060	8C
49061	2A
49062	1A
49063	3A
49064	4E
49065	8C
49066	8C
49067	8D
49068	2D
49069	2A
49070	2A
49071	8D
49072	6B
49073	8D
49074	8D
49075	8B
49076	2B
49077	6B
49078	3A
49079	8D
49080	2D
49081	3A
49082	2D
49083	3A
49084	3A
49085	8B
49086	8C
49087	20B
49088	11E
49089	3A
49090	10A
49091	5C
49092	9B
49093	2B
49094	6C
49095	10C
49096	3A
49097	3A
49098	5C
49099	3A
49100	2B
49101	6C
49102	10B
49103	2C
49104	11E
49105	6B
49106	3A
49107	2A
49108	9B
49109	11A
49110	3B
49111	9B
49112	6B
49113	4D
49114	2D
49115	6B
49116	5B
49117	2B
49119	10B
49120	6B
49121	15A
49122	15B
49123	15A
49124	10A
49125	10A
49126	15B
49127	2B
49128	1A
49129	10A
49130	8A
49131	3A
49132	9D
49133	2A
49134	10A
49135	2F
49136	8B
49137	2A
49138	4A
49139	1A
49140	8C
49141	10A
49142	3A
49143	6B
49144	5C
49145	1C
49146	4D
49147	10D
49148	4D
49149	10A
49150	2D
49151	11A
49152	10E
49153	2C
49154	2B
49155	8A
49156	9B
49157	2C
49158	2C
49159	10A
49160	3A
49161	4E
49162	2A
49163	1A
49164	1A
49165	3A
49166	6B
49167	2F
49168	4E
49169	2C
49170	8D
49171	9A
49172	6C
49173	2B
49174	4E
49175	3A
49176	10A
49177	3A
49178	8B
49179	2B
49180	3A
49181	2D
49183	9A
49184	5B
49185	9B
49186	9B
49187	9B
49188	11A
49189	3A
49190	2D
49191	2D
49192	10A
49193	2B
49194	5C
49195	3A
49196	3B
49197	10A
49198	5E
49199	10C
49200	2A
49201	2B
49202	3A
49203	2C
49204	3B
49205	2C
49207	10A
49208	2B
49209	5B
49210	5B
49211	3A
49212	9D
49213	2B
49214	9D
49216	9D
49217	15A
49218	8C
49219	8C
49220	6B
49221	10A
49222	3C
49223	15A
49224	9D
49225	9D
49226	4D
49227	9A
49228	6B
49229	2A
49230	5B
49231	10B
49232	5B
49233	3B
49234	10C
49235	6B
49236	3C
49237	2B
49238	10C
49239	8A
49240	9D
49241	5B
49242	8A
49243	4D
49244	6C
49245	3A
49246	6C
49247	8B
49248	3C
49249	1C
49250	10B
49251	6B
49252	11E
49253	8C
49254	10C
49255	10C
49256	6C
49257	10A
49258	6C
49259	3A
49260	4B
49261	6B
49262	1C
49263	5B
49264	2D
49265	3A
49266	3A
49267	5B
49268	2D
49269	11A
49270	2C
49271	2C
49272	5B
49273	10C
49274	3A
49275	5B
49276	4D
49277	1A
49278	2F
49279	3A
49280	6B
49281	8C
49282	3A
49283	3C
49284	9A
49285	9A
49286	3A
49287	8A
49288	15A
49289	15A
49290	15A
49291	6B
49292	15A
49293	8C
49294	3A
49295	3B
49296	5B
49297	8C
49298	9A
49299	10B
49300	2B
49301	3A
49302	8B
49303	10E
49304	10C
49305	9D
49306	10A
49307	2B
49308	3A
49309	3D
49310	10A
49311	10A
49312	10E
49313	3A
49314	11A
49315	9D
49316	6B
49317	10E
49318	2D
49319	2A
49320	5C
49321	2C
49322	6B
49323	1C
49324	2C
49325	3C
49326	9D
49327	3A
49328	3A
49329	21A
49330	10C
49331	9D
49332	2B
49333	8A
49334	1A
49335	3A
49337	2A
49338	8B
49339	6C
49340	2F
49341	8C
49342	2D
49343	9A
49344	1C
49345	2D
49346	2D
49347	9D
49348	10B
49349	3C
49350	2D
49351	2D
49352	2D
49353	10C
49354	3A
49355	8A
49356	3B
49357	5B
49358	4B
49359	2B
49360	21A
49361	3A
49362	3D
49363	9A
49364	3C
49365	8C
49366	2D
49367	3A
49368	2F
49369	5B
49370	5B
49371	2B
49372	2B
49373	5B
49375	1C
49376	9D
49377	21A
49378	10D
49379	25G
49381	25B
49382	25G
49383	6B
49384	2E
49385	8A
49386	9D
49387	25B
49388	3C
49389	25G
49390	25G
49391	2B
49392	25G
49393	1A
49394	25G

L.N.W.R. G2
0-8-0 7F

49395	2C
49396	5B
49397	2A
49398	1A
49399	2A
49400	2D
49401	2B
49402	3A
49403	4D
49404	2A
49405	10C
49406	2B
49407	4B

49408 2A
49409 4E
49410 2A
49411 8B
49412 2D
49413 2A
49414 2C
49415 5B
49416 2B
49417 10B
49418 4B
49419 10B
49420 10B
49421 10B
49422 10A
49423 2F
49424 10A
49425 3A
49426 2C
49427 2B
49428 2D
49429 2D
49430 2D
49431 3A
49432 2D
49433 2A
49434 2A
49435 2D
49436 2D
49437 2D
49438 1A
49439 2D
49440 2F
49441 2A
49442 10B
49443 2B
49444 2C
49445 4A
49446 2A
49447 6B
49448 1A
49449 8A
49450 5B
49451 10B
49452 2A
49453 1A
49454 1A

FOWLER 0-8-0 7F

49500 25D
49501 25B
49502 24C
49503 24C
49504 25A
49505 25A
49506 25A
49507 25E
49508 25E
49509 26F
49510 26A
49511 26A
49512 26A
49513 25A
49514 25A
49515 25A
49516 25A
49517 25A
49518 25A
49519 25A
49520 26A
49521 23B
49522 25D
49523 24C
49524 24C
49525 25A
49526 25A
49527 25E
49528 25E
49529 25A
49530 25A
49531 25A
49532 25A
49533 26A
49534 24C
49535 23B
49536 25B
49537 25G
49538 25G
49539 25C
49540 25G
49541 25A
49542 26C
49543 25A
49544 25B
49545 25A
49546 25A
49547 25G
49548 26F
49549 24B
49550 25A
49551 25G
49552 25G
49553 25G
49554 26A
49555 25D
49556 26A
49557 26D
49558 25A
49559 25A
49560 26A
49561 25A
49562 25A
49563 25B
49564 23B
49565 26A
49566 23B
49567 23B
49568 25E
49569 25E
49570 25A
49571 23B
49572 25B
49573 26C
49574 25A
49575 25A
49576 25A
49577 25A
49578 25A
49579 25D
49580 25B
49581 23B
49582 25C
49583 25B
49584 25A
49585 24C
49586 23B
49587 23B
49588 25A
49589 25A
49590 26D
49591 26D
49592 23B
49593 26F
49594 26D
49595 23B
49596 25B
49597 23B
49598 25G
49599 26B
49600 25C
49601 25D
49602 25D
49603 25A
49604 25A
49605 25A
49606 25E
49607 26A
49608 26A
49609 25A
49610 24B
49611 24C
49612 24C
49613 23B
49614 24C
49615 24C
49616 24C
49617 24C
49618 25D
49619 25D
49620 25D
49621 25A
49622 25A
49623 25A
49624 25G
49625 25A
49626 25A
49627 25A
49628 25E
49629 25A
49630 25A
49631 26B
49632 25A
49633 25A
49634 25A
49635 25A
49636 26A
49637 26A
49638 25A
49639 26A
49640 24C
49641 26C
49642 26A
49643 25A
49644 25A
49645 25A
49646 25A
49647 25A
49648 25A
49649 24C
49650 26A
49651 26A
49652 26A
49653 26A
49654 26A
49655 26A
49656 26A
49657 26A
49658 25D
49659 25D
49660 25D
49661 25D
49662 25D
49663 25D
49664 26C
49665 26D
49666 26D
49667 26D
49668 26F
49669 25A
49670 25A
49671 25A
49672 25G
49673 25G
49674 23A

HUGHES 4-6-0 5P

50412 24E
50423 24E
50429 24E
50432 24E
50442 24E
50448 24E
50455 24E

HUGHES RAIL MOTOR 0-4-0T

50617 26C

ASPINALL 2-4-2T 2P

50621 20D
50622 20A
50623 20F
50625 20G
50630 20E
50631 20E
50633 20E
50634 20E
50636 20E
50639 10B
50640 24F
50642 26C
50643 11B
50644 11B
50646 26C
50647 25A
50648 23B
50650 25A
50651 26E
50652 26E
50653 24B
50654 24B
50655 23B
50656 25A
50660 23B
50665 25F
50667 25A
50670 25D
50671 20F
50675 24F
50676 10B
50678 23C
50681 20E
50686 20G
50687 23C
50689 20A
50692 23D
50695 25A
50696 23C
50697 26C
50703 24F
50705 24F
50711 25E
50712 25D
50714 20E
50715 25F
50720 24F
50721 24E
50725 24E
50728 23C
50731 25D
50732 24F
50735 24D
50736 26A
50738 26A
50743 23C
50746 23C
50748 25A
50749 24E
50750 24E
50752 23C
50755 25A
50757 23D
50762 25F
50764 25A
50765 24F
50766 24E
50777 25A
50778 23C
50781 24D
50788 25F
50793 10B
50795 20F
50798 25D
50799 24E
50800 25A
50801 25A
50802 24F
50804 25A
50806 25A
50807 26C
50812 24F
50813 25A
50815 26C
50818 26A
50823 26D
50829 25D
50831 26C

ASPINALL/HUGHES 2-4-2T 3P

50835 25E

ASPINALL 2-4-2T 2P

50840 25F
50842 20G
50844 23D
50849 23C
50850 25D
50852 25A
50855 25F
50859 26C
50865 23C
50869 25A
50872 26D
50873 25D
50875 26D
50880 20A
50886 25F
50887 23D
50889 24E

ASPINALL/HUGHES 2-4-2T 3P

50891 25E

ASPINALL 2-4-2T 2P

50892 26D

ASPINALL/HUGHES 2-4-2T 3P

50893 24D

ASPINALL 2-4-2T 2P

50896 20G
50898 25D
50899 20G

ASPINALL/HUGHES 2-4-2T 3P

50901 20D
50903 20A
50909 25F
50925 25E
50934 25E
50943 25E
50945 24D
50950 24D
50951 24D
50952 25F
50953 24D

L.& Y.R. "PUGS" ASPINALL 0-4-0ST OF

51202 22C
51204 10E
51206 23A
51207 25C

51212	22A
51216	23A
51217	17B
51218	10B
51221	5B
51222	26A
51227	23A
51229	23A
51230	26B
51231	23A
51232	23A
51234	26A
51235	17B
51237	23A
51240	26B
51241	25C
51244	25C
51246	23A
51253	23A

ASPINALL REBUILT 0-6-0ST 2F

11304	HW
11305	HW
51307	23A
51313	6C
51316	10E
51318	8A
51319	10E
51320	25D
51321	24F
51323	25C
11324	HW
51325	23A
51336	24D
51338	26D
51342	8C
51343	23B
51345	24C
51348	26C
51353	8A
51358	25A
51361	24A
11368	HW
51371	23A
51375	23A
51376	24F
51379	26A
51381	25E
51390	25A
11394	HW
51396	23A
51397	8C
51400	26A
51404	26A
51405	8C
51408	25B
51410	24B
51412	CW
51413	23B
51415	25A
51419	26D
51423	24C
51424	26A
51425	26A
51427	8C
51429	25E
51432	25C
51436	26A
51438	26A
51439	8A
51441	6C
51443	25C
51444	8C
51445	8A
51446	CW
51447	25B
51453	25D
51457	25A
51458	25C
51460	23B
51462	23B
51464	26B
51467	24D
51468	25A
51469	8C
51470	26A
51471	10E
51472	26A
51474	26B
51475	23B
51477	24F
51479	25E
51481	26D
51482	25E
51484	25A
51486	26D
51487	26D
51488	26A
51489	26D
51490	23C
51491	10E
51492	24B
51495	10E
51496	26A
51497	24B
51498	24F
51499	24D
51500	25A
51503	25A
51504	26D
51506	24D
51510	26A
51511	26C
51512	26B
51513	26C
51514	24F
51516	25C
51519	26C
51521	25C
51524	25B
51526	24C
51530	23B

ASPINALL 0-6-0T 1F

51535	23A
51536	23A
51537	23A
51544	23B
51546	23A

BARTON WRIGHT 0-6-0 2F

52016	10B
52019	10C
52021	10A
52022	10A
52023	10A
52024	10A
52030	10C
52031	10C
52032	10A
52034	10B
52036	10C
52037	25C
52041	25C
52043	25C
52044	25C
52045	10A
52046	25A
52047	25A
52049	10C
52051	10B
52053	10A
52056	25C
52059	10C
52063	10A
52064	10A

ASPINALL 0-6-0 3F

52088	8C
52089	20D
52091	10E
52092	25A
52093	23D
52094	23B
52095	20D
52098	12E
52099	25E
52100	8B
52102	23A
52103	4A
52104	25F
52105	4A
52107	2D
52108	20C
52110	12E
52111	8A
52112	23B
52118	8B
52119	4A
52120	26A
52121	16A
52123	16A
52124	26A
52125	7D
52126	10E
52127	25F
52129	26D
52132	26A
52133	25C
52135	16A
52136	26A
52137	26B
52138	26A
52139	26D
52140	8B
52141	2D
52143	8C
52150	25A
52152	23D
52154	25A
52156	26A
52157	26C
52159	26D
52160	24C
52161	23C
52162	26B
52163	8C
52164	26D
52165	26D
52166	25D
52167	7D
52169	23D
52170	8A
52171	24C
52172	10A
52174	24E
52175	8B
52176	7B
52177	10E
52179	23B
52181	25C
52182	25A
52183	24B
52184	12E
52186	25A
52189	23D
52191	25D
52192	25D
52194	24E
52196	23B
52197	23C
52201	12E
52203	26B
52207	26A
52208	10A
52212	26C
52215	24E
52216	24A
52217	25F
52218	23B
52219	8C
52220	24B
52225	6C
52229	26A
52230	7B
52231	25D
52232	6C
52233	4A
52235	25D
52236	26C
52237	25F
52238	24A
52239	26A
52240	24F
52243	25E
52244	24C
52245	26D
52246	26D
52248	26F
52250	8B
52252	20C
52253	24D
52255	25F
52256	23C
52258	20C
52260	24D
52262	24B
52266	26A
52268	24B
52269	10A
52270	6C
52271	23C
52272	23C
52273	25D
52275	24E
52278	24B
52279	26A
52280	10E
52284	25A
52285	12E
52288	24A
52289	24D
52290	23D
52293	26B
52294	2D
52296	24C
52299	26E
52300	26A
52304	26B
52305	25A
52309	24B
52311	25D
52312	23D
52317	24C
52319	25A
52321	2D
52322	2D
52326	26F
52328	23B
52330	8B
52331	25D
52333	23B
52334	24C
52336	24C
52337	23B
52338	7D
52341	10B
52343	26A
52345	26A
52348	26C
52349	10E
52350	26C
52351	25B
52353	26B
52355	26A
52356	7D
52357	26C
52358	26A
52360	23D
52362	23B
52363	24D
52365	26C
52366	10E
52368	24C
52369	25A
52374	4A
52376	25E
52378	26F
52379	23B
52381	23C
52382	26D
52386	25A
52387	26F
52388	26E
52389	26F
52390	23B
52393	10E
52397	10E
52399	24C
52400	23C
52401	23B
52403	25F
52404	26C
52405	23B
52407	7B
52408	25D
52410	25F
52411	26B
52412	24A
52413	23D
52414	4A
52415	24E
52416	25E
52417	6A
52418	12E
52422	25F
52427	25F
52428	4A
52429	4A
52430	24E
52431	24D
52432	12B
52433	25A
52435	25A
52437	26A
52438	8C
52439	24F
52440	26E
52441	24A
52442	26E
52443	26A
52444	24D
52445	26E
52446	26C
52447	24E
52448	25D
52449	10E
52450	23A
52452	24A
52453	10E
52454	25C
52455	26D
52456	23B
52457	4A
52458	24F
52459	24E
52460	24C
52461	26B

52464 26F
52465 6C
52466 26A
52467 24C

FURNESS RAILWAY
PETTIGREW 0-6-0 3F

52494 12E
52499 12E
52501 12D
52508 12D
52509 12D
52510 12E

ASPINALL 0-6-0 3F

52515 25B
52517 26A
52518 26A
52521 25D
52522 24C
52523 23C
52524 24A
52525 4A
52526 24D
52527 23B

HUGHES 0-6-0 3F

52528 26C

ASPINALL 0-6-0 3F

52529 24B

HUGHES 0-6-0 3F

52541 24C
52542 24E
52545 26F
52549 26B
52551 12E
52554 26D
52557 23B
52558 24E
52559 20C
52561 25A
52568 25A
52569 26F
52572 24E
52574 25E
52575 25E
52576 25A
52578 26A
52579 26D
52580 26D
52581 26D
52582 23B
52583 25D
52586 26F
52587 25E
52588 23D
52590 25E
52592 25C
52598 23D
52602 23D
52607 26F
52608 26D
52609 26C
52615 26D
52616 25E
52618 10B
52619 10B

ASPINALL 0-8-0 6F

52727 23D
52782 23B
52806 23D
52821 24A
52822 24A
52825 24A
52827 23D
52828 23D
52831 24A
52834 23D
52837 23D
52839 23D

HUGHES 0-8-0 7F

52841 24B
52856 23B
52857 23B
52870 23B
52873 24B
52877 23B
52886 24B
52906 24B
52910 23B
52913 24B
52916 24B
52935 23B
52945 24B
52952 24B
52956 23B
52962 23B
52971 23B

FOWLER 2-8-0 7F

53800 22C
53801 22C
53802 22C
53803 22C
53804 22C
53805 22C
53806 22C
53807 22C
53808 22C
53809 22C
53810 22C

McINTOSH 4-4-0 2P
"DUNALASTAIR IV"

54363 32B

JONES "LOCH"
CLASS 4-4-0 2P

54379* 32B
54385* 32C

P. DRUMMOND "BEN"
CLASS 4-4-0 2P

54397* 32A
54398* 32B
54399* 32A
54401* 32A
54403* 32A
54404* 32A
54409* 32A
54410* 32C
54415* 32A
54416* 32A

McINTOSH 4-4-0 3P

54434 32B
54438 28C
54439 28C
54440 27B
54441 28A
54443 27B
54444 27B
54445 27B
54446 28C
54447 29A
54448 29A
54449 28C
54450 29D
54451 28B
54452 28B
54453 28A
54454 29D
54455 31B
54456 30B
54457 27B
54458 29A
54459 29A
54460 28A

PICKERSGILL 4-4-0
3P

54461 28C
54462 28A
54463 28C
54464 28A
54465 28A
54466 31B
54467 29A
54468 27B
54469 29A
54470 32A
54471 32A
54472 32A
54473 32C
54474 31A
54475 31A
54476 29A
54477 28C
54478 28B
54479 27B
54480 32A
54481 32C
54482 32A
54483 31A
54484 32A
54485 31B
54486 29D
54487 31A
54488 32A
54489 29A
54490 28C
54491 31B
54492 27B
54493 32B
54494 31A
54495 32A
54496 31B
54497 27B
54498 28A
54499 29A
54500 29A
54501 29A
54502 29A
54503 29A
54504 30B
54505 28C
54506 28A
54507 28B
54508 27B

PICKERSGILL 4-6-0
4P

54630 28C
54631 28A
54634 28A
54635 28A
54636 28A
54637 28A
54638 27C
54639 27C
54640 28A
54641 28A
54642 28A
54643 28A
54644 28B
54645 28A
54646 28A
54647 28A
54648 27C
54649 28A
54650 28A
54651 28A
54652 28A
54653 28A
54654 28A

C.CUMMINGS "CLAN"
CLASS 4-6-0 4P

54764* 32B
54767* 32B

P. DRUMMOND
0-4-4T 0P

55051 32A
55053 32A

McINTOSH 0-4-4T
2P

55116 27A
55117 31B
55119 31D
55121 31A
55122 31B
55123 27A
55124 31A
55125 28B
55126 31B
55127 27A
55129 31E
55130 20E
55132 30D
55133 32B
55134 28A
55135 30A
55136 31E
55138 28A
55139 28B
55140 30A
55141 27A
55142 31D
55143 30A
55144 29A
55145 31E
55146 27C

McINTOSH "439"
CLASS 0-4-4T 2P

55159 31A
55160 29D
55161 29D
55162 29D
55164 12F
55165 28B
55166 28B
55167 27A
55168 31E
55169 20E
55170 27A
55171 29A
55172 29D
55173 29C
55174 31E
55175 29A
55176 29A
55177 28B
55178 31A
55179 27A
55180 29C
55181 12F
55182 30A
55183 27A
55184 29D
55185 29D
55186 29C
55187 31C
55188 28A
55189 28B
55190 29D
55191 28A
55192 20E
55193 30A
55194 29D
55195 29D
55196 29C
55197 27A
55198 29D
55199 32A
55200 29D
55201 27A
55202 28B
55203 30B
55204 31A
55206 30A
55207 27A
55208 29A
55209 29A
55210 28B
55211 30A
55212 31B
55213 29A
55214 29D
55215 31C
55216 29A
55217 29C
55218 29A
55219 30A
55220 29B
55221 27A
55222 31B
55223 29C
55224 27A
55225 30A
55226 29C
55227 20E
55228 27A
55229 28B
55230 29D
55231 29C
55232 12F
55233 28B
55234 29B
55235 30A
55236 30B

PICKERSGILL "431"
CLASS 0-4-4T 2P

55237 12F
55238 31D
55239 12F
55240 31E

McINTOSH "439"
CLASS 0-4-4T 2P

55260 30B
55261 28C
55262 30D
55263 31C
55264 30D
55265 27A
55266 30A
55267 27A
55268 27A
55269 30A

PICKERSGILL 4-6-2T
4P

55350 12F
55351 12F
55352 12F
55353 12F
55354 12F
55355 27B
55356 12F
55359 12F
55360 12F

55361 12F

DRUMMOND 0-4-0ST OF

56010 32A
56011 32A
56020 17B
56025 ST. ROLLOX WORKS
56026 31E
56027 4A
56028 28A
56029 28A
56030 31E
56031 28A
56032 CW
56035 27B
56038 31E
56039 31E

McINTOSH 0-6-0T 2F

56151 31A
56152 31D
56153 27A
56154 31E
56155 28A
56156 27B
56157 27B
56158 31E
56159 27A
56160 27A
56161 31E
56162 27A
56163 27B
56164 31D
56165 27B
56166 27B
56167 27A
56168 31E
56169 31E
56170 31E
56171 31E
56172 27A
56173 27B

McINTOSH 0-6-0T 3F

56230 31D
56231 12A
56232 31D
56233 31A
56234 31A
56235 12A
56236 28B
56237 27C
56238 31E
56239 27A
56240 29B
56241 28A
56242 27C
56243 31D
56244 27A
56245 28A
56246 29A
56247 28A
56248 12A
56249 30A
56250 31E
56251 29B
56252 31A
56253 28B
56254 31B
56255 27C
56256 27C
56257 30D
56258 28A
56259 30C
56260 27A
56261 27A
56262 32A
56263 27A
56264 28A
56265 28A
56266 12A
56267 31D
56268 28A
56269 28A
56270 28A
56271 28A
56272 30D
56273 30D
56274 30D
56275 31D
56276 28A
56277 28A
56278 29B
56279 30C
56280 27A
56281 28A
56282 30C
56283 28B
56284 27C
56285 28A
56286 27C
56287 27C
56288 27B
56289 31A
56290 29A
56291 32A
56292 27A
56293 32A
56294 27A
56295 27A
56296 27C
56297 31E
56298 27A
56299 32A
56300 31D
56301 32C
56302 31E
56303 27C
56304 27A
56305 27A
56306 27A
56307 27A
56308 27A
56309 27C
56310 12A
56311 30C
56312 28B
56313 28B
56314 27A
56315 31E
56316 12A
56317 12A
56318 27A
56319 27C
56320 27C
56321 27C
56322 27A
56323 29C
56324 27A
56325 29C
56326 29B
56327 12A
56328 29A
56329 28B
56330 31A
56331 29A
56332 12A
56333 12A
56334 28A
56335 28A
56336 31D
56337 28A
56338 28A
56339 31E
56340 12A
56341 32A
56342 27A
56343 31B
56344 31E
56345 28A
56346 27A
56347 29A
56348 29B
56349 27A
56350 30A
56351 12H
56352 29A
56353 29A
56354 12A
56355 12A
56356 28A
56357 28A
56358 28A
56359 29B
56360 27C
56361 30A
56362 27C
56363 30D
56364 30C
56365 31B
56366 31B
56367 30D
56368 30B
56369 30A
56370 31A
56371 27C
56372 12H
56373 12A
56374 12A
56375 31D
56376 31D

P. DRUMMOND 0-6-2T 3F

56905 12A

DRUMMOND 0-6-0 2F

57230 12G
57231 28A
57232 31B
57233 31B
57234 30D
57235 30D
57236 30B
57237 27C
57238 12G
57239 27A
57240 31A
57241 30A
57242 27C
57243 31B
57244 27C
57245 31E
57246 31B
57247 28A
57249 30A
57250 27C
57251 31A
57252 31B
57253 31A
57254 31A
57255 30A
57256 28A
57257 31B
57258 31E
57259 31E
57260 27C
57261 30D
57262 30D
57263 30C
57264 31B
57265 31D
57266 30A
57267 28A
57268 27A
57269 31A
57270 28A
57271 30D
57272 28A
57273 28A
57274 30C
57275 27A
57276 30C
57277 30B
57278 28A
57279 30D
57280 27C
57282 30C
57283 29B
57284 30D
57285 31D
57286 12G
57287 31D
57288 12G
57289 28A
57290 28A
57291 28A
57292 27A
57294 31D
57295 30D
57296 31E
57298 28C
57299 28A
57300 30A
57301 28A
57302 12G
57303 28A
57304 30C
57305 31A
57306 31E
57307 27C
57308 28A
57309 30A
57310 27A
57311 31A
57312 30D
57313 28A
57314 31E
57315 30D
57316 27A
57317 27A
57318 31A
57319 27A
57320 27A
57321 27A
57322 31E
57323 28C
57324 29D
57325 28A
57326 28A
57327 28A
57328 28A
57329 12G
57330 27A
57331 30B
57332 28A
57333 31A
57334 31D
57335 27A
57336 31E
57337 12G
57338 31D
57339 29B
57340 28C
57341 31E
57342 28A
57343 12G
57344 28A
57345 29B
57346 31E
57347 27A
57348 30C
57349 12G
57350 31A
57351 30D
57352 31A
57353 30B
57354 30D
57355 30C
57356 30C
57357 30C
57358 28A
57359 30A
57360 27A
57361 27A
57362 12G
57363 28A
57364 30D
57365 27A
57366 31E
57367 27A
57368 29D
57369 27B
57370 27A
57371 31E
57372 31E
57373 31D
57374 31A
57375 12H
57377 28A
57378 12G
57379 28A
57380 31A
57381 27A
57382 27C
57383 30B
57384 27C
57385 28C
57386 28C
57387 27A
57388 27A
57389 27A
57390 30D
57391 12G
57392 30D
57393 27C
57394 31A
57395 27C
57396 31C
57397 29A
57398 27C
57399 28C
57400 29B
57401 27C
57402 31B
57403 28A
57404 28A
57405 12G
57406 28A
57407 27C
57408 27C
57409 12G
57410 27C
57411 31C
57412 27A
57413 28A
57414 28A
57415 28A
57416 28A
57417 28A
57418 28A
57419 28A
57420 27C
57421 12H
57422 31B
57423 31B

57424	31B
57425	31B
57426	31E
57427	31E
57429	31E
57430	27C
57431	27C
57432	27A
57433	27A
57434	31A
57435	28A
57436	27A
57437	28A
57438	28C
57439	27A
57440	12H
57441	29D
57442	31D
57443	27A
57444	27A
57445	12H
57446	27A
57447	27A
57448	27A
57449	29A
57450	29C
57451	28C
57452	31E
57453	31A
57454	31A
57455	31A
57456	31E
57457	31A
57458	12H
57459	27A
57460	31B
57461	28A
57462	28A
57463	27B
57464	27A
57465	27A
57466	31B
57467	27A
57468	31B
57469	31E
57470	31E
57471	31E
57472	31E
57473	29A

McINTOSH "812"
CLASS 0-6-0 3F

57550	28B
57551	27B
57552	27B
57553	28B
57554	31A
57555	27A
57556	27B
57557	31A
57558	31A
57559	28B
57560	30A
57561	30A
57562	30A
57563	12G
57564	27A
57565	28B
57566	30A
57568	29C
57569	30D
57570	30B
57571	30B
57572	30B
57573	30B
57574	30B
57575	30A
57576	28B
57577	30C
57578	28B
57579	30C
57580	30A
57581	27A
57582	28A
57583	28C
57584	28A
57585	32A
57586	32A
57587	32A
57588	28A
57589	30A
57590	30C
57591	32C
57592	12A
57593	28A
57594	30A
57595	28A
57596	30A
57597	32B
57599	28A
57600	12G
57601	12G
57602	12G
57603	31D
57604	28C
57605	12A
57606	28A
57607	31E
57608	28C
57609	27C
57611	30D
57612	31E
57613	28C
57614	30D
57615	30D
57616	30D
57617	31A
57618	28C
57619	27A
57620	32C
57621	12G
57622	32A
57623	12G
57624	30A
57625	32A
57626	12A
57627	30C
57628	30D

McINTOSH "652"
CLASS 0-6-0 3F

57629	32A
57630	27C
57631	31A
57632	27A
57633	30D
57634	32B
57635	28C
57636	12G
57637	30B
57638	28A
57639	27B
57640	30D
57641	27A
57642	29D
57643	30B
57644	30D
57645	28B

PICKERSGILL "294"
CLASS 0-6-0 3F

57650	30B
57651	30B
57652	31E
57653	29C
57654	28B
57655	28C
57658	31D
57659	28B
57661	27A
57663	27C
57665	27C
57666	28A
57667	31D
57668	28A
57669	30C
57670	28C
57671	30B
57672	30B
57673	30C
57674	28B
57679	28C
57681	28A
57682	27B
57684	30D
57686	31A
57688	30B
57689	31D
57690	27A
57691	31D

P. DRUMMOND
0-6-0 3F

57693	30A
57694	30A
57695	30A
57697	30D
57698	30A
57699	30A
57702	30A

C.CUMMINGS 4-6-0
"CLAN GOODS" 4F

57950	32A
57951	32A
57953	32A
57954	32A
57955	32A
57956	32A

"PRINCE OF WALES"
4-6-0 4P

58000*	25648	5C
58001*	25673	5C
	25722	2B
58002	25752	5C
58003	25787	5C
	25827	2B

"PRECURSOR" CLASS
4-4-0 3P

58010*	25297	6A

"GEORGE THE FIFTH"
CLASS 4-4-0 3P

	25321*	6A
58011	25350	6A
58012*	25373	6A

JOHNSON 2-4-0 1P

58020	20155	16A
58021	20185	11B
58022	20216	15B

JOHNSON 0-4-4T 1P

58030	1239	15A
58031	1246	15A
58032	1247	20A
58033	1249	19B
58034	1251	22B
58035	1252	17A
58036	1255	20E
58037	1260	15D
58038	1261	13A
58039	1272	15D
58040	1273	15D
58041	1275	20F
58042	1278	9D
58043	1287	13A
58044	1290	13A
58045	1295	15D
58046	1298	22E
58047	1303	22B
	1307	22E
58048	1315	20A
58049	1322	22E
58050	1324	16A
58051	1330	15C
58052	1337	20C
58053	1340	15D
58054	1341	16D
58055	1342	20C
58056	1344	16A
58057	1348	17B
58058	1350	16D
58059	1353	22B
58060	1357	17B
58061	1358	20F
58062	1360	13A
	1361	20F
58063	1365	22B
58064	1366	20F
58065	1367	14A
58066	1368	20C
58067	1370	19B
58068	1371	14B
58069	1373	14A
58070	1375	14A
58071	1377	19B
58072	1379	14B
58073	1382	14B
	1385	14A
58074	1389	22A
58075	1390	20C
58076	1396	19B
58077	1397	17A
58078	1402	19B
58079	1406	22C
58080	1411	22A
58081	1413	20E
58082	1416	2A
58083	1420	2A
58084	1421	9D
58085	1422	15C
58086	1423	14B
58087	1424	17B
58088	1425	22E
58089	1426	13A
58090	1429	17A
58091	1430	15D

WEBB 2-4-0T 1P

58092	6428	9D

FOWLER 0-10-0

58100	22290	21C

KIRTLEY 0-6-0 2F

58110	22630	21B
58111	22846	21B
58112	22853	21A
58113	22863	21B

JOHNSON 0-6-0 2F

58114	22900	19C
58115	22901	11B
58116	22902	2D
58117	22904	3E
58118	22907	2D
58119	22911	2A
58120	22912	11B
58121	22913	2C
58122	22915	3A
58123	22918	3A
58124	22920	3E
58125	22921	17A
58126	22924	21B
58127	22926	19C
58128	22929	19D
58129	22931	13C
58130	22932	17B
58131	22933	15D
58132	22934	17A
58133	22935	16D
58134	22940	20C
58135	22944	16D
58136	22945	20B
58137	22946	16C
58138	22947	21A
58139	22950	19A
58140	22951	19A
58141	22953	21B
58142	22954	15C
58143	22955	21B
58144	22958	17A
58145	22959	17A
58146	22963	18A
58147	22965	19C
58148	22967	17A
58149	22968	15D
58150	22969	19C
58151	22970	19A
58152	22971	2A
58153	22974	18A
58154	22975	19C
58155	22976	20E
58156	22977	20C
58157	22978	3A
58158	22982	17A
58159	22983	18A
58160	22984	17B
58161	2987	14A
58162	2988	15B
58163	2989	17C
58164	2990	14B
58165	2992	19A
58166	2993	18A
58167	2994	21A
58168	2995	18B
58169	2996	18B
58170	2997	19C
58171	2998	20E
58172	2999	15B
58173	23000	18A
58174	23001	17C
58175	23002	19C
58176	23003	18A
58177	23005	3E
58178	23006	3E
58179	23007	3E
58180	23008	3D
58181	23009	2A
58182	23010	3D
58183	23011	15B
58184	23012	13A
58185	23013	3D
58186	23014	17B
	23016	14B
58187	23018	2F
	3021	14B
58188	3023	17A
58189	3027	17D
58190	3031	19A
58191	3035	13A
58192	3037	20F
58193	3038	15B
58194	3039	15C
58195	3042	15B
58196	3044	18B
58197	3045	17D

58198 3047 19C
58199 3048 2F
58200 3049 14A
3050 20C
58201 3051 16A
58202 3052 21A
58203 3054 17D
58204 3058 19C
58205 3061 3A
58206 3062 22B
58207 3064 20C
58208 3066 19A
58209 3071 19B
58210 3073 16A
58211 3074 2F
58212 3078 20E
58213 3084 2D
58214 3090 15B
58215 3094 22A
58216 3095 17A
58217 3096 2F
58218 3098 2C
58219 3099 17D
58220 3101 19A
58221 3103 17B
58222 3108 17B
58223 3109 17D
58224 3113 17D
58225 3118 19A
58226 3119 17D
58227 3123 17A
58228 3127 17D
58229 3130 14B
58230 3134 17A
58231 3138 21A
58232 3140 19A
58233 3144 19C
58234 3149 14B
58235 3150 14A
58236 3151 17D
3153 17D
58237 3154 20C
58238 3156 20D
58239 3157 15D
58240 3161 2D
58241 3164 15D
58242 3166 15C
58243 3168 3D
58244 3171 19C
58245 3173 20B
58246 3175 17A
58247 3176 17C
58248 3177 16A
58249 3190 15C
3195 15B
58250 3196 3D
58251 3229 17C
58252 3262 16A
58253 3264 17A
58254 3270 17D
58255 3311 21A
58256 3360 17B
58257 3372 1A
58258 3377 17B
58259 3385 13A
58260 3420 14A
58261 3423 21C
3424 16C

58262 3425 19A
58263 3437 17B
58264 3445 17C
58265 3451 20C
58266 3466 19C
3473 1A
58267 3477 20F
58268 3479 17D
58269 3485 2A
58270 3489 2C
58271 3492 21C
58272 3493 1C
58273 3503 3E
58274 3508 14A
58275 3511 16A
58276 3512 19A
58277 3516 1A
58278 3517 1A
58279 3525 1A
58280 3526 1A
58281 3527 1A
58282 3533 19D
58283 3536 1A
58284 3537 17B
58285 3539 1A
58286 3543 1A
58287 3545 1A
58288 3551 3A
58289 3559 13A
58290 3561 1A
58291 3564 1A
58292 3566 20E
58293 3571 2F
58294 3592 21A
3602 16A
58295 3603 1A
58296 3617 14A
58297 3632 17B
58298 3648 15C
58299 3655 2C
58300 3688 15C
58301 3689 2F
58302 3691 1A
58303 3696 1A
58304 3703 17B
58305 3707 15D
58306 3725 1A
58307 3726 1A
58308 3738 2E
58309 3739 1A
58310 3764 14B

WEBB 0-6-0 2F

58320 28088 3C
58321 28091 CW
58322 28093 3C
28095 8D
28097 3A
58323 28100 CW
58324 28104 11B
58325 28105 3C
58326 28106 CW
58327 28107 8D
58328 28115 CW
58329 28116 11A
58330 28128 11B
58331 28133 11B
58332 28141 CW

58333 28152 3B
28153 4A
58334 28158 11A
58335 28166 11B
58336 28172 CW
58337 28191 11B
58338 28199 3A
58339 28202 11B
58340 28205 11B
58341 28216 3B
58342 28221 8D
58343 28227 CW
28230 3B
58344 28233 11B
58345 28234 3B
58346 28239 8D
58347 28245 CW
58348 28246 3C
58349 28247 3C
58350 28251 3C
58351 28253 8D
58352 28256 3C
58353 28262 8D
58354 28263 11B
58355 28271 4A
58356 28295 11B
58357 28296 11B
58358 28308 4A
58359 28309 3C
58360 28312 11B
58361 28313 3C

WEBB 18" 0-6-0 "CAULIFLOWER" 2F

58362 28318 12C
58363 28333 2D
58364 28335 7A
58365 28337 7A
58366 28338 9B
58367 28339 4A
58368 28345 2D
28350 5A
58369 28370 4A
58370 28372 12D
58371 28385 6C
58372 28392 7B
58373 28403 10A
58374 28404 7B
58375 28408 12D
28415 12D
58376 28417 10A
58377 28428 8D
58378 28430 3B
28441 12D
58379 28442 5D
58380 28443 9B
58381 28450 10A
58382 28451 6B
58383 28457 8D
58384 28458 5B
58385 28460 5D
58386 28464 5B
58387 28484 12D
58388 28487 2E
58389 28492 12C
58390 28494 10E
58391 28499 12D
58392 28505 7A

58393 28507 8D
58394 28509 10E
58395 28511 5B
58396 28512 5B
58397 28513 4A
58398 28515 12D
58399 28521 7D
58400 28525 12D
58401 28526 12D
58402 28527 8D
58403 28529 6C
58404 28531 2E
58405 28532 2D
28542 12D
58406 28543 4B
58407 28544 12D
58408 28547 12D
58409 28548 3D
58410 28549 10E
58411 28551 12C
58412 28553 7B
58413 28555 12D
58414 28556 3B
58415 28559 3D
58416 28561 12D
58417 28575 12C
58418 28580 12C
58419 28583 10E
58420 28585 8D
28586 3D
58421 28589 12C
58422 28592 10A
58423 28594 3C
28597 3C
58424 28598 8D
58425 28608 4A
58426 28611 2D
58427 28616 7D
58428 28618 6A
58429 28619 3E
58430 28622 4B

NORTH LONDON RAILWAY 0-6-0T 2F

58850 27505 17D
58851 27509 13B
58852 27510 13B
58853 27512 13B
58854 27513 6C
58855 27514 13B
58856 27515 17D
58857 27517 6C
58858 27520 13B
58859 27522 6C
27525 6C
58860 27527 13B
58861 27528 6C
58862 27530 17D
58863 27532 6C

NORTH LONDON RLY CRANE TANK 0-4-2ST

58865 27217 13B

WEBB 0-6-0ST 2F

58870 27480 CW

WEBB 0-6-2T 2F

58880 27553 4E
58881 27561 2B
58882 27562 7D
58883 27580 8C
58884 27585 7D
58885 27586 4E
58886 27591 3D
58887 27596 8A
58888 27602 7B
58889 27603 7B
58890 27619 10D
58891 27621 4B
58892 27625 4B
58893 27627 7D
58894 27635 4A
27648 4E
58895 27654 4E
58896 27669 3D
58897 27674 8A
58898 27681 8A
58899 7692 10E
58900 7699 8A
7700 4B
58901 7703 10A
58902 7710 4D
58903 7711 7D
7715 4B
58904 7720 10D
58905 7721 4D
58906 7730 8C
58907 7733 4D
58908 7737 10D
58909 7740 3E
58910 7741 4B
58911 7746 4D
58912 7751 8A
58913 7752 10E
58914 7756 10D
58915 7757 8A
58916 7759 3E
58917 7765 10E
58918 7769 10D
58919 7773 2B
58920 7780 4E
58921 7782 4E
58922 7787 8A
58923 7789 10D
58924 7791 8A
58925 7794 8B
7796 7A
58926 7799 10D
58927 7802 10D
58928 7803 8A
58929 7808 4D
7812 4D
58930 7816 8A
58931 7821 4E
58932 7822 7B
58933 7829 4D
58934 27830 2B
58935 7833 8A
58936 7836 4A
58937 7840 4D
7841 4D

L.N.W.R. STEAM RAIL CAR

29988 12F

Ex-London & North Eastern Railway Locomotives

4-6-2
A4 CLASS

60001* GHD
60002* GHD
60003* KX
60004* HAY
60005* GHD
60006* KX
60007* GRA
60008* GRA
60009* HAY
60010* KX
60011* HAY
60012* HAY
60013* KX
60014* GRA
60015* GRA
60016* GHD
60017* KX
60018* GHD

60019*	GHD
60020*	GHD
60021*	KX
60022*	GRA
60023*	GHD
60024*	HAY
60025*	KX
60026*	KX
60027*	HAY
60028*	GRA
60029*	KX
60030*	GRA
60031*	HAY
60032*	GRA
60033*	GRA
60034*	GRA

4-6-2
A3 CLASS

60035*	HAY
60036*	GHD
60037*	HAY
60038*	GHD
60039*	GRA
60040*	GHD
60041*	HAY
60042*	GHD
60043*	HAY
60044*	GRA
60045*	GHD
60046*	KX
60047*	KX
60048*	DON
60049*	DON
60050*	KX
60051*	KX
60052*	NWE
60053*	NWE
60054*	NWE
60055*	KX
60056*	KX
60057*	HAY
60058*	DON
60059*	KX
60060*	GHD
60061*	NWE
60062*	KX
60063*	DON
60064*	HAY
60065*	HAY
60066*	HAY
60067*	HAY
60068*	CAR
60069*	HTN
60070*	GHD
60071*	GHD
60072*	HTN
60073*	HTN
60074*	GHD
60075*	GHD
60076*	GHD
60077*	HTN
60078*	GHD
60079*	GHD
60080*	HTN
60081*	GHD
60082*	HTN
60083*	HTN
60084*	GHD
60085*	HTN
60086*	GHD
60087*	HAY
60088*	HTN
60089*	KX
60090*	NWE
60091*	CAR
60092*	HTN
60093*	CAR
60094*	HAY
60095*	CAR
60096*	KX
60097*	KX
60098*	KX
60099*	HAY
60100*	HAY
60101*	HAY
60102*	GRA
60103*	DON
60104*	KX
60105*	KX
60106*	GRA
60107*	KX
60108*	KX
60109*	KX
60110*	KX
60111*	NWE
60112*	KX

NOTE: 60068 CLASS A10 UNTIL DECEMBER 1948

4-6-2
A1/1 CLASS

60113*	KX

4-6-2
A2 CLASS

60500*	KX
60501*	ABD
60502*	ABD
60503*	HAY
60504*	HAY
60505*	HAY
60506*	HAY
60507*	KX
60508*	KX
60509*	HAY
60510*	HAY
60511*	HTN
60512*	HTN
60513*	KX
60514*	KX
60515*	HTN
60516*	HTN
60517*	HTN
60518*	GHD
60519*	HAY
60520*	DON
60521*	GHD
60522*	YK
60523*	KX
60524*	YK
60525*	DON

4-6-4
W1 CLASS

60700	10000	KX

2-6-2
V2 CLASS

60800*	KX
60801	GHD
60802	HTN
60803	NWE
60804	DEE
60805	GHD
60806	GHD
60807	GHD
60808	HTN
60809*	GHD
60810	GHD
60811	GHD
60812	HTN
60813	KX
60814	KX
60815	DON
60816	HAY
60817	KX
60818	KX
60819	ABD
60820	KX
60821	KX
60822	ABD
60823	KX
60824	ABD
60825	ABD
60826	DON
60827	ABD
60828	NWE
60829	KX
60830	DON
60831	DON
60832	DON
60833	GHD
60834	HAY
60835*	GHD
60836	HAY
60837	YK
60838	DEE
60839	YK
60840	DEE
60841	NWE
60842	NWE
60843	YK
60844	DEE
60845	DON
60846	DON
60847*	YK
60848	HAY
60849	DON
60850	NWE
60851	ABD
60852	DON
60853	COP
60854	NWE
60855	NWE
60856	YK
60857	DON
60858	NWE
60859	NWE
60860*	GHD
60861	DON
60862	NWE
60863	NWE
60864	DAR
60865	NWE
60866	NWE
60867	DON
60868	GHD
60869	NWE
60870	DON
60871	NWE
60872*	DON
60873*	KX
60874	NWE
60875	DON
60876	NWE
60877	DON
60878	NWE
60879	NWE
60880	DON
60881	DON
60882	HAY
60883	GHD
60884	GHD
60885	GHD
60886	HTN
60887	GHD
60888	ABD
60889	DON
60890	DON
60891	HTN
60892	KX
60893	NWE
60894	HAY
60895	HTN
60896	DON
60897	NWE
60898	ABD
60899	NWE
60900	KX
60901	YK
60902	DON
60903	KX
60904	YK
60905	NWE
60906	DON
60907	YK
60908	NWE
60909	KX
60910	GHD
60911	NWE
60912	NWE
60913	NWE
60914	KX
60915	KX
60916	NWE
60917	DON
60918	YK
60919	ABD
60920	DEE
60921	NWE
60922	KX
60923	GHD
60924	NWE
60925	YK
60926	GHD
60927	HAY
60928	DON
60929	YK
60930	DON
60931	HAY
60932	TWD
60933	YK
60934	YK
60935	DON
60936	NWE
60937	DEE
60938	NWE
60939	HTN
60940	GHD
60941	YK
60942	GHD
60943	DON
60944	HTN
60945	NWE
60946	YK
60947	HTN
60948	DON
60949	HTN
60950	NWE
60951	HAY
60952	GHD
60953	HAY
60954	YK
60955	HAY
60956	DON
60957	HTN
60958	HAY
60959	GHD
60960	YK
60961	YK
60962	YK
60963	DAR
60964	GHD
60965	GHD
60966	HTN
60967	GHD
60968	YK
60969	DEE
60970	ABD
60971	DEE
60972	HAY
60973	ABD
60974	YK
60975	YK
60976	YK
60977	YK
60978	YK
60979	YK
60980	HAY
60981	YK
60982	YK
60983	KX

4-6-0
B1 CLASS

61000*	PKS
61001*	PKS
61002*	PTH
61003*	PKS
61004*	PKS
61005*	PKS
61006*	PKS
61007*	HAY
61008*	PKS
61009*	STR
61010*	HLB
61011*	GHD
61012*	GHD
61013*	GHD
61014*	GHD
61015*	YK
61016*	YK
61017*	YK
61018*	YK
61019*	HTN
61020*	HTN
61021*	HTN
61022*	HTN
61023*	HTN
61024*	TWD
61025*	TWD
61026*	DON
61027*	NWE
61028*	NEA
61029*	KX
61030*	SKN
61031*	COP
61032*	SKN
61033*	COP
61034*	NEV
61035*	YK
61036*	GOR
61037*	DAR
61038*	DAR
61039*	DAR
61040*	NOR
61041	NOR
61042	NOR
61043	NOR
61044	NOR
61045	NOR
61046	NOR
61047	NOR
61048	NOR
61049	NOR
61050	NOR
61051	NOR
61052	NOR
61053	IPS
61054	IPS
61055	IPS
61056	IPS
61057	IPS
61058	IPS
61059	IPS
61060	NEV
61061	PTH

61062 NEV
61063 WFD
61064 KEI
61065 NEV
61066 WFD
61067 KIT
61068 NEV
61069 NEV
61070 NWE
61071 HLB
61072 HAY
61073 NWE
61074 HLB
61075 NWE
61076 HAY
61077 NEA
61078 WFD
61079 IMM
61080 HLB
61081 HAY
61082 IMM
61083 NEA
61084 HLB
61085 NEA
61086 LEI
61087 WFD
61088 WFD
61089 HIT
61090 HIT
61091 HIT
61092 HIT
61093 HIT
61094 HIT
61095 HIT
61096 HIT
61097 HIT
61098 HIT
61099 HIT
61100 GHD
61101 DEE
61102 DEE
61103 THJ
61104 PKS
61105 HIT
61106 HIT
61107 HIT
61108 WFD
61109 NEA
61110 LEI
61111 LEI
61112 KX
61113 KX
61114 KX
61115 YK
61116 EFD
61117 EFD
61118 THJ
61119 STR
61120 DON
61121 KX
61122 LEI
61123 LEI
61124 DON
61125 DON
61126 DON
61127 DON
61128 LEI
61129 KX
61130 LEI
61131 WFD
61132 KIT
61133 KIT
61134 KIT
61135 PKS
61136 KX
61137 KX
61138 KX
61139 KX
61140 NEA
61141 WFD
61142 IMM
61143 NWE
61144 NWE
61145 SHF
61146 KIT
61147 KIT
61148 KIT
61149 PKS
61150 SHF
61151 SHF
61152 SHF
61153 SHF
61154 SHF
61155 GOR
61156 GOR
61157 GOR
61158 GOR
61159 GOR
61160 GOR
61161 GOR
61162 GOR
61163 NEA
61164 NEA
61165 MEX
61166 MEX
61167 MEX
61168 MEX
61169 NEA
61170 DON
61171 GRA
61172 EFD
61173 DAR
61174 MEX
61175 GRA
61176 DAR
61177 GRA
61178 HAY
61179 SHF
61180 EFD
61181 SHF
61182 GOR
61183 SHF
61184 GOR
61185 LEI
61186 LEI
61187 LEI
61188 LEI
61189* SKN
61190 DON
61191 DON
61192 LEI
61193 DON
61194 DON
61195 IMM
61196 DON
61197 EFD
61198 TWD
61199 TWD
61200 KX
61201 DON
61202 IMM
61203 KX
61204 IMM
61205 GRA
61206 NWE
61207 NWE
61208 RET
61209 NWE
61210 NWE
61211 RET
61212 RET
61213 RET
61214 SKN
61215* HLB
61216 YK
61217 CAR
61218 NEV
61219 CAR
61220 SKN
61221* HAY
61222 CAR
61223 GOR
61224 HTN
61225 GOR
61226 STR
61227 GOR
61228 GOR
61229 BFD
61230 BFD
61231 RET
61232 STR
61233 STR
61234 STR
61235 STR
61236 STR
61237* NEV
61238* GHD
61239 YK
61240* YK
61241* HTN
61242* KIT
61243* EFD
61244* HAY
61245* HAY
61246* DON
61247* DON
61248* DON
61249* DON
61250* DON
61251* KX
61252 IPS
61253 IPS
61254 NOR
61255 HTN
61256 NEV
61257 NEV
61258 NEV
61259 NEV
61260 EFD
61261 EFD
61262 THJ
61263 DEE
61264 PKS
61265 DON
61266 KX
61267 ARD
61268 ARD
61269 LIN
61270 NOR
61271 NOR
61272 NOR
61273 DAR

4-6-0
B8 CLASS

61353 SHF
61354 SHF
61355 SHF
61357* SHF
61358* SHF

4-6-0
B7 CLASS

61360 SHF
61361 SHF
61362 SHF
61363 SHF
61364 GOR
61365 SHF
61366 GOR
61367 GOR
61368 GOR
61369 GOR
61370 GOR
61371 GOR
61372 SHF
61373 GOR
61374 GOR
61375 GOR
61376 GOR
61377 SHF
61378 SHF
61379 SHF
61380 GOR
61381 GOR
61382 GOR
61383 SHF
61384 SHF
61385 GOR
61386 SHF
61387 SHF
61388 GOR
61389 GOR
61390 GOR
61391 GOR
61392 GOR
61393 GOR
61394 GOR
61395 GOR
61396 GOR
61397 SHF

4-6-0
B16/1 CLASS

61400 YK
61401 YK
61402 YK

4-6-0
B16/3 CLASS

61403 YK

4-6-0
B16/1 CLASS

61404 YK
61405 YK

4-6-0
B16/2 CLASS

61406 YK

4-6-0
B16/3 CLASS

61407 YK

4-6-0
B16/1 CLASS

61408 YK
61409 YK
61410 YK
61411 YK
61412 YK
61413 YK
61414 YK
61415 YK
61416 YK

4-6-0
B16/3 CLASS

61417 YK
61418 YK

4-6-0
B16/1 CLASS

61419 YK

4-6-0
B16/3 CLASS

61420 YK

4-6-0
B16/2 CLASS

61421 YK

4-6-0
B16/1 CLASS

61422 YK
61423 YK
61424 YK
61425 YK
61426 YK
61427 YK
61428 YK
61429 YK
61430 YK
61431 YK
61432 YK
61433 YK
61434 YK

4-6-0
B16/2 CLASS

61435 YK

4-6-0
B16/1 CLASS

61436 YK

4-6-0
B16/2 CLASS

61437 YK
61438 YK

4-6-0
B16/3 CLASS

61439 YK

4-6-0
B16/1 CLASS

61440 YK
61441 YK
61442 YK
61443 YK

4-6-0
B16/3 CLASS

61444 YK

4-6-0
B16/1 CLASS

61445 YK
61446 YK
61447 YK

4-6-0
B16/3 CLASS

61448 YK
61449 YK

4-6-0
B16/1 CLASS

61450 YK
61451 YK
61452 YK

4-6-0
B16/3 CLASS

61453 YK
61454 YK

4-6-0
B16/2 CLASS

61455 YK

4-6-0
B16/1 CLASS

61456 YK

4-6-0
B16/2 CLASS

61457 YK

4-6-0
B16/1 CLASS

61458 YK
61459 YK
61460 YK
61461 YK
61462 YK

4-6-0
B16/3 CLASS

61463 YK
61464 YK

4-6-0
B16/1 CLASS

61465 YK
61466 YK

4-6-0
B16/3 CLASS

61467 YK
61468 YK

4-6-0
B9 CLASS

61469 STP
61470 LIV
61475 STP
61476 TFD

4-6-0
B4 CLASS

61482* ARD
61483 ARD
61485 ARD
61488 ARD

4-6-0
B3 CLASS

61497 IMM

4-6-0
B12/1 CLASS

61500 KEI
61501 KEI
61502 KEI
61503 KEI
61504 KIT
61505 KIT
61507 KIT
61508 KIT

4-6-0
B12/3 CLASS

61509 IPS
61510 STR

4-6-0
B12/1 CLASS

61511 KIT

4-6-0
B12/3 CLASS

61512 COL

4-6-0
B12/1 CLASS

61513 KIT

4-6-0
B12/3 CLASS

61514 STR
61515 STR
61516 IPS
61517 STR
61519 STR
61520 STR

4-6-0
B12/1 CLASS

61521 KIT

4-6-0
B12/3 CLASS

61523 COL

4-6-0
B12/1 CLASS

61524 KIT

4-6-0
B12/3 CLASS

61525 STR

4-6-0
B12/1 CLASS

61526 KIT
61528 KIT
61529 KIT

4-6-0
B12/3 CLASS

61530 STR

4-6-0
B12/1 CLASS

61532 KIT

4-6-0
B12/3 CLASS

61533 STR
61535 STR

4-6-0
B12/1 CLASS

61536 KIT

4-6-0
B12/3 CLASS

61537 STR
61538 STR

4-6-0
B12/1 CLASS

61539 KIT

4-6-0
B12/3 CLASS

61540 STR
61541 STR
61542 STR

4-6-0
B12/1 CLASS

61543 KIT

4-6-0
B12/3 CLASS

61545 STR
61546 STR
61547 STR
61549 STR
61550 STR

4-6-0
B12/1 CLASS

61552 KIT

4-6-0
B12/3 CLASS

61553 COL
61554 STR
61555 STR
61556 STR
61557 STR
61558 STR
61559 STR

4-6-0
B12/1 CLASS

61560 KIT

4-6-0
B12/3 CLASS

61561 IPS
61562 IPS

4-6-0
B12/1 CLASS

61563 KIT

4-6-0
B12/3 CLASS

61564 IPS
61565 STR
61566 IPS
61567 STR
61568 STR
61569 IPS
61570 IPS
61571 STR
61572 STR
61573 STR
61574 STR
61575 STR
61576 STR
61577 IPS
61578 STR
61579 STR
61580 STR

4-6-0
B17 CLASS

61600* IPS
61601* IPS
61602* IPS

4-6-0
B2 CLASS

61603* COL

4-6-0 B17 CLASS
61604* IPS
61605* STR
61606* STR

4-6-0
B2 CLASS

61607* COL

4-6-0
B17 CLASS

61608* CAM
61609* STR
61610* CAM
61611* CAM
61612* STR
61613* CAM

4-6-0
B2 CLASS

61614* COL
61615* COL
61616* COL
61617* CAM

4-6-0
B17 CLASS

61618* IPS
61619* CAM
61620* CAM
61621* CAM
61622* CAM
61623* CAM
61624* CAM
61625* NOR
61626* NOR
61627* CAM
61628* CAM
61629* NOR
61630* MAR
61631* CAM

4-6-0
B2 CLASS

61632* COL

4-6-0
B17 CLASS

61633* CAM
61634* IPS
61635* MAR
61636* MAR
61637* CAM
61638* CAM

4-6-0
B2 CLASS

61639* STR

4-6-0
B17 CLASS

61640* CAM
61641* CAM
61642* CAM
61643* CAM
61644* NOR
61645* IPS
61646* MAR
61647* LIN
61648* MAR
61649* IPS
61650* CLK
61651* CLK
61652* CLK
61653* CLK
61654* CAM
61655* STR
61656* MAR
61657* CLK
61658* STR
61659* NOR
61660* MAR
61661* MAR
61662* CLK
61663* CAM
61664* CLK
61665* CAM
61666* CAM
61667* CLK
61668* IPS
61669* CLK
61670* NOR

4-6-0
B2 CLASS

61671* CAM

4-6-0
B17 CLASS

61672* MAR

4-6-0
B5 CLASS

61680 MEX
61681 MEX
61685 MEX
61686 MEX
61688 MEX
61689 MEX
61690 MEX

2-6-2
V4 CLASS

61700* EFD
61701 EFD

2-6-0
K2 CLASS

61720 IMM
61721 STR
61722 IMM
61723 CLK
61724 IMM
61725 BOS
61726 CLK
61727 IMM
61728 IMM
61729 PKD
61730 STR
61731 BOS
61732 CLK
61733 IMM
61734 STR
61735 IMM
61736 NWE
61737 STR
61738 SL
61739 IMM
61740 STR
61741 CLK
61742 SL
61743 SL
61744 BOS
61745 STR
61746 STR
61747 NWE
61748 SL
61749 CLK
61750 CLK
61751 CLK
61752 STR
61753 STR
61754 STR
61755 BOS
61756 CLK
61757 COL
61758 CLK
61759 STR
61760 BOS
61761 STR
61762 BOS
61763 CLK
61764* EFD
61765 STR
61766 COL
61767 STR
61768 CLK
61769 CLK
61770 CLK
61771 CLK
61772* EFD
61773 CLK
61774* EFD
61775* EFD
61776 EFD
61777 STR
61778 STR
61779 EFD
61780 STR
61781* EFD
61782* FW
61783* FW
61784 EFD
61785 EFD
61786 EFD

61787	FW
61788*	FW
61789*	FW
61790*	FW
61791*	FW
61792	EFD
61793	EFD
61794*	EFD

2-6-0
K3 CLASS

61800	IMM
61801	CLK
61802	CLK
61803	IMM
61804	NWE
61805	MAR
61806	IMM
61807	LIN
61808	CLK
61809	NWE
61810	NWE
61811	NWE
61812	MAR
61813	HLD
61814	HLD
61815	MAR
61816	CLK
61817	MAR
61818	HTN
61819	HLD
61820	MAR
61821	CLK
61822	LIN
61823	STM
61824	CLK
61825	NWE
61826	CLK
61827	NWE
61828	NWE
61829	WFD
61830	MAR
61831	MAR
61832	NWE
61833	NWE
61834	NWE
61835	MAR
61836	IMM
61837	IMM
61838	IMM
61839	WFD
61840	NWE
61841	NWE
61842	IMM
61843	NWE
61844	NWE
61845	IMM
61846	MAR
61847	MAR
61848	NWE
61849	MAR
61850	NWE
61851	CAR
61852	LIN
61853	NWE
61854	CAR
61855	STM
61856	DON
61857	STM
61858	CAR
61859	LIN
61860	MAR
61861	DON
61862	NWE

2-6-0
K5 CLASS

61863	NWE

2-6-0
K3 CLASS

61864	NWE
61865	CLK
61866	MAR
61867	NWE
61868	NWE
61869	NWE
61870	WFD
61871	HLD
61872	HLD
61873	MAR
61874	HLD
61875	GHD
61876	STM
61877	NWE
61878	GHD
61879	STM
61880	NWE
61881	GHD
61882	CAR
61883	HLD
61884	HTN
61885	STM
61886	MAR
61887	MAR
61888	MAR
61889	MAR
61890	NWE
61891	IMM
61892	HLD
61893	MAR
61894	CLK
61895	ANN
61896	NWE
61897	GHD
61898	CAR
61899	HLD
61900	STM
61901	HTN
61902	HLD
61903	HLD
61904	GHD
61905	CLK
61906	HTN
61907	DON
61908	WFD
61909	STM
61910	DON
61911	STM
61912	IMM
61913	WFD
61914	MAR
61915	NWE
61916	STM
61917	HTN
61918	DON
61919	MAR
61920	HLD
61921	NOR
61922	HLD
61923	HLD
61924	STM
61925	LIN
61926	LOW
61927	HLD
61928	GHD
61929	NWE
61930	GHD
61931	STM
61932	HLD
61933	STM
61934	HLD
61935	HLD
61936	CAR
61937	CAR
61938	NWE
61939	NOR
61940	MAR
61941	HLD
61942	NOR
61943	WFD
61944	LIN
61945	HLD
61946	NWE
61947	NOR
61948	MAR
61949	LOW
61950	NWE
61951	NWE
61952	HTN
61953	NOR
61954	NWE
61955	STM
61956	WFD
61957	NOR
61958	LOW
61959	LOW
61960	LIN
61961	NWE
61962	HTN
61963	IMM
61964	LIN
61965	HLD
61966	LIN
61967	NWE
61968	STM
61969	HTN
61970	NOR
61971	NOR
61972	NWE
61973	NOR
61974	ANN
61975	ANN
61976	ANN
61977	ANN
61978	DON
61979	ANN
61980	ANN
61981	LOW
61982	LIN
61983	STM
61984	HTN
61985	GHD
61986	GHD
61987	HTN
61988	STM
61989	NOR
61990	STM
61991	STM
61992	STM

2-6-0
K4 CLASS

61993*	EFD
61994*	EFD
61995*	FW
61996*	FW

2-6-0
K1/1 CLASS

61997*	NWE

2-6-0
K4 CLASS

61998*	EFD

4-4-0
D3 CLASS

62000	GRA

4-4-0
D31 CLASS

62059	CAR
62060	CAR
62062	KIT
62064	KIT
62065	KIT
62066	KIT
62072	BGT

4-4-0
D17/2 CLASS

62111	YK
62112	YK

4-4-0
D3 CLASS

62116	CLK
62122	SL
62123	CLK
62124	SL
62125	CLK
62126	CLK
62128	NWE
62131	NWE
62132	IMM
62133	STV
62135	CLK
62137	SL
62139	IMM
62140	CLK
62143	LTH
62144	SL
62145	SL
62148	HIT

4-4-0
D2 CLASS

62150	CLK
62151	CLK
62152	YB
62153	CLK
62154	BOS
62155	MC
62156	MC
62157	MC
62160	HIT
62161	GRA
62163	HIT
62165	NWE
62167	GRA
62169	CLK
62172	GRA
62173	GRA
62175	YB
62177	CLK
62179	BOS
62180	BOS
62181	BOS
62187	CLK
62188	CLK
62189	MC
62190	NWE
62193	CLK
62194	CLK
62195	MC
62197	MC
62198	CLK
62199	CLK

4-4-0
D1 CLASS

62203	NOR
62205	DFU
62207	YB
62208	HAW
62209	STG
62214	HAY
62215	PTH

4-4-0
D41 CLASS

62225	KIT
62227	KIT
62228	KIT
62229	KIT
62230	KIT
62231	KIT
62232	KIT
62234	KEI
62235	KEI
62238	KEI
62240	KEI
62241	KIT
62242	KIT
62243	KEI
62246	KEI
62247	KEI
62248	KEI
62249	KEI
62251	KEI
62252	KEI
62255	KEI
62256	KEI

4-4-0
D40 CLASS

62260	KIT
62261	KIT
62262	KEI
62264	KEI
62265	KIT
62267	KEI
62268	KIT
62269	KIT
62270	KIT
62271	KIT
62272	KIT
62273*	KIT
62274*	KIT
62275*	KIT
62276*	KIT
62277*	KIT
62278*	KIT
62279*	KIT

4-4-0
D9 CLASS

62300	TFD
62301	TFD
62302	LIV
62303	LIV
62304	LIV
62305	TFD
62306	LIV
62307*	TFD
62308	LIV
62309	LIV
62311	WAL
62312	TFD
62313	TFD
62314	STP
62315	LIV
62317	TFD
62318	LIV
62319	LIV
62321	LIV
62322	STP
62324	LIV
62325	TFD
62329	TFD
62330	TFD
62332	LIV
62333	LIV

4-4-0
D20 CLASS

62340	SEL

62341	SEL
62342	SBK
62343	SBK
62344	TWD
62345	BRI
62347	TWD
62348	SEL
62349	BLA
62351	TWD
62352	TWD
62353	BRI
62354	TWD
62355	HLB
62357	TWD
62358	TWD
62359	WHL
62360	BLA
62361	HLB
62362	TWD
62363	SBK
62365	SKN
62366	SBK
62367	HLB
62369	HLB
62370	SBK
62371	BLA
62372	SEL
62373	SBK
62374	SEL
62375	SBK
62376	SEL
62377	TWD
62378	SEL
62379	YK
62380	TWD
62381	SEL
62382	HLB
62383	BRI
62384	WHL
62386	SEL
62387	WHL
62388	NLN
62389	SBK
62390	SKN
62391	NLN
62392	SBK
62395	SBK
62396	TWD
62397	NLN

4-4-0
D29 CLASS

62400*	STM
62401*	THJ
62402*	STM
62403*	HAY
62404*	STM
62405*	STM
62406*	THJ
62409*	DEE
62410*	DEE
62411*	POL
62412*	DEE
62413*	HAY

4-4-0
D30 CLASS

62417*	HAW
62418*	DEE
62419*	THJ
62420*	STM
62421*	STM
62422*	HAW
62423*	HAW
62424*	STM
62425*	HAW
62426*	PTH
62427*	PTH
62428*	HAW
62429*	THJ
62430*	THJ
62431*	THJ
62432*	HAW
62434*	DEE
62435*	STM
62436*	THJ
62437*	HAY
62438*	DEE
62439*	BGT
62440*	HAW
62441*	DFU
62442*	THJ

4-4-0
D32 CLASS

62443	STM
62444	STM
62445	STM
62446	THJ
62448	BLA
62449	BLA
62450	STM
62451	STM
62453	STM
62454	STM

4-4-0
D33 CLASS

62455	DFU
62457	PTH
62458	BGT
62459	DFU
62460	EFD
62461	STG
62462	EFD
62463	BGT
62464	DFU
62466	PTH

4-4-0
D34 CLASS

62467*	THJ
62468*	THJ
62469*	EFD
62470*	FW
62471*	STM
62472*	EFD
62473*	EFD
62474*	EFD
62475*	THJ
62476*	POL
62477*	EFD
62478*	THJ
62479*	EFD
62480*	FW
62481*	EFD
62482*	EFD
62483*	STM
62484*	STM
62485*	DEE
62487*	STM
62488*	STM
62489*	EFD
62490*	STM
62492*	THJ
62493*	EFD
62494*	STM
62495*	STM
62496*	EFD
62497*	EFD
62498*	EFD

4-4-0
D15 CLASS

62501	KL
62502	KL
62503	BSE
62504	KL
62505	KL
62506	KL
62507	KL
62508	BSE
62509	STR

4-4-0
D16 CLASS

62510	NOR
62511	NOR

4-4-0
D15 CLASS

62512	KL

4-4-0
D16 CLASS

62513	KL
62514	KL
62515	MC
62516	CAM
62517	YAR
62518	KL
62519	COL

4-4-0
D15 CLASS

62520	MC

4-4-0
D16 CLASS

62521	YAR
62522	NOR
62523	COL
62524	YAR
62525	CAM
62526	IPS
62527	CAM

4-4-0
D15 CLASS

62528	MC

4-4-0
D16 CLASS

62529	NOR
62530	CAM
62531	CAM
62532	STR
62533	MC
62534	SL
62535	NOR
62536	CAM

4-4-0
D15 CLASS

62538	STR

4-4-0
D16 CLASS

62539	MAR
62540	YAR
62541	NOR
62542	MAR
62543	SL
62544	YAR
62545	NOR
62546*	YAR
62547	MAR
62548	MAR
62549	CAM
62551	CAM
62552	IPS
62553	YAR
62554	NOR
62555	NOR
62556	IPS
62557	CAM
62558	SL
62559	SL
62560	IPS
62561	YB
62562	MC
62563	NOR
62564	NOR
62565	COL
62566	BSE
62567	CAM
62568	NOR
62569	KL
62570	NOR
62571	CAM
62572	SL
62573	SL
62574	CAM
62575	KL
62576	NOR
62577	NOR
62578	MC
62579	MAR
62580	YAR
62581	NOR
62582	KL
62583	NOR
62584	MAR
62585	NOR
62586	YAR
62587	STR
62588	YAR
62589	MAR
62590	IPS
62591	YAR
62592	YB
62593	LOW
62594	YAR
62596	YB
62597	YAR
62598	COL
62599	NOR
62600	NOR
62601	CAM
62602	STR
62603	MAR
62604	YAR
62605	MAR
62606	CAM
62607	CAM
62608	COL
62609	COL
62610	NOR
62611	IPS
62612	IPS
62613	YB
62614	KL
62615	BSE
62616	NOR
62617	COL
62618	CAM
62619	NOR
62620	NOR

4-4-0
D10 CLASS

62650*	NTH
62651*	TFD
62652*	NTH
62653*	LIV
62654*	SHF
62655*	NTH
62656*	TFD
62657*	SHF
62658*	LIV
62659*	SHF

4-4-0
D11 CLASS

62660*	IMM
62661*	IMM
62662*	IMM
62663*	IMM
62664*	IMM
62665*	IMM
62666*	IMM
62667*	IMM
62668*	IMM
62669*	IMM
62670*	IMM
62671*	EFD
62672*	EFD
62673*	EFD
62674*	EFD
62675*	EFD
62676*	EFD
62677*	HAY
62678*	HAY
62679*	HAY
62680*	EFD
62681*	EFD
62682*	EFD
62683*	HAY
62684*	EFD
62685*	HAY
62686*	EFD
62687*	EFD
62688*	EFD
62689*	EFD
62690*	HAY
62691*	HAY
62692*	HAY
62693*	HAY
62694*	HAY

4-4-0
D49/1 "SHIRE" CLASS

62700*	HLB
62701*	HLB
62702*	STM
62703*	HLB
62704*	THJ
62705*	HAY
62706*	HAY
62707*	HLB
62708*	THJ
62709*	HAY
62710*	HLB
62711*	HAY
62712*	HAY
62713*	DEE
62714*	PTH
62715*	STM
62716*	THJ
62717*	THJ
62718*	DEE
62719*	HAY
62720*	HLB
62721*	HAY
62722*	HLB
62723*	HLB
62724*	HLB
62725*	PTH

4-4-0
D49/2 "HUNT" CLASS

62726*	SBK
62727*	HLB

4-4-0
D49/1"SHIRE" CLASS

62728*	DEE
62729*	THJ
62730*	CAR
62731*	CAR

62732* CAR
62733* HAY
62734* CAR
62735* CAR

4-4-0
D49/2 "HUNT" CLASS

62736* GHD
62737* HLB
62738* GHD
62739* GHD
62740* YK
62741* HLB
62742* GHD
62743* HLB
62744* HLB
62745* GHD
62746* NEV
62747* GHD
62748* NEV
62749* GHD
62750* GHD
62751* YK
62752* SBK
62753* SBK
62754* HLB
62755* YK
62756* NEV
62757* HLB
62758* NEV
62759* YK
62760* YK
62761* YK
62762* SBK
62763* YK
62764* GHD
62765* NEV
62766* GHD
62767* HLB

4-4-0
D49/4 REBUILT
"HUNT" CLASS

62768* SBK

4-4-0
D49/2 "HUNT" CLASS

62769* NEV
62770* NEV
62771* GHD
62772* NEV
62773* SBK
62774* NEV
62775* NEV

2-4-0
E4 CLASS

62780 CAM
62781 CAM
62782 NOR
62783 CAM
62784 CAM
62785 BSE
62786 CAM
62787 NOR
62788 CAM
62789 NOR
62790 CAM
62791 CAM
62792 NOR
62793 NOR
62794 CAM
62795 CAM
62796 CAM
62797 NOR

4-4-2
C1 CLASS

62808 NWE
62810 GRA
62817 KX
62821 KX
62822 GRA
62828 ARD
62829 ARD
62839 NWE
62849 ARD
62854 DON
62870 GRA
62871 NWE
62875 COP
62876 GRA
62877 DON
62881 COP
62885 DON

4-4-2
C4 CLASS

62900 BOS
62901 BOS
62902 IMM
62903 IMM
62908 LIN
62909 LIN
62910 LIN
62912 LIN
62914 LIN
62915 LIN
62916 LIN
62917 LIN
62918 LIN
62919 BOS
62920 BOS
62921 BOS
62922 BOS
62923 BOS
62924 BOS
62925 BOS

4-4-2
C6 CLASS

62933 HLD
62937 GHD

4-4-2
C7 CLASS

62954 SCA
62970 HLD
62972 SCA
62973 SCA
62975 SCA
62978 DAR
62981 DAR
62982 HLD
62983 HLD
62988 HLD
62989 SCA
62992 SCA
62993 SCA
62995 HLD

0-8-0
Q4 CLASS

63200 ARD
63201 GRA
63202 BRN
63203 BRN
63204 BRN
63205 ARD
63206 GRA
63207 GRA
63210 ARD
63212 BRN
63213 ARD
63214 BRN
63216 BRN
63217 BFD
63219 BRN
63220 BRN
63221 ARD
63223 ARD
63224 ARD
63225 ARD
63226 ARD
63227 BRN
63228 GRA
63229 GRA
63231 ARD
63232 ARD
63233 BRN
63234 GRA
63235 BRN
63236 ARD
63238 BRN
63240 GRA
63241 ARD
63243 GRA

0-8-0
Q5 CLASS

63250 WHL
63251 BOR
63252 HAV
63253 WHL
63254 BOR
63255 DAR
63256 WHL
63257 BOR
63259 BOR
63260 MID
63261 BOR
63262 SEL
63263 MID
63264 BOR
63267 BOR
63268 MID
63270 HAV
63271 BOR
63272 CUD
63273 MID
63274 TDK
63275 BOR
63276 SEL
63277 DAR
63278 DAR
63279 SEL
63280 SEL
63281 WHL
63282 BOR
63283 BOR
63284 BOR
63285 MID
63286 BOR
63287 BOR
63289 BOR
63290 SEL
63291 MID
63292 MID
63293 WHL
63294 WHL
63295 MID
63296 BOR
63297 WHL
63298 BOR
63299 HAV
63300 WHL
63301 HAV
63303 WHL
63305 MID
63306 HAV
63307 DAR
63308 MID
63310 SEL
63311 CUD
63312 SEL
63313 SEL
63314 AUK
63315 AUK
63316 MID
63317 MID
63318 WHL
63319 MID
63321 BOR
63322 MID
63323 MID
63326 BOR
63327 NPT
63328 DAR
63330 DAR
63331 HAV
63332 CUD
63333 MID
63334 DAR
63335 DAR
63336 WHL
63338 NPT
63339 MID

0-8-0
Q6 CLASS

63340 HAV
63341 NPT
63342 BOR
63343 NPT
63344 NPT
63345 NPT
63346 CON
63347 NPT
63348 WHL
63349 NPT
63350 NPT
63351 TDK
63352 TDK
63353 BLA
63354 NPT
63355 NPT
63356 BLA
63357 CON
63358 NPT
63359 CON
63360 NPT
63361 CON
63362 TDK
63363 TDK
63364 MID
63365 CON
63366 NPT
63367 SKN
63368 MID
63369 SKN
63370 NPT
63371 NPT
63372 CON
63373 NPT
63374 HAV
63375 NPT
63376 BLA
63377 BOR
63378 SEL
63379 CON
63380 SKN
63381 BLA
63382 SEL
63383 WHL
63384 NPT
63385 BLA
63386 NPT
63387 SEL
63388 BOR
63389 NPT
63390 BLA
63391 BLA
63392 WHL
63393 SKN
63394 BLA
63395 WHL
63396 NPT
63397 NPT
63398 BLA
63399 BLA
63400 BOR
63401 NPT
63402 BOR
63403 BLA
63404 CON
63405 NPT
63406 SEL
63407 SKN
63408 SEL
63409 NPT
63410 WHL
63411 NPT
63412 BLA
63413 BLA
63414 WHL
63415 NPT
63416 HAV
63417 NPT
63418 CON
63419 NPT
63420 NPT
63421 WHL
63422 WHL
63423 NPT
63424 WHL
63425 NPT
63426 NPT
63427 WHL
63428 BLA
63429 SEL
63430 NPT
63431 NPT
63432 BLA
63433 CON
63434 BOR
63435 WHL
63436 SEL
63437 BLA
63438 NPT
63439 CON
63440 SEL
63441 BLA
63442 NPT
63443 NPT
63444 BLA
63445 NPT
63446 NPT
63447 SEL
63448 BLA
63449 SEL
63450 SEL
63451 SEL
63452 WHL
63453 NPT
63454 WHL
63455 CON
63456 SEL
63457 WHL
63458 NPT
63459 NPT

0-8-0
Q7 CLASS

63460 TDK
63461 TDK

63462 TDK
63463 TDK
63464 TDK
63465 TDK
63466 TDK
63467 TDK
63468 TDK
63469 TDK
63470 TDK
63471 TDK
63472 TDK
63473 TDK
63474 TDK

2-8-0
03 CLASS

63475 FRO
63476 FRO
63477 FRO
63478 FRO
63479 FRO
63480 FRO
63481 FRO
63482 FRO
63483 FRO
63484 FRO
63485 FRO
63486 FRO
63488 FRO
63489 FRO
63491 FRO
63493 FRO
63494 FRO

2-8-0
04 CLASS

63570 TUX
63571 ANN
63572 DON
63573 CLK
63574 CLK
63575 ANN
63576 MEX
63577 MEX

2-8-0
01 CLASS

63578 GOR

2-8-0
04 CLASS

63579 SHF
63580 ANN
63581 SHF
63582 ANN
63583 SHF
63584 FRO
63585 MEX
63586 DON
63587 DON
63588 SHF
63589 ANN

2-8-0
01 CLASS

63590 GOR
63591 GOR
63592 GOR

2-8-0
04 CLASS

63593 DON

2-8-0
01 CLASS

63594 DON

2-8-0
04 CLASS

63595 FRO
63596 ANN
63597 LNG
63598 DON
63599 CLK
63600 DON
63601 DON
63602 FRO
63603 TDK
63604 TUX
63605 CLK
63606 FRO
63607 DON
63608 RET
63609 STV

2-8-0
01 CLASS

63610 THJ

2-8-0
04 CLASS

63611 MEX
63612 MEX
63613 STV
63614 ANN
63615 LNG
63616 DON
63617 DON
63618 ANN

2-8-0
01 CLASS

63619 GOR

2-8-0
04 CLASS

63620 TDK
63621 DON
63622 SHF
63623 DON
63624 DON
63625 MEX
63626 FRO
63627 DON
63628 HLD
63629 SHF

2-8-0
01 CLASS

63630 GOR

2-8-0
04 CLASS

63631 ANN
63632 MEX
63633 ANN
63634 IMM
63635 ANN
63636 CLK
63637 RET
63638 ANN
63639 CLK
63640 FRO
63641 CLK
63642 FRO
63643 DON
63644 LNG
63645 FRO

2-8-0
01 CLASS

63646 GOR

2-8-0
04 CLASS

63647 DON
63648 MEX
63649 FRO

2-8-0
01 CLASS

63650 GOR

2-8-0
04 CLASS

63651 LNG

2-8-0
01 CLASS

63652 GOR

2-8-0
04 CLASS

63653 MAR
63654 RET
63655 FRO
63656 MEX
63657 DON
63658 MAR
63659 DON
63660 DON
63661 SHF
63662 ANN

2-8-0
01 CLASS

63663 GOR

2-8-0
04 CLASS

63664 HLD
63665 LNG
63666 MEX
63667 TDK
63668 DON
63669 FRO

2-8-0
01 CLASS

63670 GOR

2-8-0
04 CLASS

63671 DON
63672 MEX
63673 HLS
63674 ANN
63675 STV

2-8-0
01 CLASS

63676 TDK

2-8-0
04 CLASS

63677 LNG

2-8-0
01 CLASS

63678 GOR

2-8-0
04 CLASS

63679 IMM
63680 SHF
63681 ANN
63682 DON
63683 ARD
63684 DON
63685 ANN
63686 SHF

2-8-0
01 CLASS

63687 GOR

2-8-0
04 CLASS

63688 RET

2-8-0
01 CLASS

63689 GOR

2-8-0
04 CLASS

63690 FRO
63691 TUX
63692 IMM
63693 DON
63694 ANN
63695 CLK
63696 FRO
63697 DON
63698 DON
63699 ANN
63700 ANN
63701 MAR
63702 STV
63703 MEX
63704 CAM
63705 CAM
63706 ANN
63707 MEX
63708 CAM
63709 MEX
63710 SHF

2-8-0
01 CLASS

63711 GOR
63712 TDK

2-8-0
04 CLASS

63713 CLK
63714 SHF
63715 MEX
63716 ANN
63717 MEX
63718 CAM
63719 DON
63720 ANN
63721 CLK
63722 ANN
63723 ANN
63724 CAM

2-8-0
01 CLASS

63725 GOR

2-8-0
04 CLASS

63726 FRO
63727 MEX
63728 DON
63729 CLK
63730 CAM
63731 DON
63732 HLS
63733 SHF
63734 STV
63735 ANN
63736 RET
63737 SHF
63738 DON
63739 ANN

2-8-0
01 CLASS

63740 TDK

2-8-0
04 CLASS

63741 DON
63742 ANN
63743 ANN
63744 FRO
63745 DON
63746 STV
63747 MEX
63748 ANN
63749 STV
63750 CLK
63751 TDK

2-8-0
01 CLASS

63752 GOR

2-8-0
04 CLASS

63753 TDK
63754 TDK

2-8-0
01 CLASS

63755 TDK

2-8-0
04 CLASS

63756 ANN
63757 DON
63758 DON
63759 ANN

2-8-0
01 CLASS

63760 TDK

2-8-0
04 CLASS

63761 ANN
63762 ANN
63763 RET
63764 HLD
63765 DON
63766 SHF
63767 ANN

2-8-0
01 CLASS

63768 GOR

2-8-0
04 CLASS

63769 TDK
63770 HLD
63771 SHF
63772 HLD

2-8-0
01 CLASS

63773 GOR

2-8-0
04 CLASS

63774 RET
63775 RET
63776 MEX

2-8-0
01 CLASS

63777 GOR

2-8-0
04 CLASS

63778 FRO
63779 CAM

2-8-0
01 CLASS

63780 GOR

2-8-0
04 CLASS

63781 CLK
63782 RET
63783 SHF

2-8-0
01 CLASS

63784 GOR

2-8-0
04 CLASS

63785 RET

2-8-0
01 CLASS

63786 GOR

2-8-0
04 CLASS

63787 CLK
63788 FRO

2-8-0
01 CLASS

63789 GOR

2-8-0
04 CLASS

63790 SHF
63791 MEX

2-8-0
01 CLASS

63792 MAR

2-8-0
04 CLASS

63793 FRO
63794 ANN

2-8-0
01 CLASS

63795 GOR
63796 GOR

2-8-0
04 CLASS

63797 CLK
63798 CLK
63799 ANN
63800 DON
63801 ANN
63802 FRO

2-8-0
01 CLASS

63803 GOR

2-8-0
04 CLASS

63804 ANN
63805 ANN

2-8-0
01 CLASS

63806 THJ

2-8-0
04 CLASS

63807 MEX

2-8-0
01 CLASS

63808 GOR

2-8-0
04 CLASS

63809 ANN
63812 HLD
63813 MEX
63816 HLD

2-8-0
01 CLASS

63817 GOR

2-8-0
04 CLASS

63818 FRO
63819 TUX
63821 SHF
63822 SHF
63823 HLD
63824 FRO
63827 CLK
63828 TDK
63829 ANN
63832 DON
63833 MEX
63835 TDK
63836 CAM
63837 LNG
63838 STV
63839 CAM
63840 MEX
63841 ANN
63842 MEX
63843 HLD
63845 TDK
63846 SHF
63847 DON
63848 CLK
63849 HLS
63850 STV
63851 ANN
63852 TUX
63853 ANN

2-8-0
01 CLASS

63854 GOR

2-8-0
04 CLASS

63855 HLD
63856 TDK
63857 TDK
63858 CLK
63859 ANN
63860 SHF
63861 TUX
63862 ANN

2-8-0
01 CLASS

63863 GOR

2-8-0
04 CLASS

63864 DON

2-8-0
01 CLASS

63865 GOR

63867 MAR
63868 GOR
63869 GOR

2-8-0
04 CLASS

63870 MEX

2-8-0
01 CLASS

63872 GOR

2-8-0
04 CLASS

63873 ANN

2-8-0
01 CLASS

63874 TDK

2-8-0
04 CLASS

63876 ANN
63877 RET
63878 IMM

2-8-0
01 CLASS

63879 GOR

2-8-0
04 CLASS

63880 CAM
63881 TDK
63882 SHF
63883 DON
63884 DON
63885 TUX

2-8-0
01 CLASS

63886 GOR
63887 GOR

2-8-0
04 CLASS

63888 SHF
63889 STV

2-8-0
01 CLASS

63890 GOR

2-8-0
04 CLASS

63891 DON
63893 ANN
63894 ANN
63895 CLK
63897 CAM
63898 CAM
63899 ANN
63900 DON

2-8-0
01 CLASS

63901 GOR

2-8-0
04 CLASS

63902 IMM
63904 CAM
63905 RET
63906 MEX
63907 RET
63908 RET

63911 DON
63912 ANN
63913 CAM
63914 RET
63915 DON
63917 IMM
63920 FRO

2-8-0
02 CLASS

63921 LNG
63922 FRO
63923 LNG
63924 LNG
63925 LNG
63926 LNG
63927 LNG
63928 LNG
63929 GRA
63930 GRA
63931 GRA
63932 GRA
63933 GRA
63934 FRO
63935 GRA
63936 GRA
63937 FRO
63938 GRA
63939 FRO
63940 GRA
63941 FRO
63942 LNG
63943 LNG
63944 FRO
63945 LNG
63946 LNG
63947 MAR
63948 MAR
63949 MAR
63950 MAR
63951 MAR
63952 MAR
63953 MAR
63954 MAR
63955 MAR
63956 MAR
63957 MAR
63958 MAR
63959 MAR
63960 MAR
63961 MAR
63962 MAR
63963 FRO
63964 LNG
63965 LNG
63966 LNG
63967 LNG
63968 LNG
63969 LNG
63970 LNG
63971 LNG
63972 LNG
63973 LNG
63974 LNG
63975 FRO
63976 LNG
63977 LNG
63978 LNG
63979 LNG
63980 LNG
63981 LNG
63982 LNG
63983 LNG
63984 LNG
63985 LNG
63986 LNG
63987 LNG

0-6-0
J3 CLASS

64105 HIT
64106 NWE
64107 RET

0-6-0
J4 CLASS

64109 NWE
64110 NWE
64112 NWE

0-6-0
J3 CLASS

64114 HIT
64115 BOS
64116 ARD
64117 HIT
64118 NWE
64119 ARD

0-6-0
J4 CLASS

64120 NWE
64121 NWE

0-6-0
J3 CLASS

64122 HIT
64123 NWE
64124 RET
64125 RET
64127 ARD
64128 NWE
64129 ARD
64131 NWE
64132 BOS
64133 RET
64135 NWE
64136 NWE
64137 BOS
64140 HIT
64141 RET
64142 ARD
64145 HIT
64148 RET
64150 RET
64151 NWE
64152 RET
64153 HIT
64158 NWE

0-6-0
J4 CLASS

64160 NWE
64162 NWE

0-6-0
J3 CLASS

64163 SL

0-6-0
J4 CLASS

64167 SL

0-6-0
J6 CLASS

64170 BFD
64171 NWE
64172 GRA
64173 COP
64174 ARD
64175 GRA
64176 NWE
64177 NWE
64178 GRA
64179 DON

Built new in 1948, 7400 class 0-6-0PT No. 7436 stands in Oxford shed yard during its first year. These Collett designed engines were for passenger work, but were not fitted for push-and pull duties. No. 7436 remained at Oxford for many years, but ended up at Bristol where withdrawal took place in June 1964 from St Philip's Marsh.

R. H. G. Simpson

"Dukedog" 4-4-0 No. 9010 at Banbury shed on Sunday 18th September 1949. After rebuilding, using the frames from 'Bulldog' class No. 3402, 9010 (then carrying the number 3210 and name *Earl Cairns*) entered traffic in April 1937 and was allocated to Aberystwyth. Withdrawn in July 1957 from Oswestry.

G. W. Sharpe

LSWR M7 class 0-4-4T No. 23 stands outside Salisbury shed on Sunday 29th May 1949. This M7 had been transferred from Barnstaple to Salisbury during February 1949 and was renumbered 30023 in December the same year. Built in January 1899, withdrawal came during the week ended 7th October 1961 from Barnstaple, then coded 72E.

L. Hanson

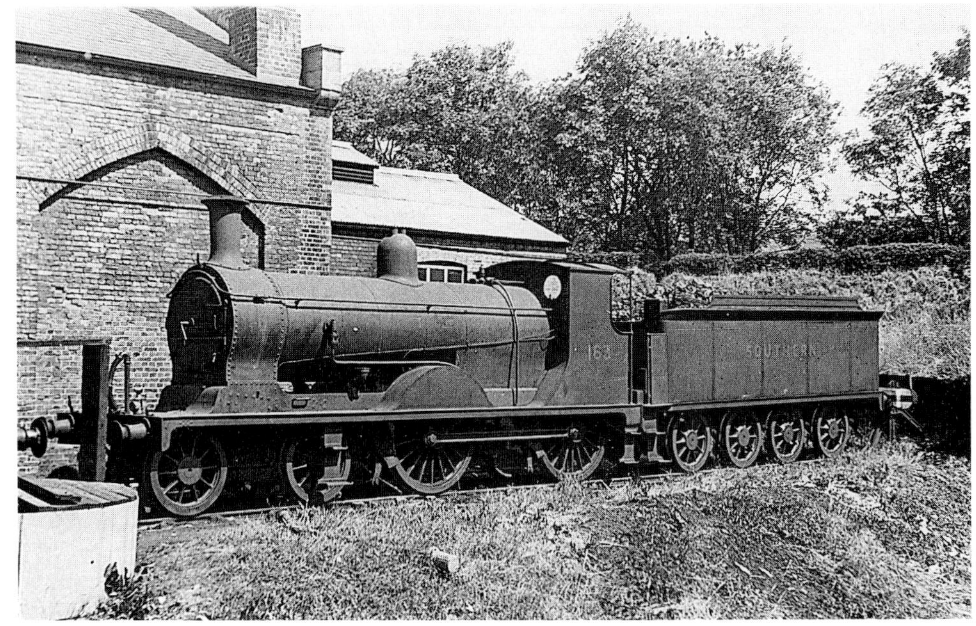

Drummond's LSWR L11 class 4-4-0 No. 163 at its home shed, Yeovil Town, in 1948. Transfer to Nine Elms took place in December 1949 when renumbering to 30163 also took place. It remained at this London shed until withdrawal during the week ended 27th October 1951. The locomotive was built in September 1903.

R. H. G. Simpson

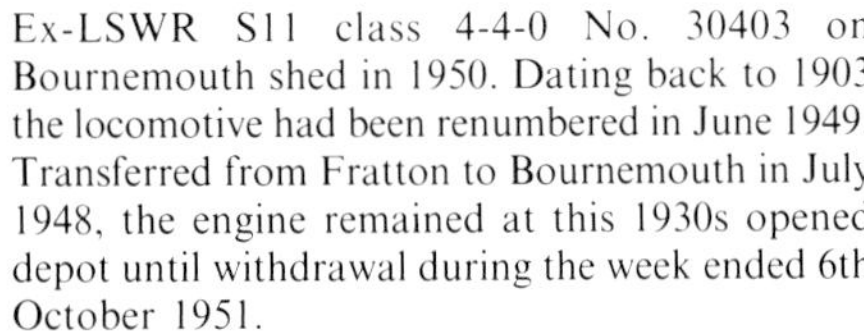

Ex-LSWR S11 class 4-4-0 No. 30403 on Bournemouth shed in 1950. Dating back to 1903 the locomotive had been renumbered in June 1949. Transferred from Fratton to Bournemouth in July 1948, the engine remained at this 1930s opened depot until withdrawal during the week ended 6th October 1951.

G. W. Sharpe

N15 'King Arthur' class 4-6-0 No. 30448 *Sir Tristram* at Exmouth Junction shed on Saturday 25th June 1949. Dating back to May 1925, this was Urie's passenger express design for the LSWR. The tenders were taken from earlier Drummond designed engines. Withdrawn from Salisbury during the week ended 27th August 1960, the locomotive was cut up at Eastleigh Works during September.

G. W. Sharpe

Dumped on its home shed Eastleigh in July 1951 is D15 class 4-4-0 No. 463 (BR No. 30463). The tender bears evidence that this locomotive had been converted for oil burning in 1946. Dating back to February 1912, the engine was withdrawn during the week ended 1st December 1951 without being reconverted to coal or renumbered and was cut up at Eastleigh Works during the following week.
G. W. Sharpe

A much happier looking D15 than the one above. Eastleigh was the home for the whole class in 1948 and remained so for a number of years. Here, No. 30466 is at home in September 1949 shortly after being renumbered. This particular locomotive was built in July 1912 and withdrawn during the week ended 30th August 1952 from Eastleigh.
G. W. Sharpe

S15 class 4-6-0 No. 506, renumbered 30506 in August 1949. This Urie, LSWR design dated back to 1920, this particular example being built in October. Feltham shed was the home for all the earlier examples in 1948 and this was the location for this photograph, taken on Sunday 25th April 1948. Withdrawal came during the week ended 5th January 1964 from Feltham but happily it survives today on the Mid-Hants Railway.
G. W. Sharpe

0395 class 0-6-0 No. 30576 at Ashford shed on Saturday 24th April 1948, freshly repainted and outshopped. This was the first of its class to be put through Ashford Works. They were more usually dealt with at Eastleigh. This Adams designed LSWR locomotive dated back to May 1883. Surprisingly in view of its works visit, it was withdrawn from Guildford shed in December 1950. The last of this class to remain in service, No. 30567, was not withdrawn until September 1959 from Feltham.
G. W. Sharpe

Axminster station is the setting for this view of Adams 0415 class 4-4-2T No. 3488 (BR No. 30583) leaving with the Lyme Regis branch train in 1948. Renumbering was not carried out until October 1949. Dating back to March 1885, this engine survived until July 1961 and was withdrawn along with the other survivor, No. 30582. This was not the end, for the Bluebell Railway purchased No. 30583 and she can still be seen working.
G. W. Sharpe

Drummond C14 class 0-4-0T No. 3741 (BR No. 30588) at Eastleigh shed along with B4 class 0-4-0T No. 91 (BR No. 30091) in August 1948. The B4 was withdrawn the same month, last shed Plymouth Friary, without being renumbered. No. 3741 was renumbered in December 1950 and was withdrawn in December 1956 from Eastleigh.
G. W. Sharpe

M7 class 0-4-4T No. 676 (BR No. 30676) at Nine Elms shed in 1948, painted in malachite green and fully lined out. This special treatment was so that the engine could be used as "Royal Shunter" at Waterloo for when any of the Royal Family were travelling. No. 676 was confined to shed duty No. 59 which enabled it to spend sufficient time in the shed to be cleaned each day. Built in November 1897, withdrawal came in July 1961 from Exmouth Junction.

G. W. Sharpe

T9 class 4-4-0 No. 30707 at Exmouth Junction shed in 1948. Drummond's design for the LSWR, this particular locomotive dated back to June 1899 and was withdrawn in March 1961 from Bournemouth shed.

G. W. Sharpe

Maunsell N15 'King Arthur' class 4-6-0 No. 30749 *Iseult* at Eastleigh shed shortly after renumbering in 1948. Built in September 1922, withdrawal came in June 1957 from Basingstoke shed. The name was later transferred to BR Standard 4-6-0 No. 73116.

G. W. Sharpe

Cheriton, near Folkestone, is the setting for this view of 'Schools' class 4-4-0 No. 929 *Malvern* on a 'down' passenger train on Saturday 17th July 1948. Built in August 1934, the engine's first home was Fratton. This was the last new design of this wheel arrangement to be built. It was a powerful and successful class and was allocated the power classification of 5P. Renumbered 30929 in January 1949, withdrawal came in December 1962, the last allocation being Brighton.

L. Hanson

Three for the price of one! The daily spectacle of trains being hauled up the steep incline out of Folkestone Harbour will always be a cherished memory for lovers of steam engines. The date is Friday 15th July 1949 and R1 class 0-6-0Ts Nos 1107 and 1337 plus R1 class 0-4-4T No. 1708 attempt the climb. No. 1708 was never renumbered into BR stock and was withdrawn during the first week in October 1952 from Faversham. Nos 31107 and 31337 were not renumbered until the 1950s and were both withdrawn from Nine Elms in August 1959 and February 1960 respectively.

L. Hanson

Another of the R1 class 0-6-0T, this time No. 1147 retaining the original round cab and fitted with cut-down boiler mountings for working the erstwhile Canterbury and Whitstable line. The date is Wednesday 13th July 1949 and it is running alongside Tram Road, Folkestone on a van train. Renumbered 31147 in June 1951, the R1 lasted until October 1958, its last shed being Ashford.

L. Hanson

H class 0-4-4T No. 31161 at Dover on Tuesday 12th July 1949. This was a Wainwright SECR design dating back to 1904, and No. 31161 was fitted out for push-pull working with a power classification of 1P. It was withdrawn during the week ended 11th November 1961 from Tunbridge Wells West.

L. Hanson

Faversham station in March 1948 with O1 class 0-6-0 No. 1379 on a string of elderly coaching stock. Stirling's design for the SECR dated as far back as 1878, but the examples inherited by British Railways had all been rebuilt with domed boilers and new cabs. No. 1379 was withdrawn during the week ended 28th April 1951 from Ashford shed, without being renumbered 31379.

G. W. Sharpe

B1 class No. 1443, allocated No. 31443 but never renumbered. The location of this photograph is not recorded but was certainly taken just after Nationalisation. These 4-4-0s were originally built with domeless boilers and represented Stirling's last design for the SER being introduced in 1898. No. 1443 was built in June as Class B and was converted to Class B1 in February 1913 and acquired an extended smokebox. This example was the last of the class to be active and was withdrawn from Reading shed during the week ended 24th February 1951.

G. W. Sharpe

E class 4-4-0 No. 31515 at Reading South shed in 1950, from where withdrawal took place in July 1951. Designed by Wainwright for the SECR the class dated back to 1905.

G. W. Sharpe

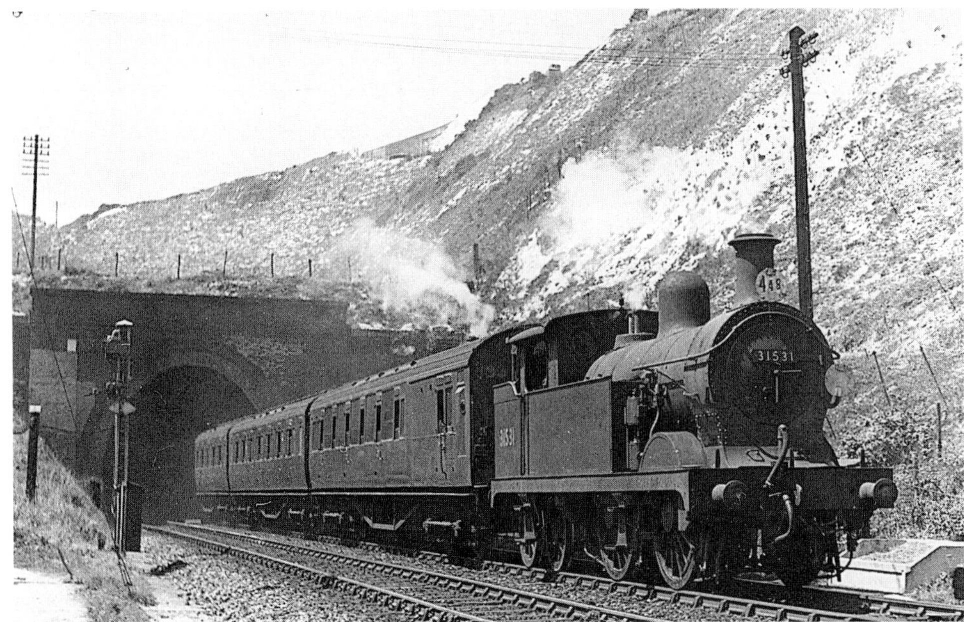

Folkestone Warren on Tuesday 12th July 1949. H class 0-4-4T No. 31531 runs past on a local passenger. Built at Ashford in July 1905, it survived until the week ended 26th March 1955, the final shed being Dover.

L. Hanson

Dover shed on 12th July 1949 finds R1 class 0-6-0T No. 1339 keeping company with P class 0-6-0T No. 31557. The R1 was renumbered in May 1951 and withdrawn from Folkestone in June 1958. No. 31557 was given its new number in May 1949 and was withdrawn in September 1957 from Stewarts Lane.

L. Hanson

Wainwright Class J 0-6-4T No. 31596 at Folkestone Warren on Thursday 14th July 1949. This was a small class of only five locomotives and had been built in 1913 for heavy outer suburban work. They served from Ashford shed for many years and it was from here that No. 31596 was withdrawn during the week ended 29th September 1951. It was the last of the class to be scrapped.
L. Hanson

Salisbury shed on Sunday 29th May 1949 finds U class 2-6-0 No. 31626 in steam and ready for work. This Maunsell design was a direct copy of earlier locomotives of this type that had been rebuilt from the ill-fated 'River' class 2-6-4Ts. No. 31626 was built in 1929, renumbered in April 1949 and withdrawn in January 1964 from Norwood Junction shed.
L. Hanson

Wandsworth in 1949 finds C class 0-6-0 No. 31719 plodding along with a freight. This was another Wainwright design, this example being built by Sharp, Stewart and Co. in January 1901. It remained in stock until May 1962 the last allocation being Bricklayers Arms shed.
G. W. Sharpe

Faversham shed in March 1948 sees D1 class 4-4-0 No. 1739 stabled out of use. This was a rebuild of Wainwright's D class with superheaters, piston valves and other modifications, creating a very different looking locomotive from the original (see the next illustration). Renumbered 31739 in 1951 the engine was withdrawn from Bricklayers Arms in November 1961.

G. W. Sharpe

An example of the original D class 4-4-0 at Folkestone Warren on Tuesday 12th July 1949. This is No. 1748 and was withdrawn without being given BR No. 31748, from Faversham in March 1951. Apart from the fitting of shorter chimneys, the unrebuilt engines remained in virtually their original condition until being scrapped.

L. Hanson

L class 4-4-0 No. 31779 at Eastleigh shed shortly after being renumbered in 1948. This was Wainwright's last design of 4-4-0 for the SECR and dated back to 1914. This example was withdrawn in July 1959 from Nine Elms shed. The last of the class, No. 31768, survived until December 1961 also at Nine Elms.

R. H. G. Simpson

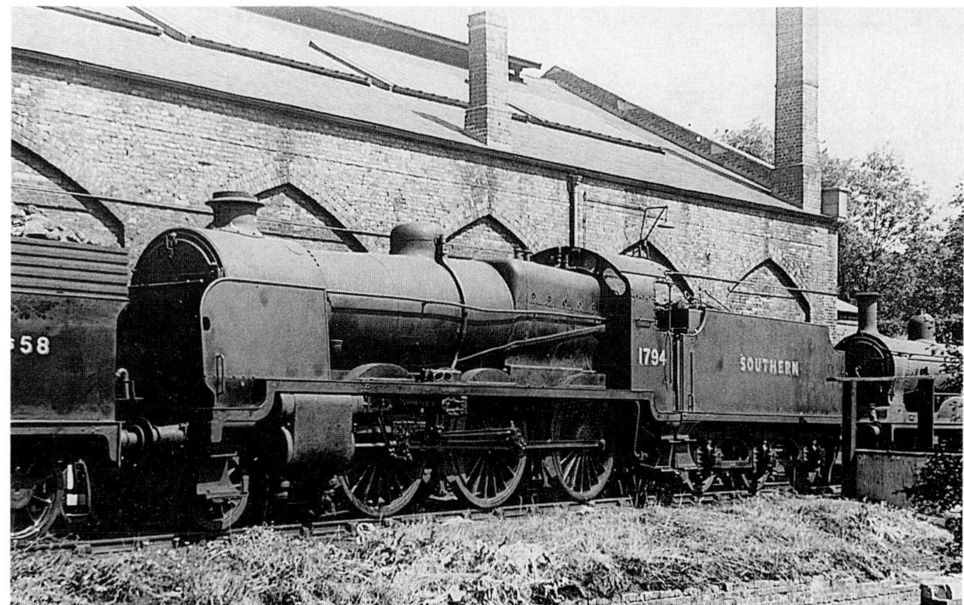

Yeovil Town shed in July 1948 has original U class 2-6-0 No. 1794 at home. Withdrawal came in June 1963 from Eastleigh shed.

R. H. G. Simpson

We return to Folkestone Warren again for this view of N class 2-6-0 No. 31821 on freight, recorded on Thursday 14th July 1949. This was a Maunsell design dating back to 1917 and was adopted as a standard type at Grouping and saw service throughout the Southern. No. 31821 was withdrawn in May 1964 from Exmouth Junction shed, which was then coded 83D and part of the Western Region.

L. Hanson

U1 class 2-6-0 No. 1902 at Cheriton on Saturday 17th July 1948. This was a modified version of the U class and No. 1902 was introduced in 1931. Renumbered 31902 in 1948, the engine was withdrawn in November 1962 from Norwood Junction shed.

L. Hanson

Bognor Regis is the location for this photograph of I1X class 4-4-2T No. 2002 in June 1950. The locomotive was in store along with Nos 2008 and 2596, all three moving on to further storage at Bricklayers Arms in July. Surprisingly, No. 2002 was returned to traffic in August 1950 and transferred to Three Bridges. This shed could not find work for her, and a further move took place in September to Brighton, from where withdrawal took place in July 1951. Never renumbered 32002, this was the last of the class to remain in service. Originally built in 1907 by Marsh for the LBSCR.

G. W. Sharpe

Another Marsh designed tank engine for the LBSCR this time I3 class 4-4-2T No. 32077. This photograph, taken on Thursday 13th October 1949, is at Eastbourne shed. The depot had lost its roof through bombing raids during the war and was never rebuilt but maintained an allocation until closure as an independent shed on 15th September 1952. The final allocation was 15 engines. No. 32077 was withdrawn from Eastbourne in March 1951.

G. W. Sharpe

N15X class 4-6-0 No. 2329 *Stephenson* at Eastleigh shed in 1948, shortly before being renumbered 32329. This locomotive started life as a Billinton design L class 4-6-4T in October 1921 but was rebuilt at Eastleigh in December 1934 to this tender engine by Maunsell. The whole class were based at Basingstoke for their BR careers, all ending their days there. On No. 32329's last day in service, Sunday 8th July 1956, it was used on the last part of an R.C.T.S. special, the "Wessex Wyvern", from Andover Junction to Waterloo, reaching 80 mph at Esher. Pretty good for a locomotive withdrawn the next day!

R. H. G. Simpson

E6 class 0-6-2T No. 32415 at Brighton shed on Saturday 24th July 1948 after a visit to the nearby works. It would work back to its home shed, Bricklayers Arms, during the following week. This was an R. J. Billinton design for the LBSCR for freight work and dated back to 1904. The BR power classification was 3F. No. 32415 was withdrawn from Dover shed in September 1961.

G. W. Sharpe

Inside Fratton roundhouse in May 1949 with Stroudley "Terrier" A1X class 0-6-0T No. 2661 nearest the camera, and a sister engine behind. Originally built in October 1875 as No. 61 and named *Sutton*, a rebuild took place in December 1912 with new boiler and various other improvements. Renumbered 32661 in May 1951, withdrawal took place in April 1963 from Eastleigh shed.

G. W. Sharpe

Bulleid's austerity Q1 class 0-6-0 No. C8 at Bricklayers Arms shed in May 1948. Unlovely to look at, they were nevertheless a powerful machine and had a power classification of 5F. No. C8 was added to stock in July 1942 and went first to Guildford shed. Renumbered 33008 in May 1951 at Ashford Works, withdrawal came in August 1963 from Feltham shed.

Photomatic

'West Country' Pacific No. 34005 *Barnstaple*, paired with an LMS tender for water pick up, leaves St Pancras on the 10.15am to Manchester on Monday 14th June 1948. This was a preliminary run before its test runs the following week during the exchanges. No. 34005, as No. 21C105, had gone new to Exmouth Junction in July 1945. Completely rebuilt in June 1957, withdrawal took place from Bournemouth shed in October 1966.

Photomatic

'Battle of Britain' Pacific No. 21C154 *Lord Beaverbrook* in full "Golden Arrow" regalia at Cheriton on Saturday 17th July 1948. This locomotive went new to Stewarts Lane in January 1947 and became No. 34054 in April 1949. Withdrawal came in September 1964 from Exmouth Junction still in original form.

L. Hanson

An 'up' express once again at Cheriton on 17th July 1948. 'Battle of Britain' class Pacific No. 34076 heads the train, then only a month old and yet to be named. It received the name *41 Squadron* in May 1949. Withdrawal came in January 1966 from Salisbury shed in original form.

L. Hanson

Exmouth Junction shed in June 1949. 'Merchant Navy' class 4-6-2 No. 35010 *Blue Star* looks ready for action on "Devon Belle" duty. Built in 1942 as No. 21C10, renumbering took place in 1948. The whole class were rebuilt under British Railways with the streamlined casing removed. No. 35010 remained in service until September 1966, the last allocation being Bournemouth, and today it is preserved at North Woolwich, East London.

G. W. Sharpe

Paddington station, Wednesday 21st April 1948. 'Merchant Navy' class 4-6-2 No. 35019 *French Line CGT* prepares to leave on the 1.30pm to Plymouth, a preliminary run before the exchange tests. New to Nine Elms in June 1945, withdrawal came in September 1965 from Weymouth.

Photomatic

On the Isle of Wight at Newport, with the shed building in the background, E1 class 0-6-0T No. 4 *Wroxall* is seen on yard shunting duty in 1948. Locomotives on the Island were later renumbered with the addition of "W" to the number. *Wroxall* was withdrawn in October 1960 from Ryde and was the last active E1 on BR.

R. H. G. Simpson

Ryde shed in 1948 has O2 class 0-4-4T No. 15 *Cowes* on show. This class remained at work on the Island until December 1966, outliving their mainland sisters by four years. This O2 did not last that long however, being withdrawn in May 1956 from Ryde.

R. H. G. Simpson

Fowler 3P class 2-6-2T No. 40025 at Cricklewood shed in 1950. Built in January 1931 as No. 15524 and renumbered 25 in 1934, renumbering into BR stock took place during the week ended 10th June 1950. The extra pipes and pumps on the boiler were part of the condensing apparatus that a number of these engines were fitted with for working through the tunnels of the London Metropolitan widened lines. No. 40025 was withdrawn from Kentish Town in December 1959.

G.W. Sharpe

64180	BOS
64181	BOS
64182	ARD
64183	DON
64184	NWE
64185	DON
64186	NWE
64187	NWE
64188	HSY
64189	NWE
64190	BOS
64191	NWE
64192	NWE
64193	DON
64194	CLK
64195	DON
64196	BOS
64197	CLK
64198	BOS
64199	CLK
64200	CLK
64201	BOS
64202	CLK
64203	BFD
64204	BOS
64205	BFD
64206	GRA
64207	NWE
64208	ARD
64209	DON
64210	BOS
64211	NWE
64212	CLK
64213	CLK
64214	ARD
64215	CLK
64216	NWE
64217	NWE
64218	DON
64219	DON
64220	NWE
64221	NWE
64222	CLK
64223	CLK
64224	CLK
64225	NWE
64226	BFD
64227	GRA
64228	NWE
64229	BOS
64230	CLK
64231	CLK
64232	DON
64233	CLK
64234	HSY
64235	NWE
64236	DON
64237	GRA
64238	NWE
64239	HSY
64240	HIT
64241	DON
64242	BOS
64243	DON
64244	BOS
64245	NWE
64246	NWE
64247	BOS
64248	BOS
64249	NWE
64250	COP
64251	HSY
64252	NWE
64253	CLK
64254	NWE
64255	DON
64256	HSY
64257	NWE
64258	DON
64259	DON
64260	COP
64261	DON
64262	DON
64263	DON
64264	DON
64265	GRA
64266	NWE
64267	ARD
64268	BFD
64269	CLK
64270	DON
64271	BFD
64272	ARD
64273	NWE
64274	BFD
64275	NWE
64276	BOS
64277	ARD
64278	NWE
64279	DON

0-6-0
J11 CLASS

64280	RET
64281	LNG
64282	RET
64283	MEX
64284	IMM
64285	LIN
64286	TUX
64287	RET
64288	MEX
64289	LNG
64290	BRN
64291	SHF
64292	ANN
64293	TUX
64294	ANN
64295	RET
64296	MEX
64297	LNG
64298	GOR
64299	TUX
64300	ANN
64301	LIN
64302	MEX
64303	LIN
64304	GOR
64305	IMM
64306	RET
64307	IMM
64308	FRO
64309	FRO
64310	TUX
64311	GOR
64312	IMM
64313	NEA
64314	IMM
64315	LIN
64316	GOR
64317	CLK
64318	ANN
64319	MEX
64320	IMM
64321	LNG
64322	GOR
64323	IMM
64324	WFD
64325	IMM
64326	GOR
64327	WFD
64328	LTH
64329	NEA
64330	WFD
64331	STV
64332	GOR
64333	LNG
64334	MEX
64335	RET
64336	STV
64337	LIN
64338	WRX
64339	FRO
64340	RET
64341	RET
64342	STV
64343	BRN
64344	TUX
64345	STV
64346	GOR
64347	RET
64348	RET
64349	RET
64350	STV
64351	STV
64352	MEX
64353	LIN
64354	ANN
64355	IMM
64356	MEX
64357	GOR
64358	LNG
64359	LIN
64360	SHF
64361	LEI
64362	FRO
64363	GOR
64364	WFD
64365	ANN
64366	BRN
64367	GOR
64368	GOR
64369	WFD
64370	ANN
64371	STV
64372	IMM
64373	STV
64374	MEX
64375	ANN
64376	LIV
64377	MEX
64378	LNG
64379	LNG
64380	RET
64381	WRX
64382	GOR
64383	GOR
64384	STV
64385	RET
64386	ANN
64387	SHF
64388	WFD
64389	LNG
64390	WFD
64391	BRN
64392	TUX
64393	RET
64394	NEA
64395	FRO
64396	LIN
64397	WAL
64398	BRN
64399	BRN
64400	MEX
64401	GOR
64402	RET
64403	MEX
64404	MEX
64405	LIV
64406	LIV
64407	FRO
64408	WFD
64409	ANN
64410	RET
64411	IMM
64412	SHF
64413	RET
64414	LNG
64415	GOR
64416	RET
64417	LIV
64418	LNG
64419	SHF
64420	LIV
64421	RET
64422	RET
64423	RET
64424	TUX
64425	RET
64426	LNG
64427	LNG
64428	STV
64429	FRO
64430	LIN
64431	ANN
64432	MEX
64433	STV
64434	GOR
64435	GOR
64436	BRN
64437	GOR
64438	WFD
64439	LTH
64440	GOR
64441	SHF
64442	MEX
64443	SHF
64444	STV
64445	SHF
64446	IMM
64447	SHF
64448	BRN
64449	MEX
64450	LNG
64451	RET
64452	BRN
64453	GOR

0-6-0
J35 CLASS

64460	KPS
64461	STG
64462	STM
64463	HAW
64464	THJ
64466	THJ
64468	BGT
64470	KPS
64471	STG
64472	KPS
64473	KPS
64474	THJ
64475	DFU
64476	DFU
64477	THJ
64478	CAR
64479	STM
64480	DFU
64482	DEE
64483	DFU
64484	POL
64485	DEE
64486	STM
64487	DFU
64488	THJ
64489	STM
64490	POL
64491	BGT
64492	STM
64493	DEE
64494	HAW
64495	THJ
64496	DFU
64497	STG
64498	KPS
64499	CAR
64500	THJ
64501	STG
64502	POL
64504	BGT
64505	DFU
64506	DEE
64507	KPS
64509	HAW
64510	BGT
64511	CAR
64512	DEE
64513	DFU
64514	THJ
64515	STM
64516	THJ
64517	STM
64518	STM
64519	STM
64520	STG
64521	THJ
64522	THJ
64523	DEE
64524	STM
64525	STG
64526	CAR
64527	STM
64528	POL
64529	BGT
64530	DEE
64531	POL
64532	STM
64533	STM
64534	BGT
64535	STM

0-6-0
J37 CLASS

64536	PTH
64537	DEE
64538	STM
64539	HAW
64540	EFD
64541	EFD
64542	STG
64543	STM
64544	STG
64545	DFU
64546	THJ
64547	STM
64548	DEE
64549	THJ
64550	THJ
64551	POL
64552	STM
64553	THJ
64554	DFU
64555	STM
64556	STG
64557	STM
64558	EFD
64559	PKD
64560	DFU
64561	DFU
64562	STM
64563	PKD
64564	THJ
64565	THJ
64566	STM
64567	DFU
64568	DFU
64569	STG
64570	POL
64571	POL
64572	STM

64573	PKD
64574	DFU
64575	DEE
64576	STM
64577	STM
64578	EFD
64579	EFD
64580	EFD
64581	EFD
64582	STM
64583	EFD
64584	PKD
64585	STG
64586	STM
64587	DEE
64588	PTH
64589	POL
64590	DFU
64591	PTH
64592	STM
64593	DEE
64594	STM
64595	STM
64596	THJ
64597	THJ
64598	THJ
64599	STM
64600	THJ
64601	EFD
64602	THJ
64603	STM
64604	DFU
64605	STM
64606	STM
64607	STM
64608	STM
64609	PKD
64610	EFD
64611	EFD
64612	THJ
64613	POL
64614	STM
64615	DEE
64616	THJ
64617	DFU
64618	THJ
64619	DEE
64620	DEE
64621	POL
64622	EFD
64623	EFD
64624	STM
64625	STM
64626	PKD
64627	DEE
64628	DFU
64629	THJ
64630	DFU
64631	DEE
64632	EFD
64633	EFD
64634	DEE
64635	THJ
64636	STM
64637	STM
64638	EFD
64639	EFD

0-6-0
J19 CLASS

64640	MAR
64641	MAR
64642	KL
64643	MAR
64644	MAR
64645	SL
64646	MAR
64647	MAR
64648	MAR
64649	CAM
64650	MAR
64651	MAR
64652	MAR
64653	MAR
64654	MAR
64655	MAR
64656	MAR
64657	MAR
64658	CAM
64659	MAR
64660	MAR
64661	MAR
64662	MAR
64663	MAR
64664	MAR
64665	MAR
64666	MAR
64667	MAR
64668	KL
64669	MAR
64670	KL
64671	MAR
64672	MAR
64673	MAR
64674	MAR

0-6-0
J20 CLASS

64675	STR
64676	CAM
64677	STR
64678	CAM
64679	CAM
64680	CAM
64681	STR
64682	STR
64683	CAM
64684	CAM
64685	STR
64686	STR
64687	CAM
64688	MAR
64689	MAR
64690	MAR
64691	STR
64692	MAR
64693	MAR
64694	MAR
64695	STR
64696	STR
64697	MAR
64698	MAR
64699	MAR

0-6-0
J39 CLASS

64700	BLA
64701	BLA
64702	LIN
64703	BLA
64704	BLA
64705	BLA
64706	SBK
64707	BLA
64708	STR
64709	BLA
64710	DAR
64711	BLA
64712	GOR
64713	DON
64714	LIV
64715	LIN
64716	CLK
64717	GOR
64718	GOR
64719	CLK
64720	CLK
64721	DON
64722	LIN
64723	TFD
64724	IPS
64725	SHF
64726	NOR
64727	PKS
64728	LIN
64729	NWE
64730	STR
64731	NOR
64732	CLK
64733	STR
64734	LIN
64735	CLK
64736	LIN
64737	DON
64738	NWE
64739	CLK
64740	GOR
64741	GOR
64742	GOR
64743	GOR
64744	GOR
64745	GOR
64746	NWE
64747	CLK
64748	NWE
64749	COP
64750	CLK
64751	ARD
64752	IPS
64753	SHF
64754	ARD
64755	GOR
64756	DAR
64757	CLK
64758	DON
64759	RET
64760	ARD
64761	NOR
64762	CLK
64763	CLK
64764	STR
64765	PKS
64766	STR
64767	STR
64768	STR
64769	STR
64770	STR
64771	STR
64772	STR
64773	STR
64774	STR
64775	STR
64776	STR
64777	STR
64778	DAR
64779	STR
64780	STR
64781	STR
64782	STR
64783	STR
64784	NOR
64785	IPS
64786	DEE
64787	STR
64788	PKS
64789	STR
64790	DEE
64791	DAR
64792	DEE
64793	IPS
64794	ABD
64795	ABD
64796	ARD
64797	NOR
64798	NOR
64799	YAR
64800	IPS
64801	ARD
64802	NOR
64803	IPS
64804	PKS
64805	CLK
64806	ARD
64807	GOR
64808	SHF
64809	SHF
64810	GOR
64811	ARD
64812	DAR
64813	BLA
64814	BLA
64815	TWD
64816	BLA
64817	BLA
64818	SBK
64819	DAR
64820	IPS
64821	DAR
64822	DEE
64823	TFD
64824	GOR
64825	ARD
64826	IPS
64827	CLK
64828	CLK
64829	IPS
64830	RET
64831	CLK
64832	CLK
64833	NOR
64834	IPS
64835	DON
64836	ARD
64837	CLK
64838	NOR
64839	STR
64840	STR
64841	IPS
64842	BLA
64843	BLA
64844	BLA
64845	SBK
64846	BLA
64847	DAR
64848	DAR
64849	BLA
64850	DAR
64851	DAR
64852	BLA
64853	BLA
64854	BLA
64855	SBK
64856	BLA
64857	SBK
64858	DAR
64859	SBK
64860	SBK
64861	SBK
64862	DAR
64863	DAR
64864	DAR
64865	DAR
64866	SBK
64867	HLD
64868	TWD
64869	DAR
64870	DAR
64871	BLA
64872	IPS
64873	STR
64874	STR
64875	CAR
64876	STR
64877	CAR
64878	SHF
64879	GOR
64880	CAR
64881	LIN
64882	NOR
64883	LIN
64884	CAR
64885	DON
64886	RET
64887	RET
64888	CAR
64889	NOR
64890	SHF
64891	DON
64892	CAR
64893	DON
64894	IPS
64895	CAR
64896	ARD
64897	DAR
64898	RET
64899	CAR
64900	IPS
64901	TFD
64902	DON
64903	SHF
64904	LIN
64905	IPS
64906	RET
64907	STR
64908	RET
64909	DON
64910	DON
64911	ARD
64912	CAR
64913	NOR
64914	HLD
64915	BLA
64916	DAR
64917	BLA
64918	GOR
64919	DAR
64920	BLA
64921	DAR
64922	SBK
64923	BLA
64924	TWD
64925	DAR
64926	BLA
64927	BLA
64928	DAR
64929	DAR
64930	CAR
64931	DAR
64932	CAR
64933	DAR
64934	BLA
64935	SBK
64936	DAR
64937	LIN
64938	DAR
64939	DAR
64940	DAR
64941	BLA
64942	DAR
64943	DAR
64944	SBK
64945	DAR
64946	CAR
64947	BLA
64948	CAR
64949	DAR
64950	DEE
64951	DON
64952	DON
64953	STR

64954	LIV
64955	CLK
64956	RET
64957	IPS
64958	IPS
64959	NOR
64960	SHF
64961	RET
64962	GOR
64963	CAR
64964	CAR
64965	NWE
64966	GOR
64967	DON
64968	NOR
64969	NWE
64970	RET
64971	LIN
64972	GOR
64973	SHF
64974	CLK
64975	ABD
64976	DON
64977	DON
64978	DAR
64979	ARD
64980	CLK
64981	CLK
64982	DAR
64983	CLK
64984	DON
64985	ARD
64986	CAR
64987	RET
64988	CLK

0-6-0
J1 CLASS

65002	NWE
65003	CLK
65004	NWE
65005	NWE
65006	NWE
65007	LEI
65008	CLK
65009	LEI
65010	CLK
65013	CLK
65014	CLK

0-6-0
J2 CLASS

65015	LEI
65016	BOS
65017	BOS
65018	LEI
65019	LEI
65020	BOS
65021	LEI
65022	LEI
65023	LEI

0-6-0
J21 CLASS

65025	BLA
65026	TWD
65027	YK
65028	KBY
65029	BLA
65030	HTN
65031	DAR
65032	AUK
65033	DAR
65035	BLA
65036	NEV
65037	NEV
65038	DAR
65039	TWD
65040	KBY
65041	NEV
65042	SEL
65043	SEL
65044	YK
65047	KBY
65049	NEV
65051	YK
65052	SKN
65056	YK
65057	SKN
65058	RET
65059	YK
65060	YK
65061	AUK
65062	BLA
65063	SBH
65064	AUK
65066	SEL
65067	TWD
65068	YK
65069	SBH
65070	RET
65072	SEL
65073	YK
65075	SEL
65076	YK
65077	NEV
65078	DAR
65079	YK
65080	BLA
65081	HTN
65082	TWD
65083	RBY
65084	MID
65086	HTN
65088	DAR
65089	SKN
65090	DAR
65091	DAR
65092	SKN
65093	SEL
65094	NEV
65095	RET
65097	NEV
65098	DAR
65099	TWD
65100	BLA
65101	BLA
65102	HTN
65103	KBY
65104	HTN
65105	SEL
65107	NEV
65108	YK
65109	NEV
65110	DAR
65111	BLA
65112	BLA
65114	HTN
65115	KBY
65116	NEV
65117	RET
65118	NEV
65119	DAR
65120	SEL
65121	YK
65122	HTN
65123	SBH

0-6-0
J10 CLASS

65126	LIV
65127	LIV
65128	WIG
65130	WAL
65131	NTH
65132	STP
65133	GOR
65134	NTH
65135	STP
65136	LIV
65137	STP
65138	NTH
65139	NTH
65140	NTH
65141	TFD
65142	NTH
65143	CHR
65144	LIV
65145	STP
65146	NTH
65147	NTH
65148	STP
65149	LIV
65151	WIG
65153	WRX
65154	STP
65155	NTH
65156	NTH
65157	STP
65158	NTH
65159	WIG
65160	STP
65161	TFD
65162	WIG
65163	LIV
65164	STP
65165	NTH
65166	NTH
65167	CHR
65168	TFD
65169	CHR
65170	WIG
65171	NTH
65172	LIV
65173	WIG
65175	WIG
65176	WIG
65177	WAL
65178	STP
65179	STP
65180	WAL
65181	STP
65182	LIV
65183	TFD
65184	TFD
65185	STP
65186	STP
65187	NTH
65188	STP
65189	WIG
65190	NTH
65191	NTH
65192	WAL
65193	STP
65194	STP
65195	WAL
65196	WIG
65197	STP
65198	STP
65199	WIG
65200	STP
65201	TFD
65202	NTH
65203	WIG
65204	TFD
65205	NTH
65208	WIG
65209	STP

0-6-0
J36 CLASS

65210	KPS
65211	BGT
65213	PTH
65214	PKD
65215	KPS
65216*	CAR
65217*	STM
65218	THJ
65220	POL
65221	EFD
65222*	POL
65224*	STM
65225	BGT
65226*	KPS
65227	EFD
65228	EFD
65229	BGT
65230	BGT
65231	BGT
65232	HAW
65233*	POL
65234	BGT
65235*	BGT
65236*	KPS
65237	FW
65238	KPS
65239	DFU
65240	HAY
65241	POL
65242	HAW
65243*	HAY
65244	POL
65245	KPS
65246	POL
65247	KPS
65248	BGT
65249	KPS
65250	BGT
65251	STM
65252	DFU
65253*	DFU
65254	BGT
65255	KPS
65256	KPS
65257	POL
65258	STM
65259	HAW
65260	KPS
65261	BGT
65264	KPS
65265	BGT
65266	KPS
65267	STM
65268*	POL
65270	EFD
65271	BGT
65273	EFD
65274	PKD
65275	POL
65276	BGT
65277	BGT
65278	BGT
65279	HAW
65280	BGT
65281	STG
65282	BGT
65283	PKD
65285	KPS
65286	STM
65287	KPS
65288	STM
65289	KPS
65290	POL
65291	THJ
65292	STM
65293	CAR
65294	KPS
65295	BLA
65296	EFD
65297	PTH
65298	PKD
65300	EFD
65303	BGT
65304	CAR
65305	STM
65306	POL
65307	STG
65308	EFD
65309	PTH
65310	STM
65311	STM
65312	CAR
65313	POL
65314	BGT
65315	EFD
65316	STM
65317	HAW
65318	BGT
65319	DEE
65320	DFU
65321	CAR
65322	STG
65323	DFU
65324	PKD
65325	KPS
65327	BGT
65328	DEE
65329	POL
65330	DEE
65331	BLA
65333	DEE
65334	STM
65335	EFD
65337	EFD
65338	POL
65339	EFD
65340	HAW
65341	BGT
65342	BGT
65343	BLA
65344	BGT
65345	THJ
65346	STG

0-6-0
J15 CLASS

65350	CAM
65351	LOW
65352	LOW
65353	LOW
65354	STR
65355	LOW
65356	CAM
65357	COL
65359	KL
65361	STR
65362	BSE
65363	STR
65364	CAM
65365	PKS
65366	CAM
65367	NOR
65368	KL
65369	CAM
65370	STR
65371	CAM
65372	MAR
65373	NOR
65374	COL
65375	STR
65376	PKS
65377	IPS
65378	KL
65379	CAM
65380	CAM
65381	STR
65382	KL
65383	CAM
65384	COL

65385 COL
65386 IPS
65387 STR
65388 STR
65389 LOW
65390 NOR
65391 CAM
65392 STR
65393 STR
65394 NOR
65395 STR
65396 KL
65397 STR
65398 NOR
65399 CAM
65400 LOW
65401 NOR
65402 STR
65404 NOR
65405 CAM
65406 CAM
65407 IPS
65408 NOR
65409 IPS
65410 CAM
65411 NOR
65412 CAM
65413 CAM
65414 COL
65415 IPS
65416 KL
65417 NOR
65418 STR
65419 MAR
65420 BSE
65421 IPS
65422 NOR
65423 IPS
65424 COL
65425 KL
65426 NOR
65427 STR
65428 IPS
65429 IPS
65430 IPS
65431 STR
65432 COL
65433 MAR
65434 STR
65435 NOR
65436 STR
65437 KL
65438 CAM
65439 MAR
65440 COL
65441 STR
65442 BSE
65443 COL
65444 STR
65445 COL
65446 STR
65447 IPS
65448 COL
65449 STR
65450 STR
65451 CAM
65452 STR
65453 PKS
65454 STR
65455 STR
65456 COL
65457 CAM
65458 PKS
65459 IPS
65460 NOR
65461 CAM
65462 LOW
65463 STR
65464 STR
65465 COL
65466 STR
65467 IPS
65468 STR
65469 YB
65470 NOR
65471 NOR
65472 YB
65473 COL
65474 CAM
65475 STR
65476 STR
65477 CAM
65478 NOR
65479 NOR

0-6-0
J5 CLASS

65480 CLK
65481 CLK
65482 CLK
65483 CLK
65484 CLK
65485 CLK
65486 WFD
65487 WFD
65488 WFD
65489 WFD
65490 CLK
65491 CLK
65492 CLK
65493 CLK
65494 CLK
65495 CLK
65496 CLK
65497 CLK
65498 CLK
65499 CLK

0-6-0
J17 CLASS

65500 STR
65501 CAM
65502 CAM
65503 CAM
65504 SL
65505 SL
65506 CAM
65507 STR
65508 STR
65509 MC
65510 IPS
65511 STR
65512 MAR
65513 MAR
65514 MC
65515 MAR
65516 NOR
65517 CAM
65518 MAR
65519 STR
65520 CAM
65521 SL
65522 COL
65523 STR
65524 MAR
65525 MAR
65526 SL
65527 KL
65528 STR
65529 KL
65530 KL
65531 COL
65532 SL
65533 SL
65534 NOR
65535 CAM
65536 STR
65537 CAM
65538 MAR
65539 COL
65540 STR
65541 STR
65542 STR
65543 STR
65544 KL
65545 SL
65546 CAM
65547 MAR
65548 KL
65549 KL
65551 MC
65552 MC
65553 NOR
65554 MAR
65555 MAR
65556 MAR
65557 MC
65558 YB
65559 YB
65560 IPS
65561 SL
65562 SL
65563 CAM
65564 COL
65565 SL
65566 MC
65567 MC
65568 MAR
65569 NOR
65570 NOR
65571 MAR
65572 KL
65573 MAR
65574 YB
65575 CAM
65576 MAR
65577 MAR
65578 NOR
65579 SL
65580 KL
65581 YB
65582 SL
65583 MAR
65584 MAR
65585 CAM
65586 MC
65587 MAR
65588 SL
65589 SL

0-6-0
J24 CLASS

65600 BOR
65601 NPT
65602 TDK
65603 BOR
65604 BOR
65606 TDK
65607 MAL
65608 NPT
65609 WBY
65611 BOR
65612 WBY
65614 DEE
65615 MAL
65617 STM
65619 HLD
65621 HLD
65622 DEE
65623 STM
65624 BOR
65625 STM
65626 NPT
65627 BOR
65628 MAL
65629 WBY
65631 HLD
65632 TDK
65633 BOR
65634 BOR
65636 MAL
65639 HLD
65640 SBK
65641 BOR
65642 MAL
65644 BOR

0-6-0
J25 CLASS

65645 NLN
65646 DAR
65647 HLD
65648 DAR
65649 HTN
65650 DAR
65651 HLD
65653 DAR
65654 HLS
65655 KBY
65656 YK
65657 BOR
65658 NLN
65659 AUK
65660 HLD
65661 BOR
65662 AUK
65663 HLD
65664 DAR
65665 AUK
65666 HLD
65667 CUD
65668 DAR
65669 KBY
65670 TDK
65671 HLD
65672 DAR
65673 KBY
65674 NLN
65675 AUK
65676 BOR
65677 AUK
65679 HLD
65680 BOR
65681 KBY
65683 AUK
65684 KBY
65685 BOR
65686 MID
65687 AUK
65688 DAR
65689 AUK
65690 HLD
65691 DAR
65692 DAR
65693 NLN
65694 TDK
65695 DAR
65696 AUK
65697 HTN
65698 HLD
65699 HLD
65700 YK
65702 MID
65703 CUD
65704 HTN
65705 HLD
65706 AUK
65707 HLS
65708 DAR
65710 MID
65712 HLD
65713 HLD
65714 CUD
65715 AUK
65716 TDK
65717 KBY
65718 AUK
65720 HTN
65721 TDK
65723 YK
65724 HLS
65725 MID
65726 MID
65727 HTN
65728 HLS

0-6-0
J26 CLASS

65730 NPT
65731 NPT
65732 WHL
65733 MID
65734 NPT
65735 NPT
65736 NPT
65737 NPT
65738 NPT
65739 NPT
65740 NPT
65741 NPT
65742 NPT
65743 NPT
65744 NPT
65745 NPT
65746 NPT
65747 WHL
65748 WHL
65749 NPT
65750 NPT
65751 NPT
65752 NPT
65753 NPT
65754 NPT
65755 NPT
65756 NPT
65757 NPT
65758 NPT
65759 NPT
65760 NPT
65761 NPT
65762 NPT
65763 NPT
65764 MID
65765 NPT
65766 NPT
65767 NPT
65768 NPT
65769 NPT
65770 NPT
65771 MID
65772 NPT
65773 NPT
65774 NPT
65775 MID
65776 MID
65777 NPT
65778 NPT
65779 MID

0-6-0
J27 CLASS

65780 PMN
65781 HTN
65782 YK
65783 NBH
65784 PMN
65785 SUN
65786 NBH
65787 HAV
65788 SKN

65789	NBH
65790	WHL
65791	PMN
65792	PMN
65793	SUN
65794	HTN
65795	HTN
65796	PMN
65797	NBH
65798	SUN
65799	NBH
65800	SKN
65801	NBH
65802	PMN
65803	WHL
65804	NBH
65805	SKN
65806	HTN
65807	SKN
65808	SBH
65809	PMN
65810	SBH
65811	NBH
65812	PMN
65813	PMN
65814	PMN
65815	PMN
65816	WHL
65817	SUN
65818	HAV
65819	NBH
65820	SUN
65821	PMN
65822	PMN
65823	SUN
65824	HTN
65825	PMN
65826	PMN
65827	SEL
65828	NBH
65829	SBH
65830	HAV
65831	PMN
65832	WHL
65833	SUN
65834	SBH
65835	SUN
65836	SEL
65837	PMN
65838	PMN
65839	PMN
65840	SUN
65841	WHL
65842	HTN
65843	SUN
65844	SEL
65845	SEL
65846	SUN
65847	SUN
65848	SEL
65849	SEL
65850	WHL
65851	NBH
65852	PMN
65853	HAV
65854	SUN
65855	HAV
65856	SUN
65857	SKN
65858	PMN
65859	HAV
65860	SKN
65861	NEV
65862	HTN
65863	HTN
65864	HTN
65865	SUN
65866	HAV
65867	NBH
65868	SAL
65869	TWD
65870	SKN
65871	WHL
65872	SUN
65873	TWD
65874	SEL
65875	SEL
65876	NBH
65877	NBH
65878	SUN
65879	NBH
65880	NBH
65881	SEL
65882	SEL
65883	NEV
65884	SUN
65885	NEV
65886	HTN
65887	SKN
65888	NEV
65889	HTN
65890	SEL
65891	SEL
65892	NBH
65893	HTN
65894	NEV

0-6-0
J38 CLASS

65900	DFU
65901	THJ
65902	THJ
65903	THJ
65904	THJ
65905	DFU
65906	STM
65907	THJ
65908	THJ
65909	DFU
65910	THJ
65911	THJ
65912	STM
65913	THJ
65914	STM
65915	STM
65916	DFU
65917	DFU
65918	STM
65919	STM
65920	STM
65921	THJ
65922	DFU
65923	DFU
65924	DFU
65925	THJ
65926	DFU
65927	STM
65928	DFU
65929	STM
65930	DFU
65931	THJ
65932	THJ
65933	DFU
65934	DFU

2-4-2T
F7 CLASS

67093	STM
67094	STM

2-4-2T
F1 CLASS

67097	GOR
67099	LIV
67100	LIV

2-4-2T
F2 CLASS

67104	ARD
67105	ANN
67106	KX
67107	ANN
67108	KX
67109	YAR
67111	KX
67112	YB
67113	KX

2-4-2T
F3 CLASS

67114	LOW
67115	CAM
67117	CAM
67119	LOW
67124	BSE
67126	LOW
67127	NOR
67128	IPS
67134	NOR
67139	NOR
67140	MC
67141	LOW
67143	IPS
67149	KL
67150	MC

2-4-2T
F4 CLASS

67151	KIT
67152	MC
67153	MC
67154	YAR
67155	MAL
67156	NOR
67157	YB
67158	LOW
67159	STR
67160	BSE
67161	STR
67162	YB
67163	LOW
67164	KIT
67165	LOW
67166	LOW
67167	LOW
67168	STR
67169	STR
67170	STR
67171	HLD
67172	STR
67173	STR
67174	NOR
67175	HLD
67176	NOR
67177	LOW
67178	NOR
67179	STR
67180	STR
67181	STR
67182	IPS
67183	STR
67184	NOR
67185	STR
67186	NOR
67187	BSE

2-4-2T
F5 CLASS

67188	COL
67189	COL
67190	COL
67191	STR
67192	STR
67193	STR
67194	STR
67195	STR
67196	STR
67197	STR
67198	STR
67199	STR
67200	STR
67201	STR
67202	STR
67203	STR
67204	PKS
67205	STR
67206	PKS
67207	COL
67208	STR
67209	STR
67210	STR
67211	STR
67212	STR
67213	COL
67214	STR
67215	STR
67216	STR
67217	STR

2-4-2T
F6 CLASS

67218	STR
67219	STR
67220	STR
67221	STR
67222	STR
67223	YB
67224	STR
67225	STR
67226	YB
67227	STR
67228	STR
67229	PKS
67230	STR
67231	STR
67232	STR
67233	YB
67234	YB
67235	YB
67236	KL
67237	BSE
67238	BSE
67239	KL

0-4-4T
G5 CLASS

67240	NEV
67241	HTN
67242	HLB
67243	SUN
67244	SBH
67245	BLA
67246	HTN
67247	SUN
67248	TWD
67249	HTN
67250	DAR
67251	SUN
67252	SUN
67253	SBK
67254	SKN
67255	BLA
67256	HLB
67257	SUN
67258	DUR
67259	BLA
67260	SUN
67261	SBH
67262	WBY
67263	DUR
67264	SUN
67265	BLA
67266	HLB
67267	SUN
67268	BLA
67269	SBK
67270	SUN
67271	WHL
67272	SKN
67273	MAL
67274	NEV
67275	MAL
67276	MAL
67277	BLA
67278	NEV
67279	HLB
67280	HLB
67281	MID
67282	HLB
67283	SUN
67284	MAL
67285	SBH
67286	SBK
67287	KIT
67288	SKN
67289	SBK
67290	NEV
67291	WHL
67292	KEI
67293	WBY
67294	SKN
67295	SBH
67296	RBY
67297	SUN
67298	DUR
67299	SUN
67300	SUN
67301	HLB
67302	WBY
67303	HTN
67304	HTN
67305	HLB
67306	AUK
67307	DUR
67308	WBY
67309	DAR
67310	SUN
67311	HLB
67312	AUK
67313	BLA
67314	WHL
67315	BLA
67316	WHL
67317	AUK
67318	SKN
67319	NEV
67320	SBH
67321	HLB
67322	STR
67323	BLA
67324	NLN
67325	BLA
67326	SBH
67327	KIT
67328	SUN
67329	BLA
67330	MAL
67331	WHL
67332	SBK
67333	HTN
67334	SBH
67335	WBY
67336	SUN
67337	NEV
67338	MID
67339	BLA
67340	HLB
67341	SBH

67342 DAR
67343 WHL
67344 NLN
67345 AUK
67346 NLN
67347 SBH
67348 SUN
67349 MAL

4-4-2T
C12 CLASS

67350 LIN
67351 LNG
67352 LTH
67353 COP
67354 MC
67355 LNG
67356 COP
67357 LNG
67358 TFD
67359 LTH
67360 CAM
67361 NWE
67362 NWE
67363 NWE
67364 LIN
67365 NWE
67366 CHR
67367 CAM
67368 NWE
67369 TFD
67370 TFD
67371 HLB
67372 COP
67373 NWE
67374 LTH
67375 CAM
67376 HSY
67377 COP
67378 TFD
67379 LTH
67380 GRA
67381 LIN
67382 GRA
67383 COP
67384 LNG
67385 CAM
67386 COP
67387 BOS
67388 COP
67389 LTH
67390 NWE
67391 HLB
67392 HLB
67393 HLB
67394 HLB
67395 HLB
67397 HLB
67398 LTH
67399 HLB

4-4-2T
C13 CLASS

67400 CHR
67401 GOR
67402 GOR
67403 GOR
67404 SHF
67405 GOR
67406 SHF
67407 GOR
67408 GOR
67409 BRN
67410 GOR
67411 BRN
67412 GOR
67413 CHR
67414 CHR
67415 GOR
67416 GOR
67417 GOR
67418 NEA
67419 GOR
67420 NEA
67421 GOR
67422 GOR
67423 GOR
67424 GOR
67425 GOR
67426 GOR
67427 GOR
67428 WRX
67429 WRX
67430 CHR
67431 GOR
67432 WRX
67433 WRX
67434 BRN
67435 WRX
67436 CHR
67437 GOR
67438 NEA
67439 GOR

4-4-2T
C14 CLASS

67440 ARD
67441 ARD
67442 ARD
67443 ARD
67444 ARD
67445 ARD
67446 ARD
67447 IPS
67448 IPS
67449 ARD
67450 IPS
67451 ARD

4-4-2T
C15 CLASS

67452 THJ
67453 DFU
67454 PKD
67455 PTH
67456 EFD
67457 HAW
67458 CAR
67459 HAW
67460 EFD
67461 DEE
67462 STG
67463 POL
67464 POL
67465 HAW
67466 DFU
67467 EFD
67468 POL
67469 DFU
67470 PKD
67471 DEE
67472 HAW
67473 HAW
67474 CAR
67475 KPS
67476 THJ
67477 HAW
67478 DFU
67479 PKD
67480 PKD
67481 CAR

4-4-2T
C16 CLASS

67482 EFD
67483 DEE
67484 DEE
67485 EFD
67486 DEE
67487 PKD
67488 PKD
67489 DEE
67490 DEE
67491 DEE
67492 STM
67493 STM
67494 STM
67495 STM
67496 STM
67497 STM
67498 DEE
67499 DEE
67500 EFD
67501 EFD
67502 EFD

2-6-2T
V1 CLASS

67600 EFD
67601 EFD
67602 EFD
67603 PKD
67604 PKD
67605 STM
67606 STM
67607 STM
67608 STM
67609 STM
67610 HAY
67611 PKD
67612 PKD
67613 PKD
67614 PKD
67615 HAY
67616 PKD
67617 STM
67618 STG
67619 PKD
67620 HAY
67621 PKD
67622 PKD
67623 PKD
67624 STM
67625 PKD
67626 PKD
67627 KPS
67628 PKD
67629 STM
67630 STM
67631 PKD
67632 PKD
67633 PKD

2-6-2T
V3 CLASS

67634 GHD

2-6-2T
V1 CLASS

67635 HTN
67636 BLA
67637 HTN
67638 MID
67639 MID
67640 HTN
67641 HTN
67642 HTN
67643 PKD
67644 DFU
67645 NEV
67646 NEV
67647 NEV
67648 PKD
67649 STM
67650 STG
67651 HTN
67652 HTN
67653 HTN
67654 HTN
67655 PKD
67656 NEV
67657 NEV
67658 BLA
67659 STM
67660 KPS
67661 DFU
67662 PKD
67663 NOR
67664 NOR
67665 NOR
67666 STM
67667 STR
67668 STR

2-6-2T
V3 CLASS

67669 STR

2-6-2T
V1 CLASS

67670 STM
67671 STR

2-6-2T
V3 CLASS

67672 STR

2-6-2T
V1 CLASS

67673 STR
67674 PKD

2-6-2T
V3 CLASS

67675 STR

2-6-2T
V1 CLASS

67676 STR
67677 STR
67678 PKD
67679 STR
67680 STR
67681 STR

2-6-2T
V3 CLASS

67682 GHD
67683 GHD
67684 MID
67685 MID
67686 MID
67687 GHD
67688 GHD
67689 GHD
67690 GHD
67691 MID

2-6-4T
L1 CLASS

67701 9000 STR

0-6-0ST
J94 CLASS

68006 IMM
68007 NPT
68008 DAR
68009 IMM
68010 BLA
68011 NPT
68012 IMM
68013 IMM
68014 BLA
68015 BLA
68016 SUN
68017 SCA
68018 IMM
68019 BLA
68020 IMM
68021 BLA
68022 IMM
68023 NPT
68024 BLA
68025 DAR
68026 IMM
68027 DAR
68028 IMM
68029 BLA
68030 IMM
68031 YK
68032 YK
68033 IMM
68034 IMM
68035 BLA
68036 BLA
68037 BLA
68038 BLA
68039 SEL
68040 SEL
68041 NPT
68042 YK
68043 YK
68044 YK
68045 YK
68046 YK
68047 DAR
68048 DAR
68049 DAR
68050 DAR
68051 DAR
68052 DAR
68053 WHL
68054 WHL
68055 WHL
68056 WHL
68057 WHL
68058 BLA
68059 BLA
68060 NPT
68061 DAR
68062 NPT
68063 GOR
68064 GOR
68065 GOR
68066 GOR
68067 GOR
68068 IMM
68069 IMM
68070 IMM
68071 IMM
68072 IMM
68073 IMM
68074 IMM
68075 IMM
68076 IMM
68077 IMM
68078 IMM
68079 IMM
68080 IMM

0-4-0ST
Y5 CLASS

68081 STRW

TRAM ENGINE
Y6 CLASS

68082 KL
68083 KL

0-4-0T
Y7 CLASS

68088 TDK
68089 TDK

0-4-0T
Y8 CLASS

68090 HLS
68091 YK

0-4-0T
Y9 CLASS

68092 STM
68093 STM
68094 KPS
68095 STM
68096 STM
68097 STM
68098 STM
68099 STM
68100 DEE
68101 DFU
68102 STM
68103 EFD
68104 POL
68105 STM
68106 KPS
68107 DEE
68108 DEE
68109 EFD
68110 DEE
68111 STM
68112 KPS
68113 POL
68114 DEE
68115 STM
68116 KPS
68117 KPS
68118 EFD
68119 STM
68120 KPS
68121 KPS
68122 STM
68123 DEE
68124 EFD

0-4-0T
Y4 CLASS

68125 STR
68126 STR
68127 STR
68128 STR
68129 STRW

TRAM ENGINE
Y10 CLASS

68186 YAR
68187 YAR

0-4-2T
Z4 CLASS

68190 KIT
68191 KIT

0-4-2T
Z5 CLASS

68192 KIT
68193 KIT

0-6-0ST
J62 CLASS

68200 WRX
68201 WRX
68203 IMM

0-6-0T
J63 CLASS

68204 IMM
68205 BID
68206 IMM
68207 BID
68208 IMM
68209 IMM
68210 IMM

0-6-0T
J65 CLASS

68211 IPS
68213 YB
68214 CAM
68215 STR

TRAM ENGINE
J70 CLASS

68216 IPS
68217 KL
68218 KL
68219 IPS
68220 KL
68221 IPS
68222 KL
68223 KL
68224 IPS
68225 IPS
68226 COL

0-6-0T
J71 CLASS

68230 YK
68231 YK
68232 HLD
68233 WHL
68234 GHD
68235 DAR
68236 DAR
68238 YK
68239 DAR
68240 YK
68242 HLD
68243 HTN
68244 WHL
68245 HTN
68246 YK
68247 GHD
68248 WHL
68249 AUK
68250 YK
68251 GHD
68252 HLD
68253 YK
68254 AUK
68255 AUK
68256 HTN
68258 WHL
68259 DAR
68260 MID
68262 GHD
68263 WHL
68264 HTN
68265 GHD
68266 TDK
68267 GHD
68268 YK
68269 AUK
68270 GHD
68271 HTN
68272 TDK
68273 HTN
68275 YK
68276 WHL
68277 HLD
68278 HTN
68279 DAR
68280 YK
68281 DAR
68282 YK
68283 GHD
68284 BLA
68285 SEL
68286 YK
68287 BOR
68288 HLD
68289 BOR
68290 WHL
68291 WHL
68292 YK
68293 YK
68294 YK
68295 WHL
68296 HLB
68297 YK
68298 YK
68299 BOR
68300 DAR
68301 WHL
68302 WHL
68303 MID
68304 HLD
68305 SKN
68306 WHL
68307 MID
68308 DAR
68309 GHD
68310 YK
68311 HLD
68312 MID
68313 SEL
68314 GHD
68316 HLD

0-6-0T
J55 CLASS

68317 DON
68319 DONW

0-6-0T
J88 CLASS

68320 STM
68321 THJ
68322 THJ
68323 THJ
68324 POL
68325 STM
68326 EFD
68327 EFD
68328 HAY
68329 KPS
68330 EFD
68331 EFD
68332 THJ
68333 EFD
68334 STM
68335 THJ
68336 EFD
68337 THJ
68338 STM
68339 HAY
68340 STM
68341 THJ
68342 STG
68343 KPS
68344 KPS
68345 EFD
68346 STG
68347 EFD
68348 STM
68349 EFD
68350 POL
68351 STG
68352 STM
68353 THJ
68354 POL

0-6-0T
J73 CLASS

68355 WHL
68356 SEL
68357 SEL
68358 WHL
68359 WHL
68360 HLA
68361 HLA
68362 SEL
68363 TWD
68364 WHL

0-6-0T
J75 CLASS

68365 WAL

0-6-0T
J60 CLASS

68366 WRX
68368 WRX

0-6-0T
J66 CLASS

68370 STRW
68371 STV
68372 CAM
68373 IPS
68374 IPS
68375 IPS
68376 LIN
68377 NOR
68378 COL
68379 STV
68380 NWE
68381 STR
68382 STV
68383 MAR
68384 NOR
68385 LIN
68386 IPS
68387 NWE
68388 STR

0-6-0T
J77 CLASS

68390 HLA
68391 DAR
68392 SBK
68393 SBK
68395 HLA
68396 NBH
68397 NBH
68398 NBH
68399 YK
68400 TWD
68401 YK
68402 HLA
68404 SBK
68405 NBH
68406 HLA
68407 SKN
68408 DAR
68409 MID
68410 DAR
68412 SKN
68413 HLA
68414 MID
68415 SBH
68416 NEV
68417 DAR
68420 SKN
68421 DAR
68422 MID
68423 MID
68424 TWD
68425 DAR
68426 NBH
68427 NPT
68428 SBH
68429 HLA
68430 HTN
68431 NPT
68432 AUK
68433 SBK
68434 SBK
68435 HLA
68436 NEV
68437 TWD
68438 SBK
68440 YK
68441 NPT

0-6-0T
J83 CLASS

68442 KPS
68443 KPS
68444 KPS
68445 KPS
68446 DEE
68447 EFD
68448 STM
68449 STM
68450 STM
68451 THJ
68452 DEE
68453 THJ
68454 STM
68455 DEE
68456 THJ
68457 HAY
68458 THJ
68459 THJ
68460 HAY
68461 KPS
68463 STM
68464 STM
68465 DFU
68466 DEE
68467 THJ
68468 EFD
68469 PTH
68470 STM
68471 POL
68472 STM
68473 HAY
68474 STM
68475 EFD
68476 EFD
68477 STM
68478 HAY
68479 EFD
68480 EFD
68481 HAY

0-6-0T
J93 CLASS

68484 SL
68488 SL
68489 MC

0-6-0T
J67 CLASS

68490 KL

0-6-0T
J69 CLASS

68491 LEI

0-6-0T
J67 CLASS

68492 STM
68493 KL

0-6-0T
J69 CLASS

68494 KL
68495 NOR

0-6-0T
J67 CLASS

68496 STR

0-6-0T
J69 CLASS

68497 BSE

0-6-0T
J67 CLASS

68498 IPS

0-6-0T
J69 CLASS

68499 CAR
68500 STR
68501 NOR
68502 KL
68503 PKD
68504 THJ
68505 STM
68507 STR
68508 STR

0-6-0T
J67 CLASS

68509 STR
68510 IPS
68511 STM
68512 HIT
68513 STR
68514 KL
68515 KL
68516 CAM
68517 CAM
68518 IPS
68519 PKS
68520 STR
68521 PKS
68522 STR
68523 STR

0-6-0T
J69 CLASS

68524 POL
68525 STM
68526 STR
68527 CLK
68528 BOS

0-6-0T
J67 CLASS

68529 LIN

0-6-0T
J69 CLASS

68530 CAM

0-6-0T
J67 CLASS

68531 WRX

0-6-0T
J69 CLASS

68532 STR
68533 POL
68534 STR
68535 THJ

0-6-0T
J67 CLASS

68536 CAM

0-6-0T
J69 CLASS

68537 LIN
68538 STR

0-6-0T
J67 CLASS

68540 TFD

0-6-0T
J69 CLASS

68541 HIT
68542 KL
68543 BOS
68544 POL
68545 STR
68546 NWE

0-6-0T
J67 CLASS

68547 LIV

0-6-0T
J69 CLASS

68548 STR
68549 STR
68550 THJ
68551 EFD
68552 EFD
68553 LIN
68554 STR
68555 THJ
68556 STR
68557 STR
68558 LIN
68559 LIV
68560 BOS
68561 STR
68562 STM
68563 STR
68565 HAT
68566 SL
68567 PKD
68568 STM
68569 STR
68570 MC
68571 PKS

0-6-0T
J67 CLASS

68572 HAT

0-6-0T
J69 CLASS

68573 STR
68574 STR
68575 STR
68576 STR
68577 STR
68578 STR
68579 BSE
68581 BOS

0-6-0T
J67 CLASS

68583 CAM
68584 WAL

0-6-0T
J69 CLASS

68585 TFD

0-6-0T
J67 CLASS

68586 NOR

0-6-0T
J69 CLASS

68587 LIN

0-6-0T
J67 CLASS

68588 NWE
68589 STR
68590 STR
68591 STR
68592 STR
68593 STR
68594 STR
68595 NOR

0-6-0T
J69 CLASS

68596 PKS

0-6-0T
J67 CLASS

68597 SL

0-6-0T
J69 CLASS

68598 GOR
68599 LIN
68600 KL
68601 STR
68602 LOW
68603 NOR
68605 HIT

0-6-0T
J67 CLASS

68606 STR

0-6-0T
J69 CLASS

68607 STR

0-6-0T
J67 CLASS

68608 STR
68609 CAM
68610 LIN
68611 LOW

0-6-0T
J69 CLASS

68612 STR
68613 STR

0-6-0T
J67 CLASS

68616 COL

0-6-0T
J69 CLASS

68617 STR
68618 LIN
68619 STR
68621 STR
68623 STM
68625 YAR
68626 STR

0-6-0T
J67 CLASS

68628 YAR

0-6-0T
J69 CLASS

68629 COL
68630 STR
68631 STR
68632 NWE
68633 STR
68635 DFU
68636 COL

0-6-0T
J68 CLASS

68638 PKS
68639 STR
68640 LOW
68641 NOR
68642 PKS
68643 STR
68644 STR
68645 CAM
68646 STR
68647 STR
68648 STR
68649 STR
68650 STR
68651 YB
68652 STR
68653 STR
68654 MAR
68655 BOS
68656 KL
68657 BOS
68658 BOS
68659 BOS
68660 PKS
68661 STR
68662 STR
68663 STR
68664 MAR
68665 STR
68666 STR

0-6-0T
J92 CLASS

68667 STRW
68668 STRW
68669 STRW

0-6-0T
J72 CLASS

68670 HLA
68671 BID
68672 NEV
68673 HLD
68674 GHD
68675 HTN
68676 HLD
68677 YK
68678 AUK
68679 BOR
68680 GHD
68681 NEV
68682 HTN
68683 HTN
68684 WHL
68685 WHL
68686 HLA
68687 HTN
68688 DAR
68689 WHL
68690 MID
68691 SUN
68692 WHL
68693 GHD
68694 WHL
68695 YK
68696 AUK
68697 WHL
68698 SUN
68699 YK
68700 KIT
68701 BID
68702 GHD
68703 WHL
68704 BOR
68705 BOR
68706 BOR
68707 SUN
68708 BOR
68709 EFD
68710 KIT
68711 MID
68712 MID
68713 MID
68714 BID
68715 YK
68716 WHL
68717 KIT
68718 SUN
68719 KIT
68720 GHD
68721 MID
68722 YK
68723 GHD
68724 HLA
68725 HTN
68726 YK
68727 BID
68728 TDK
68729 TDK
68730 SUN
68731 TDK
68732 HTN
68733 EFD
68734 WHL
68735 YK
68736 BOR
68737 BOR
68738 DAR
68739 YK
68740 MID
68741 YK
68742 WHL
68743 HTN
68744 HTN
68745 YK
68746 NEV
68747 HLA
68748 HLA
68749 KIT
68750 KIT
68751 HLA
68752 HLA
68753 HLA
68754 MID

0-6-0ST
J52 CLASS

68757 HSY
68758 HSY
68759 HSY
68760 HSY
68761 HSY
68762 CLK
68763 DON
68764 KX
68765 NWE
68766 ARD
68767 CLK
68768 CLK
68769 DON
68770 KX
68771 KX
68772 KX
68773 HSY
68774 HSY
68775 DON
68776 HSY
68777 HSY
68778 HSY
68779 CLK
68780 KX

68781	HSY
68782	DONW
68783	HSY
68784	HSY
68785	HSY
68786	DON
68787	HSY
68788	HSY
68789	NWE
68790	ARD
68791	HSY
68792	CLK
68793	HSY
68794	HSY
68795	HSY
68796	HSY
68797	KX
68798	NWE
68799	KX
68800	DON
68801	GRA
68802	KX
68803	KX
68804	DON
68805	KX
68806	DON
68807	CLK
68808	HSY
68809	KX
68810	CLK
68811	HSY
68812	CLK
68813	DON
68814	CLK
68815	HSY
68816	GRA
68817	NWE
68818	KX
68819	NWE
68820	NWE
68821	NWE
68822	KX
68823	NWE
68824	NWE
68825	HSY
68826	HSY
68827	HSY
68828	KX
68829	HSY
68830	KX
68831	KX
68832	KX
68833	HSY
68834	HSY
68835	DON
68836	DON
68837	DON
68838	KX
68839	CLK
68840	NWE
68841	DON
68842	DON
68843	DON
68844	DON
68845	DON
68846	DON
68847	DON
68848	ARD
68849	DON
68850	NWE
68851	HSY
68852	NWE
68853	HSY
68854	KX
68855	KX
68856	HSY
68857	DON
68858	CLK
68859	CLK
68860	DON
68861	KX
68862	KX
68863	CLK
68864	KX
68865	DON
68866	NWE
68867	CLK
68868	NWE
68869	DON
68870	DON
68871	ARD
68872	ARD
68873	KX
68874	KX
68875	CLK
68876	NWE
68877	GRA
68878	KX
68879	NWE
68880	NWE
68881	KX
68882	CLK
68883	HSY
68884	KX
68885	DON
68886	DON
68887	CLK
68888	KX
68889	KX

0-6-0T
J50 CLASS

68890	DON
68891	WFD
68892	BFD
68893	DON
68894	WFD
68895	BFD
68896	ARD
68897	BFD
68898	BFD
68899	DON
68900	ARD
68901	ARD
68902	BFD
68903	ARD
68904	ARD
68905	STR
68906	BFD
68907	ARD
68908	BFD
68909	ARD
68910	ARD
68911	COP
68912	BFD
68913	COP
68914	ARD
68915	ARD
68916	ARD
68917	ARD
68918	DON
68919	ARD
68920	WFD
68921	ARD
68922	BFD
68923	BFD
68924	STR
68925	ARD
68926	DON
68927	ANN
68928	SHF
68929	ANN
68930	ARD
68931	ARD
68932	BFD
68933	BFD
68934	BFD
68935	ANN
68936	DON
68937	COP
68938	ARD
68939	ARD
68940	BFD
68941	BFD
68942	BFD
68943	BFD
68944	BFD
68945	COP
68946	COP
68947	ARD
68948	ARD
68949	ARD
68950	STR
68951	ARD
68952	STM
68953	EFD
68954	EFD
68955	EFD
68956	EFD
68957	EFD
68958	EFD
68959	BFD
68960	ARD
68961	BFD
68962	FRO
68963	STR
68964	FRO
68965	STR
68966	ARD
68967	STR
68968	FRO
68969	BFD
68970	FRO
68971	FRO
68972	ANN
68973	FRO
68974	DON
68975	ANN
68976	ANN
68977	STR
68978	COP
68979	DON
68980	DON
68981	CLK
68982	CLK
68983	SHF
68984	COP
68985	DON
68986	DON
68987	DON
68988	COP
68989	DON
68990	SHF
68991	DON

2-6-4T
L3 CLASS

69050	WFD
69051	MEX
69052	NTH
69053	NEA
69054	NEA
69055	NEA
69056	NEA
69057	FRO
69058	FRO
69059	MEX
69060	NEA
69061	NEA
69062	NTH
69064	NWE
69065	MEX
69066	MEX
69067	NEA
69068	NEA
69069	WFD

2-6-4T
L2 CLASS

69070	NEA
69071	NEA

0-6-4T
M2 CLASS

69076*	NEA
69077*	NEA

0-6-2T
N12 CLASS

69089	HLS

0-6-2T
N10 CLASS

69090	GHD
69091	GHD
69092	GHD
69093	GHD
69094	HLD
69095	BLA
69096	HLD
69097	GHD
69098	HLD
69099	GHD
69100	GHD
69101	NLN
69102	GHD
69103	GHD
69104	HLD
69105	GHD
69106	GHD
69107	GHD
69108	HLD
69109	GHD

0-6-2T
N13 CLASS

69110	HLS
69111	HLS
69112	HLS
69113	HLS
69114	NEV
69115	NEV
69116	HLS
69117	NEV
69118	NEV
69119	HLS

0-6-2T
N14 CLASS

69120	EFD
69124	EFD
69125	KIT

0-6-2T
N15 CLASS

69126	EFD
69127	EFD
69128	ABD
69129	ABD
69130	STM
69131	EFD
69132	THJ
69133	STM
69134	STM
69135	DFU
69136	DFU
69137	POL
69138	EFD
69139	CAR
69140	STM
69141	KPS
69142	BGT
69143	PKD
69144	STM
69145	PKD
69146	STM
69147	STM
69148	STM
69149	STM
69150	THJ
69151	PKD
69152	STM
69153	THJ
69154	DFU
69155	CAR
69156	BGT
69157	BGT
69158	BGT
69159	BGT
69160	DFU
69161	PKD
69162	POL
69163	EFD
69164	DFU
69165	EFD
69166	EFD
69167	STM
69168	STM
69169	HAY
69170	EFD
69171	PKD
69172	STM
69173	STM
69174	CAR
69175	STM
69176	EFD
69177	EFD
69178	EFD
69179	EFD
69180	EFD
69181	EFD
69182	EFD
69183	EFD
69184	EFD
69185	CAR
69186	STM
69187	STM
69188	EFD
69189	EFD
69190	PKD
69191	EFD
69192	DFU
69193	PKD
69194	PKD
69195	PKD
69196	KPS
69197	CAR
69198	PKD
69199	PKD
69200	POL
69201	DFU
69202	DFU
69203	EFD
69204	DFU
69205	EFD
69206	KPS
69207	KPS
69208	EFD
69209	PKD
69210	PKD
69211	THJ
69212	PKD
69213	PKD
69214	PKD
69215	CAR
69216	BGT
69217	PKD
69218	CAR
69219	STM

69220	HAY
69221	DFU
69222	EFD
69223	THJ
69224	THJ

0-6-2T
N4 CLASS

69225	MEX
69226	SHF
69227	SHF
69228	SHF
69229	SHF
69230	SHF
69231	MEX
69232	SHF
69233	SHF
69234	SHF
69235	SHF
69236	SHF
69237	SHF
69239	MEX
69240	SHF
69241	SHF
69242	SHF
69243	SHF
69244	SHF
69245	SHF
69246	MEX
69247	SHF

0-6-2T
N5 CLASS

69250	LIV
69251	STP
69252	TFD
69253	BFD
69254	GOR
69255	TFD
69256	BFD
69257	NEA
69258	LIV
69259	NEA
69260	GOR
69261	BFD
69262	NTH
69263	CLK
69264	MEX
69265	WAL
69266	COP
69267	WRX
69268	BRN
69269	WFD
69270	GOR
69271	COP
69272	GOR
69273	NEA
69274	CHR
69275	TUX
69276	STP
69277	BRN
69278	BRN
69279	STV
69280	BFD
69281	CHR
69282	MEX
69283	NEA
69284	LNG
69285	BRN
69286	CLK
69287	TUX
69288	LIV
69289	BID
69290	WRX
69291	BRN
69292	STV
69293	NTH
69294	RET
69295	STV
69296	GOR
69297	MEX
69298	WAL
69299	GOR
69300	NEA
69301	STV
69302	NEA
69303	BRN
69304	TFD
69305	IMM
69306	LTH
69307	GOR
69308	GOR
69309	IMM
69310	WFD
69311	LIN
69312	CLK
69313	NEA
69314	MEX
69315	NEA
69316	MEX
69317	STP
69318	NEA
69319	LNG
69320	BRN
69321	RET
69322	IMM
69323	LNG
69324	CLK
69325	BRN
69326	WRX
69327	LNG
69328	STP
69329	WRX
69330	WRX
69331	STP
69332	STP
69333	GOR
69334	BRN
69335	NTH
69336	TFD
69337	LIV
69338	WAL
69339	LIV
69340	WRX
69341	NEA
69342	LIV
69343	TFD
69344	WAL
69345	BRN
69346	WRX
69347	GOR
69348	BRN
69349	NTH
69350	NEA
69351	STV
69352	WRX
69353	GOR
69354	NEA
69355	BRN
69356	WAL
69357	BRN
69358	NEA
69359	STP
69360	STV
69361	TFD
69362	WRX
69363	STV
69364	TFD
69365	BRN
69366	WRX
69367	BRN
69368	BRN
69369	NEA
69370	TFD

0-6-2T
N8 CLASS

69371	HTN
69372	HTN
69373	HLD
69374	HLD
69375	HLD
69376	HLD
69377	HLD
69378	TDK
69379	HLD
69380	HTN
69381	HLD
69382	HLD
69383	HLD
69384	CON
69385	HLD
69386	HLD
69387	HTN
69389	HLD
69390	HTN
69391	HLD
69392	HLD
69393	HLD
69394	CON
69395	TDK
69396	HLD
69397	HLD
69398	HLD
69399	HLD
69400	SUN
69401	HLD

0-6-2T
N9 CLASS

69410	TDK
69411	CON
69413	SUN
69414	CON
69415	DAR
69418	DAR
69419	HAV
69420	TDK
69421	SUN
69422	AUK
69423	NLN
69424	PEL
69425	SUN
69426	DAR
69427	SUN
69428	SUN
69429	SUN

0-6-2T
N1 CLASS

69430	COP
69431	HSY
69432	HSY
69433	HSY
69434	KX
69435	HSY
69436	COP
69437	BFD
69439	HSY
69440	COP
69441	HSY
69442	HSY
69443	BFD
69444	COP
69445	HSY
69446	COP
69447	BFD
69448	BFD
69449	BFD
69450	HSY
69451	HSY
69452	ARD
69453	HSY
69454	BFD
69455	HAT
69456	HSY
69457	HSY
69458	HSY
69459	BFD
69460	HSY
69461	ARD
69462	KX
69463	HSY
69464	BFD
69465	HSY
69466	KX
69467	KX
69468	KX
69469	KX
69470	HSY
69471	COP
69472	COP
69473	ARD
69474	BFD
69475	HSY
69476	KX
69477	HSY
69478	BFD
69479	BFD
69480	KX
69481	KX
69482	BFD
69483	BFD
69484	KX
69485	BFD

0-6-2T
N2 CLASS

69490	KX
69491	KX
69492	KX
69493	KX
69494	KX
69495	KX
69496	KX
69497	KX
69498	KX
69499	KX
69500	PKD
69501	CLK
69502	HAT
69503	KPS
69504	KX
69505	HSY
69506	KX
69507	PKD
69508	KPS
69509	KPS
69510	PKD
69511	KPS
69512	KX
69513	HSY
69514	PKD
69515	HIT
69516	HSY
69517	KX
69518	KPS
69519	NEA
69520	KX
69521	KX
69522	HSY
69523	KX
69524	KX
69525	KX
69526	KX
69527	KX
69528	KX
69529	KX
69530	HSY
69531	HSY
69532	KX
69533	HSY
69534	HAT
69535	KX
69536	KX
69537	HAT
69538	KX
69539	KX
69540	KX
69541	KX
69542	KX
69543	KX
69544	KX
69545	KX
69546	KX
69547	HSY
69548	KX
69549	KX
69550	CLK
69551	HAT
69552	CLK
69553	KPS
69554	HAT
69555	CLK
69556	HSY
69557	HIT
69558	HAT
69559	HAT
69560	CLK
69561	NEA
69562	PKD
69563	KPS
69564	PKD
69565	PKD
69566	HSY
69567	KX
69568	KX
69569	KX
69570	KX
69571	KX
69572	KX
69573	KX
69574	KX
69575	KX
69576	KX
69577	KX
69578	KX
69579	KX
69580	HAT
69581	KX
69582	HAT
69583	KX
69584	KX
69585	KX
69586	HAT
69587	HAT
69588	HAT
69589	KX
69590	HAT
69591	KX
69592	KX
69593	KX
69594	HAT
69595	PKD
69596	KPS

0-6-2T
N7 CLASS

69600	STR
69601	STR
69602	STR
69603	STR
69604	STR
69605	STR
69606	STR
69607	STR
69608	STR
69609	STR

69610 STR
69611 STR
69612 STR
69613 STR
69614 STR
69615 STR
69616 STR
69617 STR
69618 STR
69619 STR
69620 STR
69621 STR
69622 STR
69623 STR
69624 STR
69625 STR
69626 STR
69627 STR
69628 STR
69629 STR
69630 STR
69631 STR
69632 STR
69633 STR
69634 STR
69635 STR
69636 STR
69637 STR
69638 STR
69639 STR
69640 STR
69641 STR
69642 STR
69643 STR
69644 STR
69645 STR
69646 STR
69647 STR
69648 STR
69649 STR
69650 STR
69651 STR
69652 STR
69653 STR
69654 STR
69655 STR
69656 STR
69657 STR
69658 STR
69659 STR
69660 STR
69661 STR
69662 STR
69663 STR
69664 STR
69665 STR
69666 STR
69667 STR
69668 STR
69669 STR
69670 STR
69671 STR
69672 STR
69673 STR
69674 STR
69675 STR
69676 STR
69677 STR
69678 STR
69679 STR
69680 STR
69681 STR
69682 STR
69683 STR
69684 STR
69685 STR
69686 STR
69687 STR
69688 STR
69689 HAT
69690 HAT
69691 HAT
69692 HAT
69693 STR
69694 HAT
69695 HAT
69696 HAT
69697 STR
69698 HAT
69699 STR
69700 STR
69701 STR
69702 STR
69703 STR
69704 STR
69705 STR
69706 STR
69707 STR
69708 STR
69709 STR
69710 STR
69711 STR
69712 STR
69713 STR
69714 STR
69715 STR
69716 STR
69717 STR
69718 STR
69719 STR
69720 STR
69721 STR
69722 STR
69723 STR
69724 STR
69725 STR
69726 STR
69727 STR
69728 STR
69729 STR
69730 STR
69731 STR
69732 STR
69733 STR

4-6-2T
A7 CLASS

69770 HLD
69771 CUD
69772 HLD
69773 HLD
69774 HLS
69775 HLD
69776 HLS
69777 HLD
69778 HLD
69779 HLD
69780 HLD
69781 SKN
69782 HLD
69783 HLD
69784 HLD
69785 HLS
69786 HLD
69787 SKN
69788 HLD
69789 CUD

4-6-2T
A6 CLASS

69791 SBK
69792 WBY
69793 SBK
69794 SBK
69795 HLB
69796 HLB
69797 SBK
69798 HLB
69799 SBK

4-6-2T
A5 CLASS

69800 NEA
69801 NEA
69802 NEA
69803 NEA
69804 NEA
69805 NEA
69806 NEA
69807 NEA
69808 NEA
69809 NEA
69810 NEA
69811 NEA
69812 NEA
69813 NEA
69814 NEA
69815 NEA
69816 NEA
69817 NEA
69818 NEA
69819 NEA
69820 NEA
69821 NEA
69822 NEA
69823 NEA
69824 NEA
69825 NEA
69826 NEA
69827 NEA
69828 NEA
69829 NEA
69830 DAR
69831 DAR
69832 DAR
69833 DAR
69834 DAR
69835 DAR
69836 DAR
69837 DAR
69838 DAR
69839 DAR
69840 DAR
69841 DAR
69842 DAR

4-6-2T
A8 CLASS

69850 SUN
69851 BLA
69852 WBY
69853 BLA
69854 HLB
69855 HLB
69856 AUK
69857 BLA
69858 MID
69859 MID
69860 MID
69861 SUN
69862 WHL
69863 WHL
69864 WHL
69865 BLA
69866 HLB
69867 HLB
69868 SAL
69869 MID
69870 AUK
69871 WHL
69872 SAL
69873 HLB
69874 SUN
69875 SAL
69876 SAL
69877 AUK
69878 MID
69879 AUK
69880 MID
69881 SCA
69882 SAL
69883 SAL
69884 SAL
69885 SCA
69886 AUK
69887 SUN
69888 MID
69889 SAL
69890 HLB
69891 SAL
69892 SAL
69893 WHL
69894 SCA

0-8-4T
S1 CLASS

69900 MEX
69901 MEX
69902 MAR
69903 MAR
69904 MEX
69905 MEX

4-8-0T
T1 CLASS

69910 NPT
69911 NPT
69912 HLD
69913 NPT
69914 SEL
69915 HLD
69916 NPT
69917 NPT
69918 SKN
69919 NPT
69920 HLD
69921 NPT
69922 HLD

0-8-0T
Q1 CLASS

69925 EFD
69926 CAM
69927 EFD
69928 LNG
69929 LNG
69930 FRO
69931 GHD
69932 FRO
69933 GHD
69934 FRO
69935 FRO
69936 FRO
69937 FRO

BEYER-GARRATT
2-8-8-2T
U1 CLASS

69999 MEX

War Department (WD) 2-8-0 and 2-10-0 Locomotives

WD 2-8-0 Locomotives Allocated to BR Depots Eastern Region

90000	3000	ANN
90001	3001	TWD
90002	3002	ANN
90003	3003	MAR
90004	3004	THJ
90005	3005	IMM
90006	3006	TWD
90007	3007	MEX
90008	3008	CLK
90009	3009	MEX
90010	3010	ANN
90011	3011	MEX
90012	3012	HTN
90013	3013	MAR
90014	3014	ANN
90015	3015	MAR
90016	3016	NPT
90017	3017	THJ
90018	3018	MAR
90019	3019	THJ
90020	3020	EFD
90021	3021	CLK
90022	3022	CLK
90023	3023	MAR
90024	3024	MAR
90025	3025	CLK
90026	3026	ANN
90027	3027	CLK
90028	3028	MAR
90029	3029	MAR
90030	3030	TWD
90031	3031	NWE
90032	3032	IMM
90033	3033	WFD
90034	3034	NWE
90035	3035	MAR
90036	3036	CLK
90037	3037	MAR
90038	3038	STM
90039	3039	WFD
90040	3040	WFD
90041	3041	ABD
90042	3042	MAR
90043	3043	WFD
90044	3044	NPT
90045	3045	HTN
90046	3046	WFD
90047	3047	MEX
90048	3048	HTN
90049	3049	THJ

90050	3050	CLK
90051	3051	CLK
90052	3052	MEX
90053	3053	MAR
90054	3054	NPT
90055	3055	NWE
90056	3056	WFD
90057	3057	MEX
90058	3058	THJ
90059	3059	NWE
90060	3060	NWE
90061	3061	HTN
90062	3062	NWE
90063	3063	STM
90064	3064	NWE
90065	3065	WFD
90066	3066	NWE
90067	3067	HTN
90068	3068	CLK
90069	3069	CLK
90070	3070	NWE
90071	3071	DEE
90072	3072	TWD
90073	3073	CLK
90074	3074	NPT
90075	3075	NWE
90076	3076	HTN
90077	3077	DEE
90078	3078	HTN
90079	3079	ANN
90080	3080	WFD
90081	3081	NPT
90082	3082	HTN
90083	3083	MAR
90084	3084	CLK
90085	3085	MAR
90086	3086	HTN
90087	3087	MAR
90088	3088	NWE
90089	3089	STM
90090	3090	STM
90091	3091	NPT
90092	3092	HTN
90093	3093	NWE
90094	3094	MEX
90095	3095	WFD
90096	3096	MAR
90097	3097	ABD
90098	3098	NPT
90099	3099	HTN
90100	3100	CLK
90103	77003	NEV
90104	77004	HLS
90106	77006	NPT
90108	77008	MEX
90109	77010	NPT
90111	77013	NEV
90114	77016	NPT
90115	77017	NWE
90116	77018	HLS
90117	77019	DFU
90118	77020	MEX
90119	77022	MEX
90120	77023	MEX
90128	77031	THJ
90129	77032	HLD
90130	77034	NWE
90131	77035	MAR
90132	77036	NPT
90133	77037	CLK
90134	77039	DFU
90136	77041	CLK
90137	77042	NEV
90138	77044	STM
90139	77047	WFD
90144	77152	MEX
90145	77155	THJ
90146	77157	MEX

90150	77163	MEX
90151	77164	NWE
90153	77166	MEX
90154	77167	HLS
90155	77169	SKN
90156	77170	NEV
90158	77173	MAR
90159	77174	NPT
90160	77175	NEV
90161	77176	MEX
90162	77178	CLK
90165	77181	CLK
90166	77182	MEX
90168	77185	THJ
90169	77186	MAR
90170	77187	THJ
90172	77195	SKN
90174	77198	EFD
90175	77199	MAR
90177	77201	THJ
90180	77204	NWE
90182	77206	THJ
90183	77207	STM
90184	77208	SKN
90185	77209	CLK
90189	77215	MEX
90190	77218	HLS
90191	77221	NWE
90192	77222	EFD
90195	77227	MEX
90196	77228	MEX
90198	77230	DEE
90199	77231	DFU
90200	77232	NEV
90202	77235	WFD
90208	77248	HLD
90209	77249	MEX
90210	77252	TDK
90215	77258	MEX
90217	77260	NEV
90218	77261	WFD
90219	77302	THJ
90220	77303	MEX
90221	77305	MAR
90223	77307	NEV
90224	77309	MAR
90227	77312	STM
90228	77313	THJ
90229	77314	MEX
90230	77315	NPT
90231	77317	YK
90232	77319	MEX
90233	77320	NEV
90235	77323	NEV
90236	77324	THJ
90239	77327	MAR
90240	77328	SKN
90241	77329	YK
90244	77334	WFD
90246	77338	HLS
90248	77342	NPT
90250	77350	MEX
90251	77351	MAR
90252	77352	MEX
90253	77353	HLS
90255	77356	MEX
90256	77358	NWE
90258	77362	STM
90259	77364	MAR
90262	77371	THJ
90263	77372	NEV
90265	77375	EFD
90269	77381	STV
90270	77386	MEX
90272	77390	TDK
90273	77392	NPT
90275	77394	MEX
90276	77395	STV

90279	77401	MAR
90280	77402	MEX
90281	77404	THJ
90282	77406	THJ
90285	77411	MEX
90286	77413	MEX
90287	77414	MAR
90288	77415	MAR
90289	77416	STM
90290	77418	MEX
90291	77419	STM
90293	77424	THJ
90294	77425	MAR
90295	77426	STM
90296	77428	MEX
90298	77431	EFD
90299	77432	MAR
90300	77433	THJ
90301	77434	MEX
90302	77436	MAR
90303	77439	NEV
90304	77440	MAR
90305	77441	NPT
90306	77442	DFU
90309	77445	TDK
90311	77449	MEX
90313	70802	EFD
90314	70807	YK
90319	70817	THJ
90323	70834	HLD
90326	70839	NEV
90330	70850	MEX
90340	70871	NWE
90344	70877	SKN
90346	77263	NPT
90348	77271	NPT
90349	77274	NWE
90350	77278	THJ
90352	77283	TDK
90358	77292	WFD
90365	78514	CLK
90368	78525	CLK
90369	78526	NEV
90371	78561	STM
90373	78564	NPT
90374	78568	STM
90376	78572	STM
90377	78575	SKN
90378	78578	HLD
90382	78585	HLD
90383	78587	NEV
90384	78588	MAR
90386	78592	MAR
90387	78594	STM
90391	78598	YK
90392	78599	MAR
90393	78600	MAR
90394	78601	TDK
90400	78609	MEX
90401	78610	MEX
90403	78614	HLD
90405	78616	SKN
90409	78532	HLD
90410	78537	MEX
90411	78538	NEV
90418	78553	HLD
90421	78559	MEX
90422	3101	MAR
90423	3102	CLK
90424	3103	HTN
90425	3104	MAR
90426	3105	HTN
90427	3106	TWD
90428	3107	MAR
90429	3108	MEX
90430	3109	HTN
90431	3110	MAR
90432	3111	HTN

90433	3112	MAR
90434	3113	HTN
90435	3114	TWD
90436	3115	STM
90437	3116	WFD
90438	3117	NWE
90439	3118	NWE
90440	3119	EFD
90441	3120	EFD
90442	3121	NWE
90443	3122	MAR
90444	3123	DEE
90445	3124	HTN
90446	3125	NPT
90447	3126	STM
90448	3127	WFD
90449	3128	CLK
90450	3129	CLK
90451	3130	NPT
90452	3131	NPT
90453	3132	NWE
90454	3133	MAR
90455	3134	ABD
90456	3135	NWE
90457	3136	CLK
90458	3137	HTN
90459	3138	CLK
90460	3139	NWE
90461	3140	NPT
90462	3141	HTN
90463	3142	DEE
90464	3143	THJ
90465	3144	NPT
90466	3145	CLK
90467	3146	HTN
90468	3147	STM
90469	3148	STM
90470	3149	MEX
90471	3150	MAR
90472	3151	THJ
90473	3152	MAR
90474	3153	NWE
90475	3154	NPT
90476	3155	MAR
90477	3156	MAR
90478	3157	CLK
90479	3158	HTN
90480	3159	MAR
90481	3160	NPT
90482	3161	HTN
90483	3162	HTN
90484	3163	CLK
90485	3164	HTN
90486	3165	WFD
90487	3166	HTN
90488	3167	HTN
90489	3168	THJ
90490	3169	NWE
90491	3170	CLK
90492	3171	CLK
90493	3172	STM
90494	3173	NWE
90495	3174	NWE
90496	3175	STM
90497	3176	MEX
90498	3177	THJ
90499	3178	CLK
90500	3179	NPT
90501	3180	STM
90502	3181	NWE
90503	3182	HTN
90504	3183	WFD
90505	3184	CLK
90506	3185	MAR
90507	3186	WFD
90508	3187	MAR
90509	3188	WFD
90510	3189	NWE

90511	3190	TWD
90512	3191	CLK
90513	3192	CLK
90514	3193	NWE
90515	3194	DEE
90516	3195	WFD
90517	3196	NPT
90518	3197	HTN
90519	3198	NWE
90520	3199	WFD
90521	77050	NEV
90522	77051	MAR
90526	77055	TDK
90528	77057	WFD
90532	77061	WFD
90534	77063	THJ
90536	77066	THJ
90537	77067	HLS
90538	77068	MEX
90539	77070	THJ
90540	77071	MAR
90542	77073	DFU
90544	77075	HLS
90545	77076	EFD
90547	77078	THJ
90550	77081	NEV
90551	77085	WFD
90553	77087	DFU
90554	77088	MAR
90555	77089	STM
90559	77095	NPT
90560	77096	DFU
90567	77104	HLS
90569	77107	DFU
90571	77111	YK
90574	77118	WFD
90575	77119	DFU
90576	77120	NPT
90577	77121	NWE
90580	77124	MAR
90582	77127	MAR
90583	77128	HLS
90584	77129	NPT
90586	77135	NEV
90587	77138	HLS
90590	77144	MEX
90592	77147	STM
90594	77149	HLS
90596	77452	MEX
90597	77453	MEX
90598	77454	MEX
90599	77455	EFD
90601	77457	MAR
90602	77458	MAR
90603	77459	SKN
90605	77461	NPT
90606	77462	YK
90608	77464	MAR
90609	77465	NEV
90611	77467	TDK
90612	77468	NEV
90613	77469	NWE
90614	77470	THJ
90616	77476	THJ
90618	77480	NEV
90621	77484	NEV
90623	77488	SKN
90625	77492	NPT
90626	77494	STM
90627	77497	TDK
90628	77499	NEV
90629	77503	YK
90634	78637	STV
90636	78643	YK
90638	78650	YK
90646	78682	CLK
90647	78683	CLK
90648	78684	NEV

90653	78700	MEX	90663	79186	HLD	90676	79208	CLK	90696	79242	MEX	90709	79271	MEX
90657	78715	MEX	90665	79194	MEX	90677	79209	HLD	90697	79243	HLD	90714	79276	MEX
90659	79178	MEX	90668	79198	MAR	90683	79220	NEV	90700	79259	MEX	90727	79306	DFU
90660	79181	MAR	90670	79202	TWD	90688	79227	TDK	90703	79263	NEV	90730	79310	YK
90661	79182	TDK	90672	79204	CLK	90690	79229	THJ	90704	79264	TWD	90732*	79312	MAR
90662	79184	CLK	90674	79206	TWD	90695	79239	HLD	90705	79265	DFU	*CARRIED THE NAME "VULCAN"		

NOTE: LOCOMOTIVES 90000 - 90100 AND 90422 - 90520 PURCHASED BY THE L.N.E.R. IN 1946 AND KNOWN AS CLASS 07. THE REMAINDER WERE ON LOAN FROM THE MINISTRY OF SUPPLY.

WD 2-8-0 Locomotives Allocated to BR Depots Western Region

90101	77000	CDF	90188	77214	NA	90312	70801	SPM	90535	77064	OXY	90682	79219	OXY
90102	77001	NA	90201	77234	OXY	90315	70808	CNYD	90546	77077	TN	90685	79224	TYS
90105	77005	PDN	90205	77241	NA	90324	70836	SPM	90548	77079	OXY	90686	79225	OXY
90110	77012	BAN	90207	77247	SPM	90327	70843	DID	90561	77097	TYS	90687	79226	BHD
90112	77014	BAN	90212	77255	LA	90343	70876	SPM	90563	77099	PPRD	90691	79232	GLO
90113	77015	PDN	90214	77257	CHR	90355	77288	CDF	90565	77102	NPT	90693	79234	PDN
90123	77026	BAN	90225	77310	LLY	90356	77289	SPM	90568	77106	CDF	90694	79235	PPRD
90125	77028	OXY	90237	77325	LA	90357	77291	PDN	90572	77115	CHR	90701	79261	SPM
90135	77040	OXY	90238	77326	SPM	90359	77294	LA	90573	77116	SPM	90712	79274	STJ
90141	77049	OXY	90261	77368	RDG	90361	77297	BAN	90579	77123	CDF	90715	79278	GLO
90143	77151	OXY	90266	77378	RDG	90363	78510	NPT	90585	77130	PDN	90723	79301	SPM
90148	77161	LA	90268	77380	CDF	90364	78512	BAN	90589	77142	SPM	90725	79303	DID
90152	77165	OXY	90271	77388	CDF	90366	78521	PDN	90624	77489	LLY	90729	79309	SPM
90167	77184	PDN	90274	77393	RDG	90367	78522	RDG	90630	77508	SPM			
90173	77196	LA	90283	77407	LLY	90396	78604	BAN	90633	78632	PDN	NOTE:		
90176	77200	SPM	90284	77408	BAN	90413	78542	GLO	90642	78671	LA	ON LOAN FROM		
90178	77202	OXY	90292	77421	LA	90414	78543	CDF	90652	78695	OXY	THE MINISTRY OF		
90179	77203	GLO	90297	77429	LLY	90524	77053	CDF	90656	78714	CNYD	SUPPLY.		
90186	77210	NA	90307	77443	PPRD	90529	77058	OXF	90658	78717	LA			

WD 2-8-0 Locomotives Allocated to BR Depots Southern Region

90107	77007	BTN	90254	77355	BA	90389	78596	BA	90562	77098	FEL	90669	79199	HIT
90127	77030	FEL	90257	77359	FEL	90390	78597	HIT	90564	77101	BA	90671	79203	HIT
90142	77150	FEL	90267	77379	FEL	90408	78531	BA	90566	77103	HIT	90675	79207	FEL
90164	77180	BA	90308	77444	FEL	90523	77052	FEL	90570	77108	FEL	90678	79210	HIT
90181	77205	BA	90317	70811	AFD	90527	77056	FEL	90578	77122	FEL	90702	79262	HIT
90194	77226	BA	90332	70853	HIT	90530	77059	FEL	90604	77460	FEL	90718	79281	HIT
90213	77256	BA	90345	70878	BTN	90533	77062	FEL	90619	77481	BA			
90216	77259	BA	90347	77270	BTN	90543	77074	FEL	90622	77485	BA			
90226	77311	BA	90354	77286	BTN	90552	77086	BA	90641	78666	AFD	NOTE: ON LOAN		
90234	77321	BA	90360	77296	AFD	90556	77090	BA	90650	78688	BA	FROM THE MINISTRY		
90247	77340	BTN	90375	78569	BA	90558	77094	BA	90655	78705	AFD	OF SUPPLY.		

WD 2-10-0 Locomotives Allocated to BR Depots London Midland Region

90773	73798	12A	90774	73799	12A	NOTE: ON LOAN FROM THE MINISTRY OF SUPPLY.

WD Austerity 2-8-0 and 2-10-0 Locomotives in store — owned by the Ministry of Supply

2-8-0 s		90204	77239	90321	70829	90353	77285	90407	78624	90595	77451
90121	77024	90206	77242	90322	70833	90362	77299	90412	78541	90600	77456
90122	77025	90211	77253	90325	70838	90370	78560	90415	78544	90607	77463
90124	77027	90222	77306	90328	70845	90372	78563	90416	78546	90610	77466
90126	77029	90242	77330	90329	70849	90379	78580	90417	78551	90615	77471
90140	77048	90243	77332	90331	70851	90380	78581	90419	78554	90617	77479
90147	77160	90245	77335	90333	70857	90381	78583	90420	78556	90620	77482
90149	77162	90249	77348	90334	70859	90385	78590	90525	77054	90631	78626
90157	77171	90260	77365	90335	70860	90388	78595	90531	77060	90632	78629
90163	77179	90264	77374	90336	70864	90395	78602	90541	77072	90635	78638
90171	77192	90277	77398	90337	70865	90397	78605	90549	77080	90637	78644
90187	77212	90278	77399	90338	70866	90398	78606	90557	77092	90639	78652
90193	77225	90310	77447	90339	70867	90399	78607	90581	77126	90640	78658
90197	77229	90316	70809	90341	70874	90402	78612	90588	77141	90643	78672
90203	77237	90318	70814	90342	70875	90404	78615	90591	77145	90644	78675
		90320	70825	90351	77280	90406	78621	90593	77148	90645	78681

WD Austerity 2-8-0 Locomotives taken out of store and added to BR Operating Stock, on loan during 1948

B.R. No.	W.D. No.	TO TRAFFIC	ALLOCATION
90121	77024	Week ended 17 July	Aberdeen Ferryhill
90124	77027	April	Cardiff Canton
90149	77162	Week ended 1 May	Glasgow Eastfield
90193	77225	Week ended 7 February	Hull Dairycoates
90203	77237	Week ended 22 May	Aberdeen Ferryhill
90211	77253	Week ended 3 January	Mexborough
90222	77306	Week ended 14 February	Glasgow Eastfield
90260	77365	Week ended 15 May	Aberdeen Ferryhill
90264	77374	Week ended 15 May	Glasgow Eastfield
90278	77399	Week ended 15 May	Aberdeen Ferryhill
90399	78607	May	Newport Ebbw Junction
90549	77080	Week ended 29 May	Glasgow Eastfield
90600	77456	Week ended 1 May	Glasgow Eastfield
90689	79228	May	Newport Ebbw Junction
90716	79279	March	Severn Tunnel Junction
90717	79280	Week ended 15 May	Hull Springhead
90720	79283	May	Old Oak Common

90649 78685
90651 78689
90654 78704
90664 79190
90666 79195
90667 79196
90673 79205
90679 79213
90680 79214
90681 79215

90684 79221
90689 79228
90692 79233
90698 79244
90699 79254
90706 79266
90707 79268
90708 79269
90710 79272
90711 79273

90713 79275
90716 79279
90717 79280
90719 79282
90720 79283
90721 79294
90722 79298
90724 79302
90726 79304
90728 79307

90731 79311

2-10-0s

90750 73774
90751 73775
90752 73776
90753 73777
90754 73778
90755 73779
90756 73780

90757 73781
90758 73782
90759 73783
90760 73784
90761 73785
90762 73786
90763 73787
90764 73788
90765 73789
90766 73790

90767 73791
90768 73792
90769 73793
90770 73794
90771 73795
90772 73796

Diesel, Petrol and Electric Locomotives

Ex-LMSR Diesel Locomotives

L.M.S./ENGLISH ELECTRIC Co-Co

10000 17A

HAWTHORN-LESLIE/ ENGLISH ELECTRIC 0-6-0 SHUNTER

12000 7074 5B
12001 7076 5B
12002 7079 5B

L.M.S./ENGLISH ELECTRIC 0-6-0 SHUNTER

12003 7080 8C
12004 7081 1A
12005 7082 1A
12006 7083 18A
12007 7084 18A
12008 7085 18A
12009 7086 1A
12010 7087 1A
12011 7088 8C
12012 7089 18A
12013 7090 8C
12014 7091 5B
12015 7092 5B
12016 7093 8C

12017 7094 5B
12018 7095 5B
12019 7096 1A
12020 7097 8C
12021 7098 1A
12022 7099 1A
12023 7110 1A
12024 7111 12A
12025 7112 12A
12026 7113 12A
12027 7114 12A
12028 7115 12A
12029 7116 1A
12030 7117 1A

12031 7118 1A
12032 7119 1A

L.M.S./ENGLISH ELECTRIC CLASS 11 0-6-0 SHUNTER

12033 7120 5B
12034 7121 5B
12035 7122 5B
12036 7123 5B
12037 7124 5B
12038 7125 18A
12039 7126 21A

12040 7127 21A
12041 7128 21A
12042 7129 21A

LEYLAND DIESEL RAILCARS

29950 27C
29951 27C
29952 27C

ARMSTRONG WHITWORTH AND CO. 0-6-0 SHUNTER

13000 7058 18A

Ex-LNER Diesel, Petrol and Electric Locomotives

L.N.E.R./ENGLISH ELECTRIC CLASS DES1 0-6-0 SHUNTER

15000 8000 MAR
15001 8001 MAR
15002 8002 MAR
15003 8003 MAR

CLASS Y11 PETROL 0-4-0

15098 8188 STR
15099 8189 STR

N.E.R./B.T.H. ELECTRIC Bo-Bo

26500 6480 HTN
26501 6481 HTN

N.E.R./ENGLISH ELECTRIC CLASS EB1 ELECTRIC BO-BO

26502 6490 +

26503 6491 +
26504 6492 +
26505 6493 +
26506 6494 +
26507 6495 +
26508 6496 +
26509 6497 +
26510 6498 STR

26511 6499 +

N.E.R./ MET.VIC CLASS EE1 ELECTRIC 2-C-2

26600 6999 +

+ STORED AT SOUTH GOSFORTH CAR SHEDS.

Ex-Southern Railway Diesel and Electric Locomotives

SOUTHERN RLY/ ENGLISH ELECTRIC 0-6-0 SHUNTER

15201 1 NOR
15202 2 NOR
15203 3 NOR

SOUTHERN RAILWAY/ ENGLISH ELECTRIC

ELECTRIC Co-Co.

20001 CC1 BTN
20002 CC2 BTN

Ex-GWR Diesel Locomotives and Railcars

HAWTHORN-LESLIE/
ENGLISH ELECTRIC
0-6-0 SHUNTER

15100 2 PDN

RAILCARS

No.	Shed	No.	Shed	No.	Shed	No.	Shed	No.	Shed	No.	Shed
1	RDG	2	NPT	12	RDG	21	WEY	30	PPRD		
		3	LDR	13	CARM	22	WOS	31	WOS		
		4	LDR	14	WOS	23	NPT	32	WOS		
		5	WOS	15	CARM	24	SPM	33	STB		
		6	WOS	16	LDR	25	GLO	34	SHL		
		7	WOS	17	SHL	26	LMTN	35	RDG		
		8	STB	18	LTS	27	WOS	36	RDG		
		10	OXF	19	RDG	28	SPM	37	SPM		
		11	OXF	20	SPM	29	LMTN	38	SPM		

Locomotive Names

Ex-Great Western Railway Locomotives

EX-WESTON, CLEVEDON AND PORTISHEAD RAILWAY 0-6-0T

5 Portishead

EX-LLANELLY AND MYNYDD MAWR RAILWAY 0-6-0T

359 Hilda

"1000" COUNTY CLASS 4-6-0

1000 County of Middlesex
1001 County of Bucks
1002 County of Berks
1003 County of Wilts
1004 County of Somerset
1005 County of Devon
1006 County of Cornwall
1007 County of Brecknock
1008 County of Cardigan
1009 County of Carmarthen
1010 County of Caernarvon
1011 County of Chester
1012 County of Denbigh
1013 County of Dorset
1014 County of Glamorgan
1015 County of Gloucester
1016 County of Hants
1017 County of Hereford
1018 County of Leicester
1019 County of Merioneth
1020 County of Monmouth
1021 County of Montgomery
1022 County of Northampton
1023 County of Oxford
1024 County of Pembroke
1025 County of Radnor
1026 County of Salop
1027 County of Stafford
1028 County of Warwick
1029 County of Worcester

EX-LISKEARD AND LOOE RAILWAY 2-4-0T

1308 Lady Margaret

EX-BURRY PORT AND GWENDRAETH VALLEY RAILWAY 0-6-0T

2192 Ashburnham
2193 Burry Port
2194 Kidwelly
2196 Gwendraeth
2197 Pioneer

"2900" SAINT CLASS 4-6-0

2902 Lady of the Lake
2903 Lady of Lyons
2905 Lady Macbeth
2906 Lady of Lynn
2908 Lady of Quality
2912 Saint Ambrose
2913 Saint Andrew
2915 Saint Bartholomew
2916 Saint Benedict
2920 Saint David
2924 Saint Helena
2926 Saint Nicholas
2927 Saint Patrick
2928 Saint Sebastian
2929 Saint Stephen
2930 Saint Vincent
2931 Arlington Court
2932 Ashton Court
2933 Bibury Court
2934 Butleigh Court
2935 Caynham Court
2936 Cefntilla Court
2937 Clevedon Court
2938 Corsham Court
2939 Croome Court
2940 Dorney Court
2941 Easton Court
2942 Fawley Court
2943 Hampton Court
2944 Highnam Court
2945 Hillingdon Court
2946 Langford Court
2947 Madresfield Court
2948 Stackpole Court
2949 Stanford Court
2950 Taplow Court
2951 Tawstock Court
2952 Twineham Court
2953 Titley Court
2954 Tockenham Court
2955 Tortworth Court
2979 Quentin Durward
2980 Coeur de Lion
2981 Ivanhoe
2987 Bride of Lammermoor
2988 Rob Roy
2989 Talisman

"3300" BULLDOG CLASS 4-4-0

3341 Blasius
3363 Alfred Baldwin
3364 Frank Bibby
3376 River Plym
3379 River Fal
3391 Dominion of Canada
3393 Australia
3395 Tasmania
3396 Natal Colony
3400 Winnipeg
3401 Vancouver
3406 Calcutta
3407 Madras
3408 Bombay
3417 Lord Mildmay of Flete
3418 Sir Arthur Yorke
3430 Inchcape
3441 Blackbird
3442 Bullfinch
3443 Chaffinch
3444 Cormorant
3445 Flamingo
3446 Goldfinch
3447 Jackdaw
3448 Kingfisher
3449 Nightingale
3450 Peacock
3451 Pelican
3452 Penguin
3453 Seagull
3454 Skylark
3455 Starling

"4000" STAR CLASS 4-6-0

4003 Lode Star
4004 Morning Star
4007 Swallowfield Park
4012 Knight of the Thistle
4013 Knight of St. Patrick
4015 Knight of St. John
4017 Knight of Liége
4018 Knight of the Grand Cross
4019 Knight Templar
4020 Knight Commander
4021 British Monarch
4031 Queen Mary
4033 Queen Victoria
4034 Queen Adelaide
4035 Queen Charlotte
4036 Queen Elizabeth
4038 Queen Berengaria
4039 Queen Matilda
4040 Queen Boadicea
4041 Prince of Wales
4042 Prince Albert
4043 Prince Henry
4044 Prince George
4045 Prince John
4046 Princess Mary
4047 Princess Louise
4048 Princess Victoria
4049 Princess Maud
4050 Princess Alice
4051 Princess Helena
4052 Princess Beatrice
4053 Princess Alexandra
4054 Princess Charlotte
4055 Princess Sophia
4056 Princess Margaret

4057 Princess Elizabeth
4058 Princess Augusta
4059 Princess Patricia
4060 Princess Eugenie
4061 Glastonbury Abbey
4062 Malmesbury Abbey

"4073" CASTLE CLASS 4-6-0

100A1 Lloyd's
111 Viscount Churchill
4000 North Star
4016 The Somerset Light Infantry (Prince Albert's)
4032 Queen Alexandra
4037 The South Wales Borderers
4073 Caerphilly Castle
4074 Caldicot Castle
4075 Cardiff Castle
4076 Carmarthen Castle
4077 Chepstow Castle
4078 Pembroke Castle
4079 Pendennis Castle
4080 Powderham Castle
4081 Warwick Castle
4082 Windsor Castle
4083 Abbotsbury Castle
4084 Aberystwyth Castle
4085 Berkeley Castle
4086 Builth Castle
4087 Cardigan Castle
4088 Dartmouth Castle
4089 Donnington Castle
4090 Dorchester Castle
4091 Dudley Castle
4092 Dunraven Castle
4093 Dunster Castle
4094 Dynevor Castle
4095 Harlech Castle
4096 Highclere Castle
4097 Kenilworth Castle
4098 Kidwelly Castle
4099 Kilgerran Castle

"4900" HALL CLASS 4-6-0

4900 Saint Martin
4901 Adderley Hall
4902 Aldenham Hall
4903 Astley Hall
4904 Binnegar Hall
4905 Barton Hall
4906 Bradfield Hall
4907 Broughton Hall
4908 Broome Hall
4909 Blakesley Hall
4910 Blaisdon Hall
4912 Berrington Hall
4913 Baglan Hall
4914 Cranmore Hall
4915 Condover Hall
4916 Crumlin Hall
4917 Crosswood Hall
4918 Dartington Hall
4919 Donnington Hall
4920 Dumbleton Hall
4921 Eaton Hall
4922 Enville Hall
4923 Evenley Hall
4924 Eydon Hall
4925 Eynsham Hall
4926 Fairleigh Hall
4927 Farnborough Hall
4928 Gatacre Hall
4929 Goytrey Hall
4930 Hagley Hall
4931 Hanbury Hall
4932 Hatherton Hall
4933 Himley Hall
4934 Hindlip Hall
4935 Ketley Hall
4936 Kinlet Hall
4937 Lanelay Hall
4938 Liddington Hall
4939 Littleton Hall
4940 Ludford Hall
4941 Llangedwyn Hall
4942 Maindy Hall
4943 Marrington Hall
4944 Middleton Hall
4945 Milligan Hall
4946 Moseley Hall
4947 Nanhoran Hall
4948 Northwick Hall
4949 Packwood Hall
4950 Patshull Hall
4951 Pendeford Hall
4952 Peplow Hall
4953 Pitchford Hall
4954 Plaish Hall
4955 Plaspower Hall
4956 Plowden Hall
4957 Postlip Hall
4958 Priory Hall
4959 Purley Hall
4960 Pyle Hall
4961 Pyrland Hall
4962 Ragley Hall
4963 Rignall Hall
4964 Rodwell Hall
4965 Rood Ashton Hall
4966 Shakenhurst Hall
4967 Shirenewton Hall
4968 Shotton Hall
4969 Shrugborough Hall
4970 Sketty Hall
4971 Stanway Hall
4972 Saint Brides Hall
4973 Sweeney Hall
4974 Talgarth Hall
4975 Umberslade Hall
4976 Warfield Hall
4977 Watcombe Hall
4978 Westwood Hall
4979 Wootton Hall
4980 Wrottesley Hall
4981 Abberley Hall
4982 Acton Hall
4983 Albert Hall
4984 Albrighton Hall
4985 Allesley Hall
4986 Aston Hall
4987 Brockley Hall
4988 Bulwell Hall
4989 Cherwell Hall
4990 Clifton Hall
4991 Cobham Hall
4992 Crosby Hall
4993 Dalton Hall
4994 Downton Hall
4995 Easton Hall
4996 Eden Hall
4997 Elton Hall
4998 Eyton Hall
4999 Gopsal Hall

"4073" CASTLE CLASS 4-6-0

5000 Launceston Castle
5001 Llandovery Castle
5002 Ludlow Castle
5003 Lulworth Castle
5004 Llanstephan Castle
5005 Manorbier Castle
5006 Tregenna Castle
5007 Rougemont Castle
5008 Raglan Castle
5009 Shrewsbury Castle
5010 Restormel Castle
5011 Tintagel Castle
5012 Berry Pomeroy Castle
5013 Abergavenny Castle
5014 Goodrich Castle
5015 Kingswear Castle
5016 Montgomery Castle
5017 St. Donats Castle
5018 St. Mawes Castle
5019 Treago Castle
5020 Trematon Castle
5021 Whittington Castle
5022 Wigmore Castle
5023 Brecon Castle
5024 Carew Castle
5025 Chirk Castle
5026 Criccieth Castle
5027 Farleigh Castle
5028 Llantilio Castle
5029 Nunnery Castle
5030 Shirburn Castle
5031 Totnes Castle
5032 Usk Castle
5033 Broughton Castle
5034 Corfe Castle
5035 Coity Castle
5036 Lyonshall Castle
5037 Monmouth Castle
5038 Morlais Castle
5039 Rhuddlan Castle
5040 Stokesay Castle
5041 Tiverton Castle
5042 Winchester Castle
5043 Earl of Mount Edgcumbe
5044 Earl of Dunraven
5045 Earl of Dudley
5046 Earl of Cawdor
5047 Earl of Dartmouth
5048 Earl of Devon
5049 Earl of Plymouth
5050 Earl of St. Germans
5051 Earl Bathurst
5052 Earl of Radnor
5053 Earl of Cairns
5054 Earl of Ducie
5055 Earl of Eldon
5056 Earl of Powis
5057 Earl Waldegrave
5058 Earl of Clancarty
5059 Earl St. Aldwyn
5060 Earl of Berkeley
5061 Earl of Birkenhead
5062 Earl of Shaftesbury
5063 Earl Baldwin
5064 Bishop's Castle
5065 Newport Castle
5066 Wardour Castle
5067 St. Fagans Castle
5068 Beverston Castle
5069 Isambard Kingdom Brunel
5070 Sir Daniel Gooch
5071 Spitfire
5072 Hurricane
5073 Blenheim
5074 Hampden
5075 Wellington
5076 Gladiator
5077 Fairey Battle
5078 Beaufort
5079 Lysander
5080 Defiant
5081 Lockheed Hudson
5082 Swordfish
5083 Bath Abbey
5084 Reading Abbey

5085 Evesham Abbey
5086 Viscount Horne
5087 Tintern Abbey
5088 Llanthony Abbey
5089 Westminster Abbey
5090 Neath Abbey
5091 Cleeve Abbey
5092 Tresco Abbey
5093 Upton Castle
5094 Tretower Castle
5095 Barbury Castle
5096 Bridgwater Castle
5097 Sarum Castle
5098 Clifford Castle
5099 Compton Castle

"4900" HALL CLASS 4-6-0

5900 Hinderton Hall
5901 Hazel Hall
5902 Howick Hall
5903 Keele Hall
5904 Kelham Hall
5905 Knowsley Hall
5906 Lawton Hall
5907 Marble Hall
5908 Moreton Hall
5909 Newton Hall
5910 Park Hall
5911 Preston Hall
5912 Queen's Hall
5913 Rushton Hall
5914 Ripon Hall
5915 Trentham Hall
5916 Trinity Hall
5917 Westminster Hall
5918 Walton Hall
5919 Worsley Hall
5920 Wycliffe Hall
5921 Bingley Hall
5922 Caxton Hall
5923 Colston Hall
5924 Dinton Hall
5925 Eastcote Hall
5926 Grotrian Hall
5927 Guild Hall
5928 Haddon Hall
5929 Hanham Hall
5930 Hannington Hall
5931 Hatherley Hall
5932 Haydon Hall
5933 Kingsway Hall
5934 Kneller Hall
5935 Norton Hall
5936 Oakley Hall
5937 Stanford Hall
5938 Stanley Hall
5939 Tangley Hall
5940 Whitbourne Hall
5941 Campion Hall
5942 Doldowlod Hall
5943 Elmdon Hall
5944 Ickenham Hall
5945 Leckhampton Hall
5946 Marwell Hall
5947 Saint Benet's Hall
5948 Siddington Hall
5949 Trematon Hall
5950 Wardley Hall
5951 Clyffe Hall
5952 Cogan Hall
5953 Dunley Hall
5954 Faendre Hall
5955 Garth Hall
5956 Horsley Hall
5957 Hutton Hall
5958 Knolton Hall
5959 Mawley Hall
5960 Saint Edmund Hall
5961 Toynbee Hall
5962 Wantage Hall
5963 Wimpole Hall
5964 Wolseley Hall
5965 Woollas Hall
5966 Ashford Hall
5967 Bickmarsh Hall
5968 Cory Hall
5969 Honington Hall
5970 Hengrave Hall
5971 Merevale Hall
5972 Olton Hall
5973 Rolleston Hall
5974 Wallsworth Hall
5975 Winslow Hall
5976 Ashwicke Hall
5977 Beckford Hall
5978 Bodinnick Hall
5979 Cruckton Hall
5980 Dingley Hall
5981 Frensham Hall
5982 Harrington Hall
5983 Henley Hall
5984 Linden Hall
5985 Mostyn Hall
5986 Arbury Hall
5987 Brocket Hall
5988 Bostock Hall
5989 Cransley Hall
5990 Dorford Hall
5991 Gresham Hall
5992 Horton Hall
5993 Kirby Hall
5994 Roydon Hall
5995 Wick Hall
5996 Mytton Hall
5997 Sparkford Hall
5998 Trevor Hall
5999 Wollaton Hall

"6000" KING CLASS 4-6-0

6000 King George V
6001 King Edward VII
6002 King William IV
6003 King George IV
6004 King George III
6005 King George II
6006 King George I
6007 King William III
6008 King James II
6009 King Charles II
6010 King Charles I
6011 King James I
6012 King Edward VI
6013 King Henry VIII
6014 King Henry VII
6015 King Richard III
6016 King Edward V
6017 King Edward IV
6018 King Henry VI
6019 King Henry V
6020 King Henry IV
6021 King Richard II
6022 King Edward III
6023 King Edward II
6024 King Edward I
6025 King Henry III
6026 King John
6027 King Richard I
6028 King George VI
6029 King Edward VIII

"6800" GRANGE CLASS 4-6-0

6800 Arlington Grange
6801 Aylburton Grange
6802 Bampton Grange
6803 Bucklebury Grange
6804 Brockington Grange
6805 Broughton Grange
6806 Blackwell Grange
6807 Birchwood Grange
6808 Beenham Grange
6809 Burghclere Grange
6810 Blakemere Grange
6811 Cranbourne Grange
6812 Chesford Grange
6813 Eastbury Grange
6814 Enborne Grange
6815 Frilford Grange
6816 Frankton Grange
6817 Gwenddwr Grange
6818 Hardwick Grange
6819 Highnam Grange
6820 Kingstone Grange
6821 Leaton Grange
6822 Manton Grange
6823 Oakley Grange
6824 Ashley Grange
6825 Llanvair Grange
6826 Nannerth Grange
6827 Llanfrechfa Grange
6828 Trellech Grange
6829 Burmington Grange
6830 Buckenhill Grange
6831 Bearley Grange
6832 Brockton Grange
6833 Calcot Grange
6834 Dummer Grange
6835 Eastham Grange
6836 Estevarney Grange
6837 Forthampton Grange
6838 Goodmoor Grange
6839 Hewell Grange
6840 Hazeley Grange
6841 Marlas Grange
6842 Nunhold Grange
6843 Poulton Grange
6844 Penhydd Grange
6845 Paviland Grange
6846 Ruckley Grange
6847 Tidmarsh Grange
6848 Toddington Grange
6849 Walton Grange
6850 Cleeve Grange
6851 Hurst Grange
6852 Headbourne Grange
6853 Morehampton Grange
6854 Roundhill Grange
6855 Saighton Grange
6856 Stowe Grange
6857 Tudor Grange
6858 Woolston Grange
6859 Yiewsley Grange
6860 Aberporth Grange
6861 Crynant Grange
6862 Derwent Grange
6863 Dolhywel Grange
6864 Dymock Grange
6865 Hopton Grange
6866 Morfa Grange
6867 Peterston Grange
6868 Penrhos Grange
6869 Resolven Grange
6870 Bodicote Grange
6871 Bourton Grange
6872 Crawley Grange
6873 Caradoc Grange
6874 Haughton Grange
6875 Hindford Grange
6876 Kingsland Grange
6877 Llanfair Grange
6878 Longford Grange
6879 Overton Grange

"4900" HALL CLASS 4-6-0

6900 Abney Hall

6901 Arley Hall
6902 Butlers Hall
6903 Belmont Hall
6904 Charfield Hall
6905 Claughton Hall
6906 Chicheley Hall
6907 Davenham Hall
6908 Downham Hall
6909 Frewin Hall
6910 Gossington Hall
6911 Holker Hall
6912 Helmster Hall
6913 Levens Hall
6914 Langton Hall
6915 Mursley Hall
6916 Misterton Hall
6917 Oldlands Hall
6918 Sandon Hall
6919 Tylney Hall
6920 Barningham Hall
6921 Borwick Hall
6922 Burton Hall
6923 Croxteth Hall
6924 Grantley Hall
6925 Hackness Hall
6926 Holkham Hall
6927 Lilford Hall
6928 Underley Hall
6929 Whorlton Hall
6930 Aldersey Hall
6931 Aldborough Hall
6932 Burwarton Hall
6933 Birtles Hall
6934 Beachamwell Hall
6935 Browsholme Hall
6936 Breccles Hall
6937 Conyngham Hall
6938 Corndean Hall
6939 Calveley Hall
6940 Didlington Hall
6941 Fillongley Hall
6942 Eshton Hall
6943 Farnley Hall
6944 Fledborough Hall
6945 Glasfryn Hall
6946 Heatherden Hall
6947 Helmingham Hall
6948 Holbrooke Hall
6949 Haberfield Hall
6950 Kingsthorpe Hall
6951 Impney Hall
6952 Kimberley Hall
6953 Leighton Hall
6954 Lotherton Hall
6955 Lydcott Hall
6956 Mottram Hall
6957 Norcliffe Hall
6958 Oxburgh Hall

"6959" MODIFIED HALL CLASS 4-6-0

6959 Peatling Hall
6960 Raveningham Hall
6961 Stedham Hall
6962 Soughton Hall
6963 Throwley Hall
6964 Thornbridge Hall
6965 Thirlestaine Hall
6966 Witchingham Hall
6967 Willesley Hall
6968 Woodcock Hall
6969 Wraysbury Hall
6970 Whaddon Hall
6971 Athelhampton Hall
6972 Beningbrough Hall
6973 Bricklehampton Hall
6974 Bryngwyn Hall
6975 Capesthorne Hall
6976 Graythwaite Hall
6977 Grundisburgh Hall
6978 Haroldstone Hall
6979 Helperly Hall
6980 Llanrumney Hall

"4073" CASTLE CLASS 4-6-0

7000 Viscount Portal
7001 Sir James Milne
7002 Devizes Castle
7003 Elmley Castle
7004 Eastnor Castle
7005 Lamphey Castle
7006 Lydford Castle
7007 Great Western

"7800" MANOR CLASS 4-6-0

7800 Torquay Manor
7801 Anthony Manor
7802 Bradley Manor
7803 Barcote Manor
7804 Baydon Manor
7805 Broome Manor
7806 Cockington Manor
7807 Compton Manor
7808 Cookham Manor
7809 Childrey Manor
7810 Draycott Manor
7811 Dunley Manor
7812 Erlestoke Manor
7813 Freshford Manor
7814 Fringford Manor
7815 Fritwell Manor
7816 Frilsham Manor
7817 Garsington Manor
7818 Granville Manor
7819 Hinton Manor

"DUKE" CLASS 4-4-0

9054 Cornubia
9064 Trevithick
9065 Tre Pol and Pen
9073 Mounts Bay
9083 Comet
9084 Isle of Jersey
9087 Mercury
9091 Thames

Ex-Southern Railway Locomotives

B4 CLASS 0-4-0T

30081 Jersey
30085 Alderney
30086 Havre
30089 Trouville
30090 Caen
30093 St. Malo
30095 Honfleur
30096 Normandy
30097 Brittany
30098 Cherbourg
30101 Dinan
30102 Granville
30147 Dinard
30176 Guernsey

N15 "KING ARTHUR" CLASS 4-6-0

30448 Sir Tristram
30449 Sir Torre
30450 Sir Kay
30451 Sir Lamorak
30452 Sir Meliagrance
30453 King Arthur
30454 Queen Guinevere
30455 Sir Launcelot
30456 Sir Galahad
30457 Sir Bedivere

0458 CLASS 0-4-0T

30458 Ironside

N15 "KING ARTHUR" CLASS 4-6-0

30736 Excalibur
30737 King Uther
30738 King Pellinore
30739 King Leodegrance
30740 Merlin
30741 Joyous Gard
30742 Camelot
30743 Lyonnesse
30744 Maid of Astolat
30745 Tintagel
30746 Pendragon
30747 Elaine
30748 Vivien
30749 Iseult
30750 Morgan le Fay
30751 Etarre
30752 Linette
30753 Melisande
30754 The Green Knight
30755 The Red Knight

756 CLASS 0-6-0T

30756 A. S. Harris

757 CLASS 0-6-2T

30757 Earl of Mount Edgcumbe
30758 Lord St. Levan

N15 "KING ARTHUR" CLASS 4-6-0

30763 Sir Bors de Ganis
30764 Sir Gawain
30765 Sir Gareth
30766 Sir Geraint
30767 Sir Valence
30768 Sir Balin
30769 Sir Balan
30770 Sir Prianius
30771 Sir Sagramore
30772 Sir Percivale
30773 Sir Lavaine
30774 Sir Gaheris
30775 Sir Agravaine
30776 Sir Galagars
30777 Sir Lamiel
30778 Sir Pelleas
30779 Sir Colgrevance
30780 Sir Persant
30781 Sir Aglovale
30782 Sir Brian
30783 Sir Gillemere
30784 Sir Nerovens
30785 Sir Mador de la Porte
30786 Sir Lionel
30787 Sir Menadeuke
30788 Sir Urre of the Mount
30789 Sir Guy
30790 Sir Villiars

30791 Sir Uwaine
30792 Sir Hervis de Revel
30793 Sir Ontzlake
30794 Sir Ector de Maris
30795 Sir Dinadan
30796 Sir Dodinas le Savage
30797 Sir Blamor de Ganis
30798 Sir Hectimere
30799 Sir Ironside
30800 Sir Meleaus de Lile
30801 Sir Meliot de Logres
30802 Sir Durnore
30803 Sir Harry le Fise Lake
30804 Sir Cador of Cornwall
30805 Sir Constantine
30806 Sir Galleron

"LORD NELSON" CLASS 4-6-0

30850 Lord Nelson
30851 Sir Francis Drake
30852 Sir Walter Raleigh
30853 Sir Richard Grenville
30854 Howard of Effingham
30855 Robert Blake
30856 Lord St. Vincent
30857 Lord Howe
30858 Lord Duncan
30859 Lord Hood
30860 Lord Hawke
30861 Lord Anson
30862 Lord Collingwood
30863 Lord Rodney
30864 Sir Martin Frobisher
30865 Sir John Hawkins

V "SCHOOLS" CLASS 4-4-0

30900 Eton
30901 Winchester
30902 Wellington
30903 Charterhouse
30904 Lancing
30905 Tonbridge
30906 Sherborne
30907 Dulwich
30908 Westminster
30909 St. Paul's
30910 Merchant Taylors
30911 Dover
30912 Downside
30913 Christ's Hospital
30914 Eastbourne
30915 Brighton
30916 Whitgift
30917 Ardingly
30918 Hurstpierpoint
30919 Harrow
30920 Rugby
30921 Shrewsbury
30922 Marlborough
30923 Bradfield
30924 Haileybury
30925 Cheltenham
30926 Repton
30927 Clifton
30928 Stowe
30929 Malvern
30930 Radley
30931 King's-Wimbledon
30932 Blundells
30933 King's-Canterbury
30934 St. Lawrence
30935 Sevenoaks
30936 Cranleigh
30937 Epsom
30938 St. Olave's
30939 Leatherhead

KENT AND EAST SUSSEX RAILWAY 0-8-0T

30949 Hecate

H1 CLASS 4-4-2

32037 Selsey Bill
32038 Portland Bill
32039 Hartland Point

N15X "REMEMBRANCE" CLASS 4-6-0

32327 Trevithick
32328 Hackworth
32329 Stephenson
32330 Cudworth
32331 Beattie
32332 Stroudley
32333 Remembrance

H2 CLASS 4-4-2

32421 South Foreland
32422 North Foreland
32423 The Needles
32424 Beachy Head
32425 Trevose Head
32426 St. Alban's Head

"WEST COUNTRY"CLASS 4-6-2

34001 Exeter
34002 Salisbury
34003 Plymouth
34004 Yeovil
34005 Barnstaple
34006 Bude
34007 Wadebridge
34008 Padstow
34009 Lyme Regis
34010 Sidmouth
34011 Tavistock
34012 Launceston
34013 Okehampton
34014 Budleigh Salterton
34015 Exmouth
34016 Bodmin
34017 Ilfracombe
34018 Axminster
34019 Bideford
34020 Seaton
34021 Dartmoor
34022 Exmoor
34023 Blackmore Vale
34024 Tamar Valley
34025 Whimple
34026 Yes Tor
34027 Taw Valley
34028 Eddystone
34029 Lundy
34030 Watersmeet
34031 Torrington
34032 Camelford
34033 Chard
34034 Honiton
34035 Shaftesbury
34036 Westward Ho
34037 Clovelly
34038 Lynton
34039 Boscastle
34040 Crewkerne
34041 Wilton
34042 Dorchester
34043 Combe Martin
34044 Woolacombe
34045 Ottery St. Mary
34046 Braunton
34047 Callington
34048 Crediton

"BATTLE OF BRITAIN" CLASS 4-6-2

34049 Anti-Aircraft Command
34050 Royal Observer Corps
34051 Winston Churchill
34052 Lord Dowding
34053 Sir Keith Park
34054 Lord Beaverbrook
34055 Fighter Pilot
34056 Croydon
34057 Biggin Hill
34058 Sir Frederick Pile
34059 Sir Archibald Sinclair
34060 25 Squadron
34061 73 Squadron
34062 17 Squadron
34063 229 Squadron
34064 Fighter Command
34065 Hurricane
34066 Spitfire
34067 Tangmere
34068 Kenley
34069 Hawkinge
34070 Manston

"MERCHANT NAVY" CLASS 4-6-2

35001 Channel Packet
35002 Union Castle
35003 Royal Mail
35004 Cunard White Star
35005 Canadian Pacific
35006 Peninsular & Oriental S.N.Co.
35007 Aberdeen Commonwealth
35008 Orient Line
35009 Shaw Savill
35010 Blue Star
35011 General Steam Navigation
35012 United States Line
35013 Blue Funnel
35014 Nederland Line
35015 Rotterdam Lloyd
35016 Elders Fyffes
35017 Belgian Marine
35018 British India Line
35019 French Line C.G.T.
35020 Bibby Line

LOCOMOTIVES ALLOCATED TO THE ISLE OF WIGHT

E1 CLASS 0-6-0T

W1 Medina
W2 Yarmouth
W3 Ryde
W4 Wroxall

A1X "TERRIER" CLASS 0-6-0T

W8 Freshwater
W13 Carisbrooke

02 CLASS 0-4-4T

W14 Fishbourne
W15 Cowes
W16 Ventnor

W17 Seaview
W18 Ningwood
W19 Osborne
W20 Shanklin
W21 Sandown
W22 Brading
W23 Totland
W24 Calbourne
W25 Godshill
W26 Whitwell
W27 Merstone
W28 Ashey
W29 Alverstone
W30 Shorwell
W31 Chale
W32 Bonchurch
W33 Bembridge
W34 Newport

Ex-London, Midland & Scottish Railway Locomotives

STANIER 4-6-0 5P5F

45154 Lanarkshire Yeomanry
45156 Ayrshire Yeomanry
45157 The Glasgow Highlander
45158 Glasgow Yeomanry

PATRIOT CLASS 4-6-0 5XP

45500 Patriot
45501 St. Dunstan's
45502 Royal Naval Division
45503 The Leicestershire Regiment
45504 Royal Signals
45505 The Royal Army Ordnance Corps
45507 Royal Tank Corps
45511 Isle of Man
45512 Bunsen
45514 Holyhead
45515 Caernarvon
45516 The Bedfordshire and Hertfordshire Regiment
45518 Bradshaw
45519 Lady Godiva
45520 Llandudno
45521 Rhyl
45522 Prestatyn
45523 Bangor
45524 Blackpool
45525 Colwyn Bay
45526 Morecambe and Heysham
45527 Southport
45530 Sir Frank Ree
45531 Sir Frederick Harrison
45532 Illustrious
45533 Lord Rathmore
45534 E. Tootal Broadhurst
45535 Sir Herbert Walker, K.C.B.
45536 Private W. Wood V.C.
45537 Private E. Sykes V.C.
45538 Giggleswick
45539 E.C. Trench
45540 Sir Robert Turnbull
45541 Duke of Sutherland
45543 Home Guard
45546 Fleetwood
45548 Lytham St. Annes

JUBILEE CLASS 4-6-0 5XP

45552 Silver Jubilee
45553 Canada
45554 Ontario
45555 Quebeck
45556 Nova Scotia
45557 New Brunswick
45558 Manitoba
45559 British Columbia
45560 Prince Edward Island
45561 Saskatchewan
45562 Alberta
45563 Australia
45564 New South Wales
45565 Victoria
45566 Queensland
45567 South Australia
45568 Western Australia
45569 Tasmania
45570 New Zealand
45571 South Africa
45572 Eire
45573 Newfoundland
45574 India
45575 Madras
45576 Bombay
45577 Bengal
45578 United Provinces
45579 Punjab
45580 Burma
45581 Bihar and Orissa
45582 Central Provinces
45583 Assam
45584 North West Frontier
45585 Hyderabad
45586 Mysore
45587 Baroda
45588 Kashmir
45589 Gwalior
45590 Travancore
45591 Udaipur
45592 Indore
45593 Kolhapur
45594 Bhopal
45595 Southern Rhodesia
45596 Bahamas
45597 Barbados
45598 Basutoland
45599 Bechuanaland
45600 Bermuda
45601 British Guiana
45602 British Honduras
45603 Solomon Islands
45604 Ceylon
45605 Cyprus
45606 Falkland Islands
45607 Fiji
45608 Gibraltar
45609 Gilbert and Ellice Islands
45610 Gold Coast
45611 Hong Kong
45612 Jamaica
45613 Kenya
45614 Leeward Islands
45615 Malay States
45616 Malta, G.C.
45617 Mauritius
45618 New Hebrides
45619 Nigeria
45620 North Borneo
45621 Northern Rhodesia
45622 Nyasaland
45623 Palestine
45624 St. Helena
45625 Sarawak
45626 Seychelles
45627 Sierra Leone
45628 Somaliland
45629 Straits Settlements
45630 Swaziland
45631 Tanganyika
45632 Tonga
45633 Aden
45634 Trinidad
45635 Tobago
45636 Uganda
45637 Windward Islands
45638 Zanzibar
45639 Raleigh
45640 Frobisher
45641 Sandwich
45642 Boscawen
45643 Rodney
45644 Howe
45645 Collingwood
45646 Napier
45647 Sturdee
45648 Wemyss
45649 Hawkins
45650 Blake
45651 Shovell
45652 Hawke
45653 Barham
45654 Hood
45655 Keith
45656 Cochrane
45657 Tyrwhitt
45658 Keyes
45659 Drake
45660 Rooke
45661 Vernon
45662 Kempenfelt
45663 Jervis
45664 Nelson
45665 Lord Rutherford of Nelson
45666 Cornwallis
45667 Jellicoe
45668 Madden
45669 Fisher
45670 Howard of Effingham
45671 Prince Rupert
45672 Anson
45673 Keppel
45674 Duncan
45675 Hardy
45676 Codrington
45677 Beatty
45678 De Robeck
45679 Armada
45680 Camperdown
45681 Aboukir
45682 Trafalgar

45683 Hogue
45684 Jutland
45685 Barfleur
45686 St. Vincent
45687 Neptune
45688 Polyphemus
45689 Ajax
45690 Leander
45691 Orion
45692 Cyclops
45693 Agamemnon
45694 Bellerophon
45695 Minotaur
45696 Arethusa
45697 Achilles
45698 Mars
45699 Galatea
45700 Britannia
45701 Conqueror
45702 Colossus
45703 Thunderer
45704 Leviathan
45705 Seahorse
45706 Express
45707 Valiant
45708 Resolution
45709 Implacable
45710 Irresistible
45711 Courageous
45712 Victory
45713 Renown
45714 Revenge
45715 Invincible
45716 Swiftsure
45717 Dauntless
45718 Dreadnought
45719 Glorious
45720 Indomitable
45721 Impregnable
45722 Defence
45723 Fearless
45724 Warspite
45725 Repulse
45726 Vindictive
45727 Inflexible
45728 Defiance
45729 Furious
45730 Ocean
45731 Perseverance
45732 Sanspareil
45733 Novelty
45734 Meteor
45735 Comet
45736 Phoenix
45737 Atlas
45738 Samson
45739 Ulster
45740 Munster
45741 Leinster
45742 Connaught

ROYAL SCOT CLASS 4-6-0 6P

46100 Royal Scot
46101 Royal Scots Grey
46102 Black Watch
46103 Royal Scots Fusilier
46104 Scottish Borderer
46105 Cameron Highlander
46106 Gordon Highlander
46107 Argyll and Sutherland Highlander
46108 Seaforth Highlander
46109 Royal Engineer
46110 Grenadier Guardsman
46111 Royal Fusilier
46112 Sherwood Forester
46113 Cameronian
46114 Coldstream Guardsman
46115 Scots Guardsman
46116 Irish Guardsman
46117 Welsh Guardsman
46118 Royal Welch Fusilier
46119 Lancashire Fusilier
46120 Royal Inniskilling Fusilier
46121 H.L.I.
46122 Royal Ulster Rifleman
46123 Royal Irish Fusilier
46124 London Scottish
46125 3rd Carabinier
46126 Royal Army Service Corps
46127 Old Contemptibles
46128 The Lovat Scouts
46129 The Scottish Horse
46130 The West Yorkshire Regiment
46131 The Royal Warwickshire Regiment
46132 The King's Regiment, Liverpool
46133 The Green Howards
46134 The Cheshire Regiment
46135 The East Lancashire Regiment
46136 The Border Regiment
46137 The Prince of Wales's Volunteers (South Lancashire)
46138 The London Irish Rifleman
46139 The Welch Regiment
46140 The King's Royal Rifle Corps
46141 The North Staffordshire Regiment
46142 The York & Lancaster Regiment
46143 The South Staffordshire Regiment
46144 Honourable Artillery Company
46145 The Duke of Wellington's Regt. (West Riding)
46146 The Rifle Brigade
46147 The Northamptonshire Regiment
46148 The Manchester Regiment
46149 The Middlesex Regiment
46150 The Life Guardsman
46151 The Royal Horse Guardsman
46152 The King's Dragoon Guardsman
46153 The Royal Dragoon
46154 The Hussar
46155 The Lancer
46156 The South Wales Borderer
46157 The Royal Artilleryman
46158 The Loyal Regiment
46159 The Royal Air Force
46160 Queen Victoria's Rifleman
46161 King's Own
46162 Queen's Westminster Rifleman
46163 Civil Service Rifleman
46164 The Artists' Rifleman
46165 The Ranger (12th London Regt.)
46166 London Rifle Brigade
46167 The Hertfordshire Regiment
46168 The Girl Guide
46169 The Boy Scout
46170 British Legion

PRINCESS ROYAL CLASS
4-6-2 7P

46200 The Princess Royal
46201 Princess Elizabeth
46203 Princess Margaret Rose
46204 Princess Louise
46205 Princess Victoria
46206 Princess Marie Louise
46207 Princess Arthur of Connaught
46208 Princess Helena Victoria
46209 Princess Beatrice
46210 Lady Patricia
46211 Queen Maud
46212 Duchess of Kent

PRINCESS CORONATION
CLASS 4-6-2 7P

46220 Coronation
46221 Queen Elizabeth
46222 Queen Mary
46223 Princess Alice
46224 Princess Alexandra
46225 Duchess of Gloucester
46226 Duchess of Norfolk
46227 Duchess of Devonshire
46228 Duchess of Rutland
46229 Duchess of Hamilton
46230 Duchess of Buccleuch
46231 Duchess of Atholl
46232 Duchess of Montrose
46233 Duchess of Sutherland
46234 Duchess of Abercorn
46235 City of Birmingham
46236 City of Bradford
46237 City of Bristol
46238 City of Carlisle
46239 City of Chester
46240 City of Coventry
46241 City of Edinburgh
46242 City of Glasgow
46243 City of Lancaster
46244 King George VI
46245 City of London
46246 City of Manchester
46247 City of Liverpool
46248 City of Leeds
46249 City of Sheffield
46250 City of Lichfield

46251 City of Nottingham
46252 City of Leicester
46253 City of St. Albans
46254 City of Stoke-on-Trent
46255 City of Hereford
46256 Sir William A. Stanier F.R.S.

JONES "LOCH" CLASS
4-4-0 2P

54379 Loch Insh
54385 Loch Tay

P. DRUMMOND "BEN" CLASS
4-4-0 2P

54397 Ben-y-Gloe
54398 Ben Alder
54399 Ben Wyvis
54401 Ben Vrackie
54403 Ben Attow
54404 Ben Clebrig
54409 Ben Alisky
54410 Ben Dearg
54415 Ben Bhach Ard
54416 Ben A'Bhuird

C. CUMMINGS "CLAN" CLASS 4-6-0 4P

54764 Clan Munro
54767 Clan Mackinnon

"PRINCE OF WALES" CLASS
4-6-0 4P

58000 Queen of the Belgians
58001 Lusitania

"PRECURSOR" CLASS
4-4-0 3P

58010 Sirocco

"GEORGE THE FIFTH" CLASS
4-4-0 3P

25321 Lord Loch
58012 Ptarmigan

Named during 1948

PATRIOT CLASS 4-6-0
45506 The Royal Pioneer Corps
(15/9 - Euston Stn.)

45545 Planet
(-/10 - Crewe Works.)

Ex-London & North Eastern Railway Locomotives

A4 CLASS 4-6-2

60001 Sir Ronald Matthews
60002 Sir Murrough Wilson
60003 Andrew K. McCosh
60004 William Whitelaw
60005 Sir Charles Newton
60006 Sir Ralph Wedgwood
60007 Sir Nigel Gresley
60008 Dwight D. Eisenhower
60009 Union of South Africa
60010 Dominion of Canada
60011 Empire of India
60012 Commonwealth of Australia
60013 Dominion of New Zealand
60014 Silver Link
60015 Quicksilver
60016 Silver King
60017 Silver Fox
60018 Sparrow Hawk
60019 Bittern
60020 Guillemot
60021 Wild Swan
60022 Mallard
60023 Golden Eagle
60024 Kingfisher
60025 Falcon
60026 Miles Beevor
60027 Merlin
60028 Walter K. Whigham
60029 Woodcock
60030 Golden Fleece
60031 Golden Plover
60032 Gannet
60033 Seagull
60034 Lord Faringdon

A3 CLASS 4-6-2

60035 Windsor Lad
60036 Colombo
60037 Hyperion
60038 Firdaussi
60039 Sandwich
60040 Cameronian
60041 Salmon Trout
60042 Singapore
60043 Brown Jack
60044 Melton
60045 Lemberg
60046 Diamond Jubilee
60047 Donovan
60048 Doncaster
60049 Galtee More
60050 Persimmon
60051 Blink Bonny
60052 Prince Palatine
60053 Sansovino
60054 Prince of Wales
60055 Woolwinder
60056 Centenary
60057 Ormonde
60058 Blair Athol
60059 Tracery
60060 The Tetrarch
60061 Pretty Polly
60062 Minoru
60063 Isinglass
60064 Tagalie
60065 Knight of Thistle
60066 Merry Hampton
60067 Ladas
60068 Sir Visto
60069 Sceptre
60070 Gladiateur
60071 Tranquil
60072 Sunstar
60073 St. Gatien
60074 Harvester
60075 St. Frusquin
60076 Galopin
60077 The White Knight
60078 Night Hawk
60079 Bayardo
60080 Dick Turpin
60081 Shotover
60082 Neil Gow
60083 Sir Hugo
60084 Trigo
60085 Manna
60086 Gainsborough
60087 Blenheim
60088 Book Law
60089 Felstead
60090 Grand Parade
60091 Captain Cuttle
60092 Fairway
60093 Coronach
60094 Colorado
60095 Flamingo
60096 Papyrus
60097 Humorist
60098 Spion Kop
60099 Call Boy
60100 Spearmint
60101 Cicero
60102 Sir Frederick Banbury
60103 Flying Scotsman
60104 Solario
60105 Victor Wild
60106 Flying Fox
60107 Royal Lancer
60108 Gay Crusader
60109 Hermit
60110 Robert the Devil
60111 Enterprise
60112 St. Simon

A1/1 CLASS 4-6-2

60113 Great Northern

A2 CLASS 4-6-2

60500 Edward Thompson
60501 Cock o' the North
60502 Earl Marischal
60503 Lord President
60504 Mons Meg
60505 Thane of Fife
60506 Wolf of Badenoch
60507 Highland Chieftain
60508 Duke of Rothesay
60509 Waverley
60510 Robert the Bruce
60511 Airborne
60512 Steady Aim
60513 Dante
60514 Chamossaire
60515 Sun Stream
60516 Hycilla
60517 Ocean Swell
60518 Tehran
60519 Honeyway
60520 Owen Tudor
60521 Watling Street
60522 Straight Deal
60523 Sun Castle
60524 Herringbone
60525 A.H. Peppercorn

V2 CLASS 2-6-2

60800 Green Arrow
60809 The Snapper, The

East Yorkshire Regiment, The Duke of York's Own
60835 The Green Howard, Alexandra, Princess of Wales's Own Yorkshire Regiment
60847 St. Peter's School, York, A.D. 627
60860 Durham School
60872 King's Own Yorkshire Light Infantry
60873 Coldstreamer

B1 CLASS 4-6-0

61000 Springbok
61001 Eland
61002 Impala
61003 Gazelle
61004 Oryx
61005 Bongo
61006 Blackbuck
61007 Klipspringer
61008 Kudu
61009 Hartebeeste
61010 Wildebeeste
61011 Waterbuck
61012 Puku
61013 Topi
61014 Oribi
61015 Duiker
61016 Inyala
61017 Bushbuck
61018 Gnu
61019 Nilghai
61020 Gemsbok
61021 Reitbok
61022 Sassaby
61023 Hirola
61024 Addax
61025 Pallah
61026 Ourebi
61027 Madoqua
61028 Umseke
61029 Chamois
61030 Nyala
61031 Reedbuck
61032 Stembok
61033 Dibatag
61034 Chiru
61035 Pronghorn
61036 Ralph Assheton
61037 Jairou
61038 Blacktail
61039 Steinbok
61040 Roedeer
61189 Sir William Gray
61215 William Henton Carver
61221 Sir Alexander Erskine-Hill
61237 Geoffrey H. Kitson
61238 Leslie Runciman
61240 Harry Hinchcliffe
61241 Viscount Ridley
61242 Alexander Reith Gray
61243 Sir Harold Mitchell
61244 Strang Steel
61245 Murray of Elibank
61246 Lord Balfour of Burleigh
61247 Lord Burghley
61248 Geoffrey Gibbs
61249 FitzHerbert Wright
61250 A. Harold Bibby
61251 Oliver Bury

B8 CLASS 4-6-0

61357 Earl Kitchener of Khartoum
61358 Earl Roberts of Kandahar

B4 CLASS 4-6-0

61482 Immingham

B2 CLASS 4-6-0

61603 Framlingham
61607 Blickling
61614 Castle Hedingham
61615 Culford Hall
61616 Fallodon
61617 Ford Castle
61632 Belvoir Castle
61639 Norwich City
61671 Royal Sovereign

B17 CLASS 4-6-0

61600 Sandringham
61601 Holkham
61602 Walsingham
61604 Elveden
61605 Lincolnshire Regiment
61606 Audley End
61608 Gunton
61609 Quidenham
61610 Honingham Hall
61611 Raynham Hall
61612 Houghton Hall
61613 Woodbastwick Hall
61618 Wynyard Park
61619 Welbeck Abbey
61620 Clumber
61621 Hatfield House
61622 Alnwick Castle
61623 Lambton Castle
61624 Lumley Castle
61625 Raby Castle
61626 Brancepeth Castle
61627 Aske Hall
61628 Harewood House
61629 Naworth Castle
61630 Tottenham Hotspur
61631 Serlby Hall
61633 Kimbolton Castle
61634 Hinchingbrooke
61635 Milton
61636 Harlaxton Manor
61637 Thorpe Hall
61638 Melton Hall
61640 Somerleyton Hall
61641 Gayton Hall
61642 Kilverstone Hall
61643 Champion Lodge
61644 Earlham Hall
61645 The Suffolk Regiment
61646 Gilwell Park
61647 Helmingham Hall
61648 Arsenal
61649 Sheffield United
61650 Grimsby Town
61651 Derby County
61652 Darlington
61653 Huddersfield Town
61654 Sunderland
61655 Middlesbrough
61656 Leeds United
61657 Doncaster Rovers
61658 The Essex Regiment
61659 East Anglian
61660 Hull City
61661 Sheffield Wednesday
61662 Manchester United
61663 Everton
61664 Liverpool
61665 Leicester City
61666 Nottingham Forest
61667 Bradford
61668 Bradford City
61669 Barnsley
61670 City of London
61672 West Ham United

V4 CLASS 2-6-2

61700 Bantam Cock

K2 CLASS 2-6-0

61764 Loch Arkaig
61772 Loch Lochy
61774 Loch Garry
61775 Loch Treig
61781 Loch Morar
61782 Loch Eil
61783 Loch Sheil
61787 Loch Quoich
61788 Loch Rannoch
61789 Loch Laidon
61790 Loch Lomond
61791 Loch Laggan
61794 Loch Oich

K4 CLASS 2-6-0

61993 Loch Long
61994 The Great Marquess
61995 Cameron of Lochiel
61996 Lord of the Isles
61998 Macleod of Macleod

K1/1 CLASS 2-6-0

61997 Mac Cailin Mor

D40 CLASS 4-4-0

62273 George Davidson
62274 Benachie
62275 Sir David Stewart
62276 Andrew Bain
62277 Gordon Highlander
62278 Hatton Castle
62279 Glen Grant

D9 CLASS 4-4-0

62307 Queen Mary

D29 CLASS 4-4-0

62400 Rob Roy
62401 Dandie Dinmont
62402 Redgauntlet
62403 Sir Walter Scott
62404 Jeanie Deans
62405 The Fair Maid
62406 Meg Merrilies
62409 Helen MacGregor
62410 Ivanhoe
62411 Lady of Avenel
62412 Dirk Hatteraick
62413 Guy Mannering

D30 CLASS 4-4-0

62417 Hal o' the Wynd
62418 The Pirate
62419 Meg Dods
62420 Dominie Sampson
62421 Laird o' Monkbarns

62422 Caleb Balderstone
62423 Dugald Dalgetty
62424 Claverhouse
62425 Ellangowan
62426 Cuddie Headrigg
62427 Dumbiedykes
62428 Talisman
62429 The Abbot
62430 Jingling Geordie
62431 Kenilworth
62432 Quentin Durward
62434 Kettledrummle
62435 Norna
62436 Lord Glenvarloch
62437 Adam Woodcock
62438 Peter Poundtext
62439 Father Ambrose
62440 Wandering Willie
62441 Black Duncan
62442 Simon Glover

D34 CLASS 4-4-0

62467 Glenfinnan
62468 Glen Orchy
62469 Glen Douglas
62470 Glen Roy
62471 Glen Falloch
62472 Glen Nevis
62473 Glen Spean
62474 Glen Croe
62475 Glen Beasdale
62476 Glen Sloy
62477 Glen Dochart
62478 Glen Quoich
62479 Glen Sheil
62480 Glen Fruin
62481 Glen Ogle
62482 Glen Mamie
62483 Glen Garry
62484 Glen Lyon
62485 Glen Murran
62487 Glen Arklet
62488 Glen Aladale
62489 Glen Dessary
62490 Glen Fintaig
62492 Glen Garvin
62493 Glen Gloy
62494 Glen Gour
62495 Glen Luss
62496 Glen Loy
62497 Glen Mallie
62498 Glen Moidart

D16 CLASS 4-4-0

62546 Claud Hamilton

D10 CLASS 4-4-0

62650 Prince Henry
62651 Purdon Viccars
62652 Edwin A. Beazley
62653 Sir Edward Fraser
62654 Walter Burgh Gair
62655 The Earl of Kerry
62656 Sir Clement Royds
62657 Sir Berkeley Sheffield
62658 Prince George
62659 Worsley-Taylor

D11 CLASS 4-4-0

62660 Butler-Henderson
62661 Gerard Powys Dewhurst
62662 Prince of Wales
62663 Prince Albert
62664 Princess Mary
62665 Mons
62666 Zeebrugge
62667 Somme
62668 Jutland
62669 Ypres
62670 Marne
62671 Bailie MacWheeble
62672 Baron of Bradwardine
62673 Evan Dhu
62674 Flora MacIvor
62675 Colonel Gardiner
62676 Jonathan Oldbuck
62677 Edie Ochiltree
62678 Luckie Mucklebackit
62679 Lord Glenallan
62680 Lucy Ashton
62681 Captain Craigengelt
62682 Haystoun of Bucklaw
62683 Hobbie Elliott
62684 Wizard of the Moor
62685 Malcolm Graeme
62686 The Fiery Cross
62687 Lord James of Douglas
62688 Ellen Douglas
62689 Maid of Lorn
62690 The Lady of the Lake
62691 Laird of Balmawhapple
62692 Allan-Bane
62693 Roderick Dhu
62694 James Fitzjames

D49/1 "SHIRE" CLASS 4-4-0

62700 Yorkshire
62701 Derbyshire
62702 Oxfordshire
62703 Hertfordshire
62704 Stirlingshire
62705 Lanarkshire
62706 Forfarshire
62707 Lancashire
62708 Argyllshire
62709 Berwickshire
62710 Lincolnshire
62711 Dumbartonshire
62712 Morayshire
62713 Aberdeenshire
62714 Perthshire
62715 Roxburghshire
62716 Kincardineshire
62717 Banffshire
62718 Kinross-shire
62719 Peebles-shire
62720 Cambridgeshire
62721 Warwickshire
62722 Huntingdonshire
62723 Nottinghamshire
62724 Bedfordshire
62725 Inverness-shire

D49/2 "HUNT" CLASS 4-4-0

62726 The Meynell
62727 The Quorn

D49/1 "SHIRE" CLASS 4-4-0

62728 Cheshire
62729 Rutlandshire
62730 Berkshire
62731 Selkirkshire
62732 Dumfries-shire
62733 Northumberland
62734 Cumberland
62735 Westmorland

D49/2 "HUNT" CLASS 4-4-0

62736 The Bramham Moor
62737 The York and Ainsty
62738 The Zetland
62739 The Badsworth
62740 The Bedale
62741 The Blankney
62742 The Braes of Derwent
62743 The Cleveland
62744 The Holderness
62745 The Hurworth
62746 The Middleton
62747 The Percy
62748 The Southwold
62749 The Cottesmore
62750 The Pytchley
62751 The Albrighton
62752 The Atherstone
62753 The Belvoir
62754 The Berkeley
62755 The Bilsdale
62756 The Brocklesby
62757 The Burton
62758 The Cattistock
62759 The Craven
62760 The Cotswold
62761 The Derwent
62762 The Fernie
62763 The Fitzwilliam
62764 The Garth
62765 The Goathland
62766 The Grafton
62767 The Grove

D49/4 REBUILT "HUNT" CLASS 4-4-0

62768 The Morpeth

D49/2 "HUNT" CLASS 4-4-0

62769 The Oakley
62770 The Puckeridge
62771 The Rufford
62772 The Sinnington
62773 The South Durham
62774 The Staintondale
62775 The Tynedale

J36 CLASS 0-6-0

65216 Byng
65217 French
65222 Somme
65224 Mons
65226 Haig
65233 Plumer
65235 Gough
65236 Horne
65243 Maude
65253 Joffre
65268 Allenby

M2 CLASS 0-6-4T

69076 Robert H. Selbie
69077 Charles Jones

Locomotives Renumbered during 1948

Ex-GWR Locomotives

G.W.R. No.	B.R. No.	MONTH RENUMBERED	G.W.R. No.	B.R. No.	MONTH RENUMBERED
310	203	December	943	1142	November
317	208	September	974	1144	September
320	211	May	1373	432	November
321	215	April	3902	4948	September
324	216	March	3904	4972	October
402	304	March	3950	5955	October
408	308	December	3951	5976	November
414	219	May	3953	6953	September
420	220	November	4800	2872	September
605	91	March	4802	2862	September
610	95	September	4804	2839	October
701	1140	June	4850	2888	September
792	193	June	4852	3818	September
793	194	September	8393	5393	September
929	1141	March			

Diesel Locomotive No. 2 was renumbered 15100 in March.

Ex-Southern Railway Locomotives (30,000 added to SR No.)

The renumbering dates were not given by the Southern Region, only monthly periods during which the renumbering had taken place. For this publication the periods are; 1. 2 April to 1 June. 2. 2 June to 1 August.
3. 2 August to 4 September. 4. 5 September to 6 October.
5. 7 October to 13 November. 6. 14 November to 8 January 1949.

LOCO No.	PERIOD No.	LOCO No.	PERIOD No.	LOCO No.	PERIOD No.
29	5	254	2	451	2
35	6	260	2	452	1
36	4	270	2	455	1
38	3	274	2	456	5
39	4	276	3	461	1
55	6	284	2	468	1
56	2	286	1	469	1
59	2	310	5	470	2
60	5	315	5	471	6
62	3	316	6	472	6
66	1	317	3	475	5
67	2	320	1	476	2
72	2	327	4	477	4
74	5	330	3	478	6
86	2	333	5	480	6
104	2	334	2	484	5
105	2	335	6	485	2
106	6	339	4	486	3
107	1	350	1	487	2
115	1	357	6	489	1
119	1	374	6	490	6
121	1	375	6	492	6
132	2	377	3	493	4
134	6	382	1	495	1
156	2	396	5	496	6
159	1	399	2	497	6
160	1	400	2	500	4
166	2	406	5	501	6
173	1	407	1	504	5
175	6	417	2	505	3
177	1	419	5	509	1
179	1	420	2	514	4
183	2	423	6	515	6
193	2	425	3	517	2
200	1	428	4	520	6
213	1	429	2	521	2
221	2	431	1	523	2
231	4	432	1	530	4
232	3	434	6	534	2
241	2	438	6	535	6
243	2	442	4	537	5
244	4	446	3	538	6
248	6	448	2	539	6

LOCO No.	PERIOD No.
541	4
542	1
543	1
687	3
688	2
689	5
692	2
694	3
696	2
700	1
702	3
707	1
708	2
718	1
725	4
729	6
732	2
740	5
741	6
742	5
744	1
745	6
748	6
749	6
750	6
751	2
752	4
753	1
754	2
767	6
768	5
772	1
773	2
777	1
779	5
782	1
783	1
784	1
785	3
786	4
788	5
789	3
790	4
791	6
793	5
799	1
802	2
803	2
804	6
805	4
806	4
823	4
825	1
829	6
832	4
833	6
835	4
837	1
839	5
841	4
843	2
845	1
846	1
847	3
850	6
853	6
856	1
858	2
860	6
861	1
862	2
864	1
865	2
900	1
901	5
903	1
904	2

LOCO No.	PERIOD No.
907	3
910	6
913	4
916	6
917	1
919	2
920	5
923	4
926	1
928	2
930	2
931	5
932	2
933	2
934	3
935	6
936	2
937	4
939	1
950	2
951	5
956	2
1004	1
1005	6
1010	3
1018	1
1019	5
1027	2
1037	6
1038	2
1063	6
1067	4
1068	2
1069	1
1151	2
1154	1
1161	2
1166	2
1177	5
1218	5
1246	1
1255	6
1259	1
1268	1
1270	3
1279	2
1297	2
1298	6
1306	1
1315	2
1320	2
1326	2
1329	2
1340	4
1378	1
1400	2
1401	4
1404	1
1411	5
1412	6
1446	2
1461	4
1470	1
1477	6
1481	1
1486	2
1487	1
1488	1
1489	5
1490	1
1495	1
1500	2
1502	1
1503	5
1507	6
1511	2
1512	2

LOCO No.	PERIOD No.
1518	4
1520	2
1521	3
1530	1
1541	1
1545	6
1550	1
1555	1
1580	2
1582	3
1583	1
1585	2
1586	1
1591	2
1592	6
1593	6
1595	6
1597	2
1599	3
1610	2
1615	6
1616	3
1618	1
1620	4
1622	6
1624	3
1625	6
1628	5
1630	6
1632	2
1634	4
1636	4
1637	6
1638	5
1639	6
1666	2
1667	4
1670	6
1686	6
1687	2
1688	6
1689	5
1692	2
1697	6
1700	2
1704	2
1706	3
1710	2
1715	1
1717	6
1719	6
1722	5
1729	4
1731	2
1733	1
1734	6
1737	4
1738	6
1740	6
1743	2
1746	6
1749	1
1753	6
1756	1
1760	6
1761	1
1762	2
1763	5
1765	6
1767	2
1768	6
1769	1
1773	3
1774	6
1775	1
1779	3
1780	2

LOCO No.	PERIOD No.
1781	5
1782	2
1784	4
1786	2
1787	2
1795	6
1797	6
1800	1
1801	1
1802	2
1804	6
1810	5
1818	1
1821	6
1826	6
1827	1
1829	2
1830	6
1831	6
1833	6
1835	5
1836	6
1839	1
1840	4
1846	1
1847	2
1848	3
1850	6
1851	3
1854	1
1857	2
1861	2
1862	1
1863	1
1867	6
1868	6
1869	1
1870	1
1871	2
1873	1
1874	4
1876	4
1880	4
1890	5
1891	1
1892	4
1893	3
1896	2
1897	2
1899	6
1900	5
1902	4
1905	6
1908	1
1910	1
1916	1
1918	1
1919	6
1920	4

LOCO No.	PERIOD No.
1921	6
1922	1
1923	4
1924	2
1925	2
2005	1
2043	4
2071	2
2077	2
2081	6
2082	4
2084	3
2086	1
2087	1
2090	2
2094	6
2095	2
2096	3
2102	3
2124	1
2128	3
2129	3
2135	1
2139	1
2142	1
2145	2
2147	2
2165	2
2166	2
2300	2
2301	3
2302	6
2303	2
2326	1
2327	2
2329	6
2330	3
2332	1
2333	1
2337	4
2338	5
2344	2
2348	1
2349	3
2364	3
2365	1
2372	1
2379	2
2380	4
2389	1
2395	1
2398	1
2412	1
2415	2
2416	5
2417	6
2422	1
2424	6
2437	5

LOCO No.	PERIOD No.
2440	1
2443	2
2444	2
2445	1
2448	1
2450	3
2451	6
2453	6
2461	6
2464	3
2477	3
2479	1
2492	2
2493	2
2495	1
2496	6
2501	6
2502	1
2504	1
2506	1
2507	1
2512	6
2516	1
2520	6
2521	3
2523	1
2529	3
2532	1
2535	1
2537	5
2538	4
2539	1
2543	3
2544	4
2546	1
2547	2
2549	2
2550	6
2553	5
2558	1
2559	2
2562	1
2563	6
2565	6
2568	2
2571	3
2574	2
2576	2
2580	4
2583	5
2584	1
2585	6
2586	1
2588	5
2589	5
2591	1
2606	1
2644	2
2678	3

Ex-Southern Railway Locomotives completely Renumbered

S.R. No.	B.R. No.	PERIOD No.
3083	30565	5
3154	30567	3
3167	30570	2
3298	30587	2
3314	30585	6
3329	30586	1
3397	30571	2
3400	30572	5
3440	30576	1
3506	30580	2
3509	30581	6

S.R.No.	B.R. No.	PERIOD No.
3520	30584	1
3744	30589	3
C2	33002	6
C4	33004	5
C5	33005	6
C19	33019	1
C23	33023	6
C25	33025	1
C27	33027	2
C28	33028	6
C30	33030	3

S.R. No.	B.R. No.	PERIOD No.
C33	33033	2
C35	33035	1
C36	33036	5
C37	33037	3
C38	33038	6
C39	33039	6
C40	33040	2
21C3	35003	1
21C4	35004	1
21C5	35005	1
21C6	35006	6

21C7	35007	6
21C10	35010	6
21C11	35011	6
21C13	35013	2
21C16	35016	5
21C17	35017	1
21C18	35018	1
21C19	35019	1
21C20	35020	1
21C102	34002	6
21C103	34003	1
21C104	34004	1
21C105	34005	1
21C106	34006	1
21C111	34011	1
21C112	34012	2
21C113	34013	2
21C115	34015	1
21C116	34016	2
21C117	34017	1
21C118	34018	2
21C119	34019	1
21C120	34020	1
21C121	34021	2
21C122	34022	2
21C123	34023	1
21C124	34024	2
21C125	34025	4
21C127	34027	2
21C128	34028	6
21C130	34030	6
21C132	34032	1
21C133	34033	6
21C134	34034	2
21C136	34036	1
21C139	34039	2
21C140	34040	5
21C142	34042	1
21C143	34043	4
21C144	34044	6
21C145	34045	6
21C146	34046	5
21C148	34048	3
21C151	34051	5
21C156	34056	1
21C158	34058	6
21C160	34060	4
21C164	34064	1
21C165	34065	2
21C168	34068	5
21C169	34069	2

Also Diesel Loco. No. 2 renumbered 15202 in period 5.

Ex-LMSR Locomotives (40,000 added to LMSR No.)

LOCO. No.	RENUMBERED WEEK ENDED
1	11 September
3	28 August
4	2 October
7	30 October
10	18 September
12	3 July
16	11 December
18	20 November
20	3 July
24	31 July
26	23 October
27	5 June
33	5 June
34	28 August
35	31 December
36	10 July
37	1 May
47	5 June
48	19 June
51	13 November
53	24 April
54	25 September
63	29 May
64	1 May
65	5 June
70	9 October
75	16 October
82	29 May
83	9 October
84	19 June
86	11 December
87	14 August
89	22 May
91	6 November
92	25 September
98	6 November
99	7 August
101	16 October
105	25 September
109	20 November
110	7 August
114	27 November
115	3 July
123	23 October
125	5 June
127	18 December
130	26 June
131	15 May
132	14 August
133	24 April
134	25 December
135	14 August
138	13 November
139	30 October
143	27 November
149	1 May
150	23 October
154	1 May
155	18 September
156	5 June
158	19 June
159	27 November
162	23 October
165	19 June
167	29 May
168	4 September
170	4 September
172	10 July
173	10 July
174	11 December
176	29 May
180	26 June
181	22 May
182	17 April
184	31 December
185	6 November
186	27 November
187	2 October
188	2 October
189	17 April
194	5 June
197	31 July
198	18 September
199	4 September
200	25 December
202	15 May
205	24 April
208	25 December
209	3 July
322	3 July
323	10 July
324	20 November
332	10 July
351	25 September
356	23 October
362	28 August
370	6 November
383	14 August
396	25 December
401	14 August
405	12 June
410	16 October
411	20 November
417	4 September
418	16 October
421	11 September
424	22 May
427	27 November
433	31 December
434	14 August
438	12 June
443	25 September
444	1 May
447	10 July
450	4 September
454	20 November
458	13 November
459	26 June
463	24 April
471	18 September
472	20 November
478	9 October
482	18 September
484	6 November
486	25 December
488	20 November
497	22 May
498	7 August
500	17 April
505	21 August
508	6 November
513	15 May
515	29 May
516	15 May
522	2 October
532	1 May
533	24 April
535	5 June
537	28 August
541	7 August
546	15 May
553	3 July
556	24 July
559	28 August
562	10 July
567	18 December
570	24 April
573	28 August
574	18 September
578	9 October
582	2 October
583	26 June
584	12 June

585	3 July
587	31 July
588	16 October
589	11 December
593	24 April
596	6 November
598	16 October
601	2 October
602	25 December
604	4 September
608	26 June
611	24 July
613	8 May
618	23 October
620	8 May
621	24 April
623	16 October
624	17 April
632	4 September
633	12 June
636	17 July
641	24 April
643	4 December
646	26 June
647	28 August
649	27 November
650	9 October
651	10 July
653	19 June
655	22 May
657	25 December
658	29 May
663	5 June
664	1 May
665	3 July
667	11 September
668	17 April
670	22 May
672	15 May
674	18 December
675	25 December
679	26 June
689	22 May
692	3 July
693	1 May
694	12 June
695	8 May
696	26 June
697	29 May
726	25 September
728	5 June
740	8 May
741	21 August
745	19 June
758	7 August
900	30 October
905	21 August
908	21 August
910	24 April
911	4 December
913	4 September
914	22 May
919	3 April
920	19 June
921	19 June
924	28 August
927	28 August
929	25 September
931	14 August
933	10 July
936	5 June
937	15 May
938	3 July
1001	11 December
1003	21 August
1007	27 November
1009	25 December
1014	21 August
1017	27 November
1019	22 May
1021	11 September
1023	22 May
1034	9 October
1035	4 September
1037	8 May
1039	25 September
1046	17 July
1047	9 October
1048	25 December
1049	29 May
1050	18 December
1051	4 December
1052	18 September
1053	19 June
1055	9 October
1056	13 November
1059	11 December
1060	7 August
1062	20 November
1063	30 October
1065	22 May
1068	11 December
1070	21 August
1072	8 May
1073	3 July
1074	3 July
1076	11 September
1077	3 July
1081	10 July
1082	12 June
1083	17 April
1084	8 May
1086	23 October
1087	8 May
1089	26 June
1090	16 October
1091	15 May
1092	8 May
1094	9 October
1095	27 November
1096	12 June
1097	14 August
1098	18 December
1099	11 December
1101	15 May
1103	18 December
1106	19 June
1111	23 October
1113	5 June
1114	16 October
1115	4 September
1116	26 June
1117	31 December
1121	5 June
1122	20 November
1126	31 December
1128	13 November
1132	8 May
1133	6 November
1136	21 August
1137	24 April
1142	13 November
1143	13 November
1144	30 October
1145	17 April
1146	14 July
1147	12 June
1149	12 June
1151	13 November
1152	27 November
1154	11 September
1156	11 December
1157	5 June
1159	4 December
1162	20 November
1164	25 September
1166	26 June
1167	26 June
1168	2 October
1169	23 October
1170	15 May
1174	5 June
1176	22 May
1177	26 June
1178	18 September
1180	10 April
1181	8 May
1183	10 July
1187	18 December
1188	8 May
1192	13 November
1193	1 May
1194	26 June
1195	4 December
1196	10 July
1197	29 May
1199	25 September
1202	20 November
1203	11 December
1516	25 September
1529	10 July
1530	1 May
1532	5 June
1534	9 October
1535	3 July
1536	24 April
1537	29 May
1710	10 July
1713	21 August
1724	1 May
1739	17 April
1745	16 October
1752	4 December
1763	8 May
1769	20 November
1793	11 December
1794	20 November
1803	25 December
1804	11 September
1829	25 December
1852	22 May
1853	8 May
1854	31 July
1873	21 August
1901	4 December
1902	12 June
1903	13 November
1904	15 May
1905	14 August
1909	14 August
1981	29 May
1983	3 July
1985	1 May
1986	8 May
1988	2 October
1991	30 October
1993	31 July
2198	17 April
2199	17 April
2201	10 April
2203	17 July
2204	3 July
2205	2 October
2206	27 March
2208	24 April
2209	6 November
2212	18 December
2213	22 May
2214	1 May
2215	3 July
2220	9 October
2221	17 April
2224	1 May
2225	1 May

2227	25 September
2228	11 December
2229	29 May
2230	14 August
2231	11 September
2232	6 November
2233	23 October
2235	25 September
2237	7 August
2238	4 December
2240	18 December
2243	16 October
2248	15 May
2249	29 May
2250	22 May
2251	31 July
2252	1 May
2253	3 July
2254	22 May
2255	5 June
2256	7 August
2257	25 September
2260	31 July
2262	11 December
2267	4 December
2300	26 June
2301	6 November
2302	10 July
2303	16 October
2304	25 December
2305	22 May
2307	2 October
2311	1 May
2312	23 October
2314	1 May
2315	9 October
2316	20 November
2318	27 November
2320	15 May
2322	8 May
2324	9 October
2326	30 October
2328	4 September
2329	31 December
2331	26 June
2334	11 September
2335	2 October
2339	10 July
2340	16 October
2344	24 April
2345	4 September
2346	3 July
2347	10 July
2349	11 December
2350	30 October
2352	11 December
2358	12 June
2360	28 August
2363	29 May
2364	11 September
2370	15 May
2371	16 October
2374	7 August
2381	11 September
2383	1 May
2384	29 May
2386	29 May
2388	6 November
2389	14 August
2392	22 May
2395	25 September
2397	25 September
2398	13 November
2399	4 December
2400	9 October
2404	18 September
2405	10 July
2406	4 December
2410	11 September
2412	14 August
2414	25 September
2415	24 April
2416	3 July
2417	15 May
2418	20 March
2419	11 September
2421	28 August
2422	31 December
2425	17 April
2429	6 November
2431	15 May
2434	15 May
2435	11 September
2436	18 September
2437	26 June
2439	29 May
2441	9 October
2443	18 December
2445	27 November
2448	14 August
2450	28 August
2455	29 May
2456	11 September
2458	8 May
2459	18 December
2460	24 April
2462	3 July
2463	3 July
2464	20 November
2465	6 November
2467	9 October
2471	7 August
2472	30 October
2475	13 November
2476	12 June
2478	31 July
2479	15 May
2484	26 June
2486	18 December
2487	12 June
2489	13 November
2500	20 November
2501	2 October
2502	29 May
2503	31 July
2505	29 May
2506	11 December
2507	17 July
2508	18 December
2509	14 August
2510	15 May
2512	24 April
2513	25 December
2514	31 July
2515	27 November
2516	15 May
2517	20 November
2518	15 May
2519	7 August
2521	25 September
2522	11 December
2523	18 September
2524	11 September
2525	26 June
2526	18 September
2527	4 December
2528	10 July
2529	30 October
2530	21 August
2531	4 September
2532	17 April
2533	17 April
2534	17 July
2535	13 November
2536	23 October
2537	2 October
2540	17 April
2544	12 June
2545	24 July
2546	19 June
2547	28 August
2548	31 December
2549	23 October
2550	24 July
2552	9 October
2553	18 September
2555	20 November
2558	29 May
2559	4 December
2561	29 May
2565	3 July
2568	2 October
2569	18 December
2571	4 September
2572	12 June
2574	20 November
2575	11 September
2576	18 December
2577	8 May
2578	3 July
2580	31 July
2581	18 December
2582	30 October
2583	14 August
2585	1 May
2588	30 October
2589	10 April
2590	17 April
2592	22 May
2593	9 October
2594	25 September
2595	24 April
2596	21 August
2602	1 May
2605	19 June
2607	20 November
2608	28 August
2609	31 July
2610	19 June
2616	25 September
2617	25 December
2618	25 December
2619	18 September
2620	21 August
2621	16 October
2622	28 August
2623	8 May
2631	26 June
2632	26 June
2633	12 June
2634	7 August
2636	12 June
2638	1 May
2643	24 April
2645	5 June
2646	8 May
2647	24 April
2648	25 December
2656	25 September
2658	25 September
2659	24 April
2661	15 May
2663	22 May
2664	9 October
2666	13 November
2668	4 December
2671	24 July
2676	17 April
2677	4 December
2678	5 June
2679	9 October
2681	30 October
2684	27 November
2687	8 May

2689	4 September
2693	5 June
2698	15 May
2699	12 June
2700	18 September
2701	24 April
2706	4 September
2707	10 July
2708	2 October
2711	12 June
2712	29 May
2718	13 November
2719	7 August
2720	2 October
2722	19 June
2723	5 June
2730	19 June
2733	14 August
2734	28 August
2745	7 August
2746	16 October
2748	18 December
2749	31 December
2751	15 May
2752	20 November
2755	26 June
2757	20 November
2759	21 August
2765	23 October
2766	20 November
2771	31 July
2773	28 August
2780	22 May
2782	1 May
2784	3 July
2786	8 May
2788	28 August
2792	17 April
2794	16 October
2796	15 May
2797	5 June
2802	29 May
2803	30 October
2805	26 June
2807	27 November
2809	22 May
2810	10 July
2811	11 September
2814	9 October
2815	27 November
2818	17 April
2823	10 July
2826	18 December
2829	13 November
2830	10 April
2832	6 November
2833	10 July
2834	10 April
2836	30 October
2837	15 May
2839	27 November
2841	29 May
2846	23 October
2847	29 May
2848	3 July
2849	11 December
2851	18 September
2852	20 November
2854	5 June
2858	11 December
2859	18 December
2860	18 September
2861	12 June
2865	4 September
2868	10 July
2870	12 June
2871	9 October
2873	13 November
2874	18 December
2876	10 April
2877	28 August
2878	11 September
2879	27 November
2880	3 April
2884	5 June
2891	11 December
2892	22 May
2893	11 September
2895	16 October
2897	21 August
2898	19 June
2902	26 June
2907	23 October
2908	5 June
2910	31 December
2912	17 July
2914	8 May
2915	28 August
2918	4 September
2922	21 August
2925	26 June
2926	25 September
2927	23 October
2928	12 June
2929	2 October
2933	29 May
2935	28 August
2940	9 October
2944	14 August
2946	31 December
2947	30 October
2948	2 October
2954	22 May
2958	24 April
2961	4 September
2962	21 August
2964	8 May
2967	3 July
2968	18 December
2973	19 June
2975	12 June
2977	16 October
2978	27 November
2979	4 December
2982	23 October
2983	25 September
2984	16 October
3001	7 August
3185	16 October
3189	29 May
3193	16 October
3200	26 June
3203	15 May
3205	25 September
3211	5 June
3212	17 April
3214	31 July
3216	3 July
3219	9 October
3224	25 September
3225	7 August
3226	10 July
3232	11 December
3235	12 June
3237	17 April
3242	8 May
3243	30 October
3246	26 June
3251	4 December
3258	31 December
3259	4 September
3261	7 August
3263	24 April
3267	15 May
3273	24 April
3275	7 August
3277	31 December
3283	21 August
3294	2 October
3295	14 August
3297	5 June
3298	26 June
3299	16 October
3309	8 May
3310	17 April
3319	15 May
3326	4 December
3330	17 April
3337	13 November
3340	25 September
3341	13 November
3344	19 June
3356	1 May
3371	11 December
3374	2 October
3387	1 May
3395	23 October
3396	11 December
3400	12 June
3411	29 May
3428	14 August
3440	11 September
3446	5 June
3448	15 May
3454	12 June
3459	20 November
3464	25 September
3469	29 May
3482	19 June
3497	25 December
3499	27 November
3506	18 September
3521	8 May
3524	10 July
3531	23 October
3538	7 August
3546	20 November
3553	25 September
3565	18 September
3568	21 August
3585	16 October
3586	28 August
3599	29 May
3600	30 October
3621	18 December
3624	27 November
3627	26 June
3629	26 June
3630	4 September
3633	6 November
3636	11 September
3638	26 June
3644	5 June
3657	15 May
3665	23 October
3667	2 October
3676	23 October
3681	20 November
3683	25 December
3727	27 November
3751	18 December
3753	21 August
3754	19 June
3757	12 June
3762	15 May
3763	9 October
3765	8 May
3766	25 September
3784	19 June
3786	30 October
3787	20 November
3795	4 September
3800	8 May
3801	6 November

3806	4 September
3818	25 September
3819	5 June
3836	19 June
3838	24 April
3841	1 May
3842	6 November
3845	4 September
3846	6 November
3849	26 June
3850	12 June
3857	5 June
3858	7 August
3860	6 November
3861	5 June
3865	28 August
3869	14 August
3876	25 December
3877	6 November
3883	16 October
3884	3 July
3888	16 October
3891	25 September
3894	11 December
3896	17 April
3898	1 May
3899	18 December
3902	15 May
3908	18 December
3909	12 June
3910	24 April
3911	9 October
3912	29 May
3913	20 November
3916	7 August
3917	25 September
3921	14 August
3927	19 June
3928	4 December
3929	22 May
3933	2 October
3938	9 October
3943	14 August
3952	7 August
3953	18 December
3955	4 December
3957	25 September
3958	16 October
3960	19 June
3964	8 May
3969	4 December
3973	13 November
3976	31 December
3979	11 December
3981	16 October
3988	25 December
3990	24 July
3992	27 November
3996	6 November
3997	31 July
3999	6 November
4000	21 August
4005	31 July
4008	3 July
4013	9 October
4015	16 October
4016	17 July
4017	29 May
4020	22 May
4022	15 May
4024	12 June
4025	28 August
4030	6 November
4036	30 October
4039	25 December
4043	5 June
4048	4 September
4050	27 November
4053	26 June
4057	2 October
4058	10 July
4060	1 May
4061	11 December
4063	20 November
4072	23 October
4074	6 November
4076	24 April
4079	12 June
4080	25 December
4086	14 August
4088	18 December
4089	23 October
4095	25 December
4097	9 October
4100	4 September
4101	21 August
4102	11 December
4103	27 November
4108	30 October
4118	23 October
4119	18 September
4122	6 November
4125	20 November
4126	7 August
4127	28 August
4129	8 May
4130	13 November
4131	6 November
4136	20 November
4137	21 August
4138	3 July
4141	31 December
4146	13 November
4147	19 June
4155	19 June
4156	21 August
4158	18 December
4163	9 October
4174	27 November
4175	25 September
4177	9 October
4185	17 April
4186	18 December
4190	31 July
4197	18 December
4209	2 October
4214	6 November
4216	25 September
4217	16 October
4220	1 May
4225	7 August
4226	29 May
4228	7 August
4229	31 December
4230	14 August
4233	12 June
4234	14 August
4235	5 June
4241	12 June
4242	16 October
4247	9 October
4253	27 March
4260	8 May
4261	27 November
4265	26 June
4266	2 October
4275	17 April
4277	10 July
4281	14 August
4282	27 November
4283	10 July
4287	18 December
4293	23 October
4298	15 May
4300	17 April
4301	25 September
4304	4 September
4305	4 September
4307	1 May
4308	25 December
4309	25 September
4314	6 November
4316	22 May
4325	27 March
4326	9 October
4330	17 April
4333	4 December
4340	27 November
4344	20 November
4347	6 November
4349	12 June
4350	19 June
4355	28 August
4358	28 August
4362	12 June
4363	27 November
4366	28 August
4368	24 April
4374	25 September
4379	9 October
4380	26 June
4381	22 May
4384	13 November
4385	18 September
4386	25 December
4387	31 July
4388	31 July
4389	2 October
4390	17 April
4391	21 August
4393	21 August
4394	15 May
4398	13 November
4400	16 October
4402	10 July
4403	10 July
4416	4 September
4425	19 June
4429	28 August
4430	10 July
4438	30 October
4439	30 October
4442	29 May
4444	18 December
4446	24 April
4448	27 November
4454	30 October
4461	31 December
4462	4 December
4463	20 November
4464	7 August
4466	13 November
4469	11 December
4471	18 December
4472	12 June
4473	7 August
4475	3 July
4478	4 December
4481	4 September
4482	17 April
4483	3 July
4484	21 August
4490	28 August
4491	31 July
4497	15 May
4499	22 May
4501	29 May
4503	5 June
4509	20 November
4517	8 May
4518	9 October
4519	28 August
4523	1 May
4524	29 May

Stanier's version of the 2-6-2T, with No. 40136 seen here in very good condition at Wilmslow in 1949. Built at Derby Works it was first allocated to Blair Atholl in October 1935 as No. 136. Renumbering was carried out during the week ended 18th June 1949 and withdrawal came during the week ended 21st October 1961 from Bangor.

G.W. Sharpe

Waiting at Nuneaton Trent Valley to depart with a Coventry and Warwick train in July 1950 is another Stanier 2-6-2T, No. 40203. Built in February 1938 and first allocated to Northampton, this engine survived until July 1962 the final shed being Kentish Town. Renumbering in the 40000 series took place during the week ended 15th January 1949. The engine is seen here with a larger diameter 6B boiler which was fitted in July 1942 to improve the steaming ability. Only six of the class were so fitted, and little difference seems to have been made by this modification.

J.F. Clay

Ex-Midland 2P class 4-4-0 No. 40459 pilots an unidentified 'Royal Scot' 4-6-0 on a Leeds to Carlisle express near Hellifield in August 1948. This 2P dated back to August 1894 and after rebuilding in 1905 and 1922 with new boilers was finally withdrawn during the last week in December 1949. Hellifield was the last allocation.

G.W. Sharpe

LMS built in 1928, 2P class 4-4-0 No. 40609 ex-works at Glasgow Eastfield shed on Monday 28th February 1949 after being repaired and renumbered at Cowlairs. It left that evening to return home to Ardrossan. No. 40609 went new to Ardrossan and remained at that shed until transferred to Hurlford in April 1959 from where withdrawal took place in the week ended 2nd October 1961. Only two allocations in 33 years must be something of a record.

G.W. Sharpe

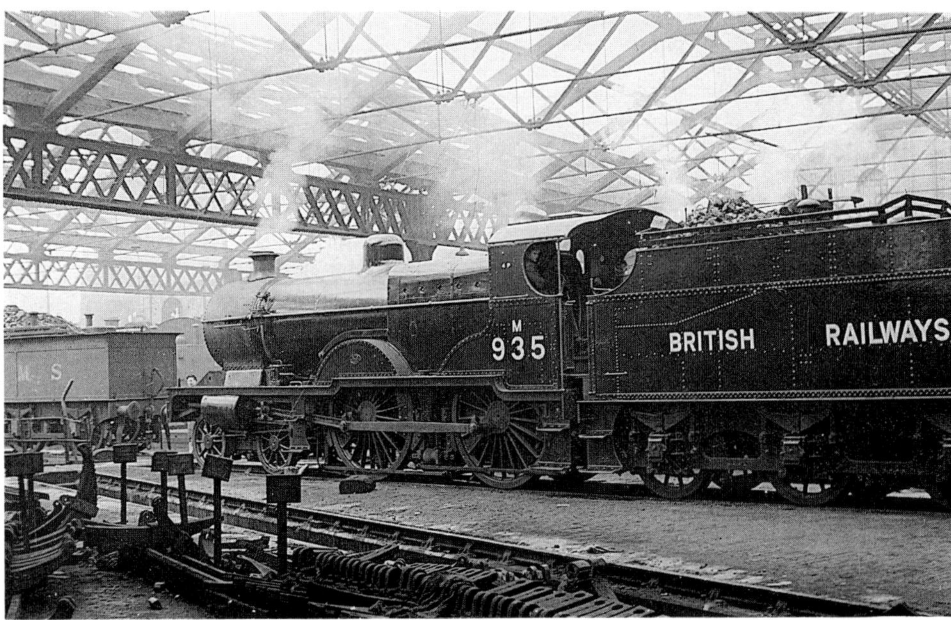

Saltley shed in March 1948. Ex-LMS 4P class 4-4-0 No. M935 is working home to Bristol Barrow Road after a visit to Derby Works. Built in 1932, the first allocation was to Derby shed and withdrawal took place during the last week of March 1958 from nearby Bournville.

R.H.G. Simpson

Burton shed was a good place to find an interesting selection of tank engines. Friday 30th July 1948 finds ex-L&YR 0-4-0T No. 11217 and ex-Midland Railway 0-4-0T No. 41536 with no work to do. The L&Y engine was renumbered during the week ended 15th April 1950. During 1948 No. 11217 (later BR No. 51217) had an interesting holiday away from shunting around the local brewery yards. During the first week in October it went to the North Eastern shed at Tweedmouth to work the North Sunderland Railway line during the time the usual locomotive, Y7 class 0-4-0T No. 68089, was away at Darlington Works for overhaul. It returned to Burton on 18th December. Withdrawal came in October 1961 from Bristol Barrow Road. No. 41536 was also withdrawn in 1961 during the first week in March from Burton.

K.C.H. Fairey

Leeds Stourton shed in May 1949. Johnson 1F class 0-6-0T No. 1838 with open cab and Belpaire boiler stands alongside the coaling stage. Renumbering took place during the week ended 17th September 1949. This engine had a long career at Stourton, remaining there until withdrawal during the last week in April 1956.

G.W. Sharpe

LTSR 4-4-2T No. 41932 at Tilbury shed on Saturday 3rd June 1950. This was a design by Whitelegg dating back to 1909 with further examples being introduced in 1923, as was No. 41932. Renumbered from 2114 during the week ended 26th February 1949, withdrawal took place from Tilbury shed during the last week of August 1951.

D.K. Jones

Fairburn 4P class 2-6-4T No. M2194 at Corkerhill shed in March 1949. This locomotive had been built at Derby and sent new to this Glasgow depot in February 1948. It remained there and other Scottish sheds in the south west of Scotland until October 1964. Transfer took it to Wakefield and then on to Darlington the next month, from where withdrawal took place in August 1965.

G.W. Sharpe

Fowler's parallel boilered design of 2-6-4T, illustrated by No. 42311. This example was built in 1928 and is seen here in 1948 at an unknown location that could possibly be on the Huddersfield to Penistone line, No. 42311 being allocated to Huddersfield at the time. Withdrawal came during the week ended 13th April 1964 from Bradford Low Moor shed.

G.W. Sharpe

Stanier's taper boiler design of 2-6-4T as exemplified by No. 2457, renumbered 42457 during the week ended 19th November 1949. Oxenholme allocated, it is seen here working a local train near Carnforth in 1948. Built in 1936 and first allocated to Liverpool Edge Hill, withdrawal took place during the week ended 17th November 1962 from Carnforth.

G.W. Sharpe

The date is Saturday 24th July 1948 and Horwich "Crab" 2-6-0 No. 2891 approaches Northampton on empties. August 1930 was the build month of this locomotive and it first carried the number 13191. This was altered to 2891 in 1934 and renumbered into BR stock during 1948. Withdrawal from Stoke shed occurred in October 1962 during the week ended the 20th.

L. Hanson

Stanier taper boilered 2-6-0 No. 42966 on a mineral train on Saturday 29th September 1951 passing Hassop station near Bakewell, which closed on 17th August 1942. This was Stanier's first design after taking over as Chief Mechanical Engineer of the LMSR. The taper boiler was a design practice brought with him from Swindon as was the combined top feed and dome. No. 42966 started life as 13266 in January 1934 and went new to Leeds Holbeck. Renumbered 2966 in 1934 and 42966 during the week ended 5th March 1949. Withdrawal came from Wolverhampton Bushbury shed during the week ended 25th July 1964.

E.R. Morten

Ivatt 4F 2-6-0 No. 43011 which was added to stock in 1948, and incorporated many modern design features to aid maintenance, including the high running plate. The double chimney was later replaced by a single. This photograph was taken at Stratford, ER shed during June 1948 whilst on loan, and as mentioned in the Introduction. No. 43011 lasted until 11th February 1967, its final home being Workington.

G.W.Sharpe

Walsall shed in 1949, with the shed roof very overdue for repair. In fact, a rebuild was not started until 1956 and the shed turned over to diesels in June 1958. Being prepared for work here is Johnson 3F class 0-6-0 No. 43214 belonging to Saltley, 21A. No. 43214 had moved from Burton to Saltley during the last week in September 1948 and remained at this allocation until withdrawal during the week ended 17th June 1961. Alongside is Walsall-owned Stanier 2-6-4T No. 42448 which had been delivered new to Aston shed in June 1936. Its withdrawal came during the first week in January 1962 from Trafford Park.

R.H.G. Simpson

Deeley 3F class 0-6-0 No. 43776 leaves Toadmoor Tunnel, Ambergate on a freight on Saturday 26th May 1951. Dating back to 1903, they were a continuation of the original Johnson design as illustrated by No. 43214. This locomotive was renumbered during the week ended 21st April 1951 and was withdrawn from Rowsley shed during the week ended 23rd November 1957.
E.R. Morton

Fowler 4F class 0-6-0 No. 3907, quite a long way from its home shed of Kirkby-in-Ashfield, being near Sowerby Bridge on a freight in February 1949. This particular example was built at Derby in 1920 and renumbered 43907 in July 1949. Kirkby was the engine's last home when withdrawn during the week ended 19th December 1959.
G.W. Sharpe

Northampton Castle station on Saturday 16th April 1949. LMS 4F class 0-6-0 No. 44379 runs past with an 'up' freight. Built in 1927 by Andrew Barclay & Sons Ltd (builder's No. 1923) for the LMSR, withdrawal came during the week ended 26th September 1964 from Kirkby-in-Ashfield.
L. Hanson

A "Black Five" variant was No. 44745, with Caprotti valve gear, and introduced in 1948 to Leeds Holbeck. Transfer took place during the week ended 9th July 1949 to Bristol Barrow Road, and this is the location for this photograph, taken around that date. Withdrawal took place from Southport shed during the week ended 24th October 1964.

R.H.G. Simpson

We move now to Sheffield Millhouses shed in June 1948 for this view of Stanier Class 5 4-6-0 No. 4986, paired with a self-weighing tender. No. 4986 had gone new to Southport shed during the week ended 19th October 1946, moving on to Liverpool Bank Hall two weeks later. Leeds Holbeck was the engine's next home, moving there by 19th April 1947 and then on to Millhouses on 14th February 1948. Its final home was Carlisle Kingmoor where withdrawal took place during the first week of May 1967.

G.W. Sharpe

Armstrong Whitworth built "Black Five" 4-6-0 (builder's No. 1258), BR No. 45217 at Glasgow Polmadie in August 1948, and one of the first to be painted in this style. When built in November 1935, Bank Hall was the first allocation. Carlisle Kingmoor was the engine's last shed when withdrawn during the week ended 26th November 1966.

G.W. Sharpe

This photograph was also taken in August 1948, on Sunday 29th at Northampton Castle station during the engine's stay at Rugby shed. Compare the livery with that of No. 45217! Another Armstrong Whitworth creation, (builder's No. 1434), No. 5379 had been delivered new to Crewe North in July 1937. Renumbered 45379 during the week ended 28th May 1949, withdrawal came at Willesden shed during the last week of July 1965. Happily, that was not the end of the story for No. 45379 survives in preservation on the Avon Valley Railway at Bitton near Bristol.

L. Hanson

Unrebuilt 'Patriot' 4-6-0 (or "Baby Scot" as they were known) No. 45516 *The Bedfordshire and Hertfordshire Regiment* (named in 1938) at home at Preston shed in 1949. Renumbered during the week ended 12th February 1949, withdrawal was actioned from Warrington Dallam shed during the week ended 22nd July 1961. Preston shed was gutted by fire on the morning of Wednesday 28th June 1961 and burning timber fell onto the tender of 2-6-0 No. 42707, setting the coal alight and then spread to the whole shed roof. Twelve other locomotives were damaged. Preston shed finally closed on Tuesday 12th September 1961.

G.W. Sharpe

Rebuilt 'Patriot' 4-6-0 No. 45522 *Prestatyn* (named in 1939) near Kingsthorpe, Northampton, on Sunday 4th June 1950. This was the last of the class to be converted with a 2A boiler and double chimney and had emerged from Crewe Works in this form during January 1949. Smoke deflector shields were fitted later. Originally built in 1933, withdrawal took place during the week ended 19th September 1964 from Manchester Longsight.

L. Hanson

Great Rocks Junction on the Midland line over the Peak is the location for this photograph of Derby-based 'Jubilee' No. 45610 *Gold Coast*. The date is Thursday 3rd May 1951 and the train is the 4.10pm Derby to Manchester stopper. No. 45610 was built at Crewe and went first to Camden shed in July 1934. Renumbered from 5610 during the week ended 11th June 1949, and renamed *Ghana* in December 1958, withdrawal was carried out from Derby shed during the second week of January 1964.

E.R. Morten

'Jubilee' No. M5714 *Revenge* at Carlisle Kingmoor shed in June 1948, paired with a smaller Fowler tender. Built at Crewe in July 1936, its first home was just down the road at Crewe North. The "M" was erased during the week ended 16th April 1949 and "4" substituted. No. 45714 was finally withdrawn from Carnforth during the week ended 20th July 1963.

G.W. Sharpe

Royal Scot itself, No. 46100 at Watford passing the engine shed on an 'up' express in September 1949. This was before the engine was rebuilt, which was carried out at Crewe in June 1950. No. 46100 was actually LMS locomotive No. 6152 with which it had exchanged identities in 1933 for its tour of Canada and America. The commemorative nameplates, including the unusual smokebox nameplate and buffer beam bell, were all a legacy from the tour. It was shipped out from Tilbury Docks on the Canadian Pacific steamship *Beaverdale* on 11th April 1933, arriving at Montreal on 21st April. Then followed a circular tour of 11,194 miles, Montreal-Cincinnati-Chicargo-Montreal. Return was again on board the *Beaverdale* casting off from Montreal at 7am on Friday 24th November. No. 46100 was the first of the class to be withdrawn during the week ended 13th October 1962 from Nottingham shed. Today, in rebuilt form, it is preserved at Bressingham, Norfolk.

G.W. Sharpe

Westbourne Park, near Paddington, during the week commencing 19th April 1948. Rebuilt 'Royal Scot' class No. 46162 *Queen's Westminster Rifleman* is returning to London with an express from Plymouth during the exchange workings. Originally built at Derby in September 1930, No. 46162 had been fitted with its new boiler and double chimney in January 1948. Withdrawal took place from Carlisle Kingmoor during the week ended 30th May 1964.

Photomatic

Stanier 'Princess Royal' class 4-6-2 No. 46203 *Princess Margaret Rose* at Ashton, Northants, on a 'down' express on Saturday 26th June 1948. This magnificent machine entered traffic at Glasgow Polmadie in July 1935 and served a distinguished career until withdrawal during the week ended 20th October 1962 from Carlisle Kingmoor. Her elegance can still be enjoyed for she is now preserved at the Midland Railway Centre at Butterley.

L. Hanson

Stanier 'Princess Coronation' or 'Duchess' class 4-6-2 No. 46227 *Duchess of Devonshire* runs past Northampton No.1 signal box on Sunday 12th August 1951 on the diverted 'down' "Royal Scot". Built originally with streamlined casing in June 1938, the first allocation was Camden. The casing was removed in 1946 and the slope at the top of the front of the boiler was the clue. No. 46227 moved from Crewe North to Polmadie during the week ended 12th June 1948 and remained at this Glasgow shed until withdrawal during the last week of December 1962.

L. Hanson

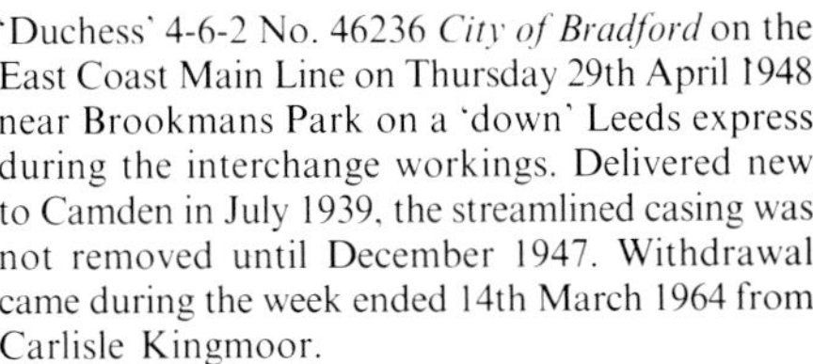

'Duchess' 4-6-2 No. 46236 *City of Bradford* on the East Coast Main Line on Thursday 29th April 1948 near Brookmans Park on a 'down' Leeds express during the interchange workings. Delivered new to Camden in July 1939, the streamlined casing was not removed until December 1947. Withdrawal came during the week ended 14th March 1964 from Carlisle Kingmoor.

Photomatic

Not all the 'Duchess' class were streamlined, and this example, No. 6253 *City of St Albans*, is one that did not receive the casing. It entered traffic during the week ended 14th September 1946 and first operated from Camden. This scene, recorded on Saturday 15th May 1948, shows the engine at Ashton coasting along on an 'up' express. Renumbered 46253 during the week ended 17th September 1949, it remained performing useful work until Crewe North decided it would run no more, during the week ended 26th January 1963.

L. Hanson

Ex-LNWR Webb 1P class 2-4-2T No. 6683 leaves Northampton on Saturday 12th June 1948 on its way to Blisworth having just passed Duston West Junction. Based at Warwick at the time, it was no doubt on loan to Northampton shed. This design dated back to 1890 and was originally a class of 160 locomotives. Renumbered 46683 during the week ended 3rd November 1951, withdrawal came from Warwick shed during the last week of February 1953.

L. Hanson

Bristol Barrow Road shed in August 1951 with Sentinel geared 4-wheeled, tank locomotive No. 47190 in the yard. This was one of two locomotives built in September 1929 for the S&DJR numbered 100 and 101. These two engines were acquired for shunting in the sidings at Radstock, and had very low cab roofs and dropped footplates due to restricted bridge clearances at Radstock. They were renumbered 7190 and 7191 on being taken over by the LMS in 1930, becoming BR Nos 47190 and 47191. No. 47190 with withdrawn in March 1961 back on S&D territory at Templecombe, and was the last of its type to remain in service on BR, No. 47191 already having been scrapped in August 1959 from Bath S&D shed.

Photomatic

Kentish Town shed in May 1948 is the setting for this portrait of Johnson 3F class 0-6-0T No. M7242, fitted with condensing apparatus. This example dated back to 1902 and became No. 47242 during the week ended 17th September 1949. Withdrawn during the last week of August 1957 from Kentish Town.

G.W. Sharpe

We return to Preston shed again for this view of the standard LMS shunter "Jinty", 3F class 0-6-0T No. M7296 in May 1948. Hunslet had built this one in 1924 (builder's No. 1461) and it had first appeared numbered 7136, becoming 7296 in the 1934 renumbering scheme. The final number, 47296, was painted on during the week ended 3rd December 1949. Withdrawal came at Bescot shed during the week ended 12th December 1959.

G.W. Sharpe

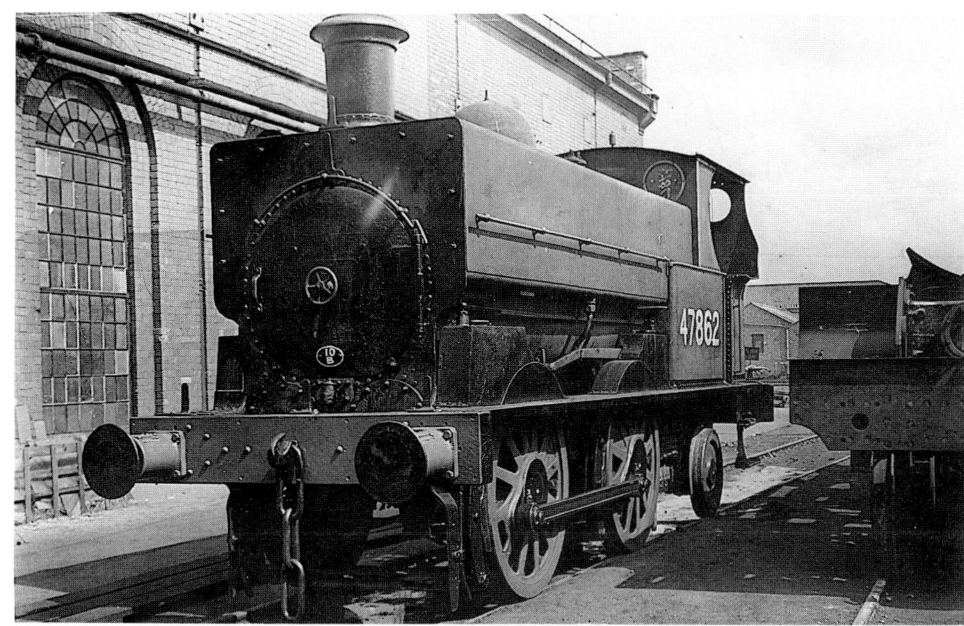

The pleasure of visiting Crewe Works was being able to see delights such as this ex-LNWR 0-4-2T, known as a "box tank". The works used unusual elderly engines as shunters and this was the job of No. 47862 in August 1949. Renumbered during the week ended 12th March 1949, it here, oddly, wears a 10B Preston shed plate. Sister engine, No. 47865 was withdrawn during the first week of November 1953, No. 47862 soldiering on until 1956, being taken out of service during the week ended 3rd November.

G.W. Sharpe

Peterborough Spital Bridge depot on Sunday 24th June 1951 plays host to Beyer-Garratt locomotive No. 47981, not long after a visit to Crewe Works by the look of the paintwork. Built by Beyer, Peacock (builder's No. 6662) in 1930, the engine was renumbered during the week ended 19th February 1949. Withdrawal from Toton came during the week ended 3rd November 1956. The last of the class to be withdrawn was No. 47994, this engine leaving Hasland shed for the last time on Friday 14th March 1958, light engine to Crewe Works for scrap.

L. Hanson

Derby shed on Sunday 9th May 1948. Stanier 8F class 2-8-0 No. M8647 sleeps away the afternoon. The tender is from an "Austerity" 2-8-0 for the usual one has been loaned out to one of the Southern Region locomotives involved in the exchange trials, as no Southern engines had tenders with water scoops, there being no troughs on the Southern Region. No. M8647 had been built at Brighton Works and entered traffic in November 1943, the first allocation being Perth shed. Renumbered 48647 during the week ended 23rd September 1950, withdrawal from Sutton Oak shed was carried out during the week ended 23rd April 1966.

L. Hanson

Stanier 8F class 2-8-0 No. 48741 rounds the curves into Buxton past East signal box with a mineral train from the Hindlow line with another 8F at the rear that had given assistance. The date is Wednesday 1st August 1951. This was one of the engines built at Darlington Works for the LNER and in February 1946 went new to Heaton shed. The LNER numbered the locomotive 3136 and changed this to 3536 in 1947. When handed over to the LMSR in 1947 it changed yet again to 8741 and finally to 48741 during the week ended 19th November 1949. The last depot to operate this engine was Heaton Mersey, withdrawal coming during the week ended 28th October 1967.

E.R. Morten

Oxford LMS shed, alongside the River Isis, is the setting for this view of ex-LNWR G1 class, 6F 0-8-0 No. 49324 in 1948. This was a sub-shed of Bletchley and remained open until 3rd December 1950 when visiting LMR engines began to use the ex-GWR shed for servicing. Known as "Super Ds" the G1 and G2 0-8-0s were the only LNWR class of any size to be taken over by BR. Remarkable survivors they were, for the last four were not withdrawn until December 1964 from Bescot. No. 49324 did not last too long into BR ownership however for it was withdrawn during the week ended 4th March 1950 from Walsall.

R.H.G. Simpson

Fowler's development of the LNWR 0-8-0 culminated in a design that was not entirely successful to say the least! Their main weakness was axlebox bearings and this resulted in high maintenance costs and poor availability. Originally a class of 175 units, scrapping commenced with a vengeance in 1949 and by the end of 1951 only 53 remained. In view of this it was surprising that the last one, No. 49508, lasted until 20th January 1962, last shed Agecroft. This example, No. 49539, was built at Crewe in 1929 and is shown near Sowerby Bridge in February 1949 when allocated to Goole. Transfer to Aintree occurred during the week ended 30th July 1949, probably in poor condition, for withdrawal was actioned from this shed during the week ended 15th October the same year.

G.W. Sharpe

Blackpool was the final home for the seven survivors of Hughes LYR 'Dreadnought' 5P class 4-6-0s. The only one to receive its BR number was 50455, pictured here at its home shed in 1949. Built at Horwich Works in July 1924, the original order was for 4-6-4Ts but this was changed in favour of tender engines. No. 50455 was the last of the class to remain active and a special excursion was arranged on Sunday 1st July 1951 from Blackpool to York and return by the Central Division of the LMR for this engine to haul. Although it had received its last intermediate repair at Horwich just before the special ran, this engine was reported to be "knocking badly and running hot". After the York trip it did very little work, spending most of its time out of use at Blackpool shed. Withdrawal took place during the first week in October 1951 after running over 750,000 miles.

G.W. Sharpe

Was this the most unusual locomotive to be acquired by BR on 1st January 1948? It is an ex-LYR Railmotor which was a combined engine and coach and was the last survivor of a class of 18 units dating back to 1906. The final duties of No. 10617 were the push-pull workings on the short branch to Horwich from Blackrod. It was withdrawn during the first week of March 1948 without being renumbered 50617.

G. W. Sharpe

In September 1910 George Hughes, Chief Mechanical Engineer of the LYR, began experiments with superheaters on goods locomotives. From the results he built 20 2-4-2 Radial tank engines for passenger work basing the design on the non-superheated 2-4-2Ts built by his predecessor, Aspinall. The first appeared in February 1911 and as they proved themselves capable engines, Hughes decided to rebuild some of the earlier 2-4-2Ts with superheaters and piston valve cylinders. No. 50925 was one of the rebuilds, originally built in March 1910 as LYR No. 1536, the rebuild was carried out in September 1914. No. 50925 is pictured at Sowerby Bridge shed in April 1949, its last home, and it was the last of the class in service being withdrawn during the week ended 9th August 1952.

G.W. Sharpe

Manchester Agecroft shed is the location for this view of LYR 0-4-0ST No. 51240 in October 1949. Known as "Pugs", the design by Aspinall dated back to 1891. Longevity was bestowed on these engines for they lasted well into the BR period, the last, No. 51218 not being withdrawn until September 1964 from Neath shed, and is now preserved. No. 51240 was finally retired during the week ended 24th April 1957 from Goole shed.

G.W. Sharpe

The Aspinall LYR F16 class 2F 0-6-0STs were rebuilds of earlier Barton Wright tender engines. This example, No. 51503, is at Sowerby Bridge shed in July 1949. It had been renumbered during the week ended 7th May 1949 and was withdrawn from Goole during the week ended 11th April 1957.

G.W. Sharpe

LOCO. No.	RENUMBERED WEEK ENDED
4525	23 October
4529	29 May
4530	4 December
4531	4 September
4535	19 June
4541	30 October
4544	30 October
4548	1 May
4550	19 June
4551	26 June
4552	23 October
4555	17 April
4556	17 April
4558	3 July
4559	1 May
4565	31 July
4566	30 October
4569	27 November
4571	2 October
4572	2 October
4575	4 December
4576	11 December
4577	25 September
4579	4 December
4581	1 May
4582	16 October
4584	19 June
4585	20 November
4587	16 October
4588	6 November
4590	17 April
4595	12 June
4596	16 October
4598	27 November
4599	30 October
4602	31 July
4606	2 October
4748	12 June
4749	12 June
4753	5 June
4758	22 May
4765	4 September
4766	22 May
4767	1 May
4768	27 November
4769	31 July
4770	16 October
4771	4 December
4772	9 October
4773	3 July
4787	27 November
4793	20 November
4795	1 May
4797	31 December
4799	15 May
4800	6 November
4803	4 December
4804	20 November
4805	10 July
4808	14 August
4809	3 July
4811	12 June
4813	4 September
4814	28 August
4815	16 October
4817	3 July
4818	23 October
4822	15 May
4825	7 August
4826	26 June
4827	14 August
4828	18 September
4829	30 October
4830	4 September
4832	28 August
4833	1 May

LOCO. No.	RENUMBERED WEEK ENDED
4834	12 June
4837	28 August
4838	14 August
4839	10 April
4844	24 April
4845	29 May
4846	22 May
4849	24 April
4851	4 December
4855	21 August
4857	7 August
4859	15 May
4861	5 June
4864	14 August
4866	5 June
4867	10 April
4870	17 April
4874	9 October
4875	25 September
4877	10 July
4878	18 September
4880	26 June
4887	31 December
4892	22 May
4893	4 December
4900	24 July
4904	6 November
4906	24 April
4910	7 August
4912	6 November
4914	3 July
4916	2 October
4918	25 December
4919	21 August
4921	2 October
4926	7 August
4928	1 May
4929	1 May
4931	15 May
4935	31 July
4937	25 December
4938	28 August
4945	4 December
4946	25 December
4948	3 July
4951	8 May
4952	17 July
4953	16 October
4954	27 November
4955	30 October
4958	19 June
4959	10 April
4962	11 September
4965	29 May
4966	9 October
4968	4 September
4970	10 July
4971	3 July
4972	18 December
4973	1 May
4974	19 June
4978	2 October
4979	11 September
4982	20 November
4983	26 June
4985	5 June
4986	18 December
4987	12 June
4988	14 August
4989	24 July
4991	8 May
4992	4 December
4993	18 December
4997	11 December
4998	12 June
4999	12 June

LOCO. No.	RENUMBERED WEEK ENDED
5002	30 October
5003	16 October
5004	22 May
5005	11 September
5007	11 December
5008	17 July
5009	15 May
5013	17 April
5014	8 May
5015	2 October
5016	4 December
5017	16 October
5019	15 May
5020	19 June
5022	10 July
5023	23 October
5026	1 May
5027	6 November
5029	25 December
5031	27 November
5033	27 November
5034	24 April
5035	31 July
5037	8 May
5038	11 December
5040	6 November
5044	19 June
5045	10 April
5047	14 August
5049	1 May
5052	15 May
5053	12 June
5054	5 June
5056	23 October
5057	8 May
5060	28 August
5061	1 May
5063	19 June
5065	2 October
5066	19 June
5067	13 November
5069	10 April
5071	7 August
5073	21 August
5074	3 July
5076	24 April
5079	8 May
5080	22 May
5081	10 April
5083	20 March
5084	10 July
5085	17 July
5086	26 June
5087	10 April
5089	16 October
5090	3 July
5091	3 July
5092	31 December
5095	31 July
5096	3 April
5097	11 December
5098	21 August
5100	29 May
5102	8 May
5109	8 May
5111	27 November
5113	8 May
5115	15 May
5116	17 April
5117	16 October
5119	24 April
5121	28 August
5122	10 April
5123	1 May
5124	1 May
5125	10 July

5126	26 June	5262	14 August	5395	26 June
5130	15 May	5263	7 August	5396	26 June
5133	2 October	5264	8 May	5397	22 May
5134	11 September	5266	19 June	5400	5 June
5135	7 August	5267	13 November	5401	31 July
5137	25 September	5268	22 May	5402	17 April
5138	20 November	5270	27 November	5403	22 May
5139	9 October	5271	2 October	5404	31 December
5141	4 September	5272	24 April	5407	20 November
5146	8 May	5275	30 October	5410	19 June
5150	18 September	5276	7 August	5411	10 April
5151	21 August	5277	14 August	5417	11 December
5153	8 May	5278	16 October	5418	28 August
5155	11 September	5279	28 August	5419	29 May
5156	18 September	5280	27 November	5422	12 June
5157	8 May	5282	5 June	5423	10 April
5158	26 June	5283	3 July	5424	25 December
5160	7 August	5285	4 September	5425	11 September
5162	17 July	5288	15 May	5428	2 October
5163	30 October	5289	2 October	5430	31 July
5164	21 August	5291	28 August	5433	22 May
5165	6 November	5292	3 April	5434	18 September
5166	1 May	5299	18 December	5436	12 June
5167	1 May	5302	14 August	5438	2 October
5168	3 April	5303	8 May	5439	21 August
5169	25 September	5305	19 June	5440	14 August
5170	22 May	5306	8 May	5442	24 April
5171	22 May	5307	23 October	5443	11 September
5172	18 December	5308	15 May	5444	31 December
5173	18 September	5309	23 October	5447	20 November
5177	15 May	5311	25 December	5448	26 June
5178	4 December	5312	8 May	5451	27 November
5179	19 June	5314	25 December	5452	20 November
5181	22 May	5316	11 September	5455	21 August
5182	23 October	5318	4 September	5456	17 April
5184	24 July	5319	15 May	5457	28 August
5185	21 August	5320	6 November	5458	20 November
5186	2 October	5321	30 October	5459	15 May
5187	13 November	5323	3 July	5460	13 November
5190	11 December	5326	10 April	5461	11 September
5192	3 July	5327	20 November	5463	23 October
5194	20 March	5328	18 September	5464	29 May
5195	3 July	5329	27 November	5467	5 June
5196	9 October	5331	24 July	5469	24 April
5202	11 December	5332	6 November	5470	20 November
5205	19 June	5333	22 May	5471	24 April
5207	4 December	5334	4 September	5472	12 June
5208	6 November	5335	9 October	5474	14 August
5210	20 November	5336	8 May	5475	3 July
5212	9 October	5337	13 November	5477	25 September
5213	3 April	5338	8 May	5478	2 October
5214	2 October	5340	25 December	5480	25 December
5215	30 October	5344	6 November	5481	6 November
5216	25 September	5345	4 December	5482	29 May
5217	29 May	5347	4 September	5483	4 September
5218	3 July	5349	21 August	5484	13 November
5219	5 June	5351	6 November	5485	9 October
5223	31 July	5355	11 September	5486	18 September
5224	21 August	5357	17 April	5487	22 May
5225	29 May	5358	12 June	5489	9 October
5229	22 May	5359	17 July	5490	26 June
5230	18 December	5360	24 April	5491	29 May
5231	5 June	5361	14 August	5492	2 October
5234	24 July	5363	17 July	5499	14 August
5236	17 April	5364	9 October	5502	20 November
5241	18 December	5365	27 March	5503	15 May
5242	21 August	5366	26 June	5504	2 October
5245	29 May	5367	1 May	5505	26 June
5248	6 November	5371	4 December	5506	4 September
5249	1 May	5373	11 September	5507	23 October
5251	3 April	5376	28 August	5510	26 June
5252	19 June	5377	29 May	5512	31 July
5253	29 May	5378	17 April	5513	12 June
5256	12 June	5380	5 June	5514	22 May
5258	26 June	5385	15 May	5515	24 April
5259	5 June	5386	31 July	5518	3 July
5260	15 May	5389	17 April	5519	4 December
5261	1 May	5394	28 August	5520	3 July

5521	14 August
5523	9 October
5525	21 August
5527	18 September
5529	7 August
5530	10 April
5531	22 May
5532	3 July
5534	31 December
5535	25 September
5536	13 November
5537	8 May
5538	26 June
5540	22 May
5541	1 May
5544	18 September
5545	6 November
5551	29 May
5554	6 November
5555	17 April
5557	15 May
5558	4 September
5559	27 November
5560	14 August
5561	15 May
5562	30 October
5565	22 May
5566	26 June
5567	6 November
5568	23 October
5569	4 December
5570	19 June
5571	16 October
5572	14 August
5573	11 September
5575	21 August
5576	19 June
5577	10 April
5578	11 December
5579	4 September
5581	17 April
5583	23 October
5584	27 March
5585	15 May
5586	3 July
5587	3 July
5589	5 June
5590	2 October
5591	25 September
5592	5 June
5593	4 December
5596	15 May
5597	28 August
5598	24 April
5599	4 September
5600	31 July
5604	10 April
5605	10 July
5607	22 May
5608	2 October
5609	14 August
5611	13 November
5612	25 December
5613	7 August
5614	1 May
5615	1 May
5616	25 September
5617	5 June
5618	15 May
5619	19 June
5620	18 September
5621	30 October
5622	19 June
5623	19 June
5624	11 September
5627	23 October
5628	4 December
5629	6 November
5630	3 July
5631	13 November
5633	18 December
5637	4 September
5638	3 July
5639	31 July
5640	29 May
5641	18 September
5642	29 May
5643	25 September
5644	20 November
5645	12 June
5646	11 December
5648	26 June
5649	14 August
5652	16 October
5653	23 October
5656	1 May
5657	21 August
5659	21 August
5660	8 May
5662	28 August
5663	7 August
5664	6 November
5666	25 December
5669	7 August
5672	7 August
5673	17 April
5674	12 June
5675	4 September
5676	2 October
5679	28 August
5680	18 September
5683	24 July
5684	9 October
5685	29 May
5687	9 October
5688	22 May
5689	27 November
5690	15 May
5692	3 July
5693	28 August
5694	17 April
5695	16 October
5696	30 October
5697	29 May
5698	25 September
5699	22 May
5700	18 December
5701	22 May
5702	26 June
5704	4 December
5706	14 August
5707	28 August
5708	28 August
5711	4 December
5712	23 October
5713	2 October
5715	1 May
5720	18 September
5721	28 August
5722	31 July
5723	29 May
5724	7 August
5725	4 December
5726	11 December
5727	26 June
5728	30 October
5729	5 June
5730	24 April
5731	18 December
5734	18 September
5735	19 June
5736	2 October
5737	13 November
5739	31 July
5740	12 June
5741	29 May
5742	13 November
6100	19 June
6101	1 May
6102	4 September
6103	23 October
6104	7 August
6105	1 May
6106	12 June
6107	3 April
6108	8 May
6109	1 May
6111	20 November
6112	11 September
6114	26 June
6116	25 September
6117	29 May
6119	31 July
6120	12 June
6121	9 October
6122	17 April
6123	26 June
6124	10 April
6125	11 September
6126	4 December
6127	1 May
6129	26 June
6130	22 May
6131	7 August
6132	24 April
6134	13 November
6135	2 October
6136	31 July
6137	8 May
6139	22 May
6141	3 July
6142	3 July
6143	4 September
6144	5 June
6145	2 October
6146	12 June
6148	26 June
6149	24 April
6151	23 October
6152	19 June
6154	17 April
6155	3 July
6157	18 December
6158	9 October
6159	18 September
6160	25 September
6161	31 July
6162	17 April
6163	20 November
6164	17 April
6165	23 October
6166	31 July
6167	18 December
6168	4 September
6169	15 May
6170	24 April
6200	14 August
6201	7 August
6203	8 May
6204	24 April
6205	22 May
6206	27 November
6208	22 May
6210	5 June
6211	5 June
6212	10 April
6220	3 July
6221	23 October
6222	25 September
6224	8 May
6225	19 June
6226	25 September
6227	8 May
6228	31 July

6229 3 July
6230 29 May
6231 29 May
6232 8 May
6233 2 October
6234 30 October
6235 29 May
6236 17 April
6237 3 July
6239 21 August
6240 26 June
6241 29 May
6242 29 May
6243 24 April
6244 28 August
6245 28 August
6246 20 November
6247 20 November
6249 17 April
6251 29 May
6256 15 May
6601 18 September
6603 13 November
6604 27 November
6620 11 December
6637 14 August
6643 18 September
6654 18 December
6658 14 August
6666 16 October
6680 7 August
6687 22 May
6712 4 September
6727 25 December
6749 6 November
6912 30 October
7003 7 August
7004 26 June
7160 6 November
7163 24 April
7164 24 April
7167 20 March
7182 11 December
7183 31 December
7201 18 September
7206 24 April
7207 12 June
7209 26 June
7210 17 July
7217 9 October
7218 31 July
7219 24 April
7220 10 July
7224 18 September
7225 20 November
7228 24 April
7247 26 June
7248 31 December
7251 5 June
7256 3 July
7259 3 July
7263 1 May
7265 24 April
7268 23 October
7274 28 August
7282 24 April
7287 21 August
7293 28 August
7297 18 December
7298 7 August
7301 14 August
7304 2 October
7305 2 October
7308 28 August
7309 25 December
7310 8 May
7313 4 December
7317 2 October
7322 5 June
7323 4 September
7326 28 August
7327 13 November
7328 3 July
7337 24 April
7344 3 July
7346 14 August
7353 6 November
7361 3 July
7362 15 May
7365 12 June
7368 22 May
7373 11 September
7384 6 November
7387 27 November
7401 27 November
7413 16 October
7418 8 May
7424 1 May
7426 7 August
7443 23 October
7446 25 December
7449 3 July
7453 7 August
7458 16 October
7470 21 August
7473 16 October
7478 23 October
7486 1 May
7493 6 November
7494 4 September
7495 4 December
7500 11 September
7504 9 October
7506 8 May
7513 19 June
7515 2 October
7516 26 June
7517 27 November
7520 21 August
7521 14 August
7527 4 September
7528 12 June
7529 28 August
7533 24 April
7536 26 June
7540 28 August
7543 25 December
7545 8 May
7547 25 September
7551 10 July
7559 31 July
7564 31 July
7565 13 November
7567 4 September
7572 15 May
7574 23 October
7576 25 December
7577 21 August
7584 11 September
7587 19 June
7588 24 April
7590 28 August
7591 21 August
7592 4 September
7599 5 June
7600 7 August
7602 30 October
7605 21 August
7606 10 July
7610 12 June
7615 9 October
7622 19 June
7626 28 August
7638 1 May
7639 6 November
7640 15 May
7643 7 August
7650 24 April
7652 20 November
7662 17 April
7665 25 September
7667 17 July
7673 30 October
7677 7 August
7865 18 September
7877 29 May
7881 11 September
7884 9 October
7896 19 June
7931 20 November
7967 11 December
7968 27 November
7969 7 August
7971 30 October
7972 26 June
7974 4 September
7975 12 June
7976 6 November
7977 11 September
7978 13 November
7979 5 June
7980 2 October
7982 18 September
7983 9 October
7984 26 June
7985 22 May
7986 25 September
7988 25 December
7990 1 May
7991 28 August
7992 19 June
7993 24 April
7997 8 May
8000 3 July
8002 11 December
8003 22 May
8004 24 April
8005 4 December
8008 3 July
8009 29 May
8017 8 May
8029 31 July
8033 15 May
8035 12 June
8037 1 May
8050 15 May
8053 15 May
8055 13 November
8063 25 December
8064 23 October
8069 13 November
8073 25 September
8076 14 August
8078 7 August
8079 21 August
8082 19 June
8083 3 July
8085 17 April
8092 4 December
8099 17 April
8100 6 November
8101 5 June
8108 18 September
8110 28 August
8111 19 June
8114 24 April
8115 11 December
8116 11 September
8117 3 July
8119 2 October
8121 17 April
8123 3 July
8125 19 June
8129 9 October

8131	8 May
8133	1 May
8135	4 September
8139	12 June
8140	3 July
8144	17 April
8145	5 June
8146	5 June
8153	29 May
8154	11 December
8155	12 June
8163	28 August
8164	19 June
8165	26 June
8167	12 June
8168	22 May
8170	18 September
8171	21 August
8172	20 November
8174	13 November
8176	25 September
8178	12 June
8180	30 October
8182	13 November
8183	1 May
8184	27 March
8187	7 August
8188	15 May
8189	26 June
8190	6 November
8191	13 November
8192	31 July
8194	11 December
8195	25 September
8197	31 December
8198	21 August
8201	2 October
8203	13 November
8204	3 July
8209	18 September
8210	11 December
8213	21 August
8214	7 August
8215	21 August
8218	21 August
8222	27 November
8223	24 April
8266	11 December
8268	7 August
8273	18 December
8277	3 July
8279	13 November
8282	16 October
8285	8 May
8293	19 June
8305	16 October
8306	3 July
8308	12 June
8319	12 June
8320	29 May
8321	25 December
8326	4 September
8330	12 June
8332	26 June
8341	8 May
8343	15 May
8346	14 August
8348	4 December
8349	25 September
8352	13 November
8353	19 June
8357	24 July
8358	20 November
8363	18 December
8364	26 June
8366	4 September
8369	9 October
8370	13 November

8371	30 October
8379	6 November
8382	16 October
8385	29 May
8386	4 December
8392	26 June
8393	16 October
8400	26 June
8402	18 September
8406	22 May
8409	25 December
8411	18 December
8413	20 November
8414	1 May
8415	31 July
8417	25 December
8420	25 December
8443	24 July
8453	15 May
8457	24 April
8465	14 August
8467	30 October
8470	24 April
8472	3 July
8474	24 April
8478	4 September
8500	24 April
8502	11 December
8507	28 August
8508	17 April
8512	30 October
8527	9 October
8532	26 June
8536	28 August
8538	29 May
8541	4 September
8600	14 August
8601	21 August
8604	15 May
8605	17 April
8606	25 December
8608	9 October
8612	24 July
8613	11 December
8614	24 April
8615	21 August
8617	30 October
8618	1 May
8621	25 December
8624	13 November
8627	1 May
8629	3 July
8633	18 September
8635	11 September
8636	17 April
8638	25 December
8639	24 April
8640	18 September
8642	15 May
8644	31 December
8648	20 November
8653	12 June
8655	20 November
8660	19 June
8661	13 November
8664	11 September
8666	18 December
8674	31 July
8675	9 October
8676	8 May
8677	21 August
8679	4 December
8680	25 September
8682	4 December
8683	4 September
8685	7 August
8688	19 June
8690	11 December

8692	9 October
8693	17 April
8699	23 October
8702	27 November
8708	6 November
8716	18 December
8721	26 June
8724	28 August
8729	10 April
8730	19 June
8748	9 October
8751	8 May
8753	3 July
8755	24 July
8758	9 October
8760	2 October
8761	1 May
8762	20 November
8765	31 July
8766	21 August
8768	5 June
8769	4 September
8770	8 May
8772	18 September
8895	27 November
8901	11 September
8905	1 May
8907	7 August
8908	22 May
8914	2 October
8917	7 August
8920	30 October
8922	24 April
8925	31 July
8929	26 June
8930	15 May
8932	2 October
8941	19 June
8942	2 October
8944	31 July
8945	8 May
8950	8 May
8952	6 November
8953	13 November
8966	21 August
9006	15 May
9008	1 May
9011	6 November
9014	28 August
9017	5 June
9028	23 October
9029	7 August
9032	29 May
9041	6 November
9046	5 June
9057	22 May
9059	14 August
9065	26 June
9069	21 August
9071	28 August
9073	3 July
9075	5 June
9079	25 September
9082	24 April
9088	11 December
9090	11 December
9092	12 June
9093	21 August
9094	18 September
9096	15 May
9104	13 November
9105	21 August
9107	19 June
9113	24 July
9115	25 September
9119	3 July
9121	28 August
9122	2 October

9126	6 November
9137	18 December
9143	8 May
9145	3 July
9148	19 June
9149	18 September
9150	28 August
9153	21 August
9154	24 July
9157	11 December
9158	1 May
9163	5 June
9164	25 December
9168	11 December
9174	11 September
9177	19 June
9178	23 October
9180	25 December
9188	7 August
9191	24 July
9200	19 June
9202	3 July
9209	14 August
9214	19 June
9216	3 July
9219	31 July
9220	22 May
9223	5 June
9228	30 October
9229	3 July
9230	25 September
9232	24 April
9235	21 August
9241	5 June
9247	8 May
9252	7 August
9261	20 November
9262	8 May
9264	4 September
9266	26 June
9267	29 May
9271	9 October
9276	27 November
9278	8 May
9279	18 September
9280	5 June
9281	9 October
9288	26 June
9291	29 May
9293	31 December
9298	27 November
9299	5 June
9306	11 September
9307	1 May
9308	16 October
9310	3 July
9313	29 May
9314	14 August
9316	13 November
9323	25 September
9324	17 April
9325	12 June
9332	4 September
9333	25 December
9339	4 September
9342	2 October
9343	5 June
9348	11 December
9351	5 June
9352	22 May
9357	15 May
9370	26 June
9373	16 October
9378	9 October
9379	5 June
9382	1 May
9389	19 June
9390	14 August
9391	12 June
9392	4 December
9393	18 September
9397	20 November
9400	12 June
9401	29 May
9403	23 October
9407	28 August
9408	4 September
9410	26 June
9411	9 October
9412	2 October
9416	18 December
9424	16 October
9425	30 October
9426	5 June
9429	9 October
9430	24 April
9431	29 May
9434	2 October
9435	1 May
9436	4 December
9438	1 May
9442	26 June
9446	4 September
9451	19 June
9452	30 October
9453	14 August
9454	6 November
9500	4 December
9501	1 May
9502	31 July
9505	12 June
9508	24 April
9509	18 December
9513	24 April
9516	14 August
9519	14 August
9520	8 May
9523	11 December
9524	3 July
9525	29 May
9526	9 October
9531	28 August
9532	16 October
9535	25 December
9536	12 June
9537	24 April
9538	26 June
9539	6 November
9540	3 July
9541	6 November
9544	10 July
9545	15 May
9548	5 June
9551	4 December
9554	23 October
9556	2 October
9560	26 June
9561	18 September
9562	26 June
9564	31 July
9566	4 September
9568	14 August
9569	11 September
9570	17 April
9574	16 October
9581	5 June
9583	14 August
9584	15 May
9586	22 May
9587	5 June
9591	25 September
9592	8 May
9593	16 October
9596	10 July
9598	4 December
9600	9 October
9602	11 December
9605	16 October
9607	8 May
9611	28 August
9612	2 October
9615	30 October
9617	19 June
9620	26 June
9622	21 August
9623	30 October
9624	13 November
9627	31 December
9628	27 November
9630	13 November
9631	19 June
9634	4 September
9635	21 August
9636	31 July
9637	26 June
9638	9 October
9640	26 June
9647	3 July
9649	18 December
9653	9 October
9655	28 August
9657	18 September
9659	12 June
9661	15 May
9663	27 November
9664	6 November
9665	7 August
9666	23 October
9668	7 August
9671	6 November
10455	25 December
10623	13 November
10630	1 May
10640	9 October
10642	15 May
10652	9 October
10654	6 November
10678	21 August
10687	7 August
10695	8 May
10712	5 June
10746	18 December
10749	31 December
10762	4 December
10766	31 July
10795	25 December
10802	21 August
10806	4 September
10812	13 November
10829	22 May
10852	24 April
10869	27 November
10872	12 June
10873	4 December
10886	22 May
10891	21 August
10893	13 November
10898	11 September
10925	25 September
10953	24 April
11202	19 June
11204	2 October
11230	27 November
11240	2 October
11246	4 December
11307	2 October
11313	1 May
11321	7 August
11323	31 July
11343	3 July
11348	9 October
11361	10 July
11404	20 November
11410	15 May

11412	9 October
11413	18 September
11423	5 June
11425	1 May
11436	23 October
11441	18 December
11446	25 September
11447	4 September
11457	11 December
11462	29 May
11474	15 May
11477	3 July
11488	20 November
11499	29 May
11500	29 May
11504	6 November
11512	10 July
11524	17 April
11526	4 September
12016	10 April
12019	10 April
12021	17 April
12022	10 April
12023	10 April
12024	10 April
12030	10 April
12031	10 April
12034	10 April
12036	10 April
12037	10 April
12041	10 April
12043	10 April
12044	10 April
12045	10 April
12047	10 April
12049	10 April
12051	10 April
12053	10 April
12056	10 April
12059	10 April
12063	10 April
12064	10 April
12088	3 July
12089	8 May
12092	10 July
12093	10 July
12095	5 June
12100	11 December
12107	19 June
12111	17 April
12118	21 August
12126	10 July
12133	24 April
12135	7 August
12136	11 September
12137	13 November
12139	16 October
12143	19 June
12154	25 December
12157	25 December
12160	1 May
12163	21 August
12166	11 September
12171	24 April
12172	25 September
12175	26 June
12177	2 October
12183	20 November
12184	19 June
12189	14 August
12191	22 May
12201	21 August
12207	3 July
12216	14 August
12218	6 November
12225	4 December
12230	6 November
12233	27 November
12237	18 December
12238	14 August
12240	15 May
12244	26 June
12268	24 April
12270	30 October
12272	11 December
12288	10 July
12296	3 July
12300	22 May
12311	12 June
12312	22 May
12330	11 December
12331	2 October
12334	5 June
12343	17 April
12345	31 July
12358	16 October
12362	25 September
12363	2 October
12368	28 August
12379	4 September
12386	28 August
12389	14 August
12390	18 September
12393	4 December
12397	8 May
12399	1 May
12400	29 May
12404	15 May
12405	28 August
12407	30 October
12408	7 August
12410	19 June
12411	1 May
12413	30 October
12427	25 September
12430	10 July
12433	9 October
12438	8 May
12441	11 September
12444	21 August
12446	31 July
12448	20 November
12449	18 September
12452	25 September
12456	28 August
12459	23 October
12461	20 November
12508	31 December
12509	7 August
12510	25 September
12522	8 May
12529	31 December
12541	9 October
12549	3 July
12557	18 December
12569	31 December
12575	22 May
12582	15 May
12583	2 October
12592	5 June
12609	10 July
12615	8 May
12727	17 April
12782	13 November
12821	8 May
12825	11 September
12831	22 May
12839	15 May
12856	23 October
12857	18 December
12870	1 May
12886	4 December
12962	7 August
13802	5 June
13804	2 October
14404	16 October
14438	10 April
14440	21 August
14444	17 April
14445	8 May
14446	4 September
14448	28 August
14453	25 September
14455	22 May
14456	5 June
14457	6 November
14458	4 December
14460	19 June
14462	27 November
14463	19 June
14464	14 August
14465	4 September
14466	17 July
14470	11 September
14471	29 May
14473	14 August
14474	20 November
14479	1 May
14480	2 October
14484	18 September
14485	1 May
14488	10 July
14491	5 June
14496	16 October
14497	30 October
14499	8 May
14504	3 April
14505	23 October
14506	17 July
14636	12 June
14638	1 May
14639	21 August
14642	22 May
14647	1 May
14649	18 September
14650	18 December
14767	21 August
15121	11 December
15124	9 October
15125	30 October
15126	3 July
15129	17 April
15138	1 May
15145	27 November
15159	18 September
15161	13 November
15165	18 December
15166	11 September
15173	5 June
15178	5 June
15180	29 May
15181	4 December
15183	13 November
15191	12 June
15196	17 July
15197	17 July
15201	25 September
15202	13 November
15204	20 November
15207	25 December
15210	22 May
15212	11 September
15219	14 August
15220	31 July
15221	28 August
15223	30 October
15228	10 July
15231	11 December
15232	12 June
15233	9 October
15240	10 July
15263	10 July
15356	17 April
15359	5 June

15360	26 June
16020	3 April
16025	21 August
16038	1 May
16153	22 May
16155	4 September
16160	26 June
16165	13 November
16169	16 October
16170	8 May
16232	16 October
16237	23 October
16238	10 April
16244	13 November
16245	12 June
16249	5 June
16254	5 June
16256	16 October
16261	15 May
16262	16 October
16263	20 March
16269	5 June
16272	24 April
16276	4 September
16277	20 March
16279	12 June
16281	24 April
16282	25 December
16283	10 April
16284	10 April
16286	27 November
16289	31 December
16297	13 November
16298	18 December
16299	31 December
16304	25 September
16310	17 April
16313	6 November
16314	4 December
16315	26 June
16320	27 March
16327	7 August
16335	8 May
16336	26 June
16340	2 October
16341	12 June
16346	19 June
16350	13 November
16359	1 May
16361	10 April
16367	18 December
16368	2 October
16369	11 September
17232	25 December
17236	25 September
17238	9 October
17243	24 April
17245	10 July
17247	25 September
17254	2 October
17256	13 November
17258	12 June
17260	3 July
17261	8 May
17264	19 June
17266	25 September
17268	8 May
17271	28 August
17272	6 November
17273	25 December
17275	25 December
17279	10 July
17284	25 December
17287	11 December
17289	17 April
17291	22 May
17292	29 May
17294	29 May
17298	8 May
17299	4 December
17307	15 May
17309	25 September
17310	15 May
17312	11 September
17315	11 September
17316	31 July
17317	17 April
17319	11 September
17320	30 October
17321	27 November
17323	17 July
17325	6 November
17329	11 September
17331	11 December
17332	3 July
17335	4 September
17337	21 August
17338	7 August
17342	3 April
17344	23 October
17351	29 May
17352	31 December
17358	26 June
17360	11 September
17361	19 June
17368	2 October
17370	28 August
17377	21 August
17385	8 May
17387	20 March
17389	29 May
17390	29 May
17391	12 June
17397	10 July
17398	3 July
17409	24 April
17417	18 December
17423	4 December
17425	17 April
17426	27 March
17430	26 June
17432	20 March
17434	20 November
17435	2 October
17436	30 October
17438	27 March
17439	26 June
17443	13 November
17445	4 September
17447	20 November
17453	14 August
17461	18 September
17463	18 September
17464	22 May
17467	7 August
17468	4 September
17472	31 December
17556	29 May
17557	6 November
17562	1 May
17566	17 July
17570	3 July
17573	8 May
17575	23 October
17576	25 September
17581	9 October
17582	24 July
17583	3 July
17588	29 May
17594	22 May
17599	14 August
17604	12 June
17608	15 May
17614	19 June
17619	10 July
17622	16 October
17631	5 June
17632	17 July
17635	19 June
17638	6 November
17643	15 May
17650	11 December
17651	2 October
17652	2 October
17653	6 November
17659	12 June
17661	19 June
17665	24 April
17669	24 July
17681	17 April
17686	17 July
17689	31 December
17690	5 June
17695	29 May
17697	16 October
17698	27 November
17951	27 November
17955	13 November
17956	27 November

Ex-LMSR Locomotives completely Renumbered

L.M.S. LOCO. No.	B.R. LOCO. No.	RENUMBERED WEEK ENDED
1249	58033	20 November
1255	58036	23 October
1261	58038	10 July
1273	58040	18 December
1340	58053	29 May
1360	58062	4 December
1375	58070	26 June
1382	58073	18 December
1411	58080	28 August
1416	58082	29 May
1422	58085	23 October
1423	58086	18 December
1426	58089	15 May
2110	41928	12 June
2112	41930	31 July
2113	41931	27 November
2115	41933	6 November
2116	41934	20 November
2118	41936	7 August
2122	41940	31 July

2125	41943	24 April
2131	41949	25 September
2135	41953	6 November
2137	41955	5 June
2138	41956	29 May
2139	41957	10 July
2140	41958	12 June
2141	41959	9 October
2142	41960	31 July
2143	41961	7 August
2144	41962	10 July
2145	41963	18 December
2146	41964	22 May
2147	41965	24 April
2148	41966	8 May
2149	41967	24 April
2150	41968	15 May
2151	41969	1 May
2152	41970	1 May
2153	41971	8 May
2154	41972	8 May
2155	41973	8 May
2156	41974	8 May
2157	41975	12 June
2158	41976	15 May
2159	41977	24 April
2160	41978	29 May
2987	58161	25 December
2990	58164	1 May
3023	58188	18 December
3027	58189	3 July
3048	58199	29 May
3051	58201	14 August
3054	58203	21 August
3074	58211	15 May
3098	58218	7 August
3108	58222	22 May
3118	58225	30 October
3150	58235	1 May
3156	58238	8 May
3161	58240	24 April
3164	58241	26 June
3175	58246	24 April
3176	58247	16 October
3190	58249	15 May
3229	58251	11 September
3262	58252	6 November
3420	58260	27 November
3445	58264	25 December
3451	58265	27 November
3493	58272	17 July
3508	58274	28 August
3517	58278	4 September
3559	58289	6 November
3571	58293	31 July
3603	58295	2 October
3691	58302	10 July
3703	58304	18 September
3725	58306	21 August
7710	58902	23 October
7737	58908	9 October
7746	58911	21 August
7759	58916	1 May
7782	58921	31 July
7791	58924	29 May
7794	58925	20 November
22630	58110	31 December
22902	58116	25 December
22915	58122	30 October
22932	58130	8 May
22946	58137	19 June
22947	58138	11 December
22958	58144	16 October
22967	58148	14 August
22974	58153	4 September
22977	58156	11 September
23002	58175	23 October
23012	58184	11 December
23013	58185	7 August
23018	58187	10 July
26616	46616	7 August
27512	58853	5 June
27515	58856	18 September
27522	58859	2 October
27527	58860	1 May
27530	58862	9 October
27553	58880	28 August
27596	58887	12 June
27603	58889	7 August
27674	58897	31 July
28091	58321	25 September
28100	58323	14 August
28106	58326	13 November
28115	58328	21 August
28141	58332	23 October
28172	58336	9 October
28227	58343	2 October
28245	58347	18 September
28253	58351	6 November
28333	58363	30 October
28428	58377	21 August
28507	58393	3 July
28512	58396	12 June
28515	58398	1 May
28548	58409	30 October

Also L.M.S. Loco. 6428 renumbered 26428 Week Ended 13 March, later to become B.R. No. 58092.

Ex-LMSR Diesel Locomotives completely Renumbered

7083	12006	17 April
7086	12009	13 November
7087	12010	8 May
7095	12018	5 June
7110	12023	29 May
7113	12026	30 October
7115	12028	18 December
7117	12030	31 December
7120	12033	10 July
7121	12034	25 December
7124	12037	14 September
7130	12043	19 June

Ex-LNER Locomotives Renumbered (60,000 added to LNER No.)

LOCO. No.	RENUMBERED WEEK ENDED
1	17 July
2	15 May
4	5 June
5	10 July
6	4 December
7	27 March
8	30 October
9	15 May
10	30 October
12	5 June
15	18 December
16	12 June

18 16 October
19 16 October
20 2 October
23 27 March
24 19 June
27 5 June
28 12 June
29 17 July
30 31 July
31 5 June
33 10 April
34 27 March
35 4 December
36 24 July
37 30 October
38 26 June
39 10 July
40 4 September
41 4 December
42 26 June
43 21 August
45 5 June
47 8 May
48 13 November
49 26 June
50 21 August
51 25 September
52 9 October
54 10 April
55 5 June
57 19 June
59 10 July
60 2 October
61 20 November
65 31 July
66 20 March
67 7 August
68 2 October
69 10 July
70 28 August
71 22 May
72 21 August
74 22 May
75 29 May
76 4 September
77 20 November
78 26 June
79 27 March
81 5 June
82 29 May
84 5 June
85 10 July
86 18 September
87 30 October
88 17 July
89 4 September
91 10 April
93 2 October
94 31 December
95 2 October
96 30 October
97 26 June
98 6 November
101 21 August
103 31 December
104 31 July
105 21 August
106 4 December
107 24 April
109 1 May
113 2 October
501 22 May
502 3 July
503 18 September
504 10 April
505 5 June
506 18 December
507 20 November
508 29 May
509 21 August
510 1 May
511 17 April
512 27 March
513 6 November
514 27 March
515 26 June
516 9 October
517 28 August
518 17 July
519 30 October
520 14 August
521 22 May
526 28 August
527 26 June
528 26 June
530 20 November
531 27 November
804 18 September
805 13 November
806 26 June
807 30 October
808 26 June
809 5 June
810 2 October
811 28 August
813 18 December
814 12 June
816 3 July
817 18 September
818 17 July
819 20 March
820 10 April
821 17 April
822 17 April
824 17 July
825 15 May
826 16 October
827 13 November
831 27 November
833 23 October
834 22 May
835 26 June
836 22 May
837 18 December
839 5 June
849 7 August
850 2 October
854 25 September
856 27 November
860 13 November
866 10 April
868 28 August
869 3 April
870 10 July
876 9 October
877 19 June
880 12 June
881 8 May
882 15 May
883 24 July
884 10 April
885 30 October
886 13 November
887 6 November
892 28 August
894 4 September
898 4 September
902 18 December
908 20 November
910 28 August
913 14 August
914 22 May
918 31 December
919 9 October
920 21 August
922 24 July
923 26 June
925 3 April
927 30 October
932 16 October
933 3 April
934 23 October
940 4 September
941 18 September
942 11 September
946 4 December
948 25 December
951 18 December
953 4 September
956 15 May
959 15 May
960 11 December
961 9 October
962 23 October
964 26 June
965 5 June
966 17 April
970 25 December
971 4 December
972 22 May
973 15 May
974 14 August
975 21 August
979 18 September
980 18 September
981 13 November
982 27 March
1000 29 May
1002 3 July
1003 25 December
1004 2 October
1008 15 May
1010 8 May
1011 24 April
1012 5 June
1013 15 May
1014 19 June
1015 18 September
1016 20 November
1017 27 November
1019 3 July
1020 10 July
1021 31 December
1023 3 July
1024 18 December
1025 25 December
1040 12 June
1041 24 April
1042 3 July
1043 17 April
1044 3 April
1045 25 September
1047 27 November
1048 24 April
1049 27 March
1050 21 August
1052 27 March
1053 31 July
1054 17 April
1057 10 April
1058 25 September
1059 5 June
1060 24 April
1063 27 March
1064 23 October
1065 27 March
1067 13 November
1069 29 May
1070 27 March
1071 1 May
1072 12 June
1074 27 March
1075 15 May
1076 27 March

1077	8 May
1078	22 May
1079	17 April
1080	28 August
1081	27 March
1083	24 July
1084	15 May
1085	7 August
1086	29 May
1087	6 November
1088	4 September
1089	20 March
1090	25 December
1092	30 October
1098	21 August
1100	7 August
1101	26 June
1102	17 July
1103	28 August
1104	25 December
1106	29 May
1107	30 October
1108	28 August
1109	2 October
1110	31 December
1111	19 June
1112	16 October
1113	22 May
1115	30 October
1116	10 July
1117	12 June
1118	14 August
1119	25 December
1120	9 October
1121	6 November
1122	17 April
1123	13 November
1124	30 October
1125	13 November
1126	4 September
1127	18 September
1128	7 August
1130	16 October
1131	25 September
1132	28 August
1133	3 April
1134	10 April
1136	18 September
1137	4 December
1138	31 December
1141	6 November
1145	18 December
1146	28 August
1147	27 November
1149	27 November
1150	18 September
1151	9 October
1153	11 December
1154	27 November
1155	18 December
1157	30 October
1159	4 September
1163	15 May
1164	4 December
1169	22 May
1172	23 October
1178	23 October
1180	4 December
1192	17 April
1195	18 December
1197	27 November
1198	9 October
1199	15 May
1204	28 August
1217	2 October
1218	20 November
1219	2 October
1222	2 October
1238	17 July
1239	25 December
1241	24 July
1245	22 May
1251	1 May
1255	27 November
1265	5 June
1266	29 May
1283	27 November
1292	26 June
1298	23 October
1323	17 July
1401	25 December
1402	2 October
1404	16 October
1406	11 September
1410	29 May
1413	8 May
1414	9 October
1418	28 August
1420	24 April
1428	13 November
1430	4 September
1432	11 December
1434	29 May
1438	18 September
1440	5 June
1441	11 December
1442	27 November
1443	9 October
1444	26 June
1446	30 October
1447	4 September
1448	9 October
1449	1 May
1453	23 October
1454	21 August
1455	17 July
1457	12 June
1459	9 October
1461	14 August
1465	27 November
1468	7 August
1497	24 April
1501	26 June
1502	12 June
1503	10 April
1504	8 May
1508	2 October
1511	15 May
1512	27 November
1513	20 March
1514	24 July
1520	11 September
1521	2 October
1523	24 April
1524	3 July
1528	13 November
1529	17 April
1533	10 April
1535	25 December
1536	31 July
1537	5 June
1539	11 September
1540	7 August
1543	6 November
1547	11 September
1549	25 December
1550	3 July
1552	16 October
1556	27 November
1558	12 June
1559	14 August
1560	2 October
1562	28 August
1563	17 April
1566	24 April
1568	9 October
1570	10 April
1571	16 October
1572	1 May
1573	7 August
1574	27 March
1575	10 April
1576	25 December
1578	29 May
1580	8 May
1600	15 May
1604	3 July
1608	1 May
1614	25 December
1615	15 May
1616	24 April
1617	26 June
1619	21 August
1620	27 November
1621	19 June
1622	8 May
1623	24 April
1624	27 November
1627	27 November
1631	23 October
1632	26 June
1633	14 August
1634	11 September
1637	18 September
1643	28 August
1646	25 December
1649	5 June
1650	16 October
1653	19 June
1654	10 April
1655	16 October
1657	31 July
1658	5 June
1659	3 April
1661	3 April
1665	3 July
1666	8 May
1670	21 August
1671	25 September
1700	30 October
1701	3 April
1721	18 September
1727	24 April
1730	25 December
1733	11 September
1734	12 June
1735	3 April
1738	8 May
1741	11 September
1743	29 May
1745	17 July
1748	1 May
1750	18 December
1754	10 April
1755	1 May
1756	11 December
1757	30 October
1758	22 May
1762	3 July
1767	12 June
1768	21 August
1769	30 October
1770	6 November
1771	1 May
1772	3 April
1774	26 June
1775	3 July
1777	26 June
1779	8 May
1781	22 May
1783	10 April
1784	30 October
1785	4 December
1786	10 April

1787	19 June	1935	3 April	2307	25 September
1788	18 September	1936	21 August	2308	12 June
1789	2 October	1937	2 October	2312	9 October
1790	17 April	1938	24 April	2313	27 March
1791	20 November	1940	27 November	2315	26 June
1792	17 July	1941	14 August	2317	11 September
1794	3 July	1946	4 September	2325	5 June
1800	10 July	1947	3 April	2332	4 September
1803	15 May	1948	1 May	2333	7 August
1804	9 October	1955	31 December	2340	3 July
1807	29 May	1958	28 August	2342	23 October
1813	16 October	1960	4 December	2347	28 August
1814	23 October	1965	10 April	2351	25 December
1815	27 November	1967	5 June	2365	18 December
1816	6 November	1968	25 September	2366	25 September
1817	27 November	1969	17 April	2371	23 October
1819	9 October	1971	27 March	2373	2 October
1820	21 August	1972	18 December	2375	9 October
1821	17 April	1973	25 September	2379	21 August
1824	10 July	1976	1 May	2387	15 May
1825	17 April	1977	20 November	2388	1 May
1827	8 May	1978	25 September	2389	3 July
1828	7 August	1983	5 June	2391	6 November
1830	26 June	1984	19 June	2392	6 November
1831	2 October	1985	24 April	2396	9 October
1834	24 April	1987	18 December	2411	3 July
1836	25 September	1988	6 November	2417	22 May
1842	6 November	1990	5 June	2418	14 August
1844	11 December	1991	26 June	2420	2 October
1845	25 December	1992	24 April	2421	8 May
1846	27 March	1993	15 May	2423	11 December
1848	20 March	1994	16 October	2424	15 May
1849	28 August	1995	3 July	2427	6 November
1850	9 October	1996	27 November	2432	20 March
1851	2 October	1998	24 April	2434	15 May
1854	20 November	2059	2 October	2436	3 July
1857	18 September	2060	16 October	2439	10 July
1858	2 October	2065	10 July	2442	27 November
1859	6 November	2072	17 July	2455	11 September
1865	11 December	2131	20 March	2457	3 April
1866	25 December	2135	19 June	2459	22 May
1867	21 August	2172	20 March	2466	25 December
1868	25 December	2203	27 March	2467	24 April
1869	16 October	2208	17 April	2468	13 November
1872	10 July	2215	20 March	2470	11 September
1874	25 December	2225	4 December	2478	27 November
1875	10 April	2227	6 November	2479	20 March
1876	6 November	2228	18 September	2482	1 May
1878	23 October	2229	1 May	2483	31 December
1881	26 June	2231	3 April	2485	29 May
1882	18 September	2232	4 September	2487	25 December
1884	11 December	2234	24 April	2488	15 May
1885	3 July	2238	27 March	2494	25 September
1887	4 September	2240	17 April	2495	11 December
1889	9 October	2242	9 October	2496	19 June
1890	4 December	2243	21 August	2497	24 April
1892	29 May	2246	16 October	2498	1 May
1893	25 December	2247	15 May	2503	27 November
1897	2 October	2249	22 May	2508	27 November
1898	2 October	2252	20 November	2509	3 April
1899	1 May	2255	8 May	2512	22 May
1902	6 November	2260	18 December	2515	25 September
1903	31 July	2261	3 July	2518	25 December
1904	8 May	2264	17 April	2520	25 December
1905	3 April	2267	2 October	2523	8 May
1906	4 September	2268	18 December	2526	10 July
1907	4 December	2270	31 December	2527	7 August
1909	7 August	2271	3 April	2528	23 October
1911	20 March	2272	4 December	2530	23 October
1912	27 March	2273	24 July	2531	28 August
1913	13 November	2275	31 July	2532	17 July
1916	10 July	2276	23 October	2534	25 December
1921	29 May	2277	13 November	2535	21 August
1922	22 May	2279	11 December	2536	27 March
1923	27 March	2300	20 March	2538	14 August
1928	15 May	2301	10 July	2540	27 November
1930	25 December	2302	4 September	2542	23 October
1932	27 November	2305	11 December	2543	22 May

2544	3 July
2546	30 October
2547	12 June
2548	5 June
2553	15 May
2555	8 May
2556	8 May
2558	4 September
2562	15 May
2566	2 October
2568	17 April
2569	24 April
2571	25 September
2574	24 April
2575	25 December
2576	12 June
2578	10 April
2579	26 June
2580	3 April
2581	7 August
2587	1 May
2588	21 August
2603	1 May
2604	19 June
2605	2 October
2609	17 April
2611	25 December
2613	25 December
2616	27 November
2617	18 September
2651	14 August
2653	27 November
2656	8 May
2658	7 August
2661	31 December
2664	3 April
2665	12 June
2668	15 May
2671	24 April
2673	27 November
2676	14 August
2677	17 April
2683	8 May
2686	10 July
2688	18 September
2690	24 July
2701	12 June
2704	17 July
2705	15 May
2706	4 September
2707	29 May
2710	16 October
2711	23 October
2713	3 July
2722	29 May
2723	16 October
2724	29 May
2728	15 May
2729	11 September
2730	2 October
2731	2 October
2732	2 October
2733	10 April
2734	2 October
2735	2 October
2737	8 May
2743	16 October
2744	16 October
2746	1 May
2747	24 April
2749	1 May
2751	12 June
2752	17 April
2753	17 April
2757	28 August
2758	27 March
2761	28 August
2762	10 April
2764	24 April
2765	3 July
2766	14 August
2768	21 August
2769	15 May
2771	24 April
2774	7 August
2775	18 September
2782	7 August
2786	12 June
2787	26 June
2788	2 October
2885	8 May
3200	9 October
3202	18 December
3204	6 November
3216	24 July
3217	1 May
3220	20 November
3223	10 April
3225	6 November
3227	13 November
3232	7 August
3236	15 May
3282	22 May
3286	15 May
3290	12 June
3313	4 December
3319	1 May
3322	6 November
3328	11 September
3333	18 September
3338	17 April
3340	18 September
3343	10 July
3344	23 October
3345	12 June
3346	4 September
3347	19 June
3349	11 September
3350	22 May
3351	19 June
3352	31 December
3354	3 July
3355	3 July
3358	6 November
3360	6 November
3361	28 August
3362	28 August
3364	2 October
3365	3 July
3367	27 November
3374	22 May
3377	19 June
3379	18 December
3380	17 July
3383	5 June
3386	11 September
3387	25 September
3388	25 December
3389	12 June
3390	6 November
3391	18 September
3392	1 May
3393	14 August
3394	29 May
3395	19 June
3397	22 May
3398	16 October
3399	18 December
3401	25 December
3402	5 June
3406	20 November
3409	8 May
3410	15 May
3413	4 December
3415	15 May
3416	30 October
3418	21 August
3419	26 June
3420	4 December
3423	31 December
3426	4 September
3429	31 December
3431	20 November
3434	21 August
3438	27 November
3447	11 December
3448	17 July
3449	28 August
3450	16 October
3451	14 August
3453	10 April
3454	21 August
3455	18 September
3459	10 April
3462	22 May
3465	19 June
3466	1 May
3468	3 July
3469	4 September
3476	27 March
3477	17 July
3478	5 June
3479	9 October
3483	17 April
3484	2 October
3485	21 August
3486	18 September
3488	31 July
3491	4 December
3493	24 July
3571	7 August
3574	21 August
3575	30 October
3579	27 March
3580	8 May
3587	10 July
3588	31 July
3591	10 July
3592	31 July
3593	26 June
3595	5 June
3603	13 November
3604	24 April
3605	10 April
3606	10 July
3607	11 September
3608	4 December
3613	9 October
3614	30 October
3615	23 October
3622	2 October
3623	10 July
3625	28 August
3626	29 May
3628	3 July
3630	12 June
3631	31 July
3634	19 June
3636	24 July
3638	2 October
3645	21 August
3652	3 April
3655	2 October
3656	19 June
3658	4 September
3661	11 December
3662	29 May
3664	8 May
3666	15 May
3670	4 September
3673	5 June
3674	24 April
3675	14 August
3678	4 September

3681	8 May
3686	24 April
3691	9 October
3692	25 September
3695	29 May
3698	17 April
3702	15 May
3706	25 December
3708	29 May
3715	5 June
3717	9 October
3718	5 June
3720	2 October
3726	26 June
3728	19 June
3729	5 June
3732	12 June
3734	21 August
3735	25 December
3738	15 May
3739	20 March
3740	3 April
3742	23 October
3744	15 May
3746	27 November
3747	10 April
3748	28 August
3749	7 August
3752	13 November
3756	31 December
3757	12 June
3758	21 August
3759	28 August
3762	4 September
3763	21 August
3764	12 June
3765	27 March
3766	22 May
3768	29 May
3771	18 December
3773	17 April
3777	1 May
3780	4 September
3781	23 October
3783	11 December
3784	7 August
3789	1 May
3791	24 July
3794	16 October
3795	18 December
3796	4 December
3799	29 May
3800	12 June
3801	9 October
3816	6 November
3822	17 April
3823	11 September
3828	18 September
3829	4 September
3833	20 March
3835	4 September
3837	18 December
3846	12 June
3848	31 December
3849	6 November
3851	18 December
3854	26 June
3855	4 September
3858	27 November
3861	1 May
3867	2 October
3869	12 June
3872	17 April
3873	4 December
3876	27 November
3881	24 April
3885	19 June
3886	6 November
3887	4 September
3890	26 June
3891	14 August
3894	20 November
3895	7 August
3899	4 December
3902	1 May
3907	19 June
3915	1 May
3917	8 May
3923	4 September
3924	6 November
3926	30 October
3928	21 August
3929	13 November
3930	1 May
3933	21 August
3934	31 July
3940	8 May
3941	25 December
3942	22 May
3943	26 June
3944	3 April
3945	23 October
3947	8 May
3954	29 May
3955	12 June
3957	26 June
3958	1 May
3961	19 June
3962	27 March
3964	15 May
3967	6 November
3968	17 July
3971	10 April
3972	25 December
3973	27 November
3974	24 July
3976	22 May
3980	17 April
3981	15 May
3982	26 June
3983	27 November
3984	18 September
3985	22 May
4105	12 June
4116	25 September
4118	25 December
4119	2 October
4122	18 December
4129	9 October
4131	16 October
4133	27 November
4137	11 December
4153	12 June
4160	13 November
4172	6 November
4173	20 March
4175	22 May
4176	23 October
4179	18 December
4183	19 June
4185	16 October
4186	6 November
4190	9 October
4193	17 April
4194	30 October
4195	10 July
4196	24 April
4199	29 May
4201	30 October
4202	2 October
4211	1 May
4213	5 June
4219	12 June
4222	29 May
4223	12 June
4225	12 June
4230	18 December
4233	1 May
4237	20 November
4240	10 April
4241	11 December
4242	1 May
4243	17 July
4244	31 December
4247	25 September
4252	14 August
4257	21 August
4258	18 September
4259	31 July
4260	24 April
4261	15 May
4263	8 May
4267	12 June
4269	9 October
4274	4 September
4277	20 March
4281	10 April
4286	20 November
4287	7 August
4292	14 August
4293	17 April
4294	27 November
4296	1 May
4298	29 May
4302	10 April
4303	26 June
4304	23 October
4306	29 May
4309	29 May
4310	18 September
4311	18 December
4317	23 October
4320	17 April
4327	4 September
4330	10 July
4331	30 October
4333	14 August
4336	10 April
4337	7 August
4339	25 September
4342	27 November
4343	29 May
4352	10 July
4354	14 August
4357	18 September
4358	6 November
4369	7 August
4374	11 September
4375	27 November
4383	4 September
4385	7 August
4388	16 October
4392	7 August
4402	5 June
4407	20 March
4410	30 October
4413	16 October
4415	24 July
4416	18 December
4417	4 December
4419	11 December
4422	5 June
4429	5 June
4433	21 August
4441	21 August
4443	2 October
4445	4 September
4450	4 December
4451	2 October
4452	20 March
4460	3 April
4461	20 March
4462	6 November
4466	18 December

4468	21 August
4471	22 May
4474	24 April
4475	18 September
4477	4 September
4478	20 March
4485	20 March
4489	22 May
4491	5 June
4492	12 June
4493	24 July
4494	12 June
4496	4 September
4498	24 April
4499	2 October
4501	10 April
4502	27 November
4504	29 May
4506	17 April
4507	3 April
4510	18 September
4511	2 October
4512	25 September
4515	18 December
4516	29 May
4517	28 August
4519	20 March
4520	17 July
4522	3 July
4523	25 September
4524	26 June
4526	2 October
4527	13 November
4530	30 October
4531	9 October
4532	7 August
4534	15 May
4536	27 November
4537	19 June
4539	28 August
4542	21 August
4543	29 May
4545	21 August
4550	3 July
4554	17 April
4557	29 May
4558	3 April
4559	15 May
4560	26 June
4566	7 August
4567	28 August
4569	7 August
4570	10 July
4575	15 May
4576	11 December
4580	8 May
4582	8 May
4585	4 December
4588	27 March
4589	10 July
4592	18 December
4593	14 August
4595	17 April
4600	10 July
4602	22 May
4607	11 December
4609	10 April
4610	10 April
4612	27 March
4613	8 May
4614	14 August
4618	6 November
4620	21 August
4621	31 December
4624	12 June
4625	17 April
4627	22 May
4628	22 May
4629	4 December
4630	25 September
4631	4 September
4633	27 March
4636	27 March
4638	15 May
4640	5 June
4641	5 June
4643	7 August
4646	9 October
4647	12 June
4649	31 July
4652	31 July
4657	1 May
4658	21 August
4662	22 May
4666	27 November
4667	4 September
4669	31 July
4678	10 April
4679	19 June
4691	21 August
4698	30 October
4701	5 June
4702	6 November
4707	15 May
4709	20 November
4712	25 December
4713	7 August
4724	31 July
4726	29 May
4727	30 October
4730	10 April
4731	3 July
4733	27 November
4734	11 December
4735	31 July
4736	29 May
4743	25 December
4744	2 October
4745	15 May
4746	23 October
4747	21 August
4750	20 November
4751	28 August
4752	10 April
4753	29 May
4755	8 May
4760	31 July
4762	20 November
4766	3 April
4767	31 July
4770	16 October
4771	23 October
4775	29 May
4778	11 December
4780	27 March
4781	14 August
4784	25 September
4787	16 October
4788	12 June
4789	18 September
4790	10 July
4791	3 July
4793	15 May
4794	15 May
4796	25 December
4797	27 March
4798	25 December
4806	18 September
4807	11 December
4808	21 August
4814	25 December
4821	3 July
4828	21 August
4829	18 September
4831	20 March
4832	5 June
4834	14 August
4839	1 May
4844	30 October
4845	22 May
4847	4 September
4848	23 October
4849	17 July
4853	29 May
4854	27 March
4855	8 May
4860	21 August
4861	1 May
4862	1 May
4864	7 August
4867	16 October
4869	13 November
4872	25 September
4873	27 November
4875	2 October
4877	17 April
4879	18 September
4880	27 March
4882	27 November
4884	2 October
4885	20 November
4887	24 July
4888	3 April
4891	26 June
4892	24 April
4893	8 May
4895	2 October
4899	3 April
4900	19 June
4904	12 June
4905	19 June
4908	7 August
4909	23 October
4911	31 July
4912	14 August
4914	17 July
4915	17 July
4916	27 November
4921	24 April
4925	19 June
4930	2 October
4932	2 October
4935	19 June
4937	3 April
4944	3 April
4947	10 April
4948	17 April
4949	27 November
4953	24 April
4954	24 April
4957	2 October
4958	24 April
4959	16 October
4962	11 December
4964	4 September
4967	24 July
4970	25 September
4972	5 June
4974	28 August
4975	18 September
4976	8 May
4977	26 June
4980	4 December
4983	2 October
4984	27 March
4985	16 October
4987	15 May
5003	23 October
5010	31 December
5016	17 July
5020	7 August
5023	22 May
5027	23 October
5028	16 October

5030	10 April
5033	11 December
5038	11 December
5039	2 October
5041	10 April
5047	7 August
5061	8 May
5064	12 June
5066	12 June
5067	19 June
5070	27 November
5075	4 September
5078	2 October
5080	6 November
5082	21 August
5084	23 October
5088	28 August
5090	13 November
5092	22 May
5097	9 October
5099	14 August
5100	11 December
5103	21 August
5104	12 June
5105	9 October
5107	1 May
5110	3 April
5118	25 September
5119	6 November
5120	13 November
5130	31 July
5133	1 May
5144	8 May
5157	11 September
5160	8 May
5161	24 April
5164	24 July
5169	9 October
5170	14 August
5171	14 August
5173	10 April
5178	12 June
5179	10 April
5189	11 September
5194	16 October
5197	27 March
5201	11 December
5205	25 December
5211	30 October
5214	27 March
5215	5 June
5216	2 October
5217	27 November
5222	24 April
5224	25 December
5225	31 July
5228	20 March
5230	22 May
5231	4 September
5233	7 August
5234	27 March
5236	27 March
5237	3 July
5239	16 October
5240	4 September
5241	1 May
5242	27 March
5243	5 June
5246	1 May
5247	31 July
5248	4 September
5249	27 March
5250	24 April
5253	25 September
5254	25 September
5258	12 June
5260	27 March
5265	9 October
5266	10 July
5267	14 August
5268	26 June
5273	17 July
5274	29 May
5277	18 September
5278	31 December
5279	12 June
5281	11 September
5283	1 May
5286	13 November
5290	11 December
5291	19 June
5292	25 December
5293	2 October
5294	1 May
5295	25 September
5300	4 December
5303	25 December
5304	2 October
5305	27 March
5308	27 November
5309	10 April
5312	10 April
5313	12 June
5315	9 October
5316	10 April
5317	4 December
5319	23 October
5320	23 October
5321	2 October
5324	17 July
5327	8 May
5330	28 August
5333	6 November
5340	9 October
5341	17 July
5342	19 June
5344	10 April
5346	11 September
5370	18 September
5378	28 August
5384	25 September
5389	25 September
5398	24 April
5404	16 October
5407	1 May
5408	25 December
5412	7 August
5417	31 July
5420	11 September
5422	28 August
5426	24 July
5430	11 September
5431	24 April
5432	27 November
5435	14 August
5447	3 July
5448	11 September
5449	2 October
5451	12 June
5456	17 April
5461	16 October
5463	17 April
5466	2 October
5467	3 April
5472	27 November
5473	26 June
5476	25 December
5477	29 May
5479	25 December
5481	4 December
5482	20 November
5486	23 October
5487	14 August
5488	27 November
5489	10 April
5498	31 December
5506	3 July
5510	25 December
5519	8 May
5520	25 September
5521	25 December
5523	23 October
5529	15 May
5531	14 August
5532	4 September
5533	31 July
5535	4 September
5536	29 May
5537	10 April
5540	18 September
5543	30 October
5545	5 June
5552	8 May
5553	11 September
5556	27 November
5558	19 June
5559	2 October
5560	19 June
5564	29 May
5566	25 December
5569	27 November
5570	12 June
5571	27 November
5575	31 July
5576	14 August
5582	11 September
5583	18 September
5584	29 May
5585	24 July
5587	30 October
5589	15 May
5619	16 October
5629	1 May
5634	16 October
5640	24 April
5642	3 April
5646	2 October
5647	14 August
5650	1 May
5654	27 November
5655	29 May
5659	4 December
5666	25 September
5669	25 September
5670	10 July
5672	22 May
5673	26 June
5676	2 October
5684	24 April
5688	11 September
5692	14 August
5695	4 September
5697	11 December
5706	6 November
5708	19 June
5710	20 November
5712	17 April
5714	26 June
5717	9 October
5718	27 March
5724	8 May
5728	19 June
5730	10 April
5733	18 December
5734	11 September
5737	14 August
5740	24 April
5741	3 July
5745	11 September
5746	11 September
5751	16 October
5752	18 September
5754	22 May
5756	1 May

Ex-LYR class 24 0-6-0T BR No. 51544 at Aintree shed in June 1951. This was an Aspinall design dating back to 1897 and intended for dock shunting. The circular metal cap on the front of this engine turned round over the top of the chimney and acted as a spark arrester. Renumbered from 11544 during the week ended 14th May 1949 but retaining LMS lettering, withdrawal took place during the first week in June 1959; last allocation Liverpool Bank Hall. The last of the class to be scrapped was No. 51537 during the third week of September 1961 from Aintree.

Photomatic

Barton Wright ex-LYR 2F class 0-6-0 No. 52053 at Wigan Springs Branch shed in May 1948, incorrectly bearing an "M". These locomotives were all renumbered early in 1948 so that confusion would not arise with the diesel shunters being built in the number series 12000 onwards. This was the only one to bear the "M" prefix, all the others being correctly dealt with. Built by Beyer, Peacock and Co. in 1887, No. 52053 survived until the first week in March 1955, the final allocation being Wakefield.

G.W. Sharpe

Aspinall's standard LYR 0-6-0s were built between 1889 and 1917, and a total of 448 were constructed. Here we see No. 52189 of this type at Sowerby Bridge shed in April 1949. This one survived until the week ended 21st August 1954, last allocation Mirfield.

G.W. Sharpe

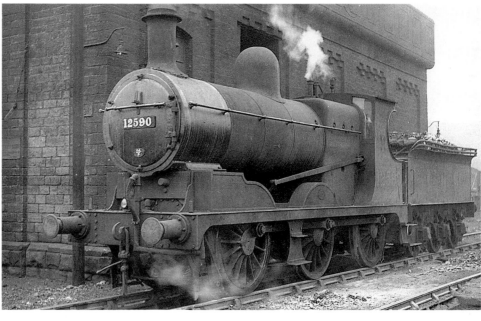

Hughes superheated version of Aspinall's basic design 0-6-0 was classified 3F. Sowerby Bridge shed is again the venue in September 1949 for this photograph of No. 12590. Withdrawn during the last week in June 1951 from Bradford Low Moor without receiving its BR number.

G.W. Sharpe

Horwich Works in October 1950, and arrived for scrapping from Wigan LY shed is Aspinall 6F class 0-8-0 No. 52727. This was the last to remain in service with the smaller 4ft 10in diameter boiler. The class originally consisted of 130 engines and this one had been built at Horwich in February 1903, works No. 839, as LYR No. 1433. It had been withdrawn during the week ended 14th October.

Photomatic

Shepton Mallet on Thursday 23rd June 1949 and S&DJR 7F class 2-8-0 No. 53810 trundles in on freight. This was the last class to be built by Fowler at Derby Works in 1925. Renumbered from 13810 during the last week in April 1949, withdrawal took place from Bath during December 1963.

G.W. Sharpe

Dumfries shed on Friday 11th June 1948 finds former Caledonian Railway McIntosh designed 'Dunalastair' class 4-4-0 No. 54445 looking smart in its new livery. The design was one that took shape back in 1910. No. 54445 had moved to Dumfries from Greenock during the week ended 3rd April 1948 and then on to Inverness during the second week in June 1950, where the engine remained until withdrawn on 18th December 1952.
G.W. Sharpe

The original Pickersgill '60' class 4-6-0s were built by the Caledonian Railway in 1916 and British Railways inherited five of these, Nos 14650 to 14654. The other batch, Nos 14630 to 14649, were built by the LMSR at St Rollox Works during 1925 and 1926. Here we see No. 14644 at Kilmarnock Works awaiting cutting up in June 1948. Still with its LMS number, it had been withdrawn from Edinburgh Dalry Road.
G.W. Sharpe

Ex-Highland Railway 0-4-4T, LMS No. 15051, at Dornoch in May 1948. It was part of a class of originally four locomotives and Nos 15051, built March 1905, and 15053, built December 1905, became BR property. They spent their time trundling back and forth between the Mound station, on the Inverness-Wick line, and Dornoch. They were sub-shedded at Dornoch, the parent depot being Helmsdale. No. 15051 was renumbered during the week ended 16th April 1949 and withdrawn on 22nd June 1956. No. 15053 became 55053 during the week ended 15th January 1949 and was withdrawn during the first week in January 1957. They were replaced by two British Railways GWR design 0-6-0PTs, Nos 1646 and 1649, which arrived in February 1957 and July 1958 respectively.
G.W. Sharpe

Grangemouth shed on 30th October 1948, with ex-CR, McIntosh 0-4-4T No. 15119 in store and looking in a poor state. This usually meant the engine was about to be withdrawn, but this was not the case this time. It survived a works visit and was renumbered 55119 during the week ended 15th January 1949. This design dated back to 1897 and all were fitted with condensing apparatus, the pipe along the boiler showing it to be still in place on this example. Withdrawal came during the second week in July 1953 from Grangemouth.

G.W. Sharpe

Grangemouth shed once again in 1948. At home is ex-Caledonian Railway McIntosh standard shunting 0-6-0T No. 16230, the first to be built in 1905. Renumbered 56230 during the week ended 25 March 1950, it remained at Grangemouth right up until withdrawal during the last week in January 1957.

G.W. Sharpe

Hurlford shed in June 1948 finds Caledonian Railway Drummond design standard goods 2F class 0-6-0 No. 17383 in the shed yard. Renumbered 57383 during the week ended 23rd July 1949, this locomotive was not withdrawn until the last week of July 1962, still at Hurlford.

G.W. Sharpe

Strathcarron, on the Inverness to Kyle of Lochalsh line, in June 1948. Cummings Highland Railway "Superheated Goods" class 5F 4-6-0 No. 17951 carries out shunting duties watched by the signalman. Built by Hawthorn Leslie (builder's No. 3287) in April 1918, renumbering took place during 1948. Withdrawal from Inverness shed took place during the week ended 24th May 1951. The last working example, No. 57954, survived until October 1952.

Photomatic

LMS No. 20155 at Nottingham shed in 1949. This was the last Midland 2-4-0 in service and was the sole survivor of a batch of Johnson 6ft 3in engines built on the opening of the Settle-Carlisle line in 1876. However, the smaller wheels did not prove to be the success expected and the engines were soon transferred south, this one being sent to Kentish Town. Originally numbered 96, it was renumbered to 155 in 1907. It was rebuilt with a G6 Belpaire boiler in 1926 and in 1933 was transferred from Bristol to Abergavenny as *Engineer South Wales*, the rectangular nameplates being fitted on the driving wheel splashers. In March 1934 it was the one Midland engine prematurely renumbered in the 20,000 list, but it reverted to 155 after a week or so. It was correctly renumbered 20155 in August 1937 by which time it had lost its nameplates. It was withdrawn from Nottingham shed during the week ended 28th October 1950 without receiving its BR number 58020. Its total mileage was quoted as 1,425,151.

G.W. Sharpe

Sunday 9th May 1948, Burton-on-Trent shed. At home is Johnson Midland Railway 1P class 0-4-4T No. 1424, renumbered 58087 during the week ended 3rd December 1949. Built by Dubs and Co. in 1900 (builder's No. 3911), this engine was withdrawn from Plaistow shed during the week ended 25th June 1955.

L. Hanson

On the Cromford and High Peak Line at Sheep Pasture in 1950. 2-4-0T No. 58092 with a good head of steam carries out its shunting duties. This was the only survivor of an original LNWR class and was built in 1877. Renumbered 26428 during 1948 and 58092 during the first week in August 1949, it was withdrawn during the second week in March 1952 from Sheep Pasture sub-shed, parent depot Buxton.

G.W. Sharpe

The Lickey Incline on Wednesday 26th September 1951, and 0-10-0 No. 58100 is doing what it was designed to do; banking a freight up the 1 in 37 to Blackwell, helped on this occasion by "Jinty" 0-6-0T No. 47638. "Big Bertha", as 58100 was known, wears the new lion and wheel emblem but the tank engine still shows LMS. Built by Fowler in 1919, weighing 73 tons 13 cwt and with a tractive effort of 43,315lb, this was a powerful and unique locomotive. Carrying the number 22290 at Nationalisation, it became No. 58100 during the last week of January 1949. At 5 am on Monday 7th May 1956 it left Bromsgrove for the last time for Derby works where withdrawal was sanctioned during the week ended 19th May. The replacement was a standard 9F class 2-10-0 No. 92079 which had gone to Toton new from Crewe Works during the last week of March 1956. The 2-10-0 went via Derby Works to have the headlamp from 58100 fitted and commenced work from Bromsgrove during the week ended 19th May.

L. Hanson

Kirtley double framed 2F class 0-6-0 No. 22630, renumbered 58110 at the end of 1948, at Derby shed on Sunday 9th May 1948. Built by Dubs and Co. in 1870 as Midland Railway No. 778, it is here seen with a round-topped firebox and Johnson type boiler and cab. Withdrawal took place during the week ended 10th November 1951 from Derby and was the last of the class.

L. Hanson

Johnson Midland 2F class 0-6-0 No. 58144 on Derby shed in 1949. The original design dated back to 1875, but this particular locomotive had been improved with a Belpaire boiler and more substantial cab. Engines from this class were remarkably long lived, the last one, No. 58182, not being withdrawn until January 1964. No. 58144 was withdrawn during the week ended 21st May 1960 from Derby shed.

G.W. Sharpe

Derby shed again, this time in July 1948, with another member of the Johnson Midland 2F 0-6-0 class, No. 58246. The difference with this one is that it was the last to retain a Johnson round-topped firebox, boiler and cab. Withdrawn during the week ended 13th June 1959 from Coalville.

G.W. Sharpe

Crewe Works yard on Sunday 27th March 1949. Ex-LNWR Webb "Coal engine" No. 58323 prepares for the coming week of works shunting duties. This was a member of a class of originally 500 locomotives built between 1873 and 1892, and the last survivors were all employed as Crewe Works shunters. No. 58323 was withdrawn during the week ended 25th April 1953. The last to go, No. 58343, was taken out of service during the week ended 3rd October 1953.

K.C.H. Fairey

Bangor station in July 1951 with Webb 18in goods "Cauliflower" 2F class 0-6-0 No. 58381 resting between duties. The first engine of this class appeared from Crewe Works in June 1880. The last three survivors, Nos 58409, 58412 and 58427, were not withdrawn until December 1955. No. 58381 was renumbered from 28450 during the week ended 24th June 1950 and withdrawn from Bangor shed during the third week of June 1952.

Photomatic

Middleton Top on the Cromford and High Peak line in 1950 finds ex-North London Railway 0-6-0T No. 58850 waiting for work. Built in December 1881, and numbered 27505 at Nationalisation, renumbering took place during the week ended 21st May 1949. Not withdrawn until the week ended 10th September 1960 from Rowsley, the engine is now preserved on the Bluebell Railway. It was the last of the class to go.

G.W. Sharpe

Birmingham New Street station, the old LNWR side, on Friday 16th June 1950. Ex LNWR Webb 0-6-2T No. 58928 is on pilot duties. Known as "Coal Tanks", these engines were built between 1881 and 1896. Renumbered from 7803 during the second week of January 1949, this engine came to Monument Lane shed, its last home, during the week ended 12th November 1949. Withdrawn during the week ended 27th January 1951.

L. Hanson

Gresley A4 class 4-6-2 No. 25 *Falcon*, with raised metal numbers and tender lettering, at York shed in June 1948. Built at Doncaster in February 1937 and numbered 4484, the first allocation was Edinburgh Haymarket. Renumbered 60025 during the week ended 28th January 1950, *Falcon* was withdrawn on 20th October 1963 from New England shed.

Photomatic

Gresley A3 class Pacific No. 60036 *Colombo* makes a fine sight on an 'up' express at Darlington in August 1948. Built at Doncaster in July 1934 and numbered 2501 the first allocation was Gateshead. Withdrawal took effect on 24th November 1964 from Darlington shed.

Photomatic

Finsbury Park in August 1948 and Class A3 No. E103 *Flying Scotsman* runs past on an express. Doncaster built in February 1923, the original number was 1472, this being changed to 4472 in 1924. Withdrawal came on 15th January 1963 from King's Cross shed and is today perhaps the most well-known preserved locomotive operating.

Photomatic

Aberdeen Ferryhill shed on Monday 7th June 1948 with an immaculate A2/2 class 4-6-2 No. 502 *Earl Marischal* on display. Originally built as a class P2/2 2-8-2 in October 1934 and numbered 2002, Edward Thompson rebuilt the locomotive to a Pacific in June 1944 and allocated it to Ferryhill. BR number 60502 was applied in 1948 and the withdrawal date was 3rd July 1961 from York.
G.W. Sharpe

Thompson A2/1 class 4-6-2 No. 509 *Waverley* at Darlington shed on Thursday 3rd June 1948. Built at Darlington in November 1944 as No. 3698 and allocated new to Darlington shed. This was Edward Thompson's first Pacific design after taking over from Sir Nigel Gresley as Chief Mechanical Engineer of the LNER. Renumbered 60509 during 1948, withdrawal came on 15th August 1960 from Edinburgh Haymarket.
G.W. Sharpe

When Edward Thompson retired in 1946, Arthur H. Peppercorn became C.M.E. This was one of his A2 class Pacifics, No. 60534 *Irish Elegance*, and was added to stock in 1948. This photograph was taken at York shed, the engine's first allocation, when only two months old. Sadly only a short life was ahead for this handsome engine, for withdrawal came on 29th December 1962 at Edinburgh St Margaret's.
Photomatic

Gresley V2 class 2-6-2 No. E958 at Dundee Tay Bridge shed in 1948. Built in October 1942 and numbered 3670, the first allocation was St Margaret's. Renumbered 60958 during the week ended 8th March 1950. The V2s were a very successful design and were recorded as hauling immense trains of twenty or more coaches during the war. No. 60958 was withdrawn from St Margaret's on 29th December 1962.

G.W. Sharpe

Thompson's B1 class 4-6-0s were the LNER equivalent of the LMS Stanier 5s. Go-anywhere engines they certainly were, and could be seen on any region, even the Southern on some occasions. This scene is St Pancras on Tuesday 15th June 1948 and No. 61251 *Oliver Bury* is leaving with a Manchester express. This was a test run during the exchanges, and the LMS dynamometer car is recording the event behind the engine's tender. This would surely have been more interesting if a V2 class 2-6-2 had been used, especially over the Derbyshire Peak route. No. 61251 was built by the North British Locomotive Company (builder's No. 26152) in October 1947 and went new to King's Cross shed. Withdrawal came on 19th April 1964 from Immingham shed.

Photomatic

Leicester Central shed in June 1948. B1 class No. 61311, then only two months old, looks smart in lined green livery. This was also a North British Locomotive Co. engine, builder's number 26212. Withdrawal took place on 16th September 1962 from Stratford shed when this London depot closed its doors to steam.

G.W. Sharpe

Robinson, LNER Class B7 4-6-0 No. 1378 on Gorton shed in 1948. This was a design for the Great Central Railway and this locomotive had been built at Gorton Works in May 1922. Its pre-1946 number had been 5470 and although allocated BR No. 61378, it was scrapped in 1948 without receiving it.

G.W. Sharpe

York shed in June 1948 with B16/3 class 4-6-0 No. 1448 in the yard. The whole class of 69 B16s were allocated to York on Nationalisation day, but by 4th November 1950 the class was divided between Leeds Neville Hill, which had 21, and York. This was a North Eastern design by Raven and this particular locomotive had been built at Darlington in May 1923 and originally numbered 2377. The B16/3 class was a rebuild by Thompson of the original locomotives with higher running plates and Walschaerts valve gear, carried out on this locomotive in July 1944. Renumbered 61448 during 1948 and withdrawn on 29th June 1964 from York.

G.W. Sharpe

Robinson's Great Central 4-6-0 express freight engines were classified B9 by the LNER and were originally a class of ten locomotives. Four survived into British Railways and No. 1475 was one of them, shown here at Liverpool Brunswick shed in 1948. Built by Beyer, Peacock and Co. (builder's No. 4812) in October 1906, and numbered 6111 by the LNER, it acquired its BR number 61475 during the week ended 12th February 1949. The engine remained in service only a short time after this, being withdrawn from Heaton Mersey shed on 16th May 1949 and was the last of the class to remain active.

G.W. Sharpe

Ardsley shed in May 1948 and Robinson, ex-Great Central Railway 4-6-0 No. 1482 *Immingham* simmers in the shed yard. Classified B4, this was another product from Beyer, Peacock's (builder's No. 4818) dating back to July 1906. The pre-1946 LNER number of this locomotive was 6097 and although allocated the number 61482 under BR this was never carried. The engine was the last of the class to be withdrawn from Ardsley on 24th November 1950.

G.W. Sharpe

B12 class 4-6-0 No. 1543 at Keith Junction in June 1948. This is a Holden, Great Eastern example in original condition, built in 1920 at Stratford, and had been sent to the Great North of Scotland section of the LNER in 1931. Its sisters in England were rebuilt by Gresley with larger round topped boilers and classified B12/3. This engine was based at Kittybrewster for many years and was withdrawn on 19th June 1953 from this shed after being renumbered 61543 in 1948.

G. W. Sharpe

Stratford shed in October 1950 with B2 class 4-6-0 No. 61603 *Framlingham* paired with a North Eastern tender. This was a rebuild by Thompson of the original 3-cylinder B17 class introduced by Gresley in 1928, this locomotive being dealt with in October 1946. The rebuild included conversion to two cylinders and B1 type boilers. No. 61603 carried the number 2803 prior to 1946 and was renumbered into BR stock during the week ended 22nd January 1949. A mass withdrawal programme was carried out of both B2 and B17 classes during 1958 to 1960. *Framlingham* was scrapped on 8th September 1958 from Cambridge shed.

G. W. Sharpe

Gresley V4 class 2-6-2 No. 61701 at Glasgow Eastfield shed in October 1948. Only two were built, the other, No. 61700 carrying the name *Bantam Cock*, and hence No. 61701 was unofficially known as "Bantam Hen". They were Gresley's last design and appeared in February and March 1941 respectively. By 1939 it was recognised by the LNER that although there was a good supply of moderately sized engines, many were of pre-Grouping design and were ageing fast. The V4 class was intended as a prototype for a new class of general purpose engine to replace the older locomotives. They had all the good features of the developed Gresley design, but on a smaller scale; the V2 wheel arrangement, wide firebox, and three cylinders with conjugated valve gear. When new, No. 61700 was sent successively to Doncaster, York, Haymarket, Stratford and Norwich sheds and performed prodigious feats of haulage for such a small engine. Had it not been for the war and Gresley's death, many more of these engines would have been built. The two engines settled in Scotland at Eastfield and for a time worked on the West Highland lines. Both were withdrawn in 1957, No. 61700 on 14th March and 61701 on 26th November, both from Aberdeen Ferryhill where they had been based since June 1954.

G.W. Sharpe

Glasgow Eastfield shed in May 1950 with Gresley K2 class 2-6-0 No. 61764 *Loch Arkaig* taking it easy. It had by then been fitted with the Eastfield shed plate, 65A. This was one of the Scottish variety of the class, fitted with a side-window cab to give crews better protection when working on such exposed lines as the West Highland. Renumbered from 1764 during the week ended 8th January 1949, withdrawal took place from Eastfield on 7th September 1961.

G.W. Sharpe

Gresley K3 class 2-6-0 No. 61990 at Eastfield shed in June 1948, just after renumbering, following a visit to Cowlairs Works. Built in February 1937, the engine went new to Edinburgh St Margaret's from where withdrawal took place on 13th October 1960.

G.W. Sharpe

K1/1 class 2-6-0 No. 1997 *MacCailin Mor* at Peterborough New England shed in June 1948. This was a rebuild by Thompson in November 1945 of the original Gresley K4 class engine built in January 1939 for the West Highland lines and was thus the prototype for the new K1s built by Thompson in 1949. This engine was delivered new to Eastfield, but when this photograph was taken the allocation was Peterborough, the transfer from Scotland being effected at the same time as the rebuild. Renumbered 61997 during the week ended 29th January 1949, the engine was sent back to Eastfield during the week ended 19th November 1949, while K2 class 2-6-0 No. 61729 returned home to New England the same week from Parkhead in exchange. Withdrawal of the K1/1 took place from Fort William shed on 12th June 1961.

G.W. Sharpe

Class D3 4-4-0 No. 62131 at Spalding in May 1948. This was an H.A. Ivatt design for the Great Northern Railway, built between 1896 and 1899. This example was slightly different in appearance to others of the type by having separate splashers over the wheels. No. 62131 was withdrawn from New England shed on 31st October 1949. The last of the class, No. 62132, went on 7th December 1950 from Boston.

Photomatic

D41 class 4-4-0 No. 62234 at Keith Junction on shunting duty in July 1949. This was a Great North of Scotland Railway engine designed by James Johnson and dating back to 1893. No. 62234 was withdrawn from Keith shed on 10th November 1949.

G.W. Sharpe

D40 class 4-4-0 No. 62277 *Gordon Highlander* at Inverurie in June 1949. This was the last Great North of Scotland Railway 4-4-0 to remain in service and is now preserved at the Glasgow Transport Museum with its first number, 49. This was based on W. Pickersgill's design of 1899, but No. 62277 was one of eight turned out by the North British Locomotive Company (builder's No. 22563) in 1920 which had extended smokeboxes and superheaters. It was withdrawn from Keith shed on 23rd June 1958, but after restoration it was used on railtours for a time and kept at Glasgow Dawsholm shed.

G.W. Sharpe

D9 class 4-4-0 No. 62333 at Liverpool Brunswick shed in 1949. This was its last allocation when withdrawn on 12th December 1949. Introduced in 1901, this was another J.G. Robinson design for the Great Central Railway. The last of the class, No. 62305, was withdrawn on 24th July 1950 from Trafford Park.

G.W. Sharpe

5757	31 December
5758	10 April
5761	2 October
5762	26 June
5763	14 August
5764	25 December
5765	10 April
5766	26 June
5767	25 September
5768	19 June
5774	10 July
5775	5 June
5779	11 September
5780	14 August
5782	5 June
5785	25 September
5786	15 May
5788	22 May
5789	28 August
5791	8 May
5792	5 June
5794	3 July
5795	20 November
5798	24 April
5799	21 August
5801	13 November
5803	23 October
5804	24 April
5808	25 December
5809	21 August
5811	29 May
5813	18 December
5814	13 November
5815	10 April
5816	12 June
5818	24 April
5820	8 May
5823	13 November
5825	17 April
5828	20 November
5830	25 December
5831	29 May
5832	6 November
5833	29 May
5835	10 July
5838	9 October
5839	6 November
5840	10 July
5841	5 June
5842	18 September
5845	1 May
5846	4 December
5847	3 April
5849	3 April
5851	17 April
5852	30 October
5854	17 April
5856	27 November
5862	7 August
5865	11 September
5866	8 May
5867	4 September
5868	21 August
5871	18 December
5872	9 October
5873	20 November
5875	10 April
5880	2 October
5882	19 June
5883	16 October
5885	20 November
5888	26 June
5889	30 October
5891	16 October
5892	25 September
5893	18 December
5905	19 June
5907	31 December
5910	14 August
5913	10 July
5914	7 August
5915	25 September
5917	8 May
5923	7 August
5929	24 July
5930	22 May
5933	10 April
7106	14 August
7107	4 September
7128	19 June
7149	27 November
7151	19 June
7152	27 November
7154	25 December
7163	23 October
7164	28 August
7165	21 August
7176	27 November
7177	21 August
7178	2 October
7182	16 October
7186	31 July
7190	25 December
7192	3 July
7193	18 September
7196	22 May
7199	27 November
7202	27 March
7203	17 April
7205	3 July
7207	29 May
7209	27 November
7211	19 June
7212	27 November
7217	21 August
7218	3 April
7222	2 October
7223	29 May
7227	4 September
7237	27 March
7242	4 December
7246	14 August
7247	10 July
7248	30 October
7250	9 October
7251	18 September
7252	21 August
7253	24 April
7254	8 May
7256	2 October
7259	19 June
7260	16 October
7261	5 June
7263	10 April
7264	5 June
7265	8 May
7266	25 September
7271	31 December
7272	14 August
7273	17 July
7275	17 April
7281	10 April
7282	18 September
7283	25 December
7284	29 May
7288	4 December
7289	28 August
7290	18 September
7293	9 October
7294	27 November
7295	7 August
7298	17 July
7299	23 October
7300	6 November
7301	17 April
7305	17 July
7307	30 October
7308	31 December
7310	26 June
7311	6 November
7312	6 November
7313	22 May
7314	23 October
7317	22 May
7318	3 July
7324	18 September
7325	6 November
7326	11 December
7329	25 September
7330	28 August
7341	20 November
7342	27 November
7344	18 September
7345	20 November
7348	4 December
7350	30 October
7352	31 July
7354	31 July
7360	8 May
7364	4 September
7366	3 April
7371	16 October
7373	27 November
7375	24 July
7380	30 October
7384	31 December
7386	25 September
7394	14 August
7398	29 May
7401	24 April
7404	26 June
7405	20 November
7407	15 May
7408	30 October
7410	24 July
7411	22 May
7413	20 March
7415	6 November
7416	8 May
7417	1 May
7419	30 October
7424	11 September
7425	8 May
7428	26 June
7430	27 March
7431	19 June
7433	1 May
7437	25 December
7438	8 May
7443	24 April
7445	2 October
7446	14 August
7447	28 August
7452	28 August
7455	10 April
7458	2 October
7460	19 June
7463	17 July
7464	11 December
7472	6 November
7474	2 October
7475	9 October
7481	2 October
7485	25 September
7486	20 November
7487	22 May
7490	27 March
7492	26 June
7498	4 September
7499	11 September
7502	13 November
7602	30 October
7603	28 August
7605	17 July

7608	10 April
7610	18 September
7613	3 July
7614	29 May
7615	19 June
7616	17 July
7618	23 October
7622	26 June
7624	28 August
7626	18 December
7628	18 September
7629	3 July
7630	17 July
7631	29 May
7632	1 May
7633	23 October
7634	20 November
7635	21 August
7636	31 December
7637	5 June
7638	21 August
7639	31 December
7640	2 October
7643	18 December
7649	22 May
7650	11 September
7659	11 September
7661	28 August
7662	6 November
7663	25 December
7665	26 June
7668	25 December
7672	17 April
7676	27 November
7677	19 June
7678	17 July
7684	17 April
7687	11 December
7688	22 May
7690	10 July
7691	12 June
8009	19 June
8014	30 October
8015	27 November
8016	25 December
8018	27 November
8020	30 October
8022	16 October
8026	18 September
8030	13 November
8033	25 September
8034	12 June
8051	25 September
8064	10 July
8068	20 March
8069	25 December
8070	8 May
8073	10 July
8075	7 August
8082	3 July
8088	9 October
8089	13 November
8093	8 May
8094	23 October
8095	21 August
8097	29 May
8100	12 June
8105	22 May
8111	20 March
8113	13 November
8114	20 November
8117	1 May
8118	3 July
8132	22 May
8133	26 June
8140	29 May
8141	23 October
8146	1 May
8150	3 July
8165	15 May
8166	7 August
8171	17 April
8179	18 December
8190	12 June
8191	28 August
8192	6 November
8204	27 November
8205	19 June
8206	10 July
8208	16 October
8221	28 August
8226	22 May
8233	18 September
8235	10 April
8240	26 June
8245	13 November
8248	3 April
8250	1 May
8256	12 June
8262	17 July
8264	25 December
8271	2 October
8275	18 December
8276	4 September
8278	1 May
8283	4 September
8290	3 April
8291	17 July
8295	13 November
8302	2 October
8305	28 August
8307	19 June
8309	25 September
8313	27 November
8319	3 July
8322	3 April
8324	12 June
8333	8 May
8346	18 September
8350	3 July
8352	5 June
8353	17 July
8356	18 September
8357	14 August
8358	5 June
8360	10 July
8364	2 October
8372	3 April
8374	25 December
8379	25 September
8385	29 May
8391	15 May
8392	8 May
8393	21 August
8395	9 October
8399	18 September
8401	4 September
8406	24 April
8423	3 July
8424	4 September
8426	13 November
8427	10 April
8434	10 July
8436	31 December
8437	23 October
8446	6 November
8447	28 August
8449	21 August
8455	10 April
8456	24 April
8457	11 September
8461	29 May
8464	10 July
8465	8 May
8466	11 September
8467	8 May
8469	18 December
8472	22 May
8476	3 April
8481	22 May
8491	24 April
8493	2 October
8498	14 August
8499	9 October
8501	25 December
8507	25 December
8518	28 August
8520	25 December
8524	25 September
8526	9 October
8529	27 March
8535	30 October
8537	24 April
8541	11 December
8542	27 November
8545	27 November
8552	12 June
8557	25 December
8565	6 November
8567	26 June
8572	4 December
8573	9 October
8581	23 October
8590	16 October
8591	27 November
8594	27 November
8595	27 November
8598	5 June
8600	27 November
8602	29 May
8603	31 July
8605	2 October
8606	31 July
8607	25 December
8609	27 November
8611	14 August
8613	29 May
8618	6 November
8621	23 October
8631	27 November
8635	17 July
8641	4 September
8643	23 October
8648	5 June
8662	10 April
8666	10 April
8671	29 May
8673	3 April
8674	10 April
8675	18 September
8676	4 December
8677	1 May
8678	30 October
8683	10 July
8686	23 October
8687	9 October
8688	5 June
8689	10 April
8691	17 April
8692	27 March
8693	16 October
8696	25 December
8698	27 November
8699	20 November
8700	19 June
8702	3 April
8704	9 October
8706	5 June
8709	15 May
8710	10 April
8711	29 May
8712	28 August
8716	19 June
8717	31 December

8722	11 September
8723	2 October
8724	8 May
8725	24 April
8728	7 August
8732	4 September
8735	17 April
8743	15 May
8744	25 September
8745	27 November
8747	22 May
8753	8 May
8758	25 September
8762	31 December
8766	24 April
8767	20 March
8769	8 May
8777	14 August
8781	30 October
8782	3 July
8783	19 June
8796	8 May
8797	3 July
8799	5 June
8802	19 June
8807	14 August
8809	28 August
8813	12 June
8815	6 November
8817	23 October
8826	7 August
8830	6 November
8831	20 November
8832	3 July
8835	18 December
8836	1 May
8837	28 August
8840	10 April
8842	4 December
8843	17 April
8844	11 December
8846	31 December
8847	15 May
8849	24 July
8853	25 September
8854	15 May
8858	26 June
8862	3 July
8865	20 March
8867	28 August
8869	6 November
8872	21 August
8873	20 November
8875	24 July
8879	17 April
8883	25 December
8884	5 June
8886	4 September
8887	18 September
8889	27 November
8890	21 August
8896	11 December
8899	26 June
8906	10 April
8917	14 August
8918	17 July
8923	25 December
8930	20 November
8932	15 May
8934	20 November
8936	19 June
8937	16 October
8940	20 March
8945	17 July
8946	5 June
8948	24 April
8953	21 August
8954	16 October
8955	26 June
8958	5 June
8960	29 May
8971	18 December
8972	4 September
8975	17 April
8977	16 October
8978	24 April
8981	4 September
8988	13 November
8989	12 June
8991	30 October
9051	6 November
9052	26 June
9054	10 April
9055	25 September
9060	1 May
9061	6 November
9062	19 June
9091	25 December
9099	20 November
9102	31 December
9109	10 July
9114	11 September
9124	25 December
9126	26 June
9130	17 July
9134	7 August
9135	14 August
9137	19 June
9139	9 October
9141	20 November
9142	17 July
9144	14 August
9145	26 June
9149	17 April
9150	21 August
9152	4 December
9153	11 September
9154	5 June
9155	2 October
9156	17 July
9158	14 August
9159	10 July
9163	11 September
9164	12 June
9167	17 July
9169	15 May
9174	2 October
9175	17 April
9178	26 June
9179	12 June
9184	30 October
9185	24 April
9186	27 March
9187	1 May
9190	12 June
9197	2 October
9198	22 May
9199	17 April
9200	25 December
9201	8 May
9203	20 November
9204	13 November
9206	19 June
9208	16 October
9210	27 November
9211	4 September
9212	24 April
9213	5 June
9215	2 October
9218	2 October
9219	15 May
9221	24 April
9223	14 August
9227	5 June
9234	7 August
9236	27 March
9237	8 May
9239	1 May
9245	12 June
9253	20 March
9254	9 October
9255	31 July
9256	19 June
9259	11 September
9267	24 July
9268	5 June
9280	17 April
9281	17 April
9282	19 June
9284	30 October
9301	20 March
9304	17 April
9311	28 August
9315	14 August
9316	16 October
9329	17 April
9332	13 November
9335	28 August
9336	11 September
9338	10 April
9341	13 November
9352	24 April
9354	20 March
9355	23 October
9360	20 November
9361	24 April
9366	19 June
9367	21 August
9368	25 September
9371	24 April
9372	16 October
9392	30 October
9418	17 April
9433	14 August
9437	13 November
9446	23 October
9447	31 December
9449	5 June
9453	19 June
9456	24 April
9459	8 May
9462	27 November
9464	14 August
9465	31 July
9468	15 May
9470	2 October
9476	15 May
9479	24 July
9481	29 May
9490	10 July
9491	24 April
9493	26 June
9494	9 October
9500	2 October
9503	7 August
9506	13 November
9508	17 April
9511	26 June
9515	28 August
9519	5 June
9521	27 November
9524	28 August
9525	24 April
9529	19 June
9532	18 September
9534	2 October
9537	14 August
9543	11 December
9545	18 December
9548	9 October
9555	25 December
9558	19 June
9560	18 December
9563	12 June

9565	26 June
9567	10 July
9568	10 April
9569	25 December
9570	23 October
9571	27 November
9575	8 May
9579	17 April
9580	17 July
9581	27 March
9582	29 May
9584	11 December
9586	31 July
9587	3 April
9590	18 September
9593	20 November
9601	9 October
9604	27 March
9605	28 August
9607	4 September
9608	3 July
9609	21 August
9611	23 October
9612	4 September
9615	29 May
9617	27 November
9618	3 July
9623	25 December
9625	25 December
9629	27 November
9634	8 May
9639	10 April
9642	19 June
9643	21 August
9646	18 September
9647	26 June
9648	22 May
9651	18 September
9653	17 July
9657	25 December
9659	27 March
9660	11 September
9661	15 May
9664	14 August
9666	4 September
9678	25 December
9679	25 September
9682	27 November
9686	19 June
9688	9 October
9692	2 October
9694	3 July
9695	3 July
9698	15 May
9699	3 July
9702	27 November
9703	3 April
9705	3 July
9706	5 June
9708	18 September
9709	14 August
9710	25 December
9713	10 April
9715	11 September
9716	28 August
9719	30 October
9725	16 October
9728	16 October
9770	3 July
9771	12 June
9776	6 November
9777	2 October
9781	21 August
9782	17 July
9783	24 April
9784	22 May
9786	17 April
9787	25 September
9788	3 July
9794	25 December
9795	14 August
9798	5 June
9801	27 November
9802	5 June
9804	3 April
9809	25 September
9810	11 December
9811	24 April
9813	14 August
9814	24 July
9815	31 July
9818	16 October
9820	9 October
9823	23 October
9824	13 November
9826	15 May
9827	10 April
9828	10 July
9829	18 September
9830	8 May
9831	11 September
9832	28 August
9833	5 June
9834	10 April
9836	15 May
9837	29 May
9840	8 May
9841	10 April
9842	25 December
9852	28 August
9854	19 June
9855	23 October
9857	10 July
9858	11 September
9860	4 September
9862	6 November
9864	17 July
9865	5 June
9866	12 June
9868	21 August
9869	18 December
9870	9 October
9872	18 December
9873	14 August
9875	10 April
9879	27 November
9881	23 October
9882	2 October
9884	17 July
9885	28 August
9887	12 June
9889	25 December
9891	23 October
9893	25 September
9901	9 October
9904	9 October
9910	3 April
9916	17 April
9917	29 May
9926	11 September
9927	17 July
9929	2 October
9933	12 June
9934	12 June
9935	18 September
9936	28 August
9937	21 August
9999	20 November

Ex-LNER Class 07 WD Austerity 2-8-0 Locomotives (60,000 added to LNER No.)

3000	12 June
3001	17 April
3002	29 May
3003	30 October
3007	30 October
3009	20 March
3010	15 May
3011	26 June
3012	17 April
3013	1 May
3015	24 July
3016	17 April
3017	4 September
3018	3 April
3019	1 May
3020	31 December
3023	28 August
3024	25 December
3026	31 July
3028	3 April
3029	2 October
3030	21 August
3033	28 August
3034	8 May
3035	21 August
3037	15 May
3038	31 July
3041	11 December
3042	9 October
3043	17 July
3045	26 June
3047	24 July
3048	15 May
3050	5 June
3051	3 April
3052	15 May
3053	19 June
3055	27 March
3057	27 March
3061	10 July
3062	5 June
3063	2 October
3064	1 May
3065	21 August
3066	13 November
3067	22 May
3068	17 July
3070	17 April
3071	8 May
3072	15 May
3073	19 June
3074	24 April
3075	27 November
3076	24 July
3077	3 July
3078	14 August
3079	26 June
3081	3 April
3082	10 April
3083	17 July
3084	4 September
3087	4 September
3089	17 April
3092	24 April
3093	17 July
3094	26 June

3097	19 June
3099	3 April
3100	13 November
3101	25 September
3102	17 July
3103	14 August
3104	3 July
3105	26 June
3106	30 October
3107	29 May
3108	24 July
3109	30 October
3110	19 June
3114	22 May
3116	19 June
3118	7 August
3120	17 April
3122	10 April
3123	3 April
3125	17 April
3126	2 October
3127	19 June
3130	24 April
3133	30 October
3137	21 August
3140	17 April
3141	5 June
3142	1 May
3144	26 June
3145	12 June
3149	8 May
3151	8 May
3152	17 April
3155	12 June
3159	3 April
3162	8 May
3163	1 May
3164	19 June
3165	24 July
3166	26 June
3167	24 April
3168	17 April
3169	24 April
3170	26 June
3173	27 March
3174	10 April
3176	19 June
3177	17 April
3178	27 March
3179	3 April
3182	17 July
3183	29 May
3185	27 November
3188	12 June
3190	5 June
3191	26 June
3192	24 July
3193	15 May
3194	17 April
3195	19 June
3196	18 September
3197	1 May

Ex-LNER Locomotives completely Renumbered

L1 CLASS 2-6-4T RENUMBERING DURING 1948

FIRST No.	B.R. No.	RENUMBERED WEEK ENDED
9000	67701	15 May
9001	67702	15 May
9002	67703	29 May
9003	67704	1 May
9004	67705	24 April
9005	67706	24 April
9006	67707	24 April
9007	67708	8 May
9008	67709	8 May
9009	67710	8 May
9010	67711	24 April
9011	67712	31 July
9012	67713	8 May
69013	67714	8 May
69014	67715	8 May
69015	67716	15 May

W1 CLASS 4-6-4 RENUMBERING

10000	60700	19 June

ELECTRIC BO-BO LOCOMOTIVE RENUMBERING

6480	26500	8 May
6481	26501	8 May

Locomotives Withdrawn during 1948

Ex-GWR Locomotives

B.R. No.	MONTH WITHDRAWN	LAST ALLOCATION
6	January	St. Philips Marsh
51	October	Cardiff East Dock
54	April	Cardiff East Dock
62	December	Newport Pill
71	December	Danygraig
184	October	Duffryn Yard
190	April	Newport Pill
198	January	Cardiff Radyr
200	July	Cardiff Canton
201*	December	Cardiff Cathays
202*	April	Treherbert
212	July	Cardiff East Dock
238	June	Cardiff Canton
248	July	Barry
259	August	Cardiff East Dock
261	August	Barry
268	April	Barry
275	April	Barry
298	July	Ferndale
410	March	Cardiff Canton
411	February	Cardiff Canton
424*	January	Newport Pill
680	December	Oswestry
783	August	Barry
906	April	Neath
1196	April	Oswestry
1197	April	Oswestry
1308	May	Oswestry
1358	February	Danygraig
1532	July	Croes Newydd
1538	November	St. Philips Marsh
1706	June	Croes Newydd
1713	June	Newport Ebbw Junction
1726	April	Newport Pill
1730	August	Tondu
1745	August	Stourbridge
1749	October	Stourbridge
1753	April	Truro
1762	April	Oxley
1769	April	Aberdare
1780	August	Croes Newydd
1867	November	Duffryn Yard
1889	December	Cardiff Canton
1900	April	St. Blazey
2356	July	Machynlleth
2569	October	Brecon
2612	January	Banbury
2623	February	Oxley

2643	July	Banbury
2656	March	Gloucester
2662	July	Chester
2665	January	Oxley
2669	May	Pontypool Road
2680	June	Hereford
2706	October	Stourbridge
2709	September	Bristol Bath Road
2714	May	Hereford
2717	October	Croes Newydd
2728	April	Pontypool Road
2730	April	Llanelly
2734	August	Newport Pill
2739	May	Pontypool Road
2746	July	Llanelly
2748	April	Taunton
2749	April	Pontypool Road
2751	April	Llanelly
2752	March	Penzance
2755	August	Taunton
2764	July	Newport Pill
2774	April	Worcester
2776	April	Plymouth Laira
2781	June	Cardiff East Dock
2785	April	Newton Abbot
2793	January	Newport Pill
2797	June	Neath
2905	April	Cardiff Canton
2913	May	Swindon
2916	July	Tyseley
2928	August	Westbury
2935	December	Swindon
2980	May	Gloucester
2988	May	Tyseley
2989	September	Chester
3002	April	Pontypool Road
3004	February	Carmarthen
3005	August	Tyseley
3006	June	Carmarthen
3008	September	Stafford Road
3009	June	Carmarthen
3013	September	St. Philips Marsh
3019	April	Westbury
3021	July	Worcester
3027	May	Worcester
3030	July	Worcester
3035	August	Westbury
3037	August	Pontypool Road
3039	August	Oxley
3046	August	St. Philips Marsh
3049	November	Tyseley
3158	April	Tyseley
3165	July	Severn Tunnel Junction
3184	July	Severn Tunnel Junction
3335	October	Exeter
3366	April	Chester
3376	September	Didcot
3379	June	Gloucester
3391	May	Plymouth Laira
3395	August	Exeter
3396	March	Didcot
3408	April	Didcot
3417	April	Wellington
3421	April	Swindon
3430	December	Newton Abbot
3431	December	Plymouth Laira
3440	June	Worcester
3442	July	Shrewsbury
3445	October	Gloucester
3446	December	Worcester
3452	April	Swindon
3585	January	Oxford
3589	August	Oxford
3597	August	Cardiff Cathays
4004	April	Oxford
4353	November	Birkenhead
4365	April	Westbury
4386	April	Birkenhead
5111	October	Stafford Road
5119	June	Southall
5121	October	Wellington
5127	May	Wellington
5128	November	Barry
5130	August	Leamington Spa
5131	October	Stourbridge
5146	May	Stourbridge
5302	May	Banbury
5320	September	Reading
5340	September	Weymouth
5343	July	Bristol Bath Road
5349	May	Banbury
5374	June	St. Philips Marsh
9006	August	Didcot
9007	July	Tyseley
9019	November	Tyseley

Note: The three locomotives that still carried their old G.W.R. numbers at withdrawal are denoted by a *. 201 carried the number 301, 202 carried 302 and 424 carried 504.

Ex-Southern Railway Locomotives

30003	September	Plymouth Friary
30009	July	Feltham
30010	August	Salisbury
30090	May	Stewarts Lane
30091	August	Plymouth Friary
30101	November	Eastleigh
30139	September	Feltham
30143	September	Yeovil Town
30145	October	Yeovil Town
30146	February	Dorchester
30150	February	Eastleigh
30176	June	Nine Elms
30239	October	Bournemouth
30261	November	Eastleigh
30271	September	Nine Elms
30278	December	Basingstoke
30279	December	Salisbury
30340	June	Yeovil Town
30343	January	Guildford
30348	August	Basingstoke
30363	June	Bournemouth
30366	October	Eastleigh
30392	October	Nine Elms
30445	November	Nine Elms
30459	November	Nine Elms
30460	November	Nine Elms
30618	January	Guildford
30627	December	Eastleigh
30629	December	Eastleigh
30636	October	Eastleigh
30672	May	Nine Elms
31002	June	Gillingham
31013	September	Reading
31014	June	Gillingham
31028	May	Reading
31031	May	Reading
31042	January	Reading
31046	October	Faversham

31051	August	Gillingham
31215	May	Gillingham
31378	November	Gillingham
31386	October	Hither Green
31388	July	Bricklayers Arms
31396	August	Tonbridge
31397	June	Bricklayers Arms
31426	August	Ashford
31437	October	Tonbridge
31438	December	Faversham
31440	December	Reading
31445	February	Stewarts Lane
31450	April	Dover
31453	October	Reading
31454	December	Stewarts Lane
31459	February	Reading
32001	July	Eastbourne
32003	July	Eastbourne
32004	November	Eastbourne
32006	July	Eastbourne
32007	September	Three Bridges
32010	July	Eastbourne
32044	September	Eastbourne
32122	May	Brighton
32164	June	Tonbridge
32239	March	Eastleigh
32259	March	Eastleigh
32269	July	Fratton
32283	November	Horsham
32286	July	Horsham
32289	July	Horsham
32308	November	Horsham
32358	November	Eastbourne
32361	March	Eastleigh
32370	September	Tonbridge
32371	October	St. Leonards
32373	November	Horsham
32377	September	Eastbourne
32383	December	St. Leonards
32397	July	Brighton
32435	May	Redhill
32598	July	Three Bridges
32599	September	Three Bridges
32601	January	Three Bridges
32604	September	Three Bridges
32605	November	Eastbourne
32609	June	Eastleigh
32699	February	Eastleigh

Note: None of the Southern Railway locomotives received their new British Railways numbers before withdrawal.

Ex-LMSR Locomotives

B.R. NO.	WITHDRAWN WEEK ENDED	LAST ALLOCATION
40408	25 December	Peterborough
40492	18 December	Crewe North
40494	18 December	Rhyl
40545	18 December	Grimesthorpe
40715	17 January	Saltley
40731	25 December	Millhouses
40736	31 January	Holbeck
40748	19 June	Holbeck
40757	8 May	Nottingham
41002	5 June	Nottingham
41018	10 July	Kentish Town
41024	2 October	Millhouses
41026	21 August	Millhouses
41027	25 September	Gloucester
41029	5 June	Saltley
41033	14 August	Derby
41036	25 September	Derby
41668	14 February	Kentish Town
41674	29 May	Kentish Town
41714	15 May	Birkenhead
41718	21 August	Burton
41759	24 January	Stourton
41762	11 September	Nottingham
41818	26 June	Birkenhead
41842	29 May	Stourton
41870	10 April	Gloucester
41893	4 September	Upper Bank
41910	18 September	Nottingham
43265	29 May	Cricklewood
43269	29 May	Buxton
43338	27 March	Rowsley
43439	19 June	Bristol Barrow Road
43573	31 January	Shrewsbury
43769	12 June	Hasland
43796	11 September	Wellingborough
43831	8 May	Toton
46605	22 May	Crewe North
46661	5 June	Walsall
46673	24 April	Warwick
46679	7 February	Walsall
46681	12 June	Crewe North
46682	3 January	Sutton Oak
46686	22 May	Watford
46691	27 March	Bangor
46692	20 March	Sutton Oak
46718	24 January	Warrington
46738	8 May	Buxton
46740	8 May	Swansea Victoria
46747	7 February	Llandudno Junction
46878	28 February	Monument Lane
46881	24 July	Bushbury
46883	22 May	Bletchley
46909	27 March	Bletchley
46920	1 May	Monument Lane
46926	14 February	Bangor
47875	28 August	Speke Junction
47887	28 August	Patricroft
47888	4 December	Springs Branch
47892	14 February	Patricroft
47930	7 August	Edge Hill
47938	21 February	Edge Hill
47948	3 July	Swansea Victoria
47954	16 October	Buxton
47956	27 November	Edge Hill
47958	4 December	Edge Hill
47959	5 June	Edge Hill
48801	27 November	Patricroft
48834	31 December	Springs Branch
48910	17 January	Warwick
48912	28 August	Patricroft
48913	28 August	Stafford
48924	11 December	Nuneaton
48939	20 November	Bushbury
48962	18 December	Springs Branch
49012	11 December	Willesden
49013	1 May	Rugby
49038	3 April	Edge Hill
49056	7 August	Walsall
49095	19 June	Patricroft
49103	12 June	Northampton
49128	20 November	Willesden
49131	31 July	Bescot
49136	28 August	Warrington
49152	2 October	Sutton Oak
49165	18 September	Bescot
49175	31 January	Bescot
49179	18 December	Coventry
49197	29 May	Springs Branch
49201	19 June	Coventry
49225	20 March	Buxton
49231	28 February	Preston

49233	22 May	Bushbury
49236	13 March	Walsall
49250	10 April	Preston
49251	31 January	Mold Junction
49272	6 March	Crewe South
49273	7 February	Patricroft
49274	10 April	Bescot
49286	24 April	Bescot
49295	14 August	Bushbury
49303	27 November	Sutton Oak
49309	3 July	Aston
49349	18 December	Walsall
49362	24 July	Aston
49383	8 May	Mold Junction
49384	18 December	Bescot
50423	3 July	Blackpool
50429	10 April	Blackpool
50617	6 March	Bolton
50631	20 November	Manningham
50667	20 March	Rhyl
50728	7 August	Southport
50800	7 August	Wakefield
50801	4 December	Wakefield
50823	4 December	Fleetwood
50835	7 August	Sowerby Bridge
50875	22 May	Fleetwood
50896	4 December	Manningham
50899	23 October	Skipton
50901	20 March	Normanton
50903	14 February	Manningham
50934	14 August	Sowerby Bridge
50943	18 December	Lower Darwen
50950	21 August	Lower Darwen
50952	19 June	Low Moor
51320	10 April	Mirfield
51342	18 September	Speke Junction
51405	11 December	Speke Junction
51427	20 November	Speke Junction
51467	13 November	Lower Darwen
51487	23 October	Bury
52032	10 January	Springs Branch
52036*	13 November	Patricroft
52046	7 February	Wakefield
52049*	9 October	Patricroft
52063*	4 September	Springs Branch
52127	19 June	Low Moor
52152	6 March	Wigan L.&Y.
52170	18 September	Edge Hill
52253	26 June	Lower Darwen
52256	21 February	Southport
52337	20 March	Aintree
52374	18 September	Shrewsbury
52401	24 January	Aintree
52417	14 February	Chester
52422	6 March	Low Moor
52457	8 May	Shrewsbury
52467	22 May	Lostock Hall
52528	27 November	Bolton
52545	13 November	Lees
52568	13 March	Wakefield
52574	30 October	Sowerby Bridge
52602	13 November	Wigan L.&.Y.
52618	15 May	Preston
52837	3 April	Wigan L.& Y.
52841	13 March-	Rose Grove
52873	8 May	Rose Grove
52877	2 October	Aintree
52935	26 June	Aintree
54363	30 October	Aviemore
54379	13 March	Aviemore
54401	16 October	Inverness
54415	8 May	Inverness
54416	21 August	Inverness
54434	17 April	Aviemore
54631	22 May	Motherwell
54637	13 March	Motherwell
54641	13 November	Motherwell
54643	7 February	Motherwell
54644	24 April	Dalry Road
54652	13 November	Motherwell
54764	14 February	Aviemore
55116	29 May	Polmadie
55117	19 June	Stirling
55130	18 September	Dundee West
55133	11 December	Aviemore
55180*	21 August	Dundee West
55190	5 June	Forfar
55351	18 December	Beattock
55355	31 January	Beattock
56270	23 October	Motherwell
56351	20 November	Stranraer
56905	17 April	Carlisle Kingmoor
57290	19 June	Motherwell
57301	22 May	Motherwell
57304	5 June	Ardrossan
57308	22 May	Motherwell
57313	31 January	Motherwell
57327	17 April	Motherwell
57330	12 June	Polmadie
57333	20 March	St. Rollox
57343	17 April	Dumfries
57371	24 July	Dawsholm
57374	22 May	St. Rollox
57380	24 April	St. Rollox
57406	31 January	Motherwell
57408	7 February	Hamilton
57421	2 October	Stranraer
57422	5 June	Stirling
57442	24 July	Grangemouth
57469	20 November	Dawsholm
57471	11 September	Dawsholm
57551	17 July	Greenock
57574	19 June	Hurlford
57578	6 November	Dalry Road
57606	11 September	Motherwell
57616	22 May	Ayr
57629	18 September	Inverness
57636	4 December	Dumfries
57639	4 September	Greenock
57641	3 April	Polmadie
57953	18 September	Inverness
58000	16 October	Stafford
58003	29 May	Stafford
58011	22 May	Chester
58012	8 May	Chester
58021	14 August	Barrow
58037	8 May	Bedford
58039	9 October	Bedford
58044	17 April	Upminster
58055	5 June	Royston
58074	2 October	Bristol Barrow Road
58081	4 September	Manningham
58141	4 September	Bournville
58150	21 August	Grimesthorpe
58205	19 June	Bescot
58210	12 June	Nottingham
58227	22 May	Derby
58250	14 August	Aston
58255	4 September	Saltley
58263	17 April	Burton
58266	15 May	Canklow
58284	25 September	Burton
58292	24 April	Manningham
58297	28 August	Burton
58301	17 April	Coventry
58320	24 July	Walsall
58324	28 August	Barrow
58325	7 August	Walsall
58331	16 October	Barrow
58337	5 June	Barrow
58339	29 May	Barrow
58345	24 April	Bushbury
58353	9 October	Widnes
58355	18 December	Shrewsbury
58356	13 November	Barrow

58357	3 July	Barrow
58358	12 June	Shrewsbury
58359	18 September	Walsall
58361	25 September	Walsall
58366	3 July	Stockport Edgeley
58370	24 July	Workington
58372	18 December	Rhyl
58374	7 August	Bangor
58385	4 September	Stoke
58386	9 October	Crewe South
58387	8 May	Workington
58390	7 August	Sutton Oak
58391	18 September	Workington
58395	29 May	Widnes
58401	16 October	Workington
58402	27 November	Widnes
58403	4 December	Bangor
58405	24 July	Workington
58408	22 May	Workington
58414	16 October	Bushbury
58423	12 June	Springs Branch
58425	25 September	Shrewsbury
58428	3 July	Chester
58870	11 December	Crewe Works
58884	13 November	Rhyl
58885	18 September	Tredegar
58893	16 October	Plodder Lane
58898	2 October	Edge Hill
58901	31 July	Springs Branch
58905	28 August	Abergavenny
58906	13 November	Abergavenny
58907	2 October	Abergavenny
58909	12 June	Monument Lane
58914	28 August	Plodder Lane
58918	24 April	Plodder Lane
58920	14 August	Tredegar
58922	31 July	Edge Hill
58930	18 September	Tredegar
58931	27 March	Tredegar
58936	22 May	Shrewsbury
58937	24 April	Abergavenny

Note: The only four locomotives to receive their new British Railways numbers before withdrawal are marked with *

The Following locomotives were not allocated new British Railways numbers as all were due for withdrawal soon after nationalisation.

1307	31 January	Highbridge
1361	21 February	Skipton
1385	10 January	Cricklewood
3021	20 March	Kentish Town
3050	28 February	Royston
3153	20 March	Rowsley
3195	13 March	Kettering
3424	6 March	Kirkby
3473	7 February	Willesden
3602	17 January	Nottingham
7700	20 March	Swansea Victoria
7715	17 January	Swansea Victoria
7796	7 February	Llandudno Junction
7812	24 January	Abergavenny
7841	7 February	Abergavenny
23016	6 March	Kentish Town
25321	7 February	Chester
25722	6 March	Stafford
25827	6 March	Stafford
27525	20 March	Birkenhead
27648	10 January	Tredegar
28095	31 January	Widnes
28097	21 February	Bescot
28153	14 February	Shrewsbury
28230	24 January	Bushbury
28350	28 February	Crewe North
28415	17 January	Workington
28441	28 February	Workington
28542	7 February	Workington
28586	24 January	Aston
28597	24 January	Walsall
29988	6 November	Beattock

Ex-LNER Locomotives

B.R. NO.	DATE WITHDRAWN	LAST ALLOCATION
61354	15 March	Darnall
61355	2 September	Darnall
61358	13 August	Darnall
61360	10 September	Darnall
61363	12 June	Darnall
61364	12 June	Gorton
61366	31 December	Gorton
61368	6 October	Gorton
61369	21 August	Gorton
61370	19 November	Gorton
61372	10 September	Darnall
61373	19 August	Gorton
61374	18 September	Gorton
61376	31 December	Gorton
61378	19 August	Darnall
61380	3 August	Gorton
61383	14 May	Darnall
61384	19 August	Darnall
61390	2 November	Gorton
61393	3 August	Gorton
61394	22 April	Gorton
61395	30 November	Gorton
61397	4 June	Darnall
61470	19 November	Brunswick
61476	19 August	Trafford Park
61488	7 October	Ardsley
61500	23 June	Keith Junction
61509	15 October	Ipswich
61517	21 October	Stratford
61680	13 November	Mexborough
61681	23 June	Mexborough
61685	6 March	Mexborough
61690	20 April	Mexborough
62062	5 March	Kittybrewster
62064	6 August	Kittybrewster
62066	10 May	Kittybrewster
62111	7 February	York
62112	7 February	York
62116	16 October	Colwick
62122	26 February	South Lynn
62124	25 November	South Lynn
62126	13 August	Colwick
62143	23 March	Louth
62144	3 August	South Lynn
62155	26 February	Melton Constable
62157	8 April	Melton Constable
62160	16 October	Hitchin
62163	16 October	Hitchin
62169	2 July	Colwick
62175	25 November	Yarmouth Beach
62187	1 October	Colwick
62189	25 November	Melton Constable
62195	26 February	Melton Constable
62198	27 August	Colwick
62205	8 November	Dunfermline
62207	8 November	Norwich

62238*	27 August	Keith Junction
62367	17 January	Botanic Gardens
62390	29 November	Stockton
62400	20 April	St. Margarets
62403	2 March	Haymarket
62409	29 October	Dundee Tay Bridge
62443	2 March	St. Margarets
62444	2 September	St. Margarets
62446	30 September	Thornton Junction
62448	2 September	Hawick
62449	13 November	Hawick
62450	26 February	St. Margarets
62453	29 May	St. Margarets
62454	30 September	St. Margarets
62463	5 March	Bathgate
62504	12 June	Kings Lynn
62560	24 September	Norwich
62563	6 August	Norwich
62583	23 November	Norwich
62600	12 June	Norwich
62602	23 September	Stratford
62808	14 February	New England
62821	2 July	Kings Cross
62829	22 July	Ardsley
62849	19 July	Ardsley
62870	14 February	Grantham
62871	21 May	New England
62876	3 January	Grantham
62914	15 March	Lincoln
62916	13 November	Lincoln
62920	3 February	Boston
62921	5 April	Boston
62922	23 June	Boston
62924	30 January	Boston
62933	6 March	Dairycoates
62937	12 March	Gateshead
62954	26 June	Scarborough
62970	27 December	Dairycoates
62972	30 August	Scarborough
62973	26 June	Scarborough
62975	10 July	Scarborough
62978	30 August	Darlington
62981	10 July	Darlington
62982	24 July	Dairycoates
62983	24 July	Dairycoates
62988	24 July	Dairycoates
62989	30 August	Scarborough
62992	1 November	Scarborough
62993	5 March	Scarborough
62995	10 July	Dairycoates
63250	26 June	West Hartlepool
63252	7 February	Haverton Hill
63253	22 November	West Hartlepool
63254	11 June	Borough Gardens
63263	1 November	Middlesbrough
63264	26 June	Borough Gardens
63268	7 February	Middlesbrough
63279	14 February	Selby
63292	8 November	Middlesbrough
63295	22 November	Middlesbrough
63298	26 February	Borough Gardens
63301	27 December	Haverton Hill
63306	20 December	Haverton Hill
63310	11 June	Selby
63315	25 March	Neville Hill
63321	6 March	Borough Gardens
63323	8 November	Middlesbrough
63327	22 November	Newport
63339	7 February	Middlesbrough
63489	22 July	Doncaster
63494	5 March	Doncaster
63921	21 May	Langwith Junction
64107	16 October	Retford
64136	25 March	New England
64145	2 March	Hitchin
64152	12 April	Retford
64167	2 July	South Lynn
65031	11 June	Darlington

65032	16 August	West Auckland
65049	2 June	Neville Hill
65056	20 December	Dairycoates
65063	14 February	South Blyth
65069	29 April	South Blyth
65104*	4 October	Northallerton
65115	26 June	Kirkby Stephen
65195	3 February	Walton
65220	23 March	Polmont
65256	14 April	Kipps
65289	23 March	Kipps
65328	23 March	Dundee Tay Bridge
65337	15 April	Eastfield
65352	29 May	Lowestoft
65368	29 May	Kings Lynn
65380	13 January	Cambridge
65381	25 November	Stratford
65383	6 February	Cambridge
65385	27 December	Stratford
65394	29 May	Norwich
65399	12 March	Cambridge
65400	18 February	Lowestoft
65410	6 February	Cambridge
65411	15 April	Norwich
65418	12 March	Stratford
65421	17 March	Ipswich
65607	27 December	Malton
65612	14 February	Whitby
65625	15 May	Borough Gardens
65626	29 November	Newport
65639	7 February	York
65641	27 September	Borough Gardens
65674	10 July	Northallerton
65704	2 June	Heaton
67093	8 November	St. Margarets
67094	8 November	St. Margarets
67097	23 March	Gorton
67105	27 August	Annesley
67106*	31 December	Annesley
67114	12 March	Lowestoft
67115	13 May	Cambridge
67117	13 May	South Lynn
67119	18 February	Lowestoft
67134	29 May	Norwich
67141	29 May	Ipswich
67143	22 July	Ipswich
67159	24 April	Stratford
67161	24 April	Stratford
67168	24 April	Stratford
67169	24 April	Stratford
67170	24 April	Stratford
67172	24 April	Stratford
67173	24 April	Stratford
67179	24 April	Stratford
67180	24 April	Stratford
67181	24 April	Stratford
67185	24 April	Stratford
67306	26 June	West Auckland
67351	1 December	Langwith Junction
67355	5 March	Langwith Junction
67358	16 January	Trafford Park
67370	30 January	Trafford Park
67378	16 January	Trafford Park
67388	6 July	Copley Hill
68081	3 April	Stratford Works
68090	15 November	Borough Gardens
68134	16 February	Doncaster Works
68135	20 September	Stratford Works
68187	13 August	Yarmouth
68213	6 February	Yarmouth Beach
68285	4 October	Selby
68317	24 December	Doncaster
68366	17 March	Wrexham Rhosddu
68368	3 August	Wrexham Rhosddu
68390	20 September	Hull Springhead
68400	4 October	South Blyth
68441	11 June	Newport
68484	20 May	South Lynn

68488	13 January	South Lynn
69070	22 October	Neasden
69071	6 October	Neasden
69076	22 October	Neasden
69077	22 October	Neasden
69089	30 August	Hull Springhead
69103	8 November	Gateshead
69110	26 June	Hull Springhead
69399	4 October	Dairycoates
69419	14 February	Haverton Hill
69792	20 December	Starbeck

Also withdrawn from Whitby on 14 February was steam railcar 2136 "Hope"

Note: The only three locomotives to receive their new British Railways numbers before withdrawal are marked with *.

New Locomotives Added to Stock during 1948

Steam Locomotives

Ex- G.W.R. design. All built at Swindon Works.

No. & TYPE	MONTH TO TRAFFIC	FIRST ALLOCATION
0-6-0 "2251" CLASS		
3218	January	Banbury
3219	January	Worcester
2-6-2T "5101" CLASS		
4160	September	Barry
4161	September	Barry
4162	September	Barry
4163	September	Barry
4164	September	Duffryn Yard
4165	October	Tyseley
4166	October	Tyseley
4167	October	Newton Abbot
4168	November	Swindon
4169	November	Swindon
0-6-0PT "6700" CLASS		
6760	November	Newport Pill
6761	November	Duffryn Yard
6762	November	Tondu
6763	November	Danygraig
6764	November	Newport Ebbw Jct.
6765	December	Cardiff East Dock
4-6-0 "6959" MODIFIED HALL CLASS		
6981	February	St. Philips Marsh
6982	January	Westbury
6983	February	Old Oak Common
6984	February	Hereford
6985	February	Oxley
6986	March	Tyseley
6987	March	Gloucester
6988	March	Weymouth
6989	March	Hereford
6990	April	Old Oak Common
6991	November	Westbury
6992	November	Gloucester
6993	December	Weymouth
6994	December	Exeter
6995	December	Taunton

No. & TYPE	MONTH TO TRAFFIC	FIRST ALLOCATION
4-6-0 "4073" CASTLE CLASS		
7008	May	Oxford
7009	May	Swansea Landore
7010	June	Old Oak Common
7011	June	Bristol Bath Road
7012	June	Swansea Landore
7013	July	Old Oak Common
7014	July	Swindon
7015	July	Bristol Bath Road
7016	August	Cardiff Canton
7017	September	Old Oak Common
0-6-0PT "7400" CLASS		
7430	August	Stourbridge
7431	August	Croes Newydd
7432	August	Stourbridge
7433	August	Croes Newydd
7434	August	Oswestry
7435	September	Stourbridge
7436	September	Oxford
7437	September	Worcester
7438	October	Danygraig
7439	October	Llanelly
0-6-0PT "5700" CLASS		
9662	April	Newport Ebbw Jct.
9663	April	Taunton
9664	April	Newport Ebbw Jct.
9665	April	St. Philips Marsh
9666	April	Neath
9667	May	Newport Ebbw Jct.
9668	May	Newton Abbot
9669	May	Croes Newydd
9670	May	Taunton
9671	June	Plymouth Laira
9672	June	Shrewsbury

Allocated names for the new locomotives from Swindon Works:

6981	Marbury Hall	6990	Witherslack Hall	7011	Banbury Castle
6982	Melmerby Hall	6991	Acton Burnell Hall	7012	Barry Castle
6983	Otterington Hall	6992	Aborfield Hall	7013	Bristol Castle
6984	Owsden Hall	6993	Arthog Hall	7014	Caerhays Castle
6985	Parwick Hall	6994	Baggrave Hall	7015	Carn Brea Castle
6986	Rydal Hall	6995	Benthall Hall	7016	Chester Castle
6987	Shervington Hall	7008	Swansea Castle	7017	G.J. Churchward
6988	Swithland Hall	7009	Athelney Castle		
6989	Wightwick Hall	7010	Avondale Castle		

Note: 7001 was renamed "Sir James Milne" from"Denbigh Castle" in February 1948. Sir James Milne was the retired General Manager of the G.W.R. Also, 7007 was renamed "Great Western" from"Ogmore Castle" in January 1948 as this was the last new locomotive constructed for the G.W.R.

Ex- Southern Railway design.

NUMBER AND TYPE	MONTH TO TRAFFIC	FIRST ALLOCATION	ALLOCATED NAME
From Brighton Works: "BATTLE OF BRITAIN" CLASS 4-6-2			
34071	April	Dover	601 Squadron
34072	April	Dover	257 Squadron
34073	May	Ramsgate	249 Squadron
34074	May	Ramsgate	46 Squadron
34075	June	Ramsgate	264 Squadron
34076	June	Ramsgate	41 Squadron
34077	July	Ramsgate	603 Squadron
34078	July	Ramsgate	222 Squadron
34079	July	Ramsgate	141 Squadron
34080	August	Ramsgate	74 Squadron
34081	September	Ramsgate	92 Squadron
34082	September	Ramsgate	615 Squadron
34083	October	Stewarts Lane	605 Squadron
34084	November	Stewarts Lane	253 Squadron
34085	November	Stewarts Lane	501 Squadron
34086	December	Ramsgate	219 Squadron
34087	December	Ramsgate	145 Squadron
34088	December	Ramsgate	213 Squadron
34089	December	Ramsgate	602 Squadron
From Eastleigh Works: "MERCHANT NAVY" CLASS 4-6-2			
35021	September	Exmouth Junction	New Zealand Line
35022	October	Exmouth Junction	Holland-America Line
35023	November	Exmouth Junction	Holland-Afrika Line
35024	November	Exmouth Junction	East Asiatic Company
35025	November	Bournemouth	Brocklebank Line
35026	December	Bournemouth	Lamport and Holt Line
35027	December	Bournemouth	Port Line
35028	December	Bournemouth	Clan Line
From Ashford Works: ENGLISH-ELECTRIC CO-CO. ELECTRIC LOCO.			
20003	October	Brighton	

Ex- L.M.S. design.

No. & TYPE	WEEK ENDED DATES TO TRAFFIC	FIRST ALLOCATION
From Crewe Works:		
Ivatt 2P 2-6-2T		
41210	21 August	Watford
41211	21 August	Northampton
41212	4 September	Bangor
41213	4 September	Bangor
41214	11 September	Crewe North
41215	11 September	Crewe North

No. & TYPE	WEEK ENDED DATES TO TRAFFIC	FIRST ALLOCATION
41216	18 September	Crewe North
41217	25 September	Crewe North
41218	18 September	Crewe North
41219	25 September	Crewe North
41220	2 October	Crewe North
41221	2 October	Crewe North
41222	2 October	Crewe North
41223	9 October	Bangor
41224	16 October	Bangor
41225	16 October	Bushbury

41226	16 October	Walsall
41227	30 October	Warwick
41228	30 October	Warwick
41229	30 October	Crewe North

From Derby Works:

Fairburn
4P 2-6-4T

42147	24 April	Fleetwood
42148	8 May	Fleetwood
42149	8 May	Sowerby Bridge
42150	15 May	Sowerby Bridge
42151	29 May	Sowerby Bridge
42152	5 June	Sowerby Bridge
42153	5 June	Sowerby Bridge
42154	12 June	Lower Darwen
42155	19 June	Rose Grove
42156	26 June	Low Moor
42157	3 July	Low Moor
42158	3 July	Lostock Hall
42159	10 July	Lostock Hall
42160	10 July	Wigan L & Y
42161	7 August	Wigan L & Y
42162	14 August	Carstairs
42163	21 August	Carstairs
42164	28 August	Hamilton
42165	4 September	Hamilton
42166	11 September	Hamilton
42167	18 September	Polmadie
42168	25 September	Polmadie
42169	2 October	Polmadie
42170	9 October	Polmadie
42171	9 October	Polmadie
42172	16 October	Polmadie
42173	23 October	Carstairs
42174	30 October	Carstairs
42175	6 November	Greenock
42176	13 November	Greenock
42177	20 November	Derby
42178	27 November	Lostock Hall
42179	4 December	Wigan L & Y
42180	11 December	Wigan L & Y
42181	18 December	Manningham
42182	25 December	Leicester Midland
42190*	17 January	Corkerhill
42191*	24 January	Corkerhill
42192*	31 January	Corkerhill
42193*	31 January	Corkerhill
42194*	7 February	Corkerhill
42195*	21 February	Corkerhill
42196*	28 February	Corkerhill
42197*	6 March	Corkerhill
42198*	13 March	Stirling
42199*	7 April	Stirling

From Horwich Works:

Ivatt
4F 2-6-0

43003*	17 January	Crewe South
43004*	24 January	Bletchley
43005*	7 February	Crewe South
43006*	14 February	Bletchley
43007*	21 February	Workington
43008*	28 February	Workington
43009*	6 March	Workington
43010*	20 March	Derby
43011	27 March	Derby
43012	10 April	Barrow Road
43013	17 April	Barrow Road
43014	24 April	Grimesthorpe
43015	8 May	Grimesthorpe
43016	16 May	Holbeck
43017	22 May	Holbeck
43018	29 May	Nottingham
43019	12 June	Nottingham
43020	18 December	Crewe South
43021	25 December	Crewe South
43022	31 December	Nuneaton

From Horwich Works:

Stanier
5P5F
4-6-0

44698	3 July	Perth
44699	10 July	Perth
44700	31 July	Perth
44701	7 August	Perth
44702	21 August	St. Rollox
44703	28 August	St. Rollox
44704	4 September	Carstairs
44705	11 September	Carstairs
44706	18 September	Corkerhill
44707	25 September	Polmadie
44708	2 October	Crewe North
44709	9 October	Crewe North
44710	16 October	Crewe North
44711	23 October	Crewe North
44712	30 October	Crewe North
44713	6 November	Crewe North
44714	13 November	Crewe North
44715	20 November	Crewe North
44716	27 November	Crewe North
44717	4 December	Crewe North

From Crewe Works:

Stanier
5P5F
4-6-0

44738	19 June	Llandudno Jct.
44739	19 June	Llandudno Jct.
44740	29 May	Crewe North
44741	12 June	Llandudno Jct.
44742	3 July	Llandudno Jct.
44743	26 June	Holbeck
44744	3 July	Holbeck
44745	3 July	Holbeck
44746	7 August	Holbeck
44747	31 July	Holbeck
44748*	7 February	Longsight
44749*	14 February	Longsight
44750*	28 February	Longsight
44751*	13 March	Longsight
44752*	20 March	Longsight
44753*	27 March	Holbeck
44754	10 April	Holbeck
44755	1 May	Derby
44756	19 June	Holbeck
44757	31 December	Holbeck

From Crewe Works:

Stanier
Princess
Coronation
8P 4-6-2

46257	22 May	Camden

Named "City of Salford"

From Crewe Works:

Ivatt
2F 2-6-0

46420	6 November	Widnes
46421	6 November	Widnes
46422	13 November	Widnes
46423	27 November	Widnes
46424	27 November	Widnes
46425	4 December	Bescot
46426	4 December	Bescot
46427	4 December	Bescot

* denotes delivered with L.M.S. number without the "4"

46428	4 December	Preston
46429	4 December	Preston
46430	11 December	Preston
46431	18 December	Willesden
46432	25 December	Willesden
46433	31 December	Willesden
46434	31 December	Willesden

Re-instated from store after return from war service in France:

L.M.S.
3F 0-6-0T

47589	23 October	Stourton
47607	20 November	Gloucester Barnwood
47611	30 October	Grimesthorpe
47659	20 November	Peterborough Spital Bridge
47660	2 October	Derby

From Doncaster Works;

A1 Class
4-6-2

60114	6 August	Kings Cross
60115	3 September	Gateshead
60116	8 October	Heaton
60117	22 October	Grantham
60118	12 November	Copley Hill
60119	26 November	Copley Hill
60120	10 December	Kings Cross
60121	22 December	York
60122	24 December	Kings Cross

From Darlington Works:

A1 Class
4-6-2

60130	28 September	Doncaster
60131	5 October	Kings Cross
60132	18 October	Gateshead
60133	30 October	Grantham
60134	5 November	Copley Hill
60135	18 November	Gateshead
60136	26 November	Copley Hill
60137	3 December	Gateshead
60138	10 December	York
60139	23 December	Kings Cross
60140	24 December	York
60141	31 December	York

From Doncaster Works;

A2 Class
4-6-2

60526*	9 January	York
60527*	30 January	Gateshead
60528*	20 February	Gateshead
60529*	20 February	Haymarket
60530*	4 March	Kings Cross
60531*	12 March	Gateshead
60532	25 March	York
60533	8 April	New England
60534	23 April	York
60535	5 May	York
60536	14 May	Copley Hill
60537	11 June	Copley Hill
60538	18 June	Gateshead
60539	27 August	Heaton

From North British Locomotive Company:

B1 Class
4-6-0

61274*	9 January	Darlington
61275*	12 January	Darlington
61276*	14 January	Darlington
61277*	16 January	Kittybrewster
61278*	19 January	Dundee
61279*	21 January	Lincoln
61280*	23 January	Lincoln
61281*	27 January	Lincoln
61282*	28 January	Colwick
61283*	2 February	Colwick
61284*	6 February	Immingham
61285*	9 February	Cambridge
61286*	9 February	Cambridge
61287*	9 February	Cambridge
61288*	16 February	Darlington
61289*	18 February	Darlington
61290*	20 February	Darlington
61291*	24 February	Darlington
61292*	25 February	Thornton Jct
61293*	27 February	Dundee
61294*	1 March	Hammerton Street
61295*	3 March	Ardsley
61296*	6 March	Ardsley
61297*	10 March	Ardsley
61298*	11 March	Leicester Central
61299*	12 March	Leicester Central
61300*	15 March	March
61301*	17 March	Cambridge
61302*	22 March	Cambridge
61303*	26 March	Darlington
61304	31 March	Dairycoates
61305	1 April	Dairycoates
61306	5 April	Dairycoates
61307	7 April	Kittybrewster
61308	9 April	Kittybrewster
61309	15 April	Ardsley
61310	19 April	Ardsley
61311	21 April	Darnall
61312	23 April	Darnall
61313	27 April	Gorton
61314	29 April	Gorton
61315	30 April	Gorton
61316	4 May	Gorton
61317	6 May	Gorton
61318	11 May	Immingham
61319	14 May	Borough Gardens
61320	18 May	Borough Gardens
61321	20 May	Borough Gardens
61322	25 May	Borough Gardens
61323	27 May	Kittybrewster
61324	1 June	Kittybrewster
61325	3 June	Immingham
61326	8 June	Gorton
61327	11 June	Gorton
61328	16 June	Immingham
61329	18 June	New England
61330	23 June	New England
61331	25 June	New England
61332	30 June	Cambridge
61333	2 July	Cambridge
61334	7 July	Norwich
61335	15 July	Stratford
61336	5 August	Stratford
61337	12 August	Neville Hill
61338	20 August	Neville Hill
61339	8 September	Neville Hill

From Gorton Works;
B1 Class
4-6-0

61340	27 November	Eastfield
61341	18 December	Eastfield

*Denotes delivered with L.N.E.R. number without the "6"

From Darlington Works:
L1 Class
2-6-4T

67702	22 January	Stratford
67703	23 January	Stratford
67704	6 February	Stratford
67705	19 February	Stratford
67706	18 February	Neasden
67707	27 February	Neasden
67708	3 March	Stratford
67709	8 March	Stratford
67710	18 March	Stratford
67711	19 March	Stratford
67712	25 March	Stratford
67713	1 April	Stratford
67714	9 April	Neasden
67715	9 April	Neasden
67716	16 April	Stratford
67717	30 April	Neasden
67718	7 May	Neasden
67719	13 May	Botanic Gardens
67720	14 May	Neasden
67721	25 May	Botanic Gardens
67722	4 June	Stratford
67723	4 June	Stratford
67724	11 June	Stratford
67725	12 June	Neasden
67726	2 July	Hitchin
67727	8 July	Botanic Gardens
67728	9 July	Botanic Gardens
67729	16 July	Stratford
67730	6 August	Botanic Gardens

From North British Locomotive Company;
L1 Class
2-6-4T

67731	26 October	Hitchin
67732	28 October	Hitchin
67733	1 November	Stratford
67734	3 November	Stratford
67735	5 November	Stratford
67736	8 November	Botanic Gardens
67737	10 November	Hitchin
67738	12 November	Hitchin
67739	17 November	Stratford
67740	17 November	Stratford
67741	19 November	Stratford
67742	22 November	Darlington
67743	24 November	Hitchin
67744	26 November	Hitchin
67745	29 November	Stratford
67746	1 December	Stratford
67747	3 December	Neasden
67748	6 December	Neasden
67749	7 December	Neasden
67750	9 December	Darlington
67751	10 December	Neasden
67752	14 December	Neasden
67753	15 December	Neasden
67754	17 December	Dairycoates
67755	21 December	Stratford
67756	22 December	Neasden
67757	23 December	Grantham
67758	27 December	Grantham
67759	29 December	Darlington
67760	30 December	Grantham

Note: 67702 to 67716 were first numbered 9001 to 9012, 69013, 69014 and 69015.

Ex-L.N.E.R. design locomotives allotted names:

A1 Class 4-6-2.

60114	W. P. Allen
60115	Meg Merrilies
60116	Hal o' the Wynd
60117	Bois Roussel
60118	Archibald Sturrock
60119	Patrick Stirling
60120	Kittiwake
60121	Silurian
60122	Curlew
60130	Kestrel
60131	Osprey
60132	Marmion
60133	Pommern
60134	Foxhunter
60135	Madge Wildfire
60136	Alcazar
60137	Redgauntlet
60138	Boswell
60139	Sea Eagle
60140	Balmoral
60141	Abbotsford

A2 Class 4-6-2

60526	Sugar Palm
60527	Sun Chariot
60528	Tudor Minstrel
60529	Pearl Diver
60530	Sayajirao
60531	Bahram
60532	Blue Peter
60533	Happy Knight
60534	Irish Elegance
60535	Hornet's Beauty
60536	Trimbush
60537	Bachelor's Button
60538	Velocity
60539	Bronzino

Diesel Locomotives

From Derby Works:

No. & TYPE	WEEK ENDED DATES TO TRAFFIC	FIRST ALLOCATION
Co-Co Diesel-Electric		
10001	10 July	Camden
0-6-0 Diesel-Electric Shunter		
12043	7 February	Saltley
12044	13 March	Saltley
12045	1 May	Toton
12046	5 June	Toton
12047	25 September	Toton
12048	18 December	Toton
12049	31 December	Crewe South

Note: 12043 and 12044 were delivered numbered 7130 and 7131.

From Swindon Works;

No. & TYPE	MONTH TO TRAFFIC	FIRST ALLOCATION
0-6-0 Diesel-Electric Shunter		
15101	April	Old Oak Common
15102	April	Old Oak Common
15103	May	Old Oak Common
15104	May	Old Oak Common
15105	July	Old Oak Common
15106	July	Old Oak Common

Narrow Gauge Locomotives in Capital Stock

NARROW GAUGE LOCOMOTIVES EX-G.W.R.

CORRIS RAILWAY 2ft 3in GAUGE

FALCON ENGINE CO. 0-4-2ST

3

KERR STUART 0-4-2ST

4

Both were kept at Maespoeth which was officially a sub-shed of Machynlleth.

Both locomotives were withdrawn in October 1948.

VALE OF RHEIDOL 1ft 11½in GAUGE

G.W. DEVELOPMENT OF V.of R. DESIGN 2-6-2T

7
8

DAVIES AND METCALFE ORIGINAL DESIGN
2-6-2T

9

No. 9 carried the number 1213.

All allocated to Aberystwyth V.of R. shed.

WELSHPOOL AND LLANFAIR RAILWAY 2ft 6in GAUGE

BEYER PEACOCK DESIGN 0-6-0T

822 The Earl
823 Countess

Both allocated to Welshpool W. & L. Shed, a sub of Oswestry.

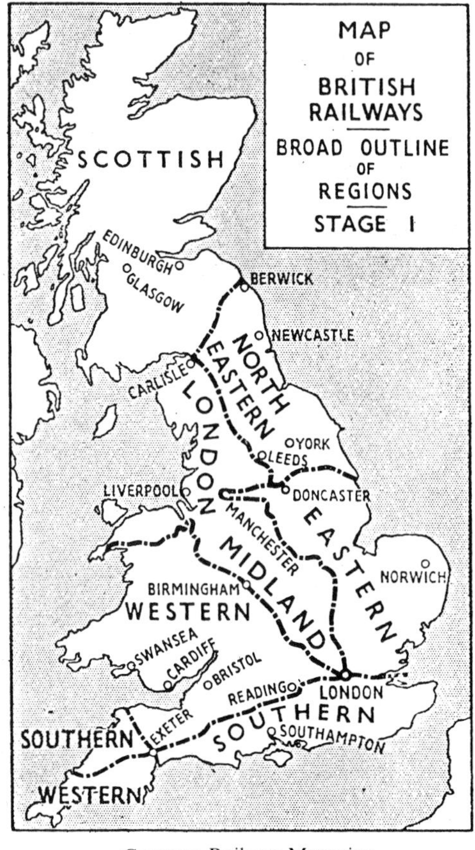

Courtesy Railway Magazine

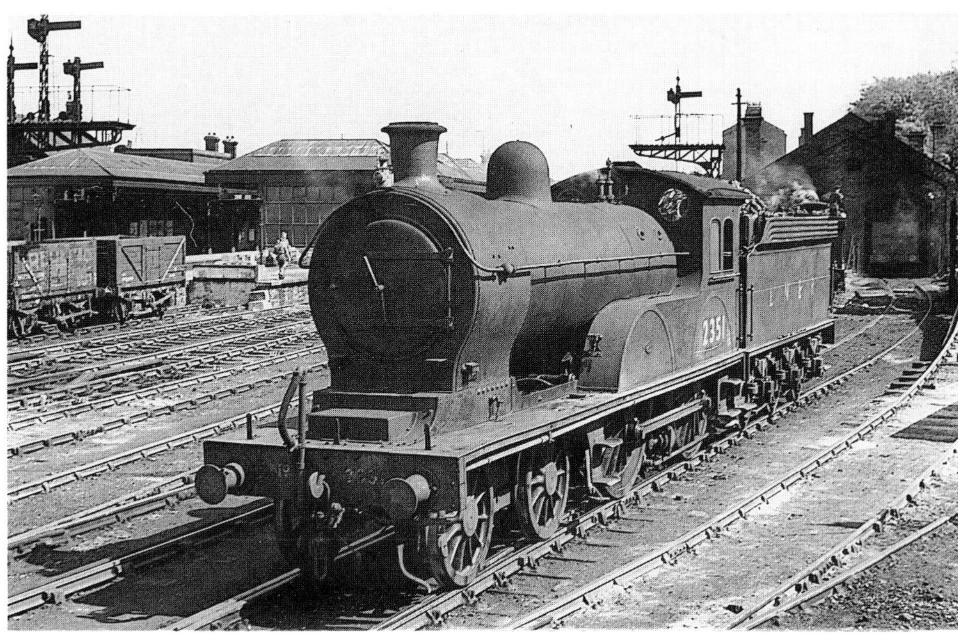

Alnmouth sub-shed in Northumberland in June 1948. Enjoying a fine day is Class D20 4-4-0 No. 2351, renumbered 62351 at the end of 1948. This was a design for the North Eastern Railway by Wilson Worsdell, dating back to 1899, and a long lived and successful class they proved to be. The last of the class, No. 62395, was not withdrawn until 20th November 1957 from Alnmouth. No. 62351 was withdrawn on 23rd November 1954, also from Alnmouth.

G.W. Sharpe

D30 'Scott' class 4-4-0 No. 62417 *Hal o' the Wynd* ex-Cowlairs Works at Glasgow Eastfield shed in June 1948, shortly after renumbering and awaiting return to Hawick. Built for the North British Railway under Locomotive Superintendent W.P. Reid, they dated back to 1913. No. 62417 was the first to be withdrawn under British Railways on 2nd January 1951 from Hawick. No more withdrawals took place until 7th January 1957 when No. 62430 was retired from Thornton Junction. The last two to go were Nos 62421 from St Margaret's and 62426 from Fort William, both on 25th June 1960.

G.W. Sharpe

D32 class 4-4-0 No. 2449 at Cowlairs Works in November 1948 after being withdrawn that month on the 13th from Hawick. Originally known as class 'K' of the North British Railway and dating back to 1906, only twelve were built. They did not last long in BR days, the last one, No. 62451, being withdrawn from St Margaret's on 29th March 1951.

G.W. Sharpe

Glasgow Eastfield shed in April 1948. D34 'Glen' class 4-4-0 No. 2469 *Glen Douglas* is on the ash pits being dealt with by one of the shed staff, complete with goggles for this most unpleasant job. Built by the North British Railway at Cowlairs in 1913, they had 6ft driving wheels which were ideal for West Highland line working. Renumbered 62469 during the week ended 24th December 1949, the engine survived until July 1959 and was withdrawn from normal duties. No official withdrawal date has been recorded, for the locomotive was put through Cowlairs Works and emerged on 24th July fully restored to its former NBR glory with original number 256. Based at Dawsholm for several years, it was used on specials. It now lies cold and silent in Glasgow Transport Museum.

G.W. Sharpe

D16/3 class 4-4-0 No. 2601 at Stratford shed in March 1948. Known as "Claud Hamilton's" the D16 class were rebuilds by Gresley from J. Holden's original class built for the Great Eastern and introduced in 1900. This example had a round topped boiler and retained the original footplating and slide valves. Renumbered 62601 during the week ended 29th April 1950, withdrawal took place on 1st January 1957 from King's Lynn. The last to be withdrawn was No. 62613 from March shed on 25th October 1960.

Photomatic

D11/2 class 4-4-0 No. 62686 *The Fiery Cross* at Eastfield shed in September 1948. This was a post-Grouping locomotive, built in October 1924 with cut down boiler mountings to conform to the Scottish loading gauge. The design was otherwise the same as the English members of the class which were J.G. Robinson's "Large Director" development of the earlier D10 4-4-0s for the Great Central. No. 62686 was withdrawn on 28th July 1961 from Eastfield.

G.W. Sharpe

D49/1 "Shire" class 4-4-0 No. 62706 *Forfarshire* at Darlington shed in September 1948 after a visit to the works. The D49 class was a Gresley design subdivided into D49/1 "Shire" and D49/2 "Hunt" titles. This example was built in December 1927 and was withdrawn on 3rd February 1958 from Thornton Junction.

Photomatic

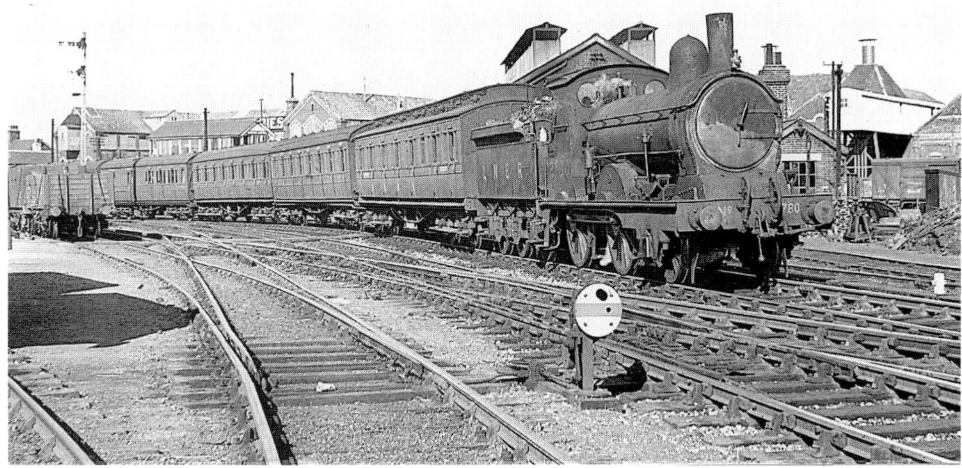

Ex-Great Eastern Railway 2-4-0, E4 class No. 2780 pulls out of Dereham on a train for Swaffham in May 1948. Just behind the locomotive can be seen the roof of the engine shed. The E4 class was a design by J. Holden first introduced in 1891. It was the practice of Stratford Works to fit some engines with an unlipped stovepipe chimney and No. 2780 has been so disfigured. Renumbered 62780 during the week ended 24th May 1950, withdrawal came on 26th September 1955 from Cambridge.

G.W. Sharpe

Q4 class 0-8-0 No. E3235 at Gorton Works in March 1948. This was a Robinson Great Central design first introduced in 1902. Scrapping of members of the class commenced in 1934 and the last, No. 63243, was condemned on 15th October 1951 at Ardsley. Withdrawal of this locomotive also took place in 1951, on 7th May, from Barnsley and still numbered with the "E".

Photomatic

Darlington shed in June 1948 finds Q5 class 0-8-0 No. 3264 awaiting entry to the works. The engine had arrived from Borough Gardens shed and was withdrawn at the works the same month on the 26th, never to receive the number 63264. This was a Wilson Worsdell 2-cylinder design for the North Eastern Railway and No. 3264 had been constructed in April 1902. None of the class survived long after Nationalisation. The last to be scrapped was No. 3326 on 3rd October 1951, Borough Gardens being once again the last allocation.

Photomatic

Q6 class 0-8-0 No. 3340 at Haverton Hill shed in February 1948. This was the first of this Vincent Raven design to be constructed in 1913. Scrapping of members of this class did not start until 1960 and the last were not withdrawn until the very end of steam in the North East. No. 63340 was withdrawn on 15th July 1963, last allocation West Auckland. The very last was No. 63395 withdrawn on 9th September 1967 from Sunderland shed and is now preserved on the North Yorkshire Moors Railway.

G.W. Sharpe

Q7 class 0-8-0 No. 63466, built 1919. This was another Raven design and the whole class was allocated to Tyne Dock for a number of years. This view is dated May 1948 and shows the engine working a 'down' empties at Darlington shortly after being renumbered. The whole class was withdrawn at the end of 1962, all from Tyne Dock shed. Their withdrawal dates were; 63467/68, 26th November, 63460/62/63/64/65/66/69/70/72 3rd December, 63461 10th December, and 63471/73/74 17th December. No. 63460 is preserved on the North Yorkshire Moors Railway as part of the National Collection.

Photomatic

Sheffield Darnall shed was a good place to get the flavour of the old Great Central for many of the Robinson designed engines could be found there. This is the location in April 1948 for 04/1 class 2-8-0 No. 3710. This locomotive was built in September 1912 and shows the basically unaltered original look of these engines. Renumbered 63710 during the week ended 28th October 1950, withdrawal came on 13th July 1959 from Darnall.

G.W. Sharpe

O1 class 2-8-0 No. 63773 leaving Acton GWR sidings on a South Wales freight test run on Tuesday, 31st August 1948. The engine was based at Hornsey at the time, and the LNER dynamometer car is the first vehicle on this exchange working. The O1 class were the Thompson rebuilds of the original O4s with B1 type 100A boilers, Walschaerts valve gear and new cylinders. No. 63773 was withdrawn on 18th October 1964 from Staveley GC shed.

Photomatic

Sheffield Darnall shed in March 1948 with J11 class 0-6-0 No. E4441. Behind the locomotive is the illuminated inspection pit. This was an attempt to improve the locomotive examination facilities at engine sheds, which were often carried out in dark and primitive conditions. Renumbered 64441 during 1948, this locomotive was officially known as J11/3 as it had been rebuilt from the original 1901 Robinson design with long-travel piston valves and higher pitched boiler. Thirty-three of the class were so dealt with. No. 64441 was withdrawn on 10th February 1961 from Retford shed.

G.W. Sharpe

Any visit to ex-LNER Scottish sheds, right through to 1965 would produce many sightings of these J37 class 0-6-0s. Newly renumbered, 64610 is at Glasgow Eastfield shed in April 1948. This was a design by W.P. Reid for the North British Railway and the first appeared in 1914. No. 64610 was made redundant on 1st February 1966 at Dunfermline. The last of the class to go were: Nos 64602, 64611, 64620 all on the 22nd April 1967 and all last operated from Dundee Tay Bridge shed.

G.W. Sharpe

J19 class 0-6-0 No. 4641 at Stratford shed in April 1948. Originally designed by S. Holden for the Great Eastern and built under A.J. Hill, they were first introduced in 1912. The whole class was rebuilt by Gresley with round-topped boilers in place of the Belpaire firebox variety first used. This engine was dealt with in October 1936, renumbered 64641 during 1948, and withdrawal came on 25th January 1960 from Norwich.

Photomatic

Gresley designed J39 class 0-6-0 No. 64920 piloting an unknown B16 class 4-6-0 on a freight at Monkton Moor on the Harrogate to Northallerton via Ripon line, which closed on 6th March 1967. It is April 1951 and the J39 now carries a shed plate, 50B Neville Hill. Built in November 1936 the engine was first allocated to Darlington. Renumbering from 4920 took place during the week ended 14th May 1949 and withdrawal on 16th November 1961 from Neville Hill.

G.W. Sharpe

J1 class 0-6-0 No. 65010 shunts at Hitchin in March 1949. It had moved here from Colwick during the week ended 19th June 1948 and remained at this allocation until withdrawal on 19th January 1953. Hitchin had the distinction of operating the last of the class, No. 65013, which was withdrawn on 22nd November 1954. The class was designed by H.A. Ivatt for the Great Northern Railway and built in 1908.

R.H.G. Simpson

Northwich shed in April 1948. J10 class 0-6-0 No. E5134 is in steam in the shed yard. Built for the Manchester, Sheffield & Lincolnshire Railway by T. Parker, they were first introduced in 1896. This example was actually classified J10/4 for it had been altered by H. Pollitt with larger bearings and a larger tender. Becoming No. 65134 during the week ended 12th March 1949, withdrawal took place on 26th December 1959 from Northwich.

G.W. Sharpe

Wigan Lower Ince shed yard in May 1948 with two J10s present, Nos 65173 and 5203. Not surprising really, for the whole allocation was 13 J10s and remained exactly the same for the whole of 1948. No. 5203 became 65203 during the week ended 26th February 1949. The shed was transferred to LMR control in 1949 and coded first 13G and then 10F, closing on Monday 24th March 1952. The locomotives were actually transferred "on loan" to the LMR with effect from 28th November 1948. On closure the entire allocation of 15 engines went to nearby Springs Branch. In December 1956 something very odd happened to the two J10s that are the subject of our photograph. Along with six of their fellow classmates they were transferred to Darlington shed. They travelled via Carnforth, Tebay and Kirkby Stephen and were in exchange for eight LMS Fowler 2-6-2Ts that the North Eastern Region had acquired and wanted to be rid of. On receipt of the J10s, Darlington withdrew the lot, No. 65173 on the 14th and No. 65203 on the 17th.

G.W. Sharpe

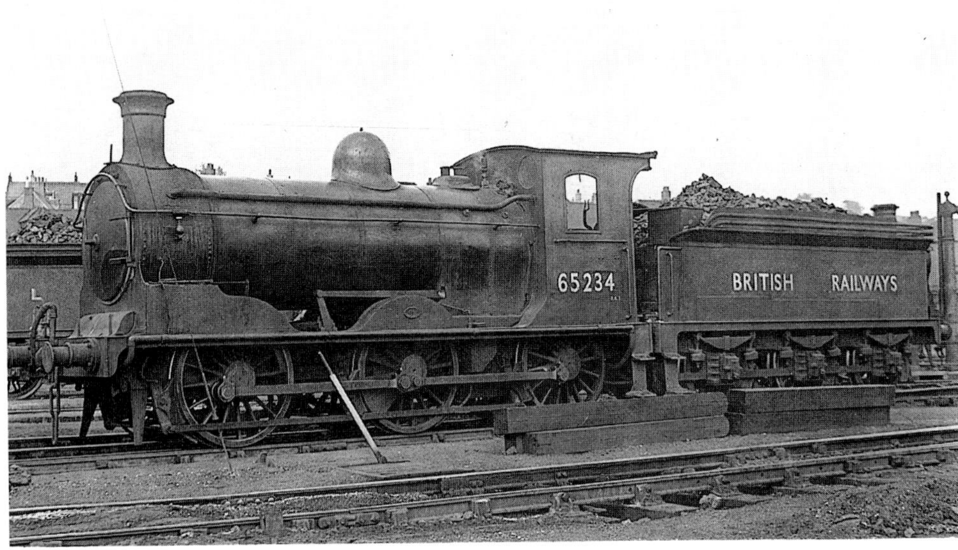

J36 class 0-6-0 No. 65234 at Bathgate shed in June 1948. This was a North British Railway engine designed by M. Holmes and first introduced in 1888. Certain members of the class were sent to France during the First World War and on return home were given commemorative names. Long-lived they certainly were, for No. 65234 was among the very last steam locomotives to be withdrawn from the Scottish Region. Its withdrawal date was 22nd April 1967 from St Margaret's, the day the shed closed and most of the remaining Scottish steam stock was withdrawn. The very last Scottish steam engines to remain in stock were also J36 0-6-0s, Nos 65288 at Dunfermline and 65345 at Thornton Junction. Both were withdrawn on 5th June that year. No. 65234 still steamed though, but only as a stationary boiler at St Margaret's until July 1967.

G.W. Sharpe

The J15 class 0-6-0 was an original design by T.W. Worsdell for the Great Eastern and first appeared in 1883. Building continued until 1913. This view shows No. 65405 at Cambridge shed in 1950. This was one of five members of the class to be fitted with a side-window and tender cab for working over the Colne Valley line (Colchester-Halstead-Haverhill). Renumbered from 5405 during the week ended 26th February 1949, withdrawal came at Neasden shed, then coded 14D, on 16th August 1958.

H.N. James

J17 class 0-6-0 No. 65532 on shunting duties at Cambridge in September 1948, the month of renumbering. This was a James Holden design for the Great Eastern and this example was built in November 1901 at Stratford Works. Originally this locomotive carried a round-topped boiler, but this was replaced by the Belpaire variety as illustrated in January 1929. This was the freight version of the "Claud Hamilton" D16 class and had the same size cylinders and identical boiler. Instead of the D16's 7ft driving wheels it had the standard diameter for GER freight engines of 4ft 11in. No. 65532 remained in service at Cambridge shed until 11th February 1962.

Photomatic

Typical of the smaller North Eastern Railway 0-6-0s is this J25 class No. 65650. Another Wilson Worsdell production, the class was first introduced in 1898. This view is at Darlington shed, by the wet ash pits, in June 1948. Withdrawn from Leeds Neville Hill on 30th September 1957.
Photomatic

Darlington Works, September 1948. J26 class 0-6-0 No. 65734 awaits permission to leave to return home to Newport, Teesside. This class was first introduced in 1904 for the North Eastern Railway and was an enlarged version of the J25 class. A considerable number of the class spent their time at Newport until the opening of the new shed at Thornaby to which they moved on 8th June 1958 when Newport closed. It was from Thornaby that No. 65734 was withdrawn on 14th October 1958.
G.W. Sharpe

Scotland was the home for the whole of the Gresley designed J38 class 0-6-0s. Here No. 65904 is at Glasgow Eastfield shed after a visit to Cowlairs Works in February 1949 where it was renumbered during the week ended the 26th. Classified 6F under BR, the class was first introduced in 1926, this one entering traffic in March that year. Two, Nos 65901 and 65929, remained until the very last few days of steam in Scotland, going on 22nd April 1967 from Thornton Junction. They were the last two Gresley engines to remain in BR stock. No. 65904 was also at Thornton Junction when retired on 23rd July 1964.
G.W. Sharpe

F3 class 2-4-2T No. 7143 at Stratford Works scrapline in August 1948 after being withdrawn on 22nd July. This was a J. Holden design for the Great Eastern and built between 1893 and 1902. The last one. No. 67127, was withdrawn on 8th April 1953 from Ipswich.

Photomatic

F4 class 2-4-2T No. 7169 again at Stratford Works scrapline in the month of withdrawal, April 1948. This was a T.W. Worsdell 1884 design for the Great Eastern and classified 1MT under BR. No. 67157, the last active member of the class, finally succumbed to more modern power on 8th June 1956 from Kittybrewster, having been transferred from Yarmouth Beach to Norwich during the week ended 24th January 1948 and then on to Kittybrewster the following week, joining two others there, Nos 67151 and 67164 (withdrawn on 28th and 27th August 1951 respectively). They were employed on the Fraserburgh to St Combs branch and were equipped with cowcatchers. Although officially withdrawn on 8th June, No. 67157 continued to work the branch until the 15th. The word of authority must have been slow in getting out to such isolated parts!

Photomatic

The North Eastern Railway 0-4-4T, designed by Wilson Worsdell and classified G5 under the LNER. Here we see No. 7336 being serviced on the ash pits at its home shed Sunderland in 1948. This locomotive was built at Darlington Works (works No. 432) in June 1901. Renumbered 67336 during the week ended 15th January 1949, withdrawal came on 22nd March 1955 from Sunderland.

G.W. Sharpe

H.A. Ivatt designed the C12 class 4-4-2T for the Great Northern Railway and they first appeared in 1898. Under the LNER they were scattered over a wide area and lasted until 1958, the final one, No. 67397 being condemned on the 6th December, last allocation Grantham. This view is at Hull Botanic Gardens shed and shows No. 7393 in July 1948. Renumbered 67393 during the week ended 8th January 1949, the engine remained at Hull until withdrawn on 20th April 1953.

Photomatic

The Chesham branch was worked by Class C13 4-4-2Ts for many years and here we see push-and-pull fitted No. 7420 doing just that in June 1948. This was a Robinson Great Central design that was first introduced in 1903. Renumbered 67420 during the week ended 21st May 1949 withdrawal came from Neasden on 13th December 1958. The last of the class was No. 67417, withdrawn from Gorton on 23rd January 1960.

G.W. Sharpe

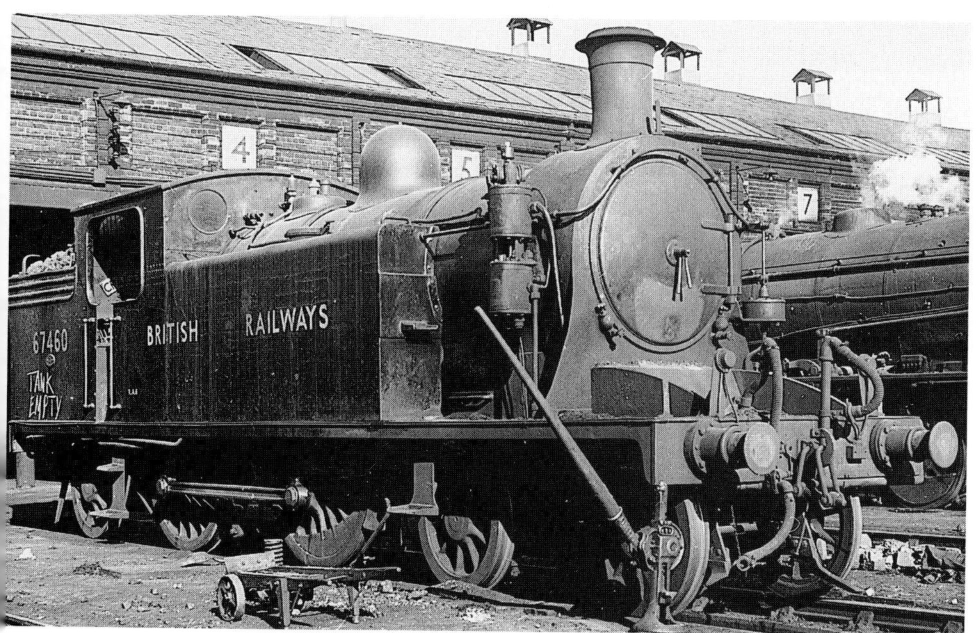

The Scottish equivalent of the English 4-4-2T, the C15 class. This is Glasgow Eastfield shed in August 1948 with No. 67460 on view. They were built in August 1912 by the Yorkshire Engine Co. (builder's No. 1073) for the North British Railway to a design by W.P. Reid. No. 67460 and classmate 67474 were the last two to be withdrawn in April 1960, both from Eastfield. No. 67460 was condemned on the 1st and No. 67474 on the 12th. Both had been push-and-pull fitted and finished their days on the Arrochar to Craigendoran workings on the West Highland lines.

G.W. Sharpe

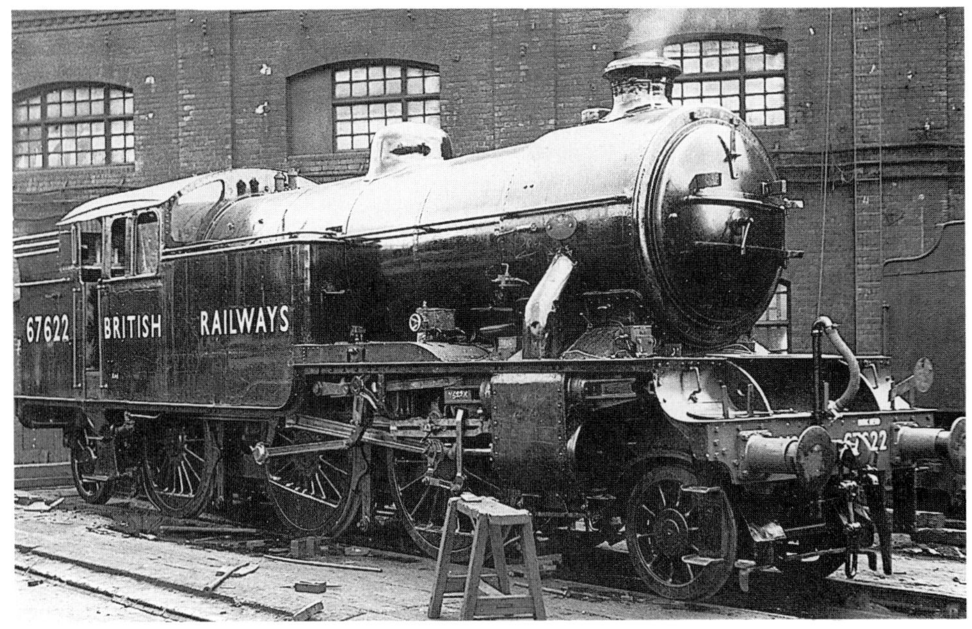

Darlington Works in June 1948. The finishing touches are made to V1 class 2-6-2T No. 67622 before returning the engine to Glasgow Parkhead shed. This locomotive had been built at Doncaster Works in October 1931 to a design by Gresley and first allocated to Helensburgh. The last allocation was Parkhead when withdrawn on 5th March 1962.

G.W. Sharpe

Thompson L1 class 2-6-4T No. 67718 at Marylebone engine stabling and servicing point in lined green livery, when nearly new in July 1948. The L1s were heavy on maintenance, particularly of the axleboxes and motion, and large scale withdrawals took place between 1960 and 1962. Those on the ex-Great Northern section of the Eastern Region earned the nickname "concrete mixers" by the men that had to work them! No. 67718 was transferred to LMR Book Stock on 2nd January 1961 and officially allocated to Gorton (9G) but was actually left in store at Peterborough New England shed for a month or so. Withdrawal from Gorton took place during the week ended 18th November 1961. The whole class had been withdrawn by the end of December 1962.

Photomatic

Y7 class 0-4-0T No. 68089, a Worsdell 1888 design for the North Eastern Railway, at Seahouses on the North Sunderland Light Railway from Chathill. This is the locomotive referred to earlier in the caption for LMS No. 11217 at Burton shed. This photograph was taken in 1951, for the engine carries a 52D Tweedmouth shedplate. When the line closed on Monday 29th October 1951 No. 68089 was made redundant. The engine was sent on to Gateshead shed where it was placed in store. Official withdrawal is recorded as 25th January 1952. It was then sold to a contractor building an outfall sewer alongside the West End Pier at Morecambe and was noted standing at the promenade on the 24th February. It was intended to use the locomotive to haul wagons of materials. The journey from Gateshead had been made by road starting on the 13th February. Sister engine No. 68088 is now preserved at the Great Central Railway, Loughborough, after being withdrawn in December 1952 and sold to the National Coal Board.

G.W. Sharpe

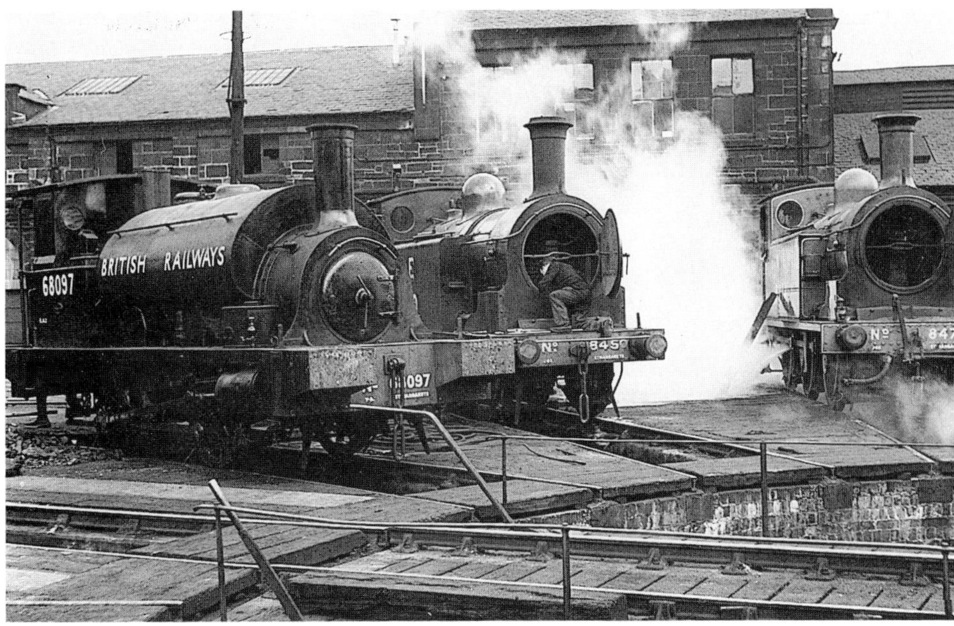

Turntable group at Edinburgh St Margaret's in June 1948. Y9 class 0-4-0ST No. 68097 keeps company with J83 0-6-0Ts Nos 8450 and 8474. All were M. Holmes designs for the North British Railway, the Y9 dating back to 1887. The two J83s were renumbered in 1950, No. 68450 during the week ended 12th August and 68474 8th July. All three lasted well into the BR era, being withdrawn from St Margaret's on the following dates: No. 68097 14th October 1958, 68450 5th December 1957 and 68474 18th April 1958.

G.W. Sharpe

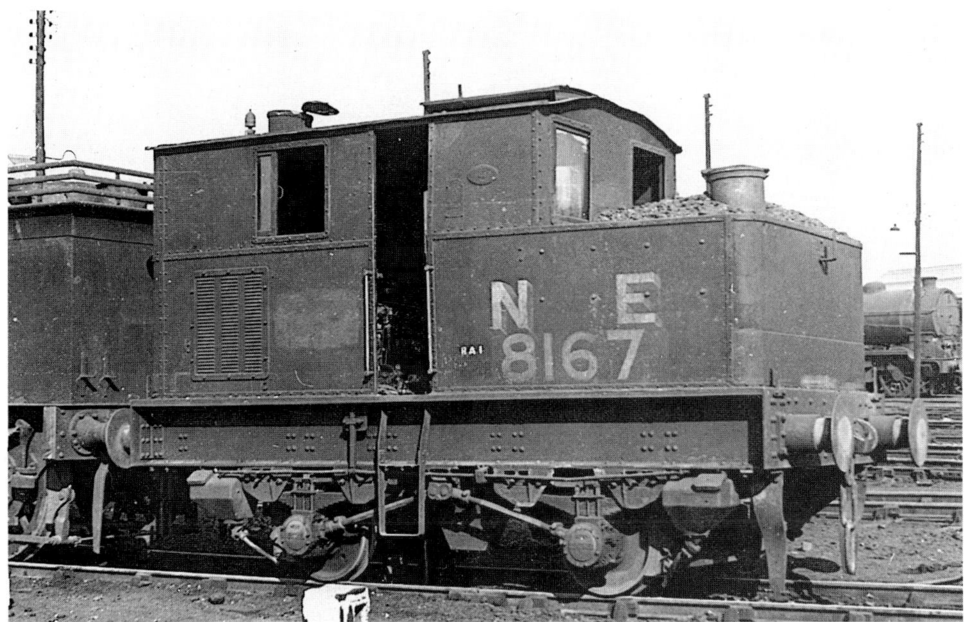

Y3 class No. 8167 at Sheffield Darnall shed in March 1948. Built by Sentinel for the LNER in September 1930 it was withdrawn from Darnall on 14th November 1949 without receiving its BR number. These odd-looking little 4-wheel locomotives had a vertical boiler and were double geared. Many were used as Departmental locomotives and finished their days shunting around the various engineers yards and numbered in Departmental stock.

Photomatic

Z4 class 0-4-2T No. 68190 at Kittybrewster shed in August 1948. This one and sister engine No. 68191 spent all their BR days at Aberdeen shunting around the docks. They were a Manning Wardle design for the Great North of Scotland Railway and were built in 1915. No. 68190 was withdrawn on 28th April 1960 and 68191 on 31st March 1959.

G.E. Sharpe

Another design of tank engine for dock shunting, this time at Immingham. On shed there in September 1948 is class J63 0-6-0T No. 8209. This was a class of only seven locomotives built in 1906 for the Great Central, and to a design by Robinson. Renumbered 68209 during the week ended 9th April 1949 it was transferred to Wrexham Rhosddu shed during December 1951 and remained there until withdrawn on 5th February 1955. The last to go was No. 68210 on 25th February 1957 from Immingham.

G.W. Sharpe

J70 class Tram Engine No. 68223 at Stratford shed shortly after renumbering during a visit to the works in August 1949. Built at Stratford in 1914, order No. P75, by J. Holden for the Great Eastern these engines were designed for the dock lines at Yarmouth and Ipswich. They were also used on the Wisbech & Upwell Tramway, and No. 68223 was later fitted with cowcatchers and side plates covering the outside cylinders for this duty. No. 68223 was withdrawn on 19th July 1955 from Yarmouth Vauxhall and the last survivor, No. 68226 was condemned the next month, on 2nd August from Colchester.

G.W. Sharpe

J. Holden's Great Eastern design LNER class J66 0-6-0T dated back to 1886 Here No. E8382 is at Stratford shed in February 1948. Renumbering to 68382 was carried out during the week ended 28th May 1949. The engine was allocated, rather surprisingly, to the ex-Great Central shed at Staveley where it remained until 30th June 1952. It was then taken out of ordinary service and transferred to Departmental stock and renumbered 31. It returned to more familiar territory as a Stratford Works shunter where it remained until final withdrawal in November 1959.

G.W. Sharpe

J77 class 0-6-0T No. 68393 shunts at Darlington after a visit to the works in August 1948. Originally built in 1874 by Neilson and Co. as an 0-4-4T to a design by E. Fletcher, it was rebuilt to the form shown here by Wilson Worsdell at Darlington in 1921. This one remained active until 4th July 1955 when it was withdrawn from Starbeck shed.

Photomatic

This is Kipps on the east side of Glasgow in July 1948 and in the background is the shed building, in urgent need of repair by the look of things! J83 class 0-6-0T No. 8444 busies itself on shunting duties over in the wagon depot sidings. This was a design by M. Holmes for the North British Railway and first introduced in 1900. They were power classified 2F under British Railways and were long lasting engines, the last, No. 68477, not being withdrawn from St Margaret's until 29th December 1962. The subject of this photograph was renumbered 68444 during the week ended 19th May 1951 and was withdrawn from Kipps on 13th January 1960.

G. W. Sharpe

May 1948 at South Lynn shed finds J69 class 0-6-0T No. 8542 out of steam and enjoying a rest. The engine had only just been transferred from King's Lynn. Originally built in 1890 by Holden for the Great Eastern at Stratford, order No. R29, a rebuild took place in 1905 to the form shown here with widened side tanks. Renumbered 68542 in 1948, withdrawal took place on 16th September 1962 from Stratford.

Photomatic

Stratford shed in July 1948 and ex-works is J52 class 0-6-0ST No. 68832, with stove-pipe chimney, waiting to return to King's Cross. This was an H. A. Ivatt build for the Great Northern Railway, based on an earlier design by his predecessor Stirling. The last of the class to be withdrawn were Nos 68869 and 68875 on 20th March 1961 from Ardsley. No. 68832 was condemned on 21st October 1957, last allocation King's Cross. G. W. Sharpe

Wortley Junction, Leeds in September 1950 with J50 class 0-6-0T No. E8921 on an empty stock working. Built in 1922, this was a Gresley design for the Great Northern Railway and they were widely scattered over the LNER with a small group operating in Scotland. This example was renumbered 68921 during the week ended 14th July 1951. Transfer south from Ardsley to Hornsey took place during October 1952 from where withdrawal came about on 26th April 1961. G. W. Sharpe

N10 class 0-6-2T No. 9106 at Hull Dairycoates shed in September 1948, after being transferred there that month from Gateshead during the week ended the 25th. The engine still carries its former allocation on the buffer beam. This was a Wilson Worsdell design first introduced in 1902 and they lasted well into the diesel era, the last three, Nos 69097, 69101 and 69109 not being withdrawn until 9th April 1962 at Gateshead. No. 9106 was renumbered during the week ended 4th June 1949 and withdrawn on 17th March 1958 from Tyne Dock.

G. W. Sharpe

Resplendent in lined out black livery at Dunfermline shed in November 1948 after a visit to Cowlairs Works, is N15 class 0-6-2T No. 69204. This was one of the first locomotives to receive a smokebox number plate as Cowlairs did not start to turn out engines so fitted until September. This was a North British Railway design by W. P. Reid, first introduced in 1910. No. 69204 was withdrawn on 16th July 1962 from Thornton Junction, while the last of the class, No. 69178, was withdrawn the same year on 29th December from Motherwell.

G. W. Sharpe

N9 class 0-6-2T No. 9423 at Sunderland shed in April 1948. The engine had been transferred here from Northallerton during the third week of January 1948. Another Wilson Worsdell design of 1893, No. 9423 did not last very long in BR ownership for withdrawal came on 9th July 1951, still at Sunderland, and never renumbered. The last active member of the class was No. 69429 which ended at Tyne Dock and was withdrawn on 4th July 1955.

G. W. Sharpe

King's Cross station on Monday 19th September 1949 finds N2 class 0-6-2T No. 69490 between duties on the engine sidings. This was one of the class designed by Gresley, fitted with condensing apparatus and small chimney for working through the tunnels to Moorgate. Scrapping of the class started in 1959, No. 69490 going on 6th July from King's Cross. They had all gone by 1962, the last being No. 69546 withdrawn from Neasden on 23rd September that year.

L. Hanson

A7 class 4-6-2T No. 69771, built in 1910, at Darlington shed in June 1948 after a visit to the works. This was a Vincent Raven design and classified 3F under BR. Allocated to Cudworth when this photograph was taken, the engine moved to Hull Dairycoates on 18th March 1950 and on to Hull Springhead in September 1954. This was the engine's last home, withdrawal coming on 8th November the same year.

Photomatic

Darlington shed in July 1948 with A5 class 4-6-2T No. 69836 alongside the ash pits. More correctly, this should be described as an A5/2 for this was a Gresley development of the Robinson, Great Central design of 1911. They were numbered under BR 69830 to 69842 and built by Hawthorn Leslie & Co. in 1925-26. To fit the LNER loading gauge they had reduced boiler mountings and lower cabs than the older GC engines. No. 69836 was withdrawn on 25th August 1958 from Botanic Gardens shed.

G. W. Sharpe

Gorton Works in October 1949 finds Q1 class 0-8-0T No. E9930 awaiting attention. It was renumbered 69930 during the week ended 19th November. This engine started life as a Robinson tender engine of class Q4 originally introduced in 1902. The engines in the Q1 class were all rebuilds by Edward Thompson from this class, the work being carried out between 1942 and 1945. The conversion from the tender engines was an economy measure during the war when further heavy shunting engines were required. It was the intention to rebuild 25 Q4s, but this was cut short to only 13 being dealt with. No. 69930 was withdrawn from Frodingham on 2nd October 1958. The last two in active service were also withdrawn from Frodingham, both in September 1959, Nos 69935 on the 3rd and 69936 on the 15th.

G. W. Sharpe

Ex-WD Austerity Locomotives

WD Austerity 2-8-0 No. 77026 at Bristol Temple Meads in 1949 on a northbound freight. This was one of the 1943 batch built by the North British Locomotive Co. Renumbered 90123 during the week ended 10th November 1951, withdrawal came in March 1965 from the ex-LMSR shed at Rose Grove.

G. W. Sharpe

Woodford Halse-based Austerity 2-8-0 No. E3199 at Neasden shed in April 1948. Originally WD No. 79308, the engine was built in 1945 at Vulcan Foundry. Renumbered to 90520 during the second week of March 1949, withdrawal came from Aintree shed in February 1965.

G. W. Sharpe

Diesel and Electric Locomotives

Ex-LMS Co-Co diesel-electric Type 3, 1,600hp locomotive No. 10000 at Northampton Castle station on Sunday 26th August 1951 on an 'up' express. Built at Derby Works in 1947 the locomotive entered traffic at Camden during the week ended 13th December. This was one of the "twins" that were the pioneers of the diesel age and were built in conjunction with the English Electric Company. No. 10001, the other member of the class, was added to stock in 1948 and was withdrawn in March 1966 from Willesden. No. 10000 had been withdrawn in December 1963 from the same depot.

L. Hanson

Saltley shed on Sunday 25th July 1948 with ex-LMS 0-6-0 diesel-electric shunter No. 7128 in the yard. Built at Derby Works it entered traffic during the week ended 18th October 1947 and went new to Saltley. Renumbered 12041 during the last week of March 1952, withdrawal came in October 1968 from Saltley, it having spent all its working life at this Birmingham depot.

K. C. H. Fairey

Three ex-LNER built 0-6-0 diesel-electric shunters, Nos 8000, 8001 and 8002, at March shed in May 1948. All three had been built in 1944, the mechanical parts built at Doncaster and the engine and electrical equipment supplied by English Electric. Similar to the LMS diesel shunters, they had the additional facility in being fitted out for use as mobile power stations if required by the provision of a double wound armature to the main generator. This enabled a 200kw industrial supply to be obtained from the diesel-generator set. As far as is known, very little use was made of this addition. These three had all been renumbered into BR stock by June 1952 becoming Nos 15000, 15001 and 15002. All three were withdrawn in 1967, No. 15001 in April and the other two in August, all from Crewe South shed.

Photomatic

One could perhaps be forgiven for thinking that this was a garden shed on wheels! It is in fact petrol engine driven Y11 class 4-wheel locomotive No. 15099 at its usual haunt of Ware goods yard in 1949. It had been renumbered 68189 in January 1949 and then to 15099 during the first week in May the same year. It had a varied career, being built in March 1921 by the Motor Rail and Tram Car Co. Ltd of Simplex Works, Bedford (builder's No. 2037), and purchased by the North British Railway in 1922. It was first used at Kelso but in July 1930 it was displaced by Y1 class Sentinel No. 9529 (which became BR No. 68138) and transferred south, being employed at Ware through until withdrawal. It was fitted with a taller cab after it had been damaged by fire. This altered its appearance considerably from its sister, illustrated next. Allocated to Stratford, withdrawal came on 21st November 1956.

G. W. Sharpe

The other "Simplex", Y11 class No. 8188, looking even more like a garden shed! This one was renumbered 15098 during the first week in May 1949 and is shown here in original condition at Brentwood, just before renumbering, in April. It had been purchased by the LNER in 1925 and was first used for shunting coal wagons at Stratford shed. Later it moved out to Brentwood, where at one time it had the unofficial name "Peggy" painted on it, and remained there until withdrawal on 4th September 1956. There was a third "Simplex" which was in Departmental Stock at Greenland Creosote Depot, West Hartlepool. It became BR No. 15097 in May 1949 from No. L4 and was withdrawn in June 1950 at Darlington Works.

Photomatic

Old Oak Common depot in 1949 with diesel-electric shunter No. 15100. This locomotive was built by Hawthorn Leslie/English Electric and purchased by the GWR in 1936. It carried the number 2 from purchase until renumbering in 1948. Withdrawn in April 1965 from Swindon shed.

Photomatic

Locomotive Shed Views

Heaton shed in June 1948. Recently renumbered ex-North Eastern Railway electric locomotive No. 26501 (with overhead and shoe pick-up) keeps company with WD 2-8-0 No. 63166, later to become 90487. This Bo-Bo Class ES1 was built in 1902 by Brush and British Thomson-Houston as a shunting engine and weighed 46 tons. It was employed on the steeply graded quayside line, Newcastle-upon-Tyne, and had its last works visit in June 1961 when it was repainted in lined green with NER and BR emblems added. Withdrawal came on 14th September 1964 fom South Gosforth along with sister locomotive No. 26500 which is now preserved in the National Railway Museum, York.

Photomatic

Blackpool Central shed yard on Sunday 22nd May 1949 with Nos 52447, (4)5717, (4)4778 and 42636 amongst others on view. Of LYR origin, it had a sub-shed at the other terminus at this seaside town, Blackpool North. On 1st January 1948 the total combined allocation was 52 locomotives. By the time this photograph was taken the shed roof was in an extremely poor state, but it was not rebuilt until 1957. Central shed closed on 2nd November 1964, the allocation having been transferred away in late September.

K. C. H. Fairey

Epping sub-shed in 1950, parent depot Stratford, with Nos 65455, 67200 and 67193 on view. A locomotive shed was built here back in 1893 by the Great Eastern Railway, but the structure shown in this illustration dated back to a rebuild in 1949. The usual allocation was around seven locomotives and the shed closed in November 1957.

Photomatic

The allocation at ex-Midland Railway **Kentish Town** shed on 1st January 1948 consisted of 113 locomotives. This view inside one of the three roundhouses, recorded on Sunday 24th July 1949, shows Nos (4)7245, 43964, (4)1672, 42325 and (40)119 around the turntable. Also present at the shed on this date were: Nos 40027, 40038, 40079, 40090, 40092, 40096, 40098, 40100, 40111, 40112, 40114, 40148, 40155, 40160, 40161, 40167, 40172, 40547, 41007, 41034, 41054, 41071, 41117, 41207, 41660, 41671, 41713, 41826, 42302, 44563, 44816, 44817, 44818, 44848, 44917, 44981, 44984, 44985, 45267, 45280, 45554, 45564, 45607, 45611, 45616, 45626, 45648, 45649, 45650, 45654, 45665, 45667, 45679, 47229, 47232, 47241, 47242, 47244, 47260, 47262, 47263, 47283, 47427, 47428, 47429, 47644, 47645, 58158, 58200 and 58229. By November 1962 the allocation was down to six steam engines, all in store. The shed finally closed around March 1963.

G. W. Sharpe

King's Cross shed in May 1949 with Class A3 No. 60059 *Tracery* and Class V2 No. 60800 *Green Arrow*. This London depot was the final home for both these engines when they were withdrawn in 1962, the V2 (now preserved) on 21st August and the A3 on 17th December. The allocation on 1st January 1948 comprised 172 locomotives, with 35 Pacifics responsible for the main express workings. King's Cross shed closed on 17th June 1963, its duties taken over by the diesel depot at Finsbury Park.

G. W. Sharpe

Slough shed was one of the smaller ex-GWR depots and is seen here in 1948. The 1st January 1948 allocation consisted of 50 tank engines, the sub-sheds at Aylesbury, Marlow and Watlington being supplied from Slough. The shed finally closed on 13th June 1964.

Author's collection

Brighton shed in 1950. Dating back to LBSCR days, the original building had a slated roof and individual arched entrances to the shed roads. This was altered in 1938 to the structure seen here with asbestos sheeting on the roof and open-ended shed front. The allocation on 1st January 1948 comprised 68 locomotives with a further 17 outstationed at Newhaven. Closure to steam traction took place on 15th June 1964. The buildings were demolished two years later.
Author's collection

Stratford in May 1948 with J69 class No. 8631, L1 No. 9000 (67701), ex-works J52 No. 68796, and another J69 on view. Dominating the background is the mechanical coaling plant.
G. W. Sharpe

Stratford shed, London, on Sunday 25th September 1949. This had the largest allocation in the country with an amazing 426 locomotives on its books on 1st January 1948 and was parent to fourteen sub-sheds. A visit to this shed was always an exciting experience, with engines coming on and off shed all the time. On Sunday 14th August 1949, for instance, at mid-day there were 254 engines at the shed. Steam working at Stratford ceased from 16th September 1962 when the remaining locomotives were withdrawn.
D. K. Jones